Restoring Trust in Sport

I0888175

In this solutions-focused collection of sport corruption case studies, leading researchers consider how to re-establish trust both within sports organisations and in the wider sporting public. Inspired by the idea of 'moral repair', the book examines significant corruption cases and the measures taken to reduce further harm or risk of recurrence.

The book has an international scope, including case study material from Europe, Asia, Africa, Australia and New Zealand, and covers important contemporary issues including whistleblowing, bribery, match-fixing, gambling, bidding for major events, and good governance. It examines the loss of trust at both national and international levels. Drawing on cutting-edge research, the book includes both on-field and off-field examples, from Olympic, non-Olympic, professional and amateur sports, as well as diverse academic and practitioner perspectives. Offering an important contribution to current debates and a source of reflection on best professional practice, *Restoring Trust in Sport* helps us to better understand why corruption happens in sport and how it can and should be addressed.

This is invaluable reading for all advanced students, researchers, managers and policy makers with an interest in integrity in sport, sport ethics, sport management, sport governance, sports law, and a useful reference for anybody working in criminology, business and management, law, sociology or political science.

Catherine Ordway is Assistant Professor in Sport Management at the University of Canberra, Australia and Senior Fellow at Melbourne Law School, The University of Melbourne, Australia.

Routledge Research in Sport and Corruption

Series Editor:

James Skinner
Loughborough University London, UK

Match-Fixing in Sport
Comparative Studies from Australia, Japan, Korea and Beyond
Edited by Stacey Steele and Hayden Opie

Corruption in Sport
Causes, Consequences, and Reform
Edited by Lisa A. Kihl

Restoring Trust in Sport
Corruption Cases and Solutions
Edited by Catherine Ordway

WADA, the World Anti-Doping Agency
A Multi-Level Legitimacy Analysis
Daniel Read, James Skinner, Daniel Lock and Aaron Smith

Restoring Trust in Sport

Corruption Cases and Solutions

Edited by
Catherine Ordway

Routledge
Taylor & Francis Group
LONDON AND NEW YORK

First published 2021
by Routledge
2 Park Square, Milton Park, Abingdon, Oxon OX14 4RN

and by Routledge
52 Vanderbilt Avenue, New York, NY 10017

Routledge is an imprint of the Taylor & Francis Group, an informa business

British Library Cataloguing-in-Publication Data
A catalogue record for this book is available from the British Library

Library of Congress Cataloging-in-Publication Data
Names: Ordway, Catherine, editor.
Title: Restoring trust in sport : corruption cases and solutions / Edited by Catherine Ordway.
Description: Abingdon, Oxon ; New York, NY : Routledge, 2020. | Includes bibliographical references and index. |
Identifiers: LCCN 2020048968 (print) | LCCN 2020048969 (ebook) | ISBN 9780367473068 (hardback) | ISBN 9781003034780 (ebook)
Subjects: LCSH: Sports--Corrupt practices--Cross-cultural studies. | Sports and state--Cross-cultural studies. | Olympics--Corrupt practices--Cross-cultural studies.
Classification: LCC GV718 .R47 2020 (print) | LCC GV718 (ebook) | DDC 796.06/9--dc23
LC record available at https://lccn.loc.gov/2020048968
LC ebook record available at https://lccn.loc.gov/2020048969

ISBN: 978-0-367-47306-8 (hbk)
ISBN: 978-0-367-61692-2 (pbk)
ISBN: 978-1-003-03478-0 (ebk)

Typeset in Galliard
by Taylor & Francis Books

Contents

Illustrations

Figures

Table

Contributors

Ruth Bayley is a PhD candidate at the Queensland University of Technology, Australia on corruption in government procurement processes and holds a Bachelor of Commerce and a Master of Business Administration. After an earlier career in procurement with the Royal Australian Air Force and the Australian Public Service, Ruth founded a training company specialising in government procurement. In this role, Ruth provides training to thousands from all levels of government. She became aware that no amount of training seemed to prevent some public officials and suppliers from acting in unethical ways in the procurement process. Ruth now focuses on her passion of building an integrity culture in government procurement.

Stefano Caneppele, PhD, is Associate Professor in the School of Criminal Justice at the University of Lausanne, Switzerland where he teaches Criminal Law courses including Sport, Criminality and Integrity. Previously he was Associate Professor at the Faculty of Political and Social Sciences, Università Cattolica del Sacro Cuore of Milan. He worked also at Transcrime on several international and national research projects (www.transcrime.it) (2002–2015). In 2006 Stefano was awarded an International PhD in Criminology from the University of Trento. In 2007, he spent six months as a Visiting Senior Lecturer at Griffith University (Australia). He is Associate Editor of the *European Journal on Criminal Policy and Research* (Springer). His research interests focus on crime analysis, crime prevention, security, organised and economic crime.

Giulia Cinaglia is a graduate in forensic science and criminology from the University of Lausanne, Switzerland. Interested in both the criminological and the forensic aspects of crime, Giulia worked on the removal of offenders' DNA profiles contained in the Swiss national database. The goal of the study was to provide empirical results for the revision of the legislation on DNA. Currently a PhD candidate at the University of Lausanne, her research focuses on 'cold cases' (unsolved crimes). Her study aims at understanding how cold cases are perceived, understood and investigated 'from the inside', based on the experiences of detectives, crime scene investigators as well as forensic scientists.

Caron Egle is a PhD candidate at the Queensland University of Technology, Australia. Caron began her career as a nurse and moved into adult education in

1985, teaching human development and adult learning in both the tertiary and vocational training sectors. In 2002 Caron founded a training company specialising in vertical leadership, organisational development and change management. This led her on a quest to discover how leaders effectively lead transformational change in turbulent and unpredictable times with high integrity, emotional mastery and wisdom. Caron is currently completing a Doctor of Education at the Queensland University of Technology on how late stage leaders facilitate complex change. She holds Bachelor of Applied Science and Master of Education degrees from the University of Canberra.

Simon Gardiner, PhD, is Professor of International Sports Law at Leeds Beckett University, UK. Simon has worked at a number of universities in the UK and in Australia. Simon has been an active researcher in the area of sports law for over 25 years and has an international reputation. His particular research interests include sports governance and the regulation of sports-related corruption. He has been involved in funded research projects with a number of bodies such as the European Union. Simon has published widely in refereed journals, numerous professional journals and is lead author of Gardiner et al., *Sports Law*, that is in its fourth edition.

Rhys Harrison is an Integrity Officer with Tennis Australia and is responsible for the development and implementation of Tennis Australia's national policies, including those for anti-corruption, anti-doping and safeguarding children. A significant part of his role includes developing and maintaining educational and training resources for the diverse stakeholders within tennis. Rhys is a member of the Australian Sports Wagering Scheme, assisting in the development of a regulatory response to safeguard the integrity of Australian sport. Rhys' prior experience with the Australian Federal Police and as an Investigator with the Victorian Commission for Gambling and Liquor Regulation (VCGLR) has provided significant in-depth practical experience. As part of his role at the VCGLR, Rhys managed the sports integrity portfolio which included reviewing integrity mechanisms for all of the major Australian sporting organisations and providing strategies to uphold the integrity of their sport.

Victoria Jamieson works at a national law firm in Canberra, having just completed her final-year Law and Commerce degrees at the University of Canberra, Australia. As part of her studies, she has engaged in international study programmes in Cambodia and Canada. Victoria is a keen sportsperson, playing football in the Australian Capital Territory Premier League, which initiated her interest in sports law. She recently achieved first-class honours in her thesis exploring how the World Anti-Doping Code could apply to non-elite athletes. She presented on this work at the Sport Management Association of Australia & New Zealand 2019 Conference in Christchurch, New Zealand.

Keiji Kawai, PhD, is a Professor of Sport Law in the Department of Policy Studies at Doshisha University in Kyoto, Japan. His book, *The Legal Status of Professional League Players* (2003), was awarded the Okinaga Prize by the

Labor Research Center. He served as Visiting Researcher at the University of Massachusetts at Amherst from 2007 to 2009. Keiji was the General Secretary of the Japan Sports Law Association from 2017 to 2019 and is also on the arbitrator panel at the Japan Sports Arbitration Agency. He was an executive board member of the Nippon Basketball League from 2013 to 2015. He is currently conducting comparative studies funded by the Japan Society for the Promotion of Science on sports accidents and compensation.

Fiona Langlois is a graduate in forensic science and crime analysis from the University of Lausanne, Switzerland. She is currently a PhD candidate in Criminology at the University of Lausanne. In her PhD, she is working on match-fixing in football. Including regular exchanges with INTERPOL, the Council of Europe, Integrity and Police Officers, her study aims at understanding the investigative techniques used by public and private bodies. She is a member of the international group Sports Integrity Analysts Forum, which promotes training, exchanges and collaboration with crime and intelligence analysts worldwide, focusing on sport issues and challenges.

Liam Lenten, PhD, has been a Senior Lecturer at the University of La Trobe, Melbourne, Australia since 2007. His research recently has centred on sports economics, specifically rules, regulation, incentives and athlete behaviour with an emphasis on various forms of cheating (doping, match-fixing, etc.), as well as using sports data to test a wide range of long-standing economic phenomena. He has published 35 peer-reviewed journal articles and has received a large International Olympic Committee grant (2017–19) on anti-doping policy. Liam has held visiting positions at a number of institutions internationally including the University of Michigan, USA, Massachusetts Institute of Technology, USA and Lancaster University, UK.

Genevieve Lim administers legislation within the Victorian Government in Melbourne, Australia relating to major sporting events, including the extension of crowd management and commercial protections. She has published articles relating to human rights in sport and the Australian response to match-fixing. Genevieve has also co-authored a chapter in the Routledge book *Match-Fixing in Sport: Comparative Studies from Australia, Japan, Korea and Beyond*. Genevieve is a qualified lawyer and has completed a Master of Laws at the University of Melbourne specialising in sports law. She is particularly interested in the significance of sport as a social and economic mechanism and emerging integrity issues in sport associated with advances in technology and increasing globalisation.

Richard Lucas, PhD, is the Principal Ethicist, The Ethics Consultancy, Australia. Richard holds a PhD in Applied Ethics and Senior Coach (Endurance Events) credentials (coaching athletics since 1983). For more than 20 years he has taught ethics to tertiary, secondary and primary education students. The tertiary teaching has been to professional, vocational and university groups in Europe and Australia. Richard has published in ethics in Information and Communications

Technology and has an interest in Artificial Intelligence. As a sports coach he is most proud of those athletes who have come closest to their potential and not those who simply achieved high performance standards easily.

James Moller is a Specialist Financial Analyst with the Victoria Police Sporting Integrity Intelligence Unit, Australia since 2013. His role specialises in the analysis of betting information for Victoria Police operations and the assessment of a range of issues relating to organised crime and the integrity of professional sport in Australia. James was also Deputy Chair of the Intelligence and Investigations Advisory Group of the Australian Sports Integrity Taskforce. This Advisory Group provided advice and guidance on the development and implementation of the enhanced intelligence and investigations capabilities of the Australian Government's new body, Sport Integrity Australia.

Thi My Dung Nguyen is a lawyer and sports administrator in Hanoi, Vietnam. She has held various positions in the Vietnam Football Federation (VFF), the Asian Football Confederation (AFC) and Federation International de Football Association over the last 20 years. She is currently Deputy CEO, PVF Football Academy (Vietnam), a Court of Arbitration for Sport arbitrator, a member of the World Athletics Disciplinary Tribunal, a co-founding member of the Women in Sports Law organisation, a member of the AFC Appeal Committee, a member of the VFF Professional Football & Club Licensing Committee, on the VFF Players' Status Committee and a member of the Disciplinary Assessment Board of the Vietnam Anti-Doping and Sports Medicine Agency. Dung also has a Master of Law (Intellectual Property) degree from the University of London International Programme.

Matt Nichol, PhD, is a Lecturer at the School of Business and Law at Central Queensland University, Australia. His research focuses on labour mobility, labour regulation and wages in professional baseball in the United States and Japan. Matt has also researched free agency and corporate governance in the Australian Football League. Matt's research utilises regulatory theory, approaches to labour and the principle that labour is not a commodity to examine the regulation of labour in professional sport. In 2019, Matt's book *Globalization, Sports Law and Labour Mobility: The Case of Professional Baseball in the United States and Japan* was published by Edward Elgar Publishing. Matt has been involved in professional and amateur baseball for a number of years and recently has been a board member of a Melbourne amateur league, a member of several baseball tribunals and worked with professional baseball teams in the Australian Baseball League, Major League Baseball and Nippon Professional Baseball.

Aderonke Ogunleye-Bello is an award-winning investigative journalist, spanning over a decade in Nigeria. Her area of speciality is sports integrity and governance. Ronke's articles have been featured in reputable media outlets throughout Africa and Europe. A passionate public speaker, Ronke has spoken at / participated in different sports events in Nigeria, Denmark, Netherlands, South Africa, Zimbabwe, Malawi, Ghana, TEDx and others. Through her non-governmental organisation, the FAME Foundation, she is using sports to advocate for girls' education and female athletes' rights. To date, more than 40 vulnerable girls in Nigeria have been awarded full scholarships through the FAME Foundation.

Bob Olukoya is a PhD researcher at the Institute for Sport Business, Loughborough University London, UK. His research at LUL focuses on exploring the impact of corruption and other integrity challenges on sponsorship within Nigerian football. Bob has over 20 years international legal practice experience spanning diverse areas such as anti-corruption, sports business development, sports infrastructure renewal, club management, sponsorship and international transfer of players. He currently teaches sport business/ management courses in London and supports grassroots sports development in Africa through his work with AFGRAS Foundation – a sports charity based in Nigeria.

Apolena Ondráčková is an external legal consultant with the Transparency International, Czech Republic chapter. Transparency International is a global non-profit, non-governmental organisation aiming to fight corruption. Apolena has a law degree from the University of Exeter, UK and Charles University in Prague, Czech Republic and she holds a Master of Laws degree. Apolena's expertise is the protection of whistleblowers, compliance and corruption. In the field of sport, she has co-authored a publication on the 'Financing of sport through (Czech) municipalities and regions' (2016).

Catherine Ordway, PhD, is Assistant Professor in Sport Management at the University of Canberra, Australia and Senior Fellow at Melbourne Law School, The University of Melbourne, Australia. Catherine is a sports lawyer, with degrees from the University of Adelaide, and played European handball at the elite level. Catherine also has a Graduate Diploma in Investigations Management from Charles Sturt University, Australia. Catherine was awarded her Sports Management PhD titled 'Protecting Sports Integrity: Sport corruption risk management strategies' in 2019 from the University of Canberra. Having also lived in Norway and Qatar, Catherine has specialised in anti-doping policy since acting for the Australian Olympic Committee in the lead-up to the Sydney 2000 Olympic Games. Catherine actively promotes women in the sports industry and is a co-founder of the Australian organisation Women on Boards, the international network, Women in Sports Law, and supports the Australian football (soccer) network Women Onside.

Erika Riedl is a Senior Legal Counsel and Researcher at the International Centre for Sports Studies (CIES) Switzerland, as well as Clerk for the Tribunal of the International Equestrian Federation. She has been working in sports integrity for over a decade and has, among other things, assisted the Cycling Independent Reform Commission in conducting an investigation concerning doping and related allegations in cycling. Erika holds a law degree, as well as an International

Master in Management, Law and Humanities of Sport. Furthermore, she has successfully completed certificates in Sports Law, in Investigations Management, and in Institutional Integrity Management.

Samantha Roberts, PhD, is an Assistant Professor of Sport & Recreation Management at Texas A&M University-Commerce, USA. She received her PhD from Coventry University, UK, where her thesis examined the managerial implications for sponsors of corruption in sport. Her research interests include toxic leadership in sport organisations, corruption and transgression in sport and trust restoration in international sport.

Elisa Solomon is an Asia-Pacific Employment Relations Specialist with Bristol Myers Squibb, and a Research Assistant with Monash University, Australia. Elisa is a lawyer with experience researching and advising on labour laws and regulations in the Asia-Pacific, and holds a Master of Laws. Having worked in both the public and the private sector in Japan, Elisa is experienced in conducting research on Japanese laws and policies. Elisa has conducted research on laws surrounding workers' protections in Japan, participation of women in Parliament, and the assessment of directors' liability in Australia and Japan. She has previously worked for the International Labour Organization in Thailand on a regional project analysing countries' compliance with the Bali Declaration.

Pim Verschuuren is a PhD candidate with the Swiss Graduate School of Public Administration at the University of Lausanne, Switzerland. Pim is analysing the implementation of whistleblowing policies within the international sports sector. As a Research Fellow at the French IRIS Institute, he has coordinated and participated to several research and awareness-raising programmes on the fight against match-fixing, the development of whistleblowing policies or the integrity of the sports betting market. He also conducted research on sports diplomacy and geopolitics for the French Ministry of Foreign Affairs. Pim graduated in International Relations and Political Science from the Free University of Amsterdam, the Netherlands and the Rennes Political Studies Institute, France.

John Young is a PhD candidate at La Trobe University, Australia. John completed a Masters of High Performance Sport (Science and Analytics) degree at the University of Canberra and achieved three Deans Medals throughout his study. He is currently studying Law at the University of New South Wales, whilst working full time as a data scientist in the horse racing industry. At an elite sports level, John has been successful in swimming, triathlon and football. He has been a staff member on national teams, has qualified athletes for the prestigious Ironman World Championships and worked with numerous elite sporting teams and corporate businesses in data science, analytics and performance evaluation roles.

Foreword

David Howman

Chair of the Board of Directors at Athletics Integrity Unit, World Athletics (formerly IAAF); Chair, Independent Oversight Group of Anti-Corruption Unit, International Cricket Council; Chair, World Squash Federation Ethics Commission; Adjunct Professor, Auckland University of Technology; and Barrister, Wellington, New Zealand.

Sport is a microcosm of society. Issues faced by sport very often mirror those occurring in society. There are many temptations placed in front of those engaged in sporting activities to take illicit short cuts to achieve immediate gains or gratification, while society is displaying an increasing norm to reward those who avoid or distract from the truth. Values are being sorely tested.

We are in the middle of tumultuous times in sport where principles of fair play and integrity are being challenged in the breach. Over recent years the public has been exposed to acts of corruption and fraud in sport ranging from the investigation and prosecution of many FIFA officials to the institutionalised doping programme in Russian sport, from Sandpapergate in cricket to fraud in thoroughbred horse racing. These events, and many others, have caused massive reputational damage to the sport and countries involved, and have significantly weakened public confidence in those entrusted to lead.

The very values of sport permeate our communities, our families, ourselves. These values include fair play, healthy competition, honesty, respect for the rules of the game, respect for officials, respect for opponents or other competitors, self-respect, ethical behaviour and so on. When these values are ignored or not followed there is the possibility of corruption, injustice, fixing of points or results, bullying, sexual harassment, cheating and doping. The integrity of sport is broken, reputations are lost, and recovery of that lost reputation is very difficult if not impossible.

Several sports which have been rattled by corruption and scandal, have responded in a positive way in order to regain public belief. Independent integrity units have been established with varying mandates, and a few countries have likewise responded positively, notably Australia with the creation of Sport Integrity Australia.

However, there has yet to be a coordinated international response to broader corruption issues. Following the Festina doping scandal at the 1998 Tour de France, the IOC, together with governments of the world, formed an international regulator/monitor called the World Anti-Doping Agency, in 1999. Now we need to look at how to expand this type of international response.

The key question is whether sport will designate greater and coordinated resources, both human and financial, to those currently investigating breaches of integrity? Or will the scandals continue unabated?

Integrity must come from the top. The leaders who govern sports are expected to do so with a high degree of integrity. Should they fail, they let down the athletes, the sport and the public. It is important that integrity breaches by top sport officials be independently investigated and scrutinised in an open and transparent fashion, and that any sanction process be as robust as that meted out to athletes who break the rules.

Where there is money there is greed, and with sport betting, supply of steroids, and other banned substances, there are ready markets for easy money. Organised crime has advanced its foray into sport, including at the top levels. While a body of knowledge on how to combat cheating in sport is growing, it is not being shared and implemented at the same rate. Talk fests are not enough. Every day organised criminals can see new opportunities; efforts to combat them are not improving at the same speed, so ill-gotten gains keep increasing and criminal activity continues with impunity.

This book is not only timely but also significant, in that it gathers considered thoughts as to how these challenges might be addressed, together with analysis on how they can be confronted. It is one thing to identify a problem, yet quite another to answer it in a significant way. This book does that with leading minds in the sport integrity area contributing to expose the issues and provide positive solutions for sport to regain public confidence. The individual case studies give a global snapshot of recent controversies and provide an interesting insight into the growing world of research in sport integrity.

Restoring Trust in Sport: Corruption Cases and Solutions is a very valuable contribution to this important part of sport and will provide readers with novel material as to how these matters might be addressed in their own settings.

David Howman CNZM
28 May 2020

Acknowledgements

Thank you to my original PhD primary supervisor, Allan Edwards, and his Loughborough University colleague, and Routledge series editor, James Skinner, for optimistically suggesting that I could simultaneously finish my PhD and start putting together the stellar cast to contribute to this edited book. Thank you too to Richard Lucas, who as my stand-in PhD primary supervisor, introduced me to the Ethics of Care and the work of Margaret Urban Walker on 'moral repair' which inspired the approach to this book. Originally it was planned that Richard and I would co-edit this book, but unfortunately Richard's health has meant that he has had to take a step back. Thank you for all your time and editing advice throughout, Richard!

Rather than a book of misery, focusing on all the ills in sport, I wanted to find best practice examples from around the world that different sports and nations could learn from. Ambitiously, I aimed to bring in people who hadn't written together before, to capture the excellent work being done that was not otherwise being presented in regular conference programmes. It is hoped that this book demonstrates the benefits of transdisciplinary perspectives and ideas from around the world, drawing on lessons from industries beyond sport. It has certainly not been without its challenges to bring authors with different languages, writing styles and theoretical frameworks together. It has been personally rewarding for me to learn so much from each of the contributors – including those who were unable for various reasons to see the whole journey through – and those friends and colleagues who have generously provided ideas, support and constructive critiques. Thank you all.

With a keen eye on diversity, there are contributing authors from each of the continents, and a proactive desire to promote early career researchers – particularly women – so there is a broad age and experience range represented in our cohort. In the case studies chosen, the range of sports is also varied. They include Olympic and non-Olympic sports, and sports at the professional and amateur levels. There are summer and winter sports represented, team and individual sports, as well as horse racing[1] and the challenges faced in the multi-sport Major Games environment. The types of corruption and the solutions recommended have also varied to provide ideas for readers to apply in their own settings. Perhaps this will lead to further editions featuring an even broader diversity of solutions to corruption challenges reflecting the kaleidoscope of cultures, abilities, genders and ages throughout the sport ecosystem.

It is my hope that if this pandemic and 'pause' on sport the world over has a silver lining, it is that we take the time to remember the joy, fun, friendship and fitness sport can bring to everyone. In this downtime, we should refocus our efforts on finding inclusive and connected sport products for all. The colossal wealth in the sport industry must be redistributed to support the whole sporting community, particularly those most vulnerable and in need of all the benefits sport brings. This is an opportunity to rethink our reward system and develop an Ethics of Care approach based on fairness. No longer can the over-inflated salaries for the privileged few, athletes and administrators, be sustained, while community sport, and even the major events, rely heavily on tired and ageing volunteers. The greed, cheating and corrupt practices by people in positions of trust, whether by those who already have too much, or those who have too little, need to be held up to the light in order for trust in the sports industry to be restored. New ways of working, new ways of thinking, new structures, new products and a new relatedness based on care and wellness is needed.

The final big thank you is reserved for my home cheer squad; my son Joshan, and my man Sandy. I look forward to more fun, better 'integration',[2] fruitful collaborations and, ultimately, sports organisations and ethical leaders we can all feel proud of.

Catherine Ordway
Canberra, Australia: 6 July 2020

Notes

1 Noting that my colleague, Dr Adam Masters, likes to (half) joke that horse racing is not a sport until the jockey carries the horse across the line!

2 As distinct from "balance": thank you for the reminder Maria Clarke, sports lawyer.

1 Restoring trust in sport

Corruption cases and solutions

Catherine Ordway and Richard Lucas

In 2013, then UEFA (European football) General Secretary, now international President of FIFA, Gianni Infantino, referred to match-fixing as a 'cancer' which threatens football's integrity (Chaplin, 2013). Fast-forward to 2020 when this book is being drafted during the COVID-19 lockdown, it is meaningful to refer to the challenge of 'corruption in sport' as an umbrella term, which match-fixing is a part, as a 'pandemic' (Porta, 2014, p. 179). The medical metaphor is appropriate: corruption can be regarded as an infectious disease that crosses international borders and is present in every nation and every sport. How to tackle corruption in sport then is a 'wicked' challenge in that it is both an 'unresolved societal issue' and 'no discipline alone can satisfactorily resolve it' (Viret, 2019, p. 3). While most of the media and academic writing is about 'integrity in sport', no one has adequately defined what that means. This book then focuses on trust, a topic that is more closely impacted by corruption than integrity. The fact that trust is a casualty of corruption is less spoken and written about, particularly in the sport space, and so warrants greater attention.

Groundwork

The underlying driver of this book is that it should be focused on solving the threats challenging sport. While some segments of the sport ecosystem are undoubtedly business-centred, corrupt practices demean the fundamental reasons that people engage in sport: fun, friendship, health, skills development, teamwork, a sense of achievement and a host of other reasons. At its heart, corrupt leadership steals not just the money and power in sport, but undermines those values, and creates an environment of fear and distrust.

While this book is about how the loss of trust can be regained, it is important to demonstrate that the loss of trust can come from corruption and that it is ubiquitous: every sport, everywhere. To do this, chapter authors were engaged from a range of countries with an emphasis on diversity in the researchers, and the case studies, by gender, sport, culture, discipline and age. This book showcases best practice examples from around the world which can, in turn, be adapted to suit the different sports and regions where they are played. Featuring 13 women and 11 men, the contributing authors from across the globe write about sports as diverse as biathlon, *sumo*, rugby league, horse racing, road cycling, golf, tennis, ice hockey and, of course, the world game, football. These sports are represented in case studies from eight countries: South Korea, Japan, Vietnam, Nigeria, the Czech Republic, Great Britain, New Zealand and Australia. This is through the eyes of five professions: sport administrators, lawyers, journalists, policymakers, and law enforcement officers working together with academic scholars from nine broad disciplines: business, criminology, economics, ethics, law, political science, psychology, sociology and sport management. Truly interdisciplinary with a world view!

Transdisciplinary approach

This book has taken on the 'transdisciplinarity' approach advocated by Marjolaine Viret: 'where the emphasis is on policy-oriented work that involves practitioners and stakeholders of the community in the process (as opposed to academic experts only)' (2019, p. 3). Viret has looked at applying interdisciplinary tools to improve anti-doping efforts (Viret, 2019), while this book more comprehensively situates doping within a broader framework of corruption. It is hoped that the goal-oriented approach of writing word-limited chapters gave the contributing authors the opportunity to both 'introspectively' consider the 'positions and implicit biases' of their own disciplines, and to 'integrate' a new, melded understanding into practical, and ideally, unique, solutions (Viret, 2019 pp. 4–5). The contributing authors were challenged to identify a case study(s) that most usefully demonstrated the type of corruption chosen and the solution recommended. The brief then for each of the chapter teams was to structure the case study along the lines of:

- What was the wrongdoing?
- How did that impact on trust?
- What was the response from the responsible authority/ sport organisation in attempting to 'restore trust'?
- Did it go far enough? Are there other recommendations going forward?

The brief to each chapter author(s) was to focus on a particular sport and a documented example of corruption through a case study, to arrive at a unique solution for regaining trust.

Corruption

The 'Overview of corruption in sport around the world' following (Chapter 2 in this volume) by our University of Lausanne colleagues, Caneppele, Cinaglia and Langlois, sets the scene and outlines the frequency and extent of corruption (as well as the challenge of determining whether corruption has occurred). For the purposes of this book, 'Corruption', as Miller (2018) writes; 'is exemplified by a very wide and diverse array of phenomena …' (Miller, 2018, p. 4) including '… bribery, nepotism, false testimony, cheating, abuse of authority and so on' (Miller,

2018, p. 40). Miller goes on to say that corruption: 'involves the despoiling of the moral character of persons and ... role occupants *qua* institutional role occupants' (Miller, 2018, p. 7).

This overview then provides a snapshot of corruption cases and serves to set the scene relating to the types and prevalence of sports corruption worldwide for the remainder of the book. It outlines the results of a Database of Corruption Cases in Sport (DACCS) research project. This project has been collecting and analysing information since 2017, and involves:

- Collection: collecting cases of corruption in sport reported by the media;
- Identification: classifying the main characteristics of corrupt behaviour; and
- Analysis: analysing the responses by sport institutions, sport justice and criminal justice systems.

This chapter provides an overview of 230 cases of corruption in sport around the world that were reported in open source media in 2016 and 2017. The DACCS results show that corrupt behaviour exists in many countries and that sport, as well as public institutions, are active in countering corrupt conduct.

Each chapter thereafter focuses on publicly reported case studies involving an instance of corruption, defined in line with either Miller's definition above, or the sport-specific definition of 'corruption' proposed by Masters and Graycar: 'the deviation from public expectations that sports will be played and administered in an honest manner' (Masters & Graycar, 2015, p. 57). This book distinguishes between 'on-field' and 'off-field' corruption. On-field corruption has been considered in sports ranging from cycling and golf to football and tennis. Off-field corruption has been defined using the United Nations Convention Against Corruption (UNCAC) (UN, 2005). The UNCAC does not provide a legal definition of 'corruption', but in this spirit, and in accordance with the 10th Principle of the UN Global Compact (2004), namely that: 'Businesses should work against corruption in all its forms, including extortion and bribery', contributing authors were also encouraged to choose from case studies examining sports organisations, athletes, coaches and administrators involved (as the perpetrator and/or victim) in extortion and bribery associated with event hosting rights, in relation to player selection or transfers, fraud and misappropriation of membership organisation funds, 'pork barrelling', nepotism, ticketing and procurement impropriety, and/or poor accountability and governance.

All of this should seem very familiar: all, and more, of these corrupt behaviours have been exhibited across many sports and at all levels. These examples involve individuals as athletes, officials, coaches, fans, administrators, sponsors and commentators. The essence of corruption lies in moral failure. Moral failure always results in a loss of trust.

Trust

Trust is important, but it can also be dangerous. With trust comes acceptance and vulnerability. If trusted, a person can inflict more harm than if someone is kept at a distance, and treated with caution or distrust. That is why betraying trust is so devastating. Trust is important because it allows us to form relationships with people and to depend on them (McLeod, 2015, p. 1). In the case of organisations, rather than individuals, as set out in Chapter 5 by Jamieson and Ordway, trust creates the environment for a Social Licence to Operate.

It has long been recognised that betraying a person's trust is the worst thing one can do. In Canto XXXIV of the *Divine Comedy*, Dante describes in graphic detail that the greatest punishment (in the 4th Round of the Ninth circle of Hell) is reserved for those who have betrayed: 'That upper spirit, Who hath worst punishment … Is Judas, he that hath his head within / And plies the feet without' (Dante, 1320, p. 233). While Dante does not assist in defining what is meant by 'trust', according to the Oxford English Dictionary (1993), 'trust' is defined as:

> 1. firm belief in the reliability, truth, or ability of someone or something: acceptance of the truth of a statement without evidence or investigation.

To lose trust is to betray; to not do what one has promised; to tell things that are not true; truth. It will be clear from the cases described in this book that the moral failures necessarily lead to a loss of trust. It is not enough, however, to describe the betrayal. It was also required of the contributing authors that they direct their minds to analyse the response to the case study chosen by decision-makers at the time (should there have been a response), and to also canvass possible, improved, solutions for the restoration of that breach of trust.

The theme running throughout this book of 'restoring trust', and hence its title, has been inspired by the work of Margaret Urban Walker and her concept of 'moral repair' (2001). Based on an Ethics of Care approach (Gilligan, 1982), which Walker (Care Ethics Research Consortium, 2010) defined as follows:

> I believe an ethic of care examines closely the implications of human dependency, vulnerability, and interdependence, and insists on four goods: responsiveness to human needs; responsibility and competence in meeting needs; valuing connection and relationship itself; and valuing of caring labor and activities.

A note on integrity

While it is not the focus of this book, it is clear that the term 'sport integrity' is in common usage, so a few words seem to be in order.

For example, prior to a new Government agency, Sport Integrity Australia (SIA), being established on 1 July 2020, the National Integrity of Sport Unit (NISU) provided national oversight, monitoring and coordination of efforts to protect the integrity of sport in Australia from threats of match-fixing, doping and other forms of corruption. NISU defined sports integrity as:

> The manifestation of the ethics and values which promote community confidence in sports, including:
>
> - fair and honest performances and outcomes, unaffected by illegitimate enhancements or external interests; and
> - positive conduct by athletes, administrators, officials, supporters and other stakeholders, on and off the sporting arena, which enhances the reputation and standing of the sporting contest and of sport overall. (NISU 2016)

This definition, which resonates with the concept of a 'good citizen' (e.g. Dalton, 2015; McCuaig & Hay, 2013), raises more questions than it answers. For example, it is not clear what is meant by 'manifestation', or how it should be measured. It is also not explained what are the ethics and values that 'promote confidence', community or otherwise. Promoting *confidence* may be a branding and marketing concern but does not relate to ethics. The reference to 'illegitimate' is also not defined to clarify whether it relates to behaviour not authorised by law, or otherwise specified standards or rules (as distinct from integrity nor ethics). The astute reader will notice that none of this says what integrity (of a sport) *actually* is. Therein lies the difficulty. It is this failure to use integrity to bring positive moral behaviour back into sport that inspired our focus here on trust.

The related concept of the 'spirit of sport', is defined by the World Anti-Doping Agency (WADA) in the *World Anti-Doping Code* (attributed to Angela Schneider), and includes the concept of 'integrity'. David Howman, who also kindly provided the Foreword to this book, when Director General of WADA, in his speech to the Australian & New Zealand Sports Law Association said:

> The intrinsic values of sport, often referred to as 'the spirit of sport' is the celebration of the human spirit, body and mind, and is characterised by values such as ethics, honesty, respect for rules, self-respect and respect for others, fair play and healthy competition. If sport is void of these values (and others) it might be argued it is no longer sport. (Howman, 2015)

This values-based expression is then overlaid by the: 'normative, formal, or rule-based definition of the integrity of a sporting competition' proposed by Ordway and Opie (2016):

> the audience is entitled to rely on the outcome of a match or competition on the basis that it has been played in accordance with the sport rules. This suggests that the outcome, or elements of the competition leading to the outcome, have not been affected by either cheating to win (e.g., by doping) or cheating to lose (e.g., match-fixing). In that sense, not only does the competition have integrity, but so do the athletes who participate in it. (pp. 40–1)

Contributing authors were then referred to, and asked to challenge, the options outlined under the heading: 'Solutions: Anti-corruption Strategies and Their Application to Sport' by Ordway and Opie (2016) as follows:

1. Leadership: ethical decision-making
2. Partnerships: information-sharing and inter-agency collaboration
3. Good governance: transparency and accountability (including gender equity)
4. Awareness and education
5. Sport industry regulatory frameworks
6. Early warning systems
7. Whistleblowing and reporting systems
8. Integrity units, officials and networks
9. Legislation and the role of penal measures
10. Asset protection: athlete welfare; and
11. Research and facilitation of new ideas and approaches

in determining how best to 'restore trust' in the organisation, and in the sporting public, impacted by the chosen case study.

Chapters' structure

To allow the reader to make comparisons between each of the cases of corruption, the individual chapters contain these elements:

- *The Facts:* Each case has described the background to the corruption.
- *The Corruption:* Each case has classified the corruption, pointing out the peculiarities of the case.
- *The Loss:* The chapter will show how the corruption resulted in a loss of trust; trust in whom for individuals and, trust in which group, for organisations.
- *The Repair:* Many chapters do not have a happy ending. Where there was a good news story, the author(s) have described what took place to restore trust. Where there was not, the author(s) have made suggestions on what possible future solutions may be considered.
- *Conclusion:* Each chapter has wrapped up their case by discussing the future. The authors have attempted to outline what lasting impact will result from the corruption, loss of trust, and attempts to make it right.
- *Questions:* Each case study chapter has at the end posed three questions to focus the mind of the reader as follows:

    1. *Trust loss* – In whom (or, in which group) has trust been lost in this case?
    2. *Trust correction* – How, if attempted, has the restoration of trust been tried?; and;
    3. *Lessons learned* – How could the lessons from this case be applied to other sports, nations, states, other districts for the same sport, or other sports to prevent a further loss of trust or at least to restore trust?

Case studies chosen

Case studies have long been recognised as useful tools for teaching and learning, both for students and for practitioners. The book has been divided into two parts, based on whether the case studies are from the international or national levels.

Part I: International organisations

The four chapters in this section provide an example of a loss of trust at a global scale, through the 23rd Winter Olympic Games, PyeongChang 2018 (South Korea) procurement disgrace, the International Biathlon Union bribery scandal, the World Anti-Doping Agency Code over-reach, and the International Cycling Union doping culture.

PyeongChang 2018 Winter Olympic Games

The Bayley and Egle chapter on the PyeongChang 2018 Winter Olympic Games outlines the loss of trust where the lack of ethical leadership within the host organising committee and sponsors, combined with lax procurement processes for the Games infrastructure, created unfairness and abuse of power and process. The conflicts of interest exposed during the procurement processes for the 2018 PyeongChang Winter Olympic Games led to prosecutions and convictions, the impeachment of the President of South Korea for corruption, and difficulties for the organising committee, POCOG, in conducting its business. This situation reduced trust and integrity for the PyeongChang Games. The chapter considers how concepts of ethical leadership, particularly action-logics, can be introduced into the procurement decision-making process to avoid such problems in the future. These approaches can help to ensure that trust is restored to, and maintained in, procurement processes for other major international sporting events.

International Biathlon Union

The chapter by Riedl analyses the International Biathlon Union's (IBU) response to bribery allegations through its Code of Ethics regulatory mechanism. Focusing on recent events impacting on the IBU, this chapter analyses and evaluates the responses by the IBU, looking mainly into the IBU Integrity Code and the creation of the Independent Integrity Unit. This chapter further compares the IBU Integrity Code with the codes of conduct/codes of ethics of the remaining International Olympic Winter Sports Federations. In addition, this chapter includes recommendations on how the regulations could be strengthened from an anti-corruption perspective, and discusses whether the responses are sufficient and adequate to regain trust after the biathlon scandal.

World Anti-Doping Code

The chapter by Jamieson and Ordway then provides an example from New Zealand where it is argued that the World Anti-Doping Code (WADC) unfairly prevents the national anti-doping organisations (NADOs) from exercising a proportionate discretion. While 'cheating in sport by using drugs' clearly falls within the definition of corruption (Miller, 2018), it is argued instead that the abuse of power in this case study relates to the failure of the WADC to distinguish between competitors 'cheating in sport' and people unintentionally caught up in the contractual anti-doping process. The deliberately broad definition of 'Athlete' combined with the lack of discretion to determine appropriate sanctions for those inadvertently captured combines to amount to an abuse of power and consequent breach of trust. The actors enforcing the WADC, primarily the NADOs, are arguably not permitted to exercise a discretion to determine appropriate and proportionate responses to those cases falling outside the range of people participating in competitive sport. The NADOs are usually taxpayer funded entities, and have legitimacy through their 'social licence' to protect clean sport. The publicly funded resources available to the NADOs are finite. This chapter argued that the public confidence, or trust, in the work of NADOs under the WADC is undermined where NADOs are seen to be heavy-handed or excessive in their treatment of non-elite or recreational athletes. It also has the effect of working counter to public policy expectations for non-elite participants in sport. It is argued here that rewording the WADC from an Ethics of Care perspective (Gilligan, 1982) would allow the transparent exercise of discretion and thereby restore trust in the WADC by the athletes and the public in order to focus anti-doping efforts in the areas of greatest need.

International Cycling Federation

The final international organisation included in this section is the International Cycling Federation (UCI), the world governing body for cycling. The question that is raised here by Roberts and Ordway is whether the success of Team Sky (now Team Ineos) has assisted the UCI to overcome some of the distrust caused by decades of doping in men's professional road cycling. No one sport has faced greater scrutiny from stakeholders in the sport industry than cycling and, in particular, road cycling. A history of the use of performance-enhancing drugs has tarnished the legacies of some of the sport's biggest names and most high-profile races, like the Tour de France.

After admissions from arguably the sport's most well-known name, Lance Armstrong, one team seemingly at the forefront of success in professional road cycling, winning all three of the Grand Tours since 2012, including winning seven of the last eight Tours de France (2012–2019) is Team Sky. These successes have repeatedly been questioned by the media and other stakeholders and, given the context, it is hardly surprising. This chapter discusses how the culture of cycling has altered the dialogue of success in the sport, so that distrust in any success is automatic. How Team Sky have been perceived within this dialogue, and what they, in particular, have done and can do to try to restore trust in performances and, indeed, governance of the sport more broadly is examined.

Part II: National responses

The seven chapters in this section provide an example of a loss of trust at the national level, through: match-fixing in Japanese *sumo*, Australian tennis, Australian rugby league and Vietnamese football, selection bribery in Czech ice hockey and Nigerian football, and athlete (horse) substitution in Australian racing.

Japanese sumo

Professional *sumo* in Japan provides a different perspective on corruption in sport due to the long-standing and, until recently, accepted tradition of match-fixing in *makuuchi* and *jûryô*, the two highest divisions of wrestling known as *sekitori*. As sports gambling is generally illegal under Japan's Criminal Code, match-fixing in *sumo* is not related to gambling. Instead fixing is largely the result of the promotion rules, where *rikishi* ('wrestlers') with a losing record in one of the six annual tournaments face demotion in rank and division, and with it, the loss of status and income of competing in *sekitori*. Here, the matches are fixed to maintain the status of wrestlers. Evidence surfaced in the 1990s and 2000s of match-fixing involving wrestlers with above expected winning records when facing a losing record in the last days of a tournament. A police investigation into illegal gambling in baseball in 2011 led to evidence of fixing involving a number of *rikishi* and resulted in an investigation by the Japan Sumo Association that confirmed the first official cases of match-fixing in *sumo*. This chapter by Nichol, Solomon and Kawai has examined the cultural, institutional and *sumo* specific factors that encourage fixing and how trust was restored with the public, fans and sponsors after the 2011 fixing scandal.

Czech Republic ice hockey

Although the promotion of whistleblowing is becoming a global issue, through major scandals revealed by insiders, such as the Snowden disclosures (von Solms et al., 2015), or the Panama Papers (O'Donovan, et al., 2019), political recognition and legal protection of whistleblowers is still lacking. The sport environment is no exception. Recent prominent corruption cases in international sports have highlighted the strong organisational silence (or 'omerta') that can prevail in some sport settings, and the high level of retaliation that whistleblowers face as official dissenters. Sport organisations have started to set up whistleblowing (or reporting) mechanisms to enable individuals to signal corrupt behaviours occurring on or off the field, such as match-fixing or corruption. However, it still has to be demonstrated to what extent these tools can be trusted by sport actors.

This chapter, by Ondráčková, from Transparency International, and Verschuuren, underlines the specificities of the sport sector with regard to the implementation of whistleblowing and compliance processes. Lessons from the 'good practice' case study in Czech ice hockey will explain why reliable and trustworthy reporting policies are specifically needed and how to build them. In this case, the national ice hockey federation established a formal cooperation with a national chapter of Transparency International. The independent and neutral organisation not only collects and pre-handles reports but also coordinates integrity awareness programmes and acts as a mediator and adviser for sport actors facing integrity issues. The chapter concludes with concrete recommendations to consider and adapt such solutions in other (national or international) sport contexts. Although the promotion of whistleblowing is becoming a global issue, political recognition and legal protection of whistleblowers are still lacking. Recent prominent corruption cases in international sports have highlighted the strong organisational silence and the high level of retaliation that whistleblowers face. Does this restore trust and, while it is the right thing to do, is it safe to blow the whistle?

Australian tennis

Tennis Australia works collaboratively with the international Tennis Integrity Unit (TIU) and the Victoria Police Sporting Integrity Intelligence Unit (SIIU). The TIU is the anti-corruption body with oversight for professional tennis around the world. The TIU is responsible for enforcing the sport's zero-tolerance policy on betting-related corruption. In doing so, it has three main strategic priorities – preventing corruption from taking place; investigation and prosecution of offenders; and delivering anti-corruption education for players and stakeholders to recognise and report corrupt activity. The TIU is an operationally independent organisation based in London. A global review of integrity in tennis has recently been undertaken and a report released by the Independent Review of Integrity in Tennis in December 2018. The SIIU has assisted in meeting with the review panel, as well as providing submissions with recommendations for improvements to the TIU. Partnerships and inter-agency collaboration will be highlighted in this case study analysing the collaborative approach used, through Harrison from Tennis Australia, and Moller from the SIIU.

Vietnamese football

Football in Vietnam has a long and distinguished history of corruption. This chapter by Nguyen and Gardiner examines cases of betting-related match-fixing which involved national and club players in Vietnam. The actions taken by authorities, football federation and clubs to combat this type of corruption in football showed initial results in a new generation of professional players who focused on developing their career, images and good reputation. Trust of fans and sponsors has been improved. However, there is still more that needs to be done to maintain the good results achieved. As such, recommendations are directed at a more systematic and global approach to prevent and combat corruption by focusing on education and communication, giving assistance and support to players; having in place early warning, whistleblowing and reporting mechanisms; making timely investigation and appropriate disciplinary action, as well as improvement in rules and regulations. Will these measures restore trust in the players and in the men's football league?

Nigeria and football

This chapter presents another football story by Olukoya and Ogunleye-Bello: a Nigerian National team coach accepted a 'gift' from a journalist posing as a player's agent. This 'gift' was intended (by the fake player's agent) to facilitate the selection of the fake player's agent footballer into the national team. If team selection is not based on merit and the 'gift' influenced the coaches' recommendation then clearly the coach has subverted the trust that the public, sports administrators and all the other players have assumed would be in place when selections were made.

This case study was used to illustrate how 'moral repair' Walker (2001) and 'Ethics of Care' (Gilligan, 1982) can be a complementary part of the predominantly punitive and retributive justice system in Nigeria. Football is no doubt the number one sport in Nigeria and it unifies the nation the way nothing else does. The Super Eagles and the Super Falcons (male and female national teams respectively) are well loved in the country and have enjoyed great successes in Africa and world football. Football coaches in Nigeria, especially those working with the national teams, are high-profile and subjected to close scrutiny notably during the period in the lead up to continental and international tournaments. The dominant narrative (within the media and fans), however, is that the players' selection process had been corrupted. Players are chosen not entirely based on their ability on the field but for their capacity to bribe the coach. There was no empirical evidence of this practice, however, until this case surfaced. The chapter focuses on the aftermath of the discovery of the coach's behaviour, analysing how the wrongdoing was dealt with by the football authorities. The authors consider whether the attempts at 'restoring trust' have been aided through the care and justice principles inherent in Walker and Gilligan's work, rather than focusing on punishment and retribution for the coach. The chapter concludes with recommendations on what could be done to discourage similar behaviour in future to restore trust in the fairness of future selections.

Australian rugby league

While 'cheating to win' (doping) and 'cheating to lose' (match-fixing) involve very different behaviours (Ordway & Opie, 2016), this chapter has analysed the extent to which a possible new incentive-based strategy, conditional retirement funds, tested in the anti-doping environment, may also assist to reduce the risk of match-fixing. It is intended to address financial vulnerabilities that make some athletes more susceptible to untoward influences. Financial vulnerability post-retirement can make some athletes more amenable to approaches leading to match-fixing while still playing. Athletes are vulnerable for a range of reasons, including addictions, secrets, poverty and greed. Here, Ordway and Lenten propose a novel, punitive strategy, conditional superannuation.

Some athletes do not participate in retirement or superannuation schemes; they look for other ways to secure their future. To reduce their financial exposure some athletes resort to match-fixing as an income hedge. For athlete employees, however, this proposal can be seen as an additional punitive measure, as is legislated for public servants and other persons in positions of trust, such as Australian Federal Police Officers. This policy also allows building in a retrospective component to penalties by confiscating earlier (ill-gotten) earnings. For those not already having superannuation payments included in their packages, it could be negotiated as an additional payment to assist in alleviating future financial stress often experienced by retired (and untainted) professional sportspeople. Will freeing athletes from the worries of financial security in retirement reduce match-fixing and restore trust in a fair contest?

Australian horse racing

It is said that Australians will bet on two flies crawling up a wall. There are many examples of gamblers attempting to change the odds of a race to favour themselves. Some attempts at manipulation are legal but questionable morally, while others breach sport and criminal regulations. In the case of Fine Cotton, the Australian horse racing industry was scandalised by an instance of match-fixing involving horse substitution. While the replacement of a fast horse for a reputedly slow one in a thoroughbred race was not unknown, the case of Fine Cotton was breathtaking for the ineptitude of the fix and for exposing entrenched corruption in Queensland law enforcement agencies. Restoring trust in the horse racing industry after this incident involved not only investigating the conduct and punishing the perpetrators but addressing systemic organisational corruption in Queensland more broadly. This example of match-fixing holds a significant place in public memory and Lim and Young provide insights into addressing integrity problems that lie beyond the control of sporting regulators. How can a punter (or anyone, for that matter) trust that a race is genuine?

Where to from here?

In the final chapter, Ordway considers why this all matters, and what we have learnt from the various case studies on how trust was lost and then restored (or not). What is the current state of effective trust restoration, and what more needs to be done? Is sport doomed to cynicism and mere entertainment? In entertainment the very notion of trust, in the content at least, is of no interest. Nobody puts any importance on the truth or veracity of an actor's words. The only measure is: how entertaining has it been? Surely sport is not to be reduced to mere entertainment. As will be demonstrated throughout this book, and as expressed best by then Liverpool manager, Bill Shankly, when asked about football: 'Some people believe [sport] is a matter of life and death, I am very disappointed with that attitude. I can assure you it is much, much more important than that' (bracket added, Bona, 2015). We hope that this book is a contribution to restoring trust in all those people who share Shankly's view.

References

Bona, E. (2015, 29 September). Bill Shankly remembered: 11 brilliant quotes from Liverpool's iconic manager. *The Liverpool Echo*. Retrieved from https://www.liverpoolecho.co.uk/news/liverpool-news/bill-shankly-remembered-11-brilliant-10156199

Care Ethics Research Consortium. (2010, 3 May). Margaret Urban Walker, Interviews. Care Ethics Research Consortium. Retrieved from https://care857567951.wordpress.com/2010/05/03/margaret-urban-walker/

Chaplin, M. (2013, 18 January). UEFA determined to combat match-fixing. UEFA. Retrieved from https://www.uefa.com/insideuefa/about-uefa/legal-justice/news/newsid=1912418.html

Dalton, R. J. (2015). *The good citizen: How a younger generation is reshaping American politics.* Washington, DC: CQ Press.

Dante, A. (1320). *Divine comedy; Volume inferno.* Retrieved from https://www.sacred-texts.com/chr/dante/in34.htm

Gilligan, C. (1982). *In a different voice.* Cambridge, MA: Harvard University Press.

Howman, D. (2015, 15 October). Speech by WADA Director General, David Howman, Challenges to the integrity of sport, Melbourne. World Anti-Doping Agency. Retrieved from https://www.wada-ama.org/en/media/news/2015-10/speech-by-wada-director-general-david-howman-challenges-to-the-integrity-of-sport

Masters, A.& Graycar, A.(2015). *Corruption in sport – a new field for public policy.* United Nations Office on Drugs and CrimeSymposium of the Anti - Corruption Academic (ACAD) InitiativeMoscow, 30–31 October 2015, pp. 56–68. Retrieved fromhttps://www.researchgate.net/publication/304541091_Corruption_in_Sport_A_new_field_for_public_policy

McCuaig, L., & Hay, P. J. (2013). Principled pursuits of 'the good citizen' in health and physical education. *Physical Education and Sport Pedagogy*, 18(3), 282–297.

McLeod, C. (2015). Trust. *Stanford encyclopedia of philosophy.* Palo Alto, CA: Stanford University Press. Retrieved from http://plato.stanford.edu/archives/fall2015/entries/trust/

Miller, S. (2018, 21 September). Corruption. *Stanford encyclopedia of philosophy.* Palo Alto, CA: Stanford University Press. Retrieved from https://plato.stanford.edu/archives/win2018/entries/corruption/

NISU. (2016, 3 August). National Integrity of Sport Unit, Department of Health, Australian Government. Retrieved from https://www1.health.gov.au/internet/main/publishing.nsf/Content/national-integrity-of-sport-unit

O'Donovan, J., Wagner, H. F., & Zeume, S. (2019). The value of offshore secrets: Evidence from the Panama Papers. *The Review of Financial Studies*, 32(11), 4117–4155.

O'Hara, K. (2004). *Trust: From Socrates to spin.* Crow's Nest, NSW: Allen & Unwin.

Ordway, C. & Opie, H. (2016). Integrity and corruption in sport. In N. Schulenkorf & S. Frawley (Eds.), *Critical issues in global sport management* (pp. 60–85). Abingdon: Routledge.

Oxford University Press. (1993). *The Compact Oxford English Dictionary* (2nd ed.). Oxford: Clarendon Press.

Porta, M. (Ed.). (2014). *A dictionary of epidemiology.* Oxford: Oxford University Press.

UN. (2004). UN global compact 10th principle against corruption. United Nations. Retrieved from https://www.unglobalcompact.org/library/2031

UN. (2005). United Nations convention against corruption. United Nations. Retrieved from https://www.unodc.org/unodc/en/corruption/uncac.html

Viret, M. (2019). Using interdisciplinary tools to improve anti-doping: Utopia or necessity?. *Int Sports Law J.* Retrieved from https://doi.org/10.1007/s40318-019-00161-8

von Solms, S., & van Heerden, R. (2015, February). The consequences of Edward Snowden NSA related information disclosures. In *Iccws 2015-The Proceedings of the 10th International Conference on Cyber Warfare and Security: ICCWS2015* (p. 358). Academic Conferences Limited. Retrieved from https://www.researchgate.net/publication/275019554 The_Consequences_of_Edward_Snowden_NSA_Related_Information_Disclosures

Walker, M. U. (2001). Moral repair and its limits. Retrieved from http://epublications.marquette.edu/cgi/viewcontent.cgi?article=1151&context=phil_fac

2 An overview of corruption in sport around the world

Stefano Caneppele, Giulia Cinaglia and Fiona Langlois

This chapter provides an overview of 230 cases of corruption in sport around the world that were reported in open source media in 2016 and 2017. These cases come from the Database on Alleged Cases of Corruption in Sport (DACCS).[1] Results show that corrupt behaviour exists in many countries and that sport as well as public institutions are active in countering corrupt conduct. Match manipulation remains the main concern, and the most popular sports disciplines (i.e. soccer, tennis and cricket) are the ones most affected by the topic. Corrupt conduct with event bidding and contracts follows the awarding cycle for major sports events, while the other corrupt behaviours – often associated with sports bodies' mismanagement – appears to be publicly reported more often now than in the past, partly because of previous scandals and partly because of increased levels of media coverage.

Introduction

Sport has always played an important role in society because of its collective, cultural and educational functions. Indeed, sport is a sort of social glue, bringing together all kinds of individuals and communities with a diverse range of abilities and backgrounds in the collective spirit of equality, honesty, hard work, discipline, teamwork and mutual respect (Barbary, Dyer, & Frandano, 2011). These intrinsic values, together with sport's global reach and iconic athletes, contribute to the popularity of sport among amateurs and professionals, participants and observers alike. Beside its social impact, sport is also a continuously evolving business. Over the past few decades, there has been a huge increase in team revenues, player salaries, ticket prices, merchandising and tournament prizes (Schulenkorf & Frawley, 2017). Nowadays, the global sports industry is worth an estimated US$1.3 trillion (Première Ligue, UCPF, & EY, 2017) and its impact on the world economy is ceaselessly growing. In the last few decades, the significant increase in professionalisation, globalisation and commercialisation of sport has had a positive effect, but it has also generated several sports scandals. The years 2015 and 2016 raised the media's attention with a series of crises in football (with 'FIFA Gate'), in tennis (with the BBC and BuzzFeed News allegations about match-fixing), and at the Winter Olympic Games (with the alleged state-run doping programme in

Russia). All these scandals have contributed to the public debate on the integrity of sport. Nonetheless, even though harmful behaviour is easily recognised, the concept of integrity itself is still blurry (Cleret et al., 2015). According to the different definitions of sports integrity in the literature (see, e.g. Treagus, Cover, & Beasley, 2011), a sport with integrity can be defined as an inclusive sport; it is characterised by the equal treatment of everyone, regardless of age, colour, gender, race or sexual orientation. The environment is respectful and fair, it is not harmful and nor does it pose any risk to the health or the safety of any people involved, whether they be athletes or members of the public (Sport Australia, n.d., Hemphill & Wilson-Evered, 2016). The main assumption is that corruption in sport undermines sport integrity.

Many definitions of corruption exist, and different scholars have debated over them (see, e.g. Miller, 2018). Likewise, corruption in sport is a multifaceted phenomenon. Several authors have grouped corrupt behaviour into two categories: on-field and off-field corruption (Figure 2.1; see, e.g. Barbary et al., 2011; Chappelet, 2017). On-field corruption refers to any behaviour likely to modify the outcome of a competition (e.g. doping, match-fixing through betting or non-betting acts, etc.). Off-field corruption includes two subcategories. The first group includes all the corrupt behaviour aimed at manipulating the adjudication, preparation and conduct of sports events (e.g. vote-buying, bribery in the awarding of construction work, etc.). The second group comprises corrupt behaviours that affect the way in which a sports organisation is managed (e.g. through vote rigging, ticketing, embezzlement related to player transfers, etc.). Indeed, sports corruption is a complex phenomenon that consists of behaviour that directly impacts athletic performance or the outcome of a competition (e.g. by altering a match) as well as behaviours detected in public and private organisations (e.g. bribery, fraud and tax evasion schemes). Corrupt behaviour undermines the role of sport, but there is still a dearth of knowledge about the size and the characteristics of this phenomenon. For these reasons, the Council of Europe, through the Enlarged Partial Agreement on Sport, decided in 2017 to start collecting data on cases of sports corruption.

In spring 2017, the Enlarged Partial Agreement on Sport launched a project to build a database on alleged cases of corruption in sport. The DACCS project aimed to (a) record alleged cases of corruption in sport reported in the media, and (b) monitor the responses given both by the institutions involved (i.e. disciplinary

Figure 2.1 Typologies of on-field and off-field corrupt behaviour (source of icons: Flaticon.com).

sanctions) and by criminal justice systems. The goal was twofold: establish an initial corpus of cases of corruption and then monitor how they have been managed by sports and national institutions. The DACCS project identified six general categories of corruption in sport: (a) manipulation of competitions, (b) doping (c), event bids, (d) contracts, (e) elections, and (f) other. Generally, the 'manipulation of competitions', and otherwise referred to throughout this book as 'match-fixing', relates to events where the score or other match-related occurrences (e.g. red cards) are known before the end of the match. 'Doping' refers to corruption in doping cases only (e.g. blackmail and the extortion of athletes or manipulation of the test results), while 'event bids' refers to corruption in bids to host sport competitions or meetings. Moreover, 'contracts' refers to fraud and embezzlement that may happen in a sports institution during the awarding of business-related contracts, and 'election' refers to cases in which the election of sports institution representatives has been manipulated through fraud or corruption. Finally, 'other' refers to all other sporting cases related to corruption that do not fit the previous typology.[2] The School of Criminal Justice at the University of Lausanne was appointed to run the pilot study. Since very few studies have treated corruption in sport empirically, this exploratory research focused on providing an overview of the issue of corruption in sports. The exploratory approach helps the researcher become familiar with the topic and better understand it, while also painting a picture of the situation (Neuman, 2014). A pilot study was then conducted to develop a methodology for collecting cases of sports corruption through open sources (Caneppele, Cinaglia, Sperrer, & Langlois, 2019).

Data and method

The DACCS project covers a two-year period (2016–2017). Initial data collection was completed in 2017 on 2016 cases, while a second round occurred in 2018 on 2017 cases. Although the study targeted articles appearing in 2016 and 2017, some of the cases mentioned happened before those years.

Given the lack of official statistics on the phenomenon, the study used open sources in order to retrieve articles that reported on alleged cases of corruption in sport. More specifically, the research replicated the approach followed by Aniello and Caneppele (2018) to study the sale of stolen goods on online platforms. An automated system to retrieve and extract media articles through a series of selected keywords was put in place (Table 2.1). The extraction was carried out through the EMM (Europe Media Monitor) News Brief.[3] It was decided that all available media on the EMM News Brief would be taken into consideration. The extraction process generated Excel files that were cleaned to remove duplicates and false positive cases. A second review occurred in which researchers read the articles and manually deleted false positives, links that were no longer active, and duplicates. It was commonplace for several articles to mention the same fact. In these circumstances, the research team kept only the most accurate, detailed and relevant article(s). The selected corpus of articles served as the source of information that populated the database, resulting in 230 relevant cases.

Table 2.1 Corruption in sport: Selected keywords

ON-FIELD CORRUPTION		*OFF-FIELD CORRUPTION*			
Behaviours directly impacting sports results		**Behaviours influencing the adjudication, preparation and conduct of sports events**		**Behaviours affecting the appointment and management of sports organisations**	
Manipulation of competitions	***Corruptive behaviours doping-related***	***Corruptive behaviours at Event bids & at Contracts***	***Ticketing***	***Corruptive behaviour at election***	***Other corruptive behaviours***
'Match manipulation' AND sport	Black-mailing AND sport	'Vote bribes' AND sport	'Ticketing fraud' AND sport	'Election fraud' AND sport	Fraud AND sport
Match-fixing AND sport gambling	Extortion AND sport	'Money laundering' AND sport	'Ticketing scam' AND sport	'Vote rigging' AND sport	Transfer of players fraud
Spot-fixing AND sport	Corruption AND sport	'Vote rigging' AND sport			Fraud in player market
Tanking AND sport		Corruption AND sport			Corruption AND sport
		'Vote-buying' AND sport			Bribery AND sport
		Bribery AND sport			
		'Vote rigging' AND sport			

The DACCS considers cases of corruption as a unit of analysis. For each case, there are three categories of variables: (a) metadata, (b) the case's general information, and (c) the disciplinary/judicial follow-up on the case. The first category – metadata – includes the case identification number, which is unique; the source(s) that reported the case; and the source reliability score, which varies depending on the existence of formal proceedings or decisions made on the case. The second category covers general information about the case and provides a short description of what was reported. It consists of variables on the type(s) of alleged corrupt conduct, the year in which it took place, the name and the number of the countries in which the case occurred, the sports disciplines involved, the entities allegedly involved, and whether the case was linked to other cases. The third category focuses on the social reaction of sports organisations and law enforcement to the (alleged) corruption. Variables refer to the existence of any disciplinary and judicial investigations open on the case. They also cover the output of these investigations in terms of any sanctions on or the acquittal of the parties involved.

Data was analysed using descriptive and comparative statistical analysis, and examples of in-depth analysis are provided at the end of the results section. For descriptive comparisons, the analyses used frequency distribution and cross tabulation among pairs of selected variables (e.g. sports disciplines and type of corrupt behaviour). This chapter provides two visual examples for in-depth analysis. All Figures were created either through Tableau Desktop software (Figures 2.2, 2.3, 2.4 and 2.5) or through IBM® i2 Analyst's Notebook® (Figures 2.6, 2.7 and 2.8). The examples have been selected to show how information from DACCS cases can be displayed to establish links among different cases and to explain complex cases.

Results

The data collection exercise on cases of corruption in sport reported a total of 230 cases published in the media in the years 2016–2017; however, cases recorded in the DACCS occurred between 2000 and 2017.

Corruption in sport has been detected across all continents. Figure 2.2 shows the countries affected by cases of corruption in sport. The map represents the places where the alleged corruption has happened, but in some cases, corrupt behaviour has a multi-country dimension, and it is difficult to clearly determine crime localisation. Corrupt behaviour exists in various African, Asian and European countries, as cases of corruption are spread across multiple nations, while the United States and Brazil seem to have the highest concentrations of cases in the Americas. In Oceania, Australia has the most recurrent number of cases of alleged sport corruption reported by open source media. Australia also recorded the highest total number of cases (17), followed by Brazil (14), India (14), the United States (12), and the United Kingdom (12). As mentioned above, alleged cases of sports corruption can affect multiple countries, as corruption easily assumes a transnational dimension. This is particularly true when corrupt behaviour involves international federations or mega-events.

Figure 2.3 illustrates the frequency distribution by category of corrupt behaviour. The category that occurs most often is the manipulation of competitions (95 cases), followed by doping-related events (32), and corrupt event bidding (22). The category 'Other' includes 66 cases. The analysis reveals that match manipulation is by far the main problem. It affects several sports, small and large competitions, and wealthy as well as poor countries. As 'Other' includes a large range of corrupt behaviours, it is difficult to describe this category in detail, even though it is possible to assess which sports disciplines are most affected by corruption (Figure 2.4).

The DACCS detected corrupt behaviour in 26 sports disciplines. European football (soccer) is the sport with the most frequent number of cases, followed by: tennis, athletics and cricket. Under the label 'Olympics' there are corrupt behaviours related to the awarding and management of Olympic events. Manipulation of competition occurs frequently in soccer, tennis and cricket, while doping-related activities are mostly observed in athletics. Most disciplines recorded one or two types of corrupt behaviours. Only six sports had more than three.

Figure 2.2 Countries affected by cases of sports corruption.

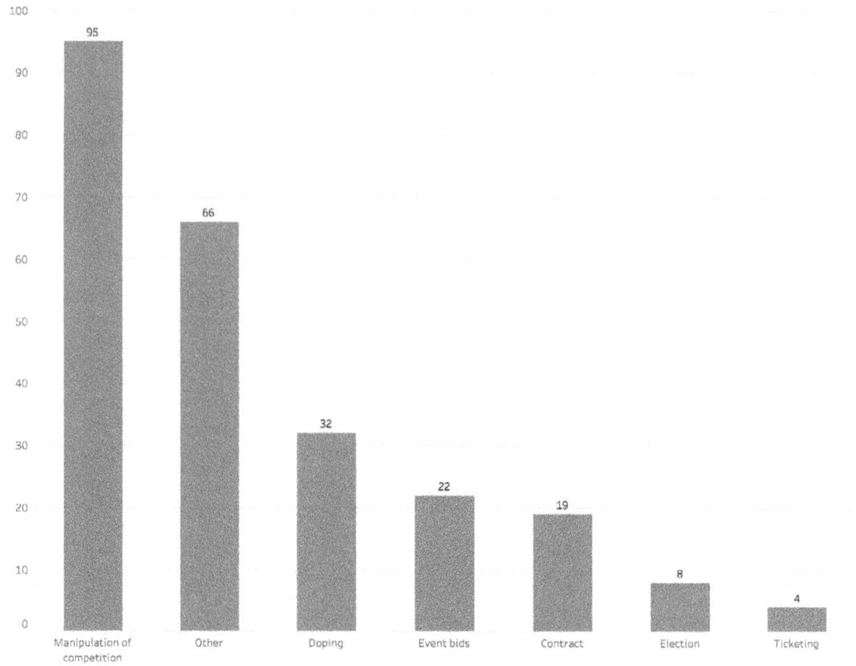

Figure 2.3 Types of corrupt behaviour in sport. Cases detected through open source media in 2016 and 2017 (N = 230).

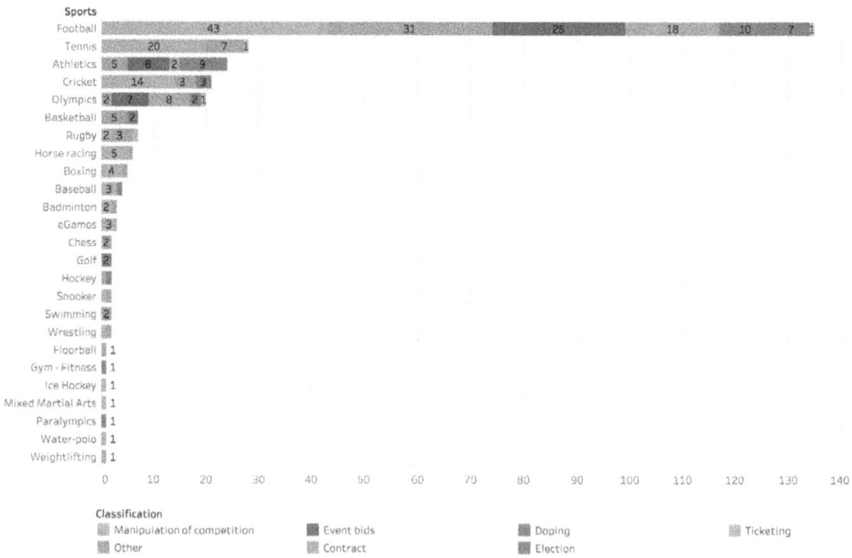

Figure 2.4 Corrupt behaviour according to sports disciplines in the DACCS.

Additionally, the DACCS monitors the reaction of sports federations and public bodies against corrupt behaviour (Figure 2.5). In general, sports authorities frequently use disciplinary sanctions, while law enforcement intervention (and then judicial sanctions) is left to the most serious cases. Currently, it is impossible to give a detailed overview of the social reaction to corruption in sport since the cases covered are recent and some of them are still going through judicial procedures.

Corrupt behaviour in sport may be analysed in depth to better understand how such criminal events occur, and this analysis looks at individuals and their roles or behaviour within a corrupt scheme. This section presents two examples concerning cricket (Figure 2.6) and basketball (Figures 2.7 and 2.8). Figure 2.6 shows that individual DACCS cases can be linked to reveal match-fixing patterns.

The selected cases refer to one cricket scandal in the 2017 Pakistan Super League competition. In a nutshell, some active players from a Super League cricket team conspired with bookmakers ('bookies') to manipulate their matches.

In case 1, cricketer NJ acted as a broker between active players and bookies. He was identified and banned from cricket by the Pakistan Cricket Board because of a conspiracy to match-fix and because of his refusal to cooperate during the investigation.

In case 2, a man (whose identity is unknown) – linked to an international betting syndicate – convinced two players, KL and SK, to fix a match during the Pakistan Super League competition in 2017. The three were arrested, convicted and given disciplinary sanctions.

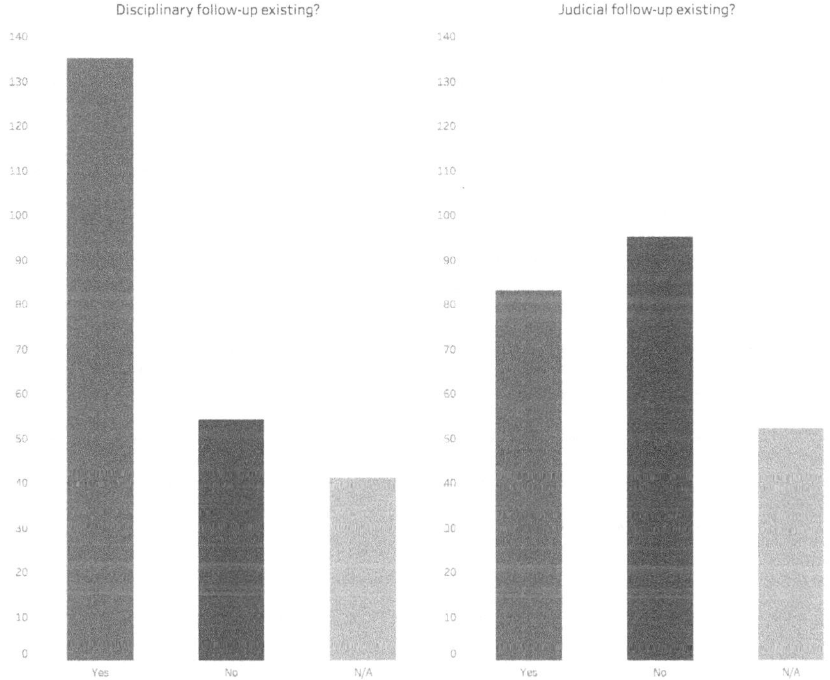

Figure 2.5 Existence of disciplinary or judicial procedure on corrupt DACCS cases.

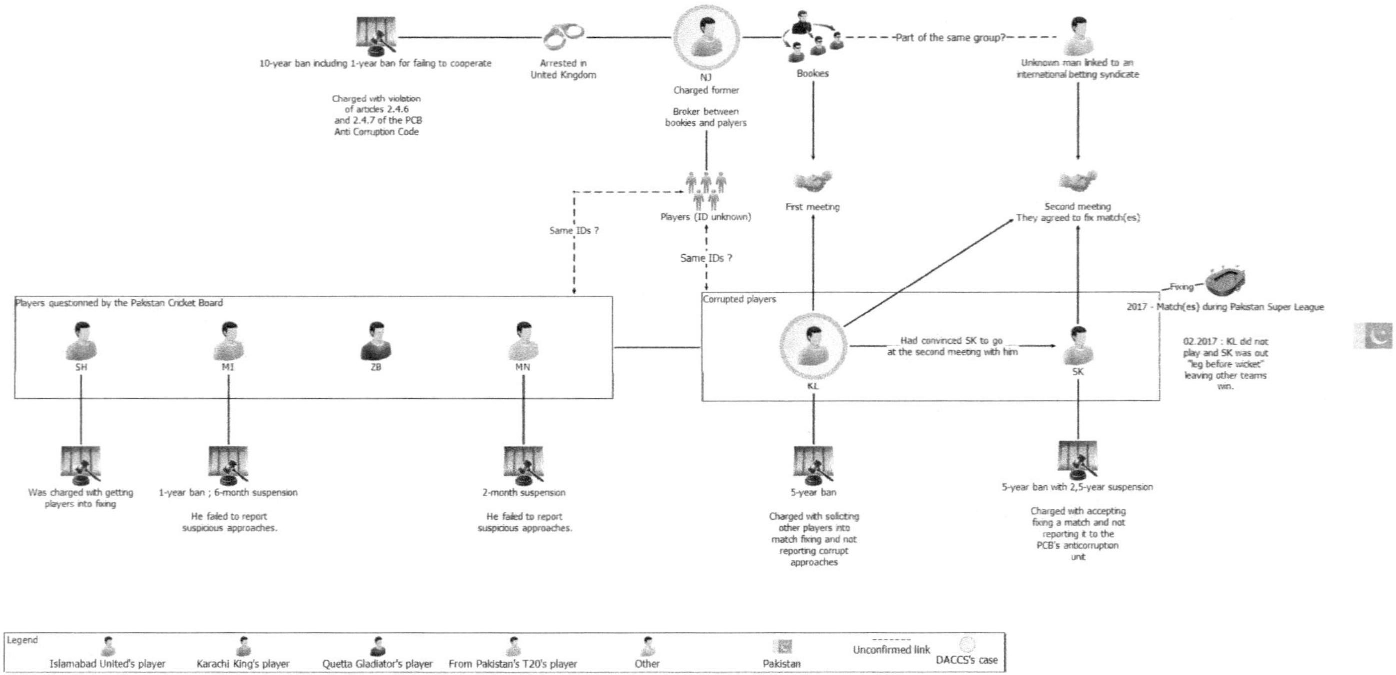

Figure 2.6 In-depth analysis of 2017 match-fixing cases in cricket.

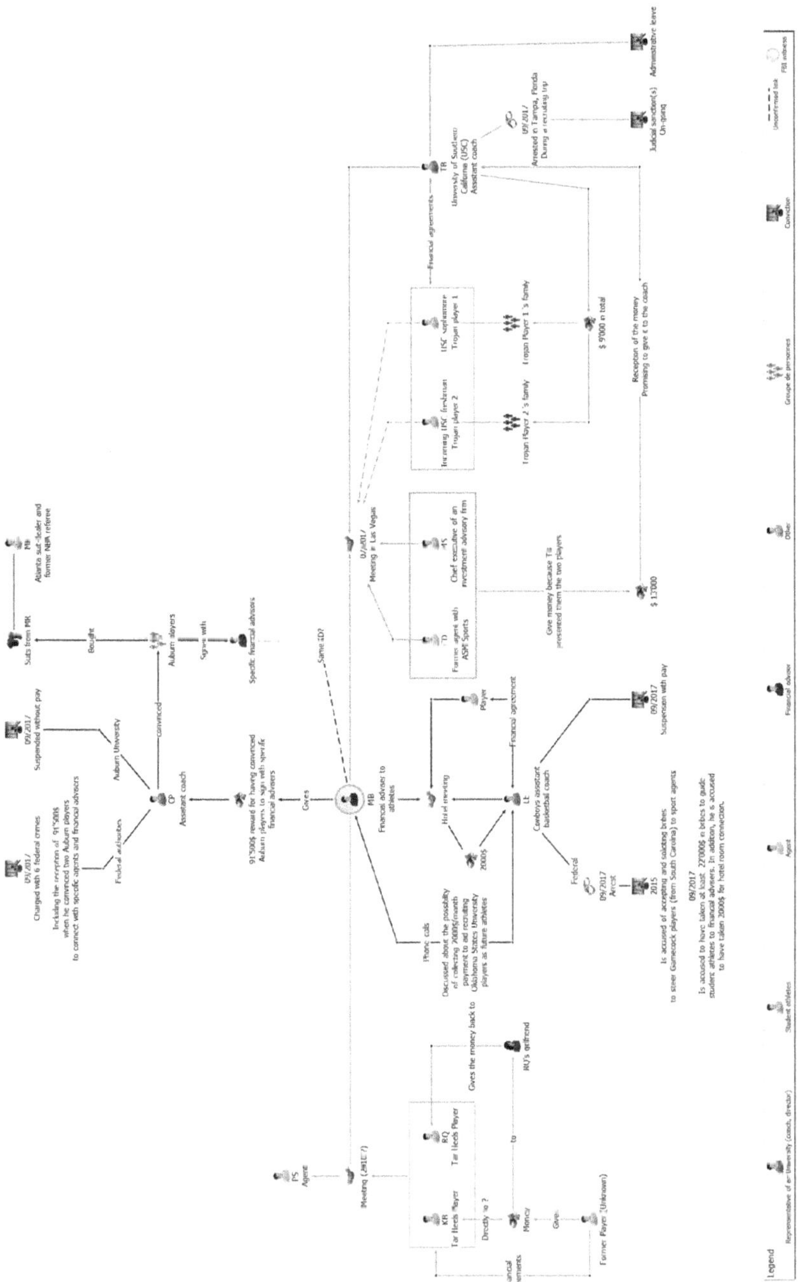

Figure 2.7 In-depth analysis of U.S. college basketball fraud scheme (part 1).

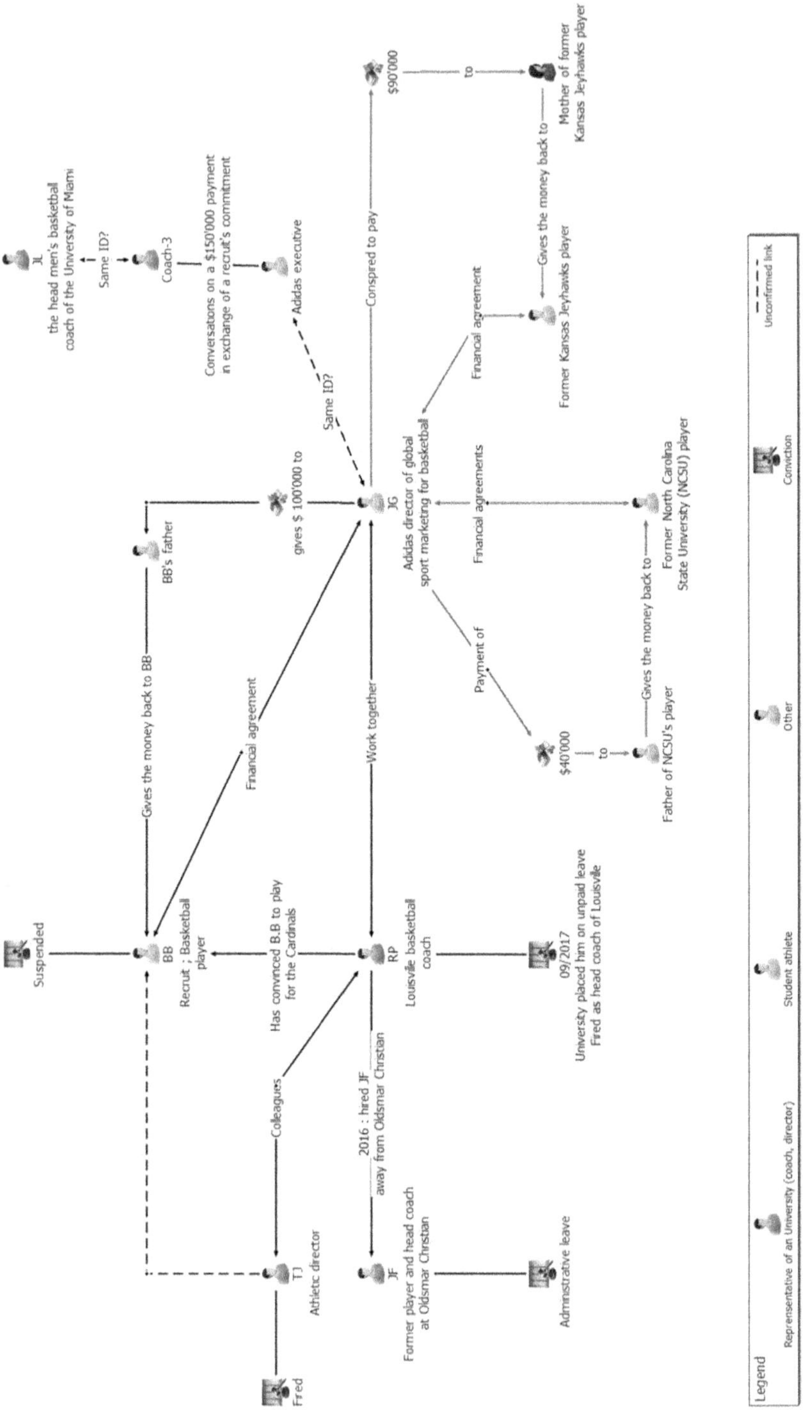

Figure 2.8 In-depth analysis of U.S. college basketball fraud scheme (part 2).

The media reported that these two cases were part of the same scandal. It is known that NJ was a player on the same team as KL and SK. Our open sources did not reveal who attempted to approach the players in question. These players have been sanctioned for not reporting these suspicious instances of contact to the authorities.

Visualisation schemes can also facilitate the understanding of complex cases that may involve many people or may cover a long period of time. The other selected case refers to the U.S. college basketball scandal. It involved 9 universities, and at least 27 individuals. Briefly described, the basketball scandal centred on coaches and financial advisers convincing student athletes to play basketball for specific universities in return for money. The scandal is quite well detailed as the Federal Bureau of Investigation – the authority investigating the case – had a witness (MB), a key actor in the corrupt network. He cooperated with authorities after his arrest in 2010. The arrest of MB in 2010 was linked to a previous case of corruption in sport involving two North Carolina Tar Heels players. Figures 2.7 and 2.8 provide a global view of this complex case involving 27 people (witnesses, athletes, financial advisers, etc.). The figures show those who allegedly perpetrated the crimes as well as their *modi operandi*. For example, two players who agreed to play for a specific university received a sum of money through their family or relatives. This system was put in place to dissimulate the fraud, and thus reduce the risk of detection.

In this case, both the Federal Bureau of Investigation and several universities responded to the allegations of the corrupt behaviour. Following this basketball scandal, the internal investigations conducted by the universities also led to disciplinary sanctions.

Discussion

The study presented cross-sectional and in-depth analysis of cases of corruption in sport published in open source media throughout 2016 and 2017. The database showed that open sources can provide many pieces of information that can be strategically put together to create further knowledge about the types of corruption in sport. The most popular sports in the world, football, tennis, athletics and cricket, are also the most susceptible to corruption. Geographically, the map on corruption in sport does not necessarily indicate the countries in which such corruption is most prevalent. On the contrary, it may represent countries in which public opinion, media, sport federations and the state have acted to tackle the phenomenon. For example, the creation of special investigative police units or internal sports integrity units – which start investigations and attract media coverage – may help explain geographic and sport over-representation on the map. Conversely, countries without any reported cases of corruption should not necessarily be considered beacons of stronger integrity in sport. This is particularly the case if investigations are not carried out and media interest in sport corruption is low.

This exploratory study provided information that suggest research hypotheses that are worth testing once the database has been further consolidated. The first group of hypotheses focus on the concentration of corrupt conduct (by time, place and sport type). First, the DACCS data seem to suggest that some corrupt behaviour may be clustered in time-cycles, especially around mega-events. For example, event bidding has firm deadlines. Therefore, corrupt behaviour associated with the manipulation of event bidding should then correlate to this timeline. Second, the DACCS data appears to suggest that some corrupt behaviour may be clustered by geographic areas (e.g. football competition manipulation in Eastern Europe and cricket competition manipulation in India and Pakistan). Third, the DACCS data seemingly confirms that some sports disciplines see more corrupt conduct than others. For example, betting-related competition manipulation looks to be more common in football, tennis and cricket. According to Forrest, McHale, and McAuley (2008), this is explained by the high liquidity in these sports betting markets. High liquidity makes it easier for fraudsters to hide their bets, and it makes it harder to detect anomalous betting patterns.

The second group of hypotheses centres on the concept of social reaction, criminal adaptation and crime displacement. In particular, they consider how the reaction of the sport and governmental environment against corruption impacts criminal behaviour. One hypothesis is that when a social system strengthens its control, corrupt behaviour will adapt to the circumstances. Another hypothesis is that corrupt conduct evolves. It is reshaped according to environmental opportunities (e.g. this occurs when people change their modus operandi; see, e.g. Caneppele, Langlois, & Verschuuren, 2020). A more robust dataset over a longer time period will also allow testing of the hypothesis that sanctioning attitudes vary among different sports and national authorities. Such a dataset will make it possible to assess whether these attitudes have changed over a number of years.

Conclusion

This chapter provided an overview of cases of corruption in sport detected through open source media. The DACCS initiative is the first systematic attempt to build an international knowledge platform on the phenomenon. Based on articles published in 2016 and 2017 by English-speaking open source media, the DACCS recorded 230 cases of corruption in sport, mainly occurring between 2015 and 2017.

Results showed that corrupt behaviours exist in many countries and that sport organisations, as well as public institutions, are active in countering corrupt conduct.

Competition manipulation remains the main concern, and the wealthiest sports disciplines (i.e. football, tennis and cricket) are more concerned about corruption than other sports. Corrupt conduct concerning event bidding and contracts follows the awarding cycle for major sports events, while other corrupt behaviour – often associated with sports bodies' mismanagement – appeared to be publicly reported more often now than in the past. This rise in reported corrupt behaviour can be accounted for partly due to previous scandals and partly because of increased levels of media coverage (Caneppele, Cinaglia, Sperrer, & Langlois, 2019).

The DACCS may also be useful for in-depth analysis, displaying links among cases and showing similar *modi operandi*. Nevertheless, the authors are aware that much can be done to improve data flow, quality and accuracy. The taxonomy of corrupt behaviour can be improved and defined more in detail. The category 'Other' can be disentangled to provide more nuanced pieces of information on various conduct. This may allow researchers to develop more specific keywords that subsequently reduce redundancy during the data collection process. The use of multiple languages (e.g. English, Spanish, French and German) may reduce the amount of non-detected cases that have been published online but not extracted. In general, using an open source for research purposes has many advantages – such as data availability and the sample size – but it also presents challenges, particularly when it comes to the collection and processing of data. In particular, two main problems related to sample size have been observed: a large number of false positives and data volatility (e.g. links to websites were often no longer active at the time of extraction). The solution to overcoming these issues lies in the use of an automated system for data processing (corresponding to data extraction, data selection and data classification). Although this kind of system will save time, it must be developed and tested to ensure its usefulness and reliability.

Other limitations can be reduced, but they will continue to exist. For complex cases, it is difficult to disentangle which corrupt behaviour happened where; it is difficult to assess in which countries such behaviour was perpetrated and by whom. Ideally, the unit of analysis should refer to a specific instance of corrupt conduct, but for competition manipulation it is rare for a researcher to know anything more than the fact that a specific match was highlighted as 'suspicious' when monitored by sports institutions and/or law enforcement. In other cases, allegations cover multiple matches without being specific. Only a portion of cases end with sanctions that allow researchers to link the conduct to an event. Further, an investigation will likely take one, two, three, or more years, and it is sometimes hard to monitor the social response over this extended period, especially when updates are scattered over time.

It is also important to note that DACCS cases do not, and never will, represent a full picture of corruption in sport. The 230 cases detected here do not reflect the real size of the problem, and they may not reflect its actual geographical distribution. Even with a more effective and sophisticated detection system, it is acknowledged that the DACCS will be a better measure of public sensitivity to corruption than of actual figures on corrupt behaviour in sport around the world. The DACCS does not cover cases that are unknown to the media (e.g. those known exclusively by the police, sports bodies, non-governmental organisations, or isolated individuals) or those that are not published online. In this sense, the database should be viewed more as a measure of social reaction by sports federations and law enforcement. However, this very same limitation would appear when measuring corruption in any sector and in any part of the world. Despite this last point, systematic data collection allows for greater comprehension of a phenomenon. An in-depth analysis of the DACCS cases may provide relevant information on actors, *modi operandi*, and links among different cases, making it possible to identify patterns in crime and recidivism. Further research and data collection exercises may contribute to improving the accuracy, the quantity of cases, and the quality of this database. Gathering a greater volume of data will facilitate more sophisticated analyses on different corrupt behaviours in sport.

Notes

1 The Database on Alleged Cases of Corruption in Sport (DACCS) is an initiative supported by the Council of Europe through the Enlarged Partial Agreement on Sport.

2 Cases of Anti-Doping Rule Violations are excluded from the DACCS open-source statistics since the World Anti-Doping Agency publishes statistical reports based on official data from anti-doping organisations and laboratories (Article 14.4 of the World Anti-Doping Code). Tax evasion by players, of other sport representatives, or infringements of sport regulations on third-party ownership agreements are outside the scope of the DACCS unless they are related to cases of corruption – for example, in the running of a sports institution.

3 The EMM News Brief is a system that was set up by the European Commission in 2014 that gathers about 300,000 articles each day from around the world, in 70 different languages. The system is updated every 10 minutes all day long (EU, 2016), ensuring almost instantaneous news coverage.

References

Aniello, S., & Caneppele, S. (2018). Selling stolen goods on the online markets: An explorative study. *Global Crime*, 19(1), 42–62.

Barbary, V., Dyer, D., & Frandano, P. (2011). *Guarding the game: Preserving the integrity of sport.* London: Monitor Quest.

Caneppele, S., Cinaglia, G., Sperrer, C., & Langlois, F. (2019). Menaces à l'intégrité du sport et sources ouvertes: une étude exploratoire. *Criminologie*, 52(2), 110–140.

Caneppele, S., Langlois, F., & Verschuuren, P. (2020). Those who counter match-fixing fraudsters: Voices from a multistakeholder ecosystem. *Crime, Law and Social Change*, 74, 13–26.

Chappelet, J.-L. (2017). Pour un cadre global de lutte contre la corruption dans le sport. *Jurisport*, 181(12), 19–22.

Cleret L., McNamee, M., & Page, S. (2015). 'Sports integrity' needs sports ethics (and sports philosophers and sports ethicists too). *Sport, Ethics and Philosophy*, 9(1), 1–5.

EU. (2016). Europe Media Monitor. European Commission Joint Research Centre Directorate. Retrieved from https://emm.newsbrief.eu/overview/emm_newsletter_201612.pdf

Forrest, D., McHale, I., & McAuley, K. (2008). 'Say it ain't so': Betting-related malpractice in sport. *International Journal of Sport Finance*, 3(3), 156–166.

Hemphill, D., & Wilson-Evered, E. (2016). *Sport integrity readiness kit.* Melbourne, Australia: Victoria University.

Miller, S. (2018). Corruption. *The Stanford encyclopedia of philosophy.* E. N. Zalta (Ed.). Retrieved from https://plato.stanford.edu/archives/win2018/entries/corruption/

Neuman, W. L. (2014). What are the major types of social research? In W. L. Neuman (Ed.), *Social research methods: Qualitative and quantitative approaches* (7th ed., pp. 25–54). Harlow, UK: Pearson Education.

Première Ligue, UCPF, & EY. (2017). Baromètre 2017 des impacts économiques et sociaux du football professionnel. Retrieved from https://www.ey.com/fr/fr/newsroom/news-releases/communique-de-presse-ey-barometre-2017-des-impacts-economiques-et-sociaux-du-football-professionnel

Schulenkorf, N., & Frawley, S. (2017). *Critical issues in global sport management.* London: Routledge.

Sport Australia (n.d.) Safe and Inclusive Sport. Retrieved from https://www.sportaus.gov.au/integrity_in_sport

Treagus, M., Cover, R., & Beasley, C. (2011). Integrity in sport literature review. Retrieved from www.ausport.gov.au/__data/assets/pdf_file/0011/516782/Integrity_in_Sport_Literature_Review-.pdf

Part I

International responses

3 Ethical leadership in Major Games procurement processes

Ruth Bayley and Caron Egle

Introduction

Sporting organisations worldwide now operate in a global economy that is characterised by increasing volatility, uncertainty, complexity and ambiguity (Johansen, 2010; Lawrence, 2013; Petrie, 2011), turbulence (Briggs & Peat, 1999), change and urgency (Jaworski & Scharmer, 2000). For sporting organisations to survive, sustain and grow they need to focus on maximising economic efficiency and profit, adapt to rapid changes in technology, markets, and competition, and innovate and reinvent themselves, whilst maintaining trust and integrity in their operations. A new type of leadership is required to successfully navigate this complex changing environment (Jaworski, 2012; Jokinen, 2005; Scharmer, 2009; Senge, Scharmer, Jaworski, & Flowers, 2004; Wheatley, 2006).

A downside of the complex environment for sporting organisations is that it often produces an environment ripe for inefficiency, fraud, corruption and misconduct to flourish. This behaviour in procurement relating to sporting events is a significant and complex global problem with substantial financial and non-financial impacts. This qualitative case study examines the nature of such inefficiency, fraud, corruption and misconduct, and makes prevention recommendations, including the incorporation of new ethical leadership concepts, incorporating trust and integrity, into procurement decision-making.

Procurement relating to sporting events may include the acquisition of goods and services, and infrastructure construction. Sporting events usually operate to tight deadlines and involve significant resource investment, often of public funds. The investment of public funds means that public sector procurement expectations very often apply to procurement relating to sporting events (Arrowsmith, Bayley, Gorezynska, Idoko, Kay, 2019), such as found this case study. These conditions provide opportunities for a range of problems, including procurement processes which deviate from normal standards of probity or which do not result in a value for money outcome (Arrowsmith et al., 2019; International Partnership Against Corruption in Sport, 2017).

Procurement relating to sporting events comprises a range of activities, including initial needs assessment, budget allocations and market research; preparation of specifications and other documents for approaching the market; evaluation of responses received from potential suppliers and awarding contracts. Contract implementation and administration, contract variations, and auditing and evaluation of the procurement process are also usually included (Kühn & Sherman, 2014; Organisation for Economic Cooperation and Development, 2016).

Fraud, corruption and misconduct

The terms fraud, corruption and misconduct are frequently used interchangeably in the literature to describe situations where procurement has not been conducted to the expected standard of probity. Although there are differences between the constructs of fraud, corruption and misconduct, mainly relating to the degree of seriousness and the intent of the perpetrator, a number of common underlying themes exist. These include improper behaviour that is contrary to a code of conduct, policy or legislation; lack of transparency; seeking or receiving an improper benefit from one's position; allowing irrelevant extraneous factors to influence decision-making; and misusing official information for personal advantage.

As mentioned, fraud, corruption and misconduct are related constructs. For example, all fraud is corrupt, but not all corruption is fraud. Corruption that is not fraud could, for example, consist of a public official having an undisclosed conflict of interest. In a similar way, all corruption is misconduct, but not all misconduct is corrupt. Misconduct that is not corrupt could, for example, consist of players or officials engaging in lewd behaviour that offends community standards (Kontominas, 2018) or posting images on social media that bring the sporting organisation into disrepute (Burgess & Dunlevie, 2018; Proszenko, 2016). Each of these behaviours is linked to forms of power and power relationships, and has implications for trust. For simplicity of expression, this chapter will use the term 'procurement corruption' to inclusively describe instances of fraud, corruption or misconduct that occur in procurement relating to sporting events.

Common types of corruption in procurement relating to sporting events

Procurement fraud includes price fixing; bid rigging; cover pricing; false, double or duplicate invoicing; overpayment; false payment; altered payment details or diverted payments; bribes or kickbacks; and delivery of inferior or sub-standard substitute products (UK National Fraud Authority, 2013). This is an effective description of public sector procurement *fraud*, but is narrower than the concept of *corruption* in procurement relating to sporting events, as previously discussed.

A complete definition of corruption in procurement relating to sporting events must also include the concepts of a public or sporting official having an undeclared conflict of interest; soliciting or accepting gifts or hospitality in exchange for favourable decisions or providing unauthorised access to insider information. To encapsulate these broader concepts, we generated a working definition of corruption in procurement relating to sporting events that was adopted for this chapter – 'an act or omission by a party involved in the procurement process relating to a sporting event that is intended to, has the effect, or the appearance of, improperly influencing that process for gain'.

Impact of procurement corruption

Procurement corruption causes financial loss that depletes the availability of resources for delivering other goods and services to stakeholders (Jorna & Smith, 2015; Minister for Justice, 2014; UK National Fraud Authority, 2013). Procurement corruption also has significant non-financial costs, including reputational damage and loss of trust and confidence in organisations that undermine their integrity, credibility, trust and good reputation (PricewaterhouseCoopers, 2011, 2015; The Ethics Centre, 2018; UK National Fraud Authority, 2013). It may result in social, emotional and psychological impacts on victims (Jorna & Smith, 2015; UK National Fraud Authority, 2013) and may damage relationships between organisations and their regulators (PricewaterhouseCoopers, 2011) or sponsors, players and supporters (The Ethics Centre, 2018).

Therefore, there is substantial value in considering ways to prevent, detect and treat corruption in procurement relating to sporting events.

New ethical leadership

Evidence supports that there is corruption in procurement relating to sporting events (Arrowsmith et al., 2019; Butler, 2018; Matheson et al., 2018; Rutherford & Shine, 2018; Choe, 2018; Spiro, 2018). New ethical leadership is needed to combat this corruption. There are a number of leadership theories that speak to the ethical and moral component of leadership, including authentic transformational leadership (Burns, 2005), ethical-charismatic leadership (Howell & Avolio, 1992) and authentic leadership (Avolio & Gardner, 2005).

Ethical leadership is defined as 'the demonstration of normatively appropriate conduct through personal actions and interpersonal relationships, and the promotion of such conduct to stakeholders through two-way communication, reinforcement and decision-making' (Brown, Treviño & Harrison, 2005, p. 120). Traditional approaches describing ethical leadership have focused on what ethical leaders should be doing, and the antecedents and consequences to ethical leadership (Brown & Treviño, 2006). Authentic leaders and their relationships with their stakeholders are characterised by 'transparency, openness and trust; guidance toward worthy objectives; and an emphasis on follower development' (Day, Harrison & Halpin 2009, p. 81)

Authentic, ethical decision-making results from the process of self-awareness and reflection with increasing maturity where authentic leaders develop mental models that facilitate the moral recognition required to address ethical dilemmas (May, Chan, Hodges & Avolio, 2003, p. 253).

The development of authentic, ethical leaders focuses heavily on the seminal work of Bandura (1986), describing social learning theory to explain the antecedents and consequences of ethical reasoning, where people learn ethical leadership by observing and 'emulating the attitudes, values and behaviours of attractive and credible models' (Brown & Treviño, 2006, p. 597). While this is of value, it fails to describe how people cognitively construct their meaning-making schemas to engage with ethics and integrity issues to develop moral capacity (the recognition of a moral issue), moral courage (the fortitude to convert moral intention in to actions regardless of pressure from either ones internal or external environment) (May et al., 2003, p. 255), and moral resilience (one's ability to adapt in positive ways in the face of significant threat or risk to acting with integrity for sustainable moral behaviour) (Day et al., 2009). Nor does it provide a structured and transparent roadmap for this development to more mature, complex stages of thinking that predetermine true ethical leadership.

This chapter proffers adult constructive development (Kegan, 1994) as a useful theoretical perspective for exploring the issues of ethical leadership and ethical leadership development. Adult constructive development describes levels of cognitive, emotional and relational capabilities (Cook-Greuter, 2002) that enable people to make ethical decisions from a self-transforming perspective (where one can step back from and reflect on the limits of one's own ideology or personal authority) (Kegan, 1994; Kegan & Lahey, 2009) and highlights how compromises to ethical decision-making come from less sophisticated, earlier stages of meaning-making. Research into adult cognitive stage development indicates that leaders operating from more mature and complex stages of thinking or meaning-making, referred to as action-logic stages (Torbert, 2003, 2010), demonstrate higher ethical leadership standards.

Developed from the earlier work of Cook-Greuter (2002), Rooke and Torbert (2005) utilise the action-logic model as a holistic stage development framework to develop a person's thinking capability to increasing more complex stages. A stage relates to a structure of thinking rather than the content of thinking. Each stage becomes increasingly more complex, incorporating the previous level and expanding awareness and capability as it increases the way a person makes sense of reality. The seven leadership action-logic stages that describe vertical stage thinking and their implications for trust and integrity are Opportunist, Diplomat, Expert, Achiever, Redefining, Transforming and Alchemical.

The Opportunist action-logic focuses on immediate needs and opportunities can be manipulative and wants to win in any way possible. They have little sensitivity to ethical issues except when they pose a threat for personal foreseeable gain and respond to punitive consequences. The Opportunist mantra that challenges integrity is ***it's all about me. Rules are meant to be broken.***

The Diplomat action-logic wants to belong and comply with the dominant rules by rigidly conforming. They avoid conflict and being seen as wrong, losing face or status, or upsetting others. They follow the dominant norms and their mantra that challenges integrity is ***I don't rock the boat so I will fit in.***

The Expert action-logic focuses on their craft mastery, expertise and procedure. With black and white thinking, they seek efficiency, and therefore consider ethical issues from a technical, specialised perspective. They have high regard for rational rules and regulations rather than principles and as such like to contribute to the development and implementation of ethical/integrity knowledge and frameworks. The Expert mantra that challenges integrity is ***the rules are the rules.***

The Achiever action-logic is driven to meet strategic goals through harnessing teams and deliver results. They focus is effectiveness and efficiency for timely outcomes and results rather than rules. The Achiever mantra that challenges integrity is ***results not rules, and the end justifies the means.***

The Redefining action-logic interweaves competing personal and organisational action-logics. They innovate to merge strategy and performance and are committed to continual personal growth. They are reflective, questioning preconceived notions, norms and frameworks and develop creative solutions, especially to integrity issues. They are collaborative, encourages participative employee engagement, and broader systemic vision of integrity issues. The Redefining mantra that addresses integrity is ***it's about both process and results – inconvenient truth.***

The Transforming action-logic generates personal and organisational transformations. They exercise the power of mutual inquiry, vigilance and vulnerability and are conscious of paradox. They recognise the value of principle for making good decisions and experiences dilemmas and paradox as generative. The Transforming action-logic champions large in-depth change in values and habits within organisations to drive culture change over the longer term. They consider the social, economic, environmental and psychological aspects of integrity to lead the real integration of the principles of integrity and ethics across the organisation. Their integrity mantra is ***it's about a culture of integrity.***

The alchemical action-logic integrates material, spiritual and social transformations, demonstrating deep concern for truth, authenticity and transparency. They focus on awareness, thought, action and effects and have a complex and integrated vision. They practice personal integrity with passion, compassion and dispassion, disrupting received norms in multiple territories – individual, interpersonal, social and subtle. They are actively involved in various organisations and events that support integrity and ethical standards and causes. We refer to the alchemist's mantra as ***the getting to Gandhi!***

The development of later stage thinking

The development of action-logics is through the differentiation of subjective engagement to objective reflection. There are three primary developmental processes that expedite the development through the stages, without which one can take up to ten years (and sometimes never) to move to the next stage. These are heat experiences, colliding perspectives, and increased sense making (Petrie, 2015). ***Heat Experiences*** occur when the leader faces a complex situation that disrupts and disorients their habitual way of thinking and acting. They discover that their current way of thinking and making sense of the world is not adequate for the challenges they face. Their mind begins to open and search for new and better ways to make sense of the challenges. ***Colliding Perspectives*** occur when the leader is exposed to people with different worldviews, opinions, beliefs, backgrounds, experiences and training. This provides contrast, and both challenges their existing mental models and increases the range of perspectives through which they can see the world. ***Elevated Sensemaking*** occurs when the leader uses a process or a coach to help people navigate, integrate and make sense of these new perspectives and experiences from more elevated stages of development (later action-logic stages). Each of these serve to support the development of leaders and teams to later action-logic stages and therefore develop organisational cultures of high integrity.

The next section explores a sporting event case study through the various action-logic lenses using an approach modelled on the ethics of care framework (Gilligan, 1982). The case study demonstrates that the people involved in the corruption made behavioural choices from earlier action-logics stages, particularly that of Opportunist. Strategies will be identified to foster later stage leadership thinking to contribute to transformational change.

Case study: The construction programme for PyeongChang 2018 Winter Olympic Games

Local news media reported allegations of conflict of interest relating to venues to be used for the PyeongChang 2018 Winter Olympic Games. The allegations included that Ms Choi Soon-sil (a close friend of the president of South Korea, Ms Park Geun-hye) and a member of Ms Choi's family, were allowed by Ms Park to exert undue influence on policy decisions (Butler, 2018; Rutherford & Shine, 2018). Other allegations included that foundations and companies linked to Ms Choi were awarded contracts for sporting venues for the Games (Butler, 2018; Rutherford & Shine, 2018). It was also alleged that the head of Samsung, Mr Lee Jae-yong, had provided funds and a horse to support Ms Choi's daughter in her international equestrian career in return for political favours from Ms Park and her government, including sponsorship opportunities (BBC News, 2018; Choe, 2018; Lee & Choi, 2018).

In 2018, Samsung, which was a worldwide Olympic Partner, announced that it would gift a Samsung mobile phone to all competitors and officials of the International Olympics Committee (IOC) and POCOG (Samsung Newsroom, 2018).

The president's friend, Ms Choi, was subsequently charged with abuse of power and fraud in connection with projects such as building facilities and developing sporting talent for Olympic and Asian Games (Rutherford & Shine, 2018) and accepting bribes (BBC News, 2018). In February 2018, Ms Choi was fined approximately US$16M and was sentenced by a South Korean Court to 20 years imprisonment for corruption (BBC News, 2018).

In December 2016, the South Korean National Assembly impeached Ms Park. This decision was upheld by the Constitutional Court in March 2017, removing her from office (Choe, 2018). Ms Park was subsequently sentenced to 24 years imprisonment for abuse of power and corruption (Haas, 2018; Choe, 2018). In both cases, the courts' corruption findings were wider than just the corruption in procurement relating to the PyeongChang Winter Olympic Games (BBC News, 2018; Haas, 2018; Rutherford & Shine, 2018).

In August 2017, Mr Lee Jae-yong received a 5-year sentence for paying US$6.7 million in bribes to Ms Park and Ms Choi for political influence (BBC News, 2017; Choe, 2018). Two other Samsung executives were also convicted at the same trial (BBC News, 2017). Mr Lee Jae-yong's jail term was suspended in February 2018 (Lee & Choi, 2018).

How did this impact trust?

These corruption allegations and the subsequent legal and political actions led to significant negative global media reporting about corrupt practices associated with the Games as identified above. Additionally, it can only be damaging to public trust and confidence in the integrity of an international sporting event when the president of the host country is impeached and jailed for corruption in connection with procurement practices for that event. Further, a wide web of significant conflicts of interest in connection with procurement for the event was revealed by this case. As the procurements were all conducted under public procurement rules, there was also potential for a loss of trust in the public procurement process.

What was the response of the sporting body?

In November 2016, the President of the PyeongChang Organising Committee for the 2018 Olympic & Paralympic Winter Games (POCOG), Mr Lee Hee-beom, strenuously denied allegations of corruption in Games contracts, and stated that he had conducted an internal review of all contracts associated with POCOG. He claimed that this revealed no issues with any of the contracts (Rutherford & Shine, 2018). Mr Lee Hee-beom said that procurement for the Games was conducted cleanly and without improper interference using the public procurement process (Rutherford & Shine, 2018; Sport Business, 2017).

Trust in POCOG must have been damaged by the conflicts of interest and the associated media reporting. For example, the Korea News Gazette (2016) reported that POCOG's marketing and promotion activities were impacted by the scandal and that POCOG had subsequent difficulties in signing business deals and gaining sponsors. Additionally, the public and the media are notoriously sceptical of internal reviews (Rutherford and Shine, 2018; Sport Business, 2017). This scepticism seems warranted given that the internal finding of no procurement irregularities was clearly inconsistent with the facts reported by the media, the outcomes in the various South Korean courts and the views of the South Korean National Assembly.

What action-logic stages applied to the key participants in this case?

Ms Choi Soon-sil (friend of the president of South Korea) used her friend's power and influence for personal benefit to herself, her family and organisations that she controlled. She diverted money intended for other purposes to herself and accepted bribes. These actions demonstrate Opportunist action-logic thinking.

Ms Park Geun-hye (impeached president of South Korea) used her power to favour a very close friend, turned a blind eye to wrongdoing and accepted bribes. These actions demonstrate Diplomat action-logic thinking.

Mr Lee Jae-yong (head of Samsung) paid bribes for business advancement and power, which were consistent with the Korean cultural practice of *chaebol* (see below) and could be seen as just doing what needed to be done to succeed in business. These actions demonstrate Achiever action-logic thinking.

Mr Lee-Hee-beom (president of POCOG) said there was no wrongdoing, persistently relied on an internal review that found no wrongdoing, despite mounting external evidence that there was, and said that all procurement for the PyeongChang Winter Olympic Games had been done in accordance with the rules. These actions demonstrate Expert action-logic thinking.

What should they have done?

The next section of this chapter applies the principles of new ethical leadership and action-logics to the case to present some alternative actions that could have been taken to prevent or minimise the potential for procurement corruption connected with the Games. We propose three main suggestions for improving integrity and trust for procurement for sporting events. These are to build an explicit culture of integrity and trust, to harness the power and influence of positional authority to model, promote and enforce a culture of integrity and trust, and looking to other sporting domains and even outside sport for transferrable learnings about integrity and trust.

Building an explicit culture of integrity and trust – application of new ethical leadership to the case

This case highlights conflict of interest between family, friends and business/political connections as a form of procurement corruption. It is vital to recognise, when operating globally, that different cultures have different normalised expectations about standards of ethical behaviour in relation to conflicts of interest. Conflicts of interest are socially defined according to the shared expectations of members of a group or national culture.

As demonstrated by this case, actual or perceived conflicts of interest can seriously damage the integrity of procurement processes in relation to sporting events, and may also have significant impacts on the individuals, as well as causing reputational damage for sporting organisations. Conflicts of interest that are not managed effectively can erode trust within an organisation, and also with external stakeholders and the community.

In South Korea, it has been suggested that there is some level of cultural acceptance of close ties between business and politicians, known as *chaebol* (Haas, 2018; Spiro, 2018). This is probably also not unusual in other cultures, with concerns about similar business and political corruption relating to the Rio 2016 Olympic Games (Talbot, 2016). Another commonly identified area of conflict of interest in procurement relating to sporting events concerns seeking benefits for friends and family. This type of conflict of interest was demonstrated in this case study, and has also affected the 2002 Salt Lake City Winter Olympics (Lashmar, 1999; Pearlstein, 1999), the 2004 Athens Olympic Games (Schmitt, 2010), the 2016 Rio Olympic Games (Schmitt, 2010; Talbot, 2016) and 2016 Rio FIFA World Cup (Chade, 2017).

To deal with the problem of actual and perceived conflicts of interest, officials with procurement responsibilities need to formally and explicitly create a transparent integrity culture which rejects or quarantines these conflicts. This is effectively the minimum standard of behaviour necessary to generate and maintain trust in the procurement process. Leaders should actively and transparently identify a consensus minimum standard of ethical behaviour that will apply to procurement processes, regardless of the cultural background of the officials conducting the procurement. Leaders must clearly articulate which relationships (for example family, friends, business, political connections etc.) would be too close to allow the perception of ethical procurement. These relationships must be transparently quarantined during procurement processes. This approach requires thinking from the post-conventional action-logic stages of Redefining and Transforming. At the Redefining stage, the leader must recognise, reconcile and react to the inconvenient truth that a culture of trust and integrity requires both adherence to proper process and getting timely results. The leader must also deal with the reality that officials may be caught between their public and their private obligations and must make ethical decisions that maintain trust in the procurement process. At the Transforming action-logic stage, the leader creates and maintains a culture of trust and integrity by refusing to walk past (ignore) situations which do not contribute to, support and enhance a trust and integrity culture. The Transforming leader must also work towards embedding and integrating a trust and integrity culture into the whole organisation or across organisations, not just the procurement function.

Harnessing the power and influence of positional leadership – application of new ethical leadership to case

To achieve results with integrity, leaders must model ethical behaviour from at least a Redefining stage of thinking, because followers at the Diplomat action-logic stage ('I don't rock the boat') are adept at intuiting the tacit norms that apply to procurement processes. Diplomat followers will align their behaviour to fit with the tacit or implicit norms, even if these norms are different to the espoused norms and values of the organisation. Those followers at the Expert action-logic stage will be devoted to following rules and processes ('the rules are the rules'), and this may lead to overly bureaucratic procurement processes that focus on the rules at the expense of results, and 'letter of the law' rather than 'spirit of the law' compliance with procurement rules. Those followers at Achiever action-logic stage will focus on results, often thinking that the ends justify the means. Achievers may seek original and innovative ways to get those results, even if the rules have to be bent, re-interpreted or even ignored along the way. They may see awarding a contract to a close associate as a way to get a better, faster result. To minimise procurement corruption, a minimum requirement is to focus on **both** process and results, and it can be challenging to simultaneously achieve both.

Leaders demonstrating Redefining thinking will ask questions about the procurement process such as 'How else could we do this?', 'What will happen if we do this?', 'What will happen if we don't do this?' 'What will not happen if we don't do this?'. Redefining leaders will recognise the potential for a clash of moral values in procurement processes by acknowledging the different obligations on sporting officials including to their family, friends, ethnic group, community, business connections, and the like, as well as to their sporting organisation. To maintain trust in the process, both internally and externally, these relationships must be transparently identified and their impact on the perceived and actual integrity of the procurement process discussed. A shared consensus process and standard of ethics for procurement activities must be developed, often over an iteration of 'heat' events. These heat events must be analysed and discussed with courage aimed at creating new norms (Diplomat); new processes, ethical frameworks and procurement and integrity policies (Expert) and balancing these with results (Achiever). Transforming leaders will be needed to embed, reinforce, consolidate, integrate and adapt the new norms so that a culture of trust and integrity can develop and thrive.

One of the greatest challenges for developing a culture of trust and integrity using this approach is that it takes time to build the necessary trust for this type of change. Most sporting events operate to a timeframe that is inconsistent with truly transformational leadership. This means that a lasting culture of integrity can only be achieved by a transformational leader who has a vision beyond their own event, and who builds mechanisms and channels for creating a living legacy of trust and integrity that extends beyond any single event.

This vision for transformational change could begin to potentially encompass broader organisational, environmental, social or economic change such as contributing to the United Nations Sustainable Development Goals including Goal 12 (Responsible consumption and production) (United Nations, 2019a) and Goal 16 (Peace, justice and strong institutions) (United Nations, 2019b) through a reduction in corruption and responsible procurement practices, particularly in the supply chains, for major sporting events. The content of the international standard ISO 20400:2017 Sustainable Procurement – Guidance International Organisation for Standardisation (International Standards Organisation, 2017) outlines practical ways in which the procurement process can contribute to a number of the Sustainable Development Goals, including Goals 12 and 16.

Looking across sporting domains and also outside sport – application of new ethical leadership to case

A major problem with an inculcated integrity gap is that, for most people, the routine acceptance of unethical activities and the corrupting influence of organisational culture may become so common that it can blunt the individual's awareness of the existence of an integrity gap (De Graaf, 2007; Jones, 1991). In many sporting organisations, otherwise ethical individuals may behave corruptly in order to fit in (Diplomat), or because the corrupt behaviour is so normalised and widespread in the organisation that it is longer even recognised as corrupt (Ashforth & Anand, 2003; Ashforth, Gioia, Robinson, & Treviño, 2008; Gottschalk, 2012; Greil & Rudy, 1984; Punch, 2000). If the moral dimensions of an issue are not recognised, ethical decision-making processes cannot be engaged (Bandura, 1986, 2006; Hunt & Vitell, 1986; Jones, 1991). People who behave unethically can thus avoid perceiving themselves as corrupt by casting their corrupt actions as normal and reasonable business activities (Achiever), sanctioned by their organisation (Expert), done by everyone else (Diplomat), and often undertaken under pressure, with incomplete or contradictory information (Anand, Ashforth, & Joshi, 2004; Gottschalk, 2012; Heath, 2008). This occurs particularly at earlier action-logic stages because of the unilateral views of power and the unquestioning nature of their engagement with the issues.

It is extremely difficult for insiders to notice and address an institutionalised integrity gap once it is normalised in an organisation. Even if an integrity gap is noticed, it is often rationalised away (Ashforth & Anand, 2003; Balch & Armstrong, 2010; Sims & Brinkmann, 2003). Leaders may be so personally embedded into the corrupt organisational practice that they cannot realistically or credibly identify and address it (Anand et al., 2004; Balch & Armstrong, 2010; Sims & Brinkmann, 2003). This implies that external scrutiny should be a major part of corruption prevention and detection (Gao, Greenberg, & Wong-on-wing, 2015). This would involve asking different questions, originating from the Redefining and Transforming action-logic stages to question the existing modus operandi.

For these reasons, officials charged with undertaking procurement for sporting events often cannot even see the integrity gap that is so obvious to outsiders (Chade, 2017; Lashmar, 1999; Schmitt, 2010; Spiro, 2018). The integrity gap can only be identified and bridged by internal officials who are aware of the possibility that a gap may exist (Redefining and Transforming), and who actively scan other sporting domains or those outside sport for examples of good practice and transferrable lessons to learn. This requires the ability to reflect on one's own engagement with integrity from a Redefining perspective. However, if the normalisation of unethical behaviour is so strong that the insiders cannot perceive the integrity gap, then an outsider view, from other sporting domains, or even from outside sports organisations entirely, is necessary.

This external intervention must aim to create a tensional contrast leading to new perspectives, that will assist in bridging the integrity gap. It is important to select external reviewers from post-conventional action-logic stages. If the reviewer's lens is Expert, then the contrast will be seen as right/wrong. If the lens is from Achiever action-logics, the reviewer will be narrowly focused on achieving results in a timely manner. If the lens utilised is from a minimum of Redefining post-conventional thinking, then the reviewer will be able to take on multiple perspectives and sit with the contrast, until a solution that reconciles the needs for proper process, for great results and for the inclusion of multiple perspectives can be grasped. This approach ultimately provides the best opportunity for Transforming actual or potential sports procurement corruption to greater integrity at the individual, organisational and ultimately the cultural/societal level – a lofty vision.

Implications for major sporting events

At the moment, the effectiveness and probity of host city bids and subsequent preparations for hosting the Olympic Games, including procurement processes and construction programmes, is the responsibility of International Olympic Committee Coordination Commissions (International Olympic Committee, 2020). This is effectively an internal review, and may be subject to the shortcomings outlined above. The review process might be more effective if provided by a more broadly based stakeholder group such as the Independent Partnership Against Corruption in Sport or a genuinely independent external organisation such as the United Nations Office on Drugs and Crime (UNODC) or the United Nations Environment Programme (UNEP) through its commitment to the Sustainable Development Goals, in particular Goal 12.7 in relation to sustainable public procurement practices (United Nations, 2019a). Ultimately, regardless of the body that auspices the review, individuals appointed to Organising Committees, Coordination Commissions, national sporting bodies, review panels or any other probity organisation for a major sporting event, could benefit from receiving training and mentorship in new ethical leadership techniques such as those described in this chapter.

Conclusions

Procurement in relation to sporting events is an area ripe with opportunities for corruption, particularly for actual and perceived conflicts of interest, as demonstrated by this case study. For public and private trust to be restored, sporting organisations must show that they are serious about identifying and tackling any integrity gap before it results in actual or perceived corruption in procurement for the event.

The actions suggested in this chapter to prevent, identify and manage integrity gaps, and thus to build and maintain trust, include building an integrity culture; harnessing positional power; and looking across sporting domains and outside sport for good exemplars and transferrable lessons to learn. To be effective, these actions must be led, modelled and implemented by leaders and officials who are operating at post-conventional action-logic stages of Redefining and Transforming. This can assist in avoiding the integrity pitfalls of Diplomat thinking, where individuals want to fit in to a normalised corrupt culture leading to rationalised organisational integrity gaps; Expert thinking, where excessive reliance on rules and process leads to simplistic approaches to complex problems and a focus on process over results (meaning anticipated value for money may not be attained); and Achiever thinking where focusing only on results without attention to proper process leads to an ends justifies the means approach (leading to accusations of unfair, unaccountable and opaque processes). This is at odds with the requirements of public procurement processes, social corporate responsibility and the expectations of the public. The integrity pitfalls of all these action-logic stages can result in trust being damaged inside an organisation and also with its external stakeholders and the community. It also prevents procurement processes for major sporting events contributing effectively to broader desirable social outcomes, such as making contribution to the United Nations Sustainable Development Goals (United Nations 2019a, 2019b) and makes it difficult for major sporting events to meet the International Partnership Against Corruption in Sports (2017) expectations (Arrowsmith et al., 2019).

Building and maintaining a culture of trust and integrity in procurement for sporting events requires new ethical leadership where real, perceived or potential integrity issues can be explored, considered and challenged through heat experiences, colliding perspectives and the increased sense making that arises from considering multiple perspectives. The power dynamics associated with each action-logic stage of thinking reinforce the need for transformational development so that leaders can lead from the post-conventional stages of thinking. This development takes personal and organisational courage, wisdom, passion, compassion and commitment – all of which can be facilitated with post-conventional development, training, coaching and consulting using new ethical leadership approaches.

Questions

i *Trust loss* – In whom (or, in which group) has trust been lost in this case?

ii *Trust correction* – How, if attempted, has the restoration of trust been tried?; and;

iii *Lessons learned* – How could the lessons from this case be applied to other sports, nations, states, other districts for the same sport, or other sports to prevent a further loss of trust or at least to restore trust?

References

Anand, V., Ashforth, B. E., & Joshi, M. (2004). Business as usual: The acceptance and perception of corruption in organizations. *Academy of Management Executive*, 18(2), 39–53. www.jstor.org/action/showPublication?journalCode=acadmanaexe2

Arrowsmith, S., Bayley, R., Gorezynska, A., Idoko, J., Kay, S., Lopes, J. F., … Thurston, A. (2019). Procuring infrastructure for international sporting events: Mapping the field for IPACS and beyond. *Public Procurement Law Review*, 6, 257–318.

Ashforth, B. E., & Anand, V. (2003). The normalization of corruption in organizations. *Research in Organizational Behavior*, 25(0), 1–52.

Ashforth, B. E., Gioia, D. A., Robinson, S. L., & Treviño, L. K. (2008). Re-reviewing organizational corruption. *Academy of Management Review*, 33(3), 670–684.

Avolio, B. J., & Gardner, W. L. (2005). Authentic leadership development: Getting to the root of positive forms of leadership. *The Leadership Quarterly* 16, 315–338.

Balch, D. R., & Armstrong, R. W. (2010). Ethical marginality: The Icarus syndrome and banality of wrongdoing. *Journal of Business Ethics*, 92(2), 291–303.

Bandura, A. (1986). *Social foundations of thought and action: A social cognitive theory.* Englewood Cliffs, NJ: Prentice Hall.

Bandura, A. (2006). Going global with social cognitive theory: From prospect to paydirt. In S. I. Donaldson, D. L. Berger & K. Pezdek (Eds.), *Applied psychology: New frontiers and rewarding careers* (pp. 53–80). Mahwah, NJ: Lawrence Erlbaum Associates.

BBC News. (2017, 25 August). Samsung heir Lee Jae-yong jailed for corruption. Retrieved from https://www.bbc.com/news/business-41033568

BBC News. (2018, 13 February). South Korea jails Choi Soon-sil, friend to Park Geun-hye, for corruption. Retrieved from https://www.bbc.com/news/world-asia-43042862

Briggs, J., & Peat, F. D. (1999). *The seven life lessons of chaos.* New York: Harper Perennial.

Brown, M. E., & Treviño, L. K. (2006). Ethical Leadership: A review and future directions. *The Leadership Quarterly* 17, 595–616.

Brown, M. E., Treviño, L. K., & Harrison, D. A. (2005). Ethical leadership: A social learning perspective for construct development and testing. *Organizational Behavior and Human Decision Processes*, 97(2), 117–134.

Burgess, G., & Dunlevie, J. (2018, 19 September). Blackface stunt football players apologise for mocking Williams sisters. Retrieved from https://www.abc.net.au/news/2018-09-19/blackface-mad-monday-stunt-by-football-players/10281160

Burns, J. M. (2005). Leadership. *Leadership*, 1(11), 11–12.

Butler, N. (2018, 2 November). Pyeongchang 2018 venue implicated in political scandal engulfing South Korean Government. Retrieved from https://www.insidethegames.biz/articles/1043259/pyeongchang-2018-venue-implicated-in-political-scandal-engulfing-south-korean-government

Chade, J. (2017, 23 April). Stadium deals, corruption and bribery: the questions at the heart of Brazil's Olympic and World Cup 'miracle'. *The Observer.* Retrieved from https://www.theguardian.com/sport/2017/apr/23/brazil-olympic-world-cup-corruption-bribery

Choe, S. (2018, 6 April). Park Geun-hye, South Korea's ousted president, gets 24 years in prison. *The New York Times.* Retrieved from https://www.nytimes.com/2018/04/06/world/asia/park-geun-hye-south-korea.html

Cook-Greuter, S. R. (2002). A detailed description of the development of nine action-logics (adapted and expanded) A detailed description of the successive stages of ego-development. Retrieved from www.cook-greuter.com

Day, D. V., Harrison, M. M., & Halpin, S. M. (2009). *An integrative approach to leader development: Connecting adult development, identity and expertise.* New York: Psychology Press.

De Graaf, G. (2007). Causes of corruption: Towards a contextual theory of corruption. *Public Administration Quarterly*, 31(1), 39–86. Retrieved from http://jpart.oxfordjournals.org/

Gao, J., Greenberg, R., & Wong-on-wing, B. (2015). Whistleblowing intentions of lower-level employees: The effect of reporting channel, bystanders, and wrongdoer power status. *Journal of Business Ethics*, 126(1), 85–99.

Gilligan, C. (1982). *In a different voice.* Cambridge, MA: Harvard University Press.

Gottschalk, P. (2012). Rotten apples versus rotten barrels in white collar crime: A qualitative analysis of white collar offenders in Norway. *International Journal of Criminal Justice Sciences*, 7(2), 575–590. Retrieved from www.sascv.org/ijcjs/

Greil, A. L., & Rudy, D. R. (1984). Social cocoons: Encapsulation and identity transformation organizations. *Sociological Inquiry*, 54(3), 260–278.

Haas, B. (2018, 6 April). South Korea: former president Park Geun-hye sentenced to 24 years in jail. *The Guardian*. Retrieved from https://www.theguardian.com/world/2018/apr/06/former-south-korea-president-park-geun-hye-guilty-of-corruption

Heath, J. (2008). Business ethics and moral motivation: A criminological perspective. *Journal of Business Ethics*, 83(4), 595–614.

Howell, J. M., & Avolio, B. J. (1992). The ethics of charismatic leadership: Submission or liberation? *The Executive*, 6(2) 43–54.

Hunt, S. D., & Vitell, S. J. (1986). A general theory of marketing ethics. *Journal of Macromarketing*, 6(1), 5.

International Olympic Committee. (2020). Coordination commissions. Retrieved from https://www.olympic.org/coordination-commissions

International Organization for Standardization. (2017). ISO20400:2017 Sustainable procurement – guidance. Retrieved from https://www.iso.org/standard/63026.html

International Partnership Against Corruption in Sport. (2017). Terms of reference of the task force for reducing the risk of corruption in procurement relating to sporting events and infrastructure. Retrieved from https://www.oecd.org/corruption/IPACS-Task-force-No1-TOR.pdf

Jaworski, J. (2012). *The advent of stage IV leadership*. Austin, TX: Generon International, LLC.

Jaworski, J., & Scharmer, C. (2000). *Leadership in the new economy: Sensing and actualizing emerging futures*. Austin, TX: Generon Consulting.

Johansen, B. (2010). *Leaders make the future: Ten new leadership skills for an uncertain world*. San Fransisco, CA: Berrett-Koehler.

Jokinen, T. (2005). Global leadership competencies: A review and discussion. *Journal of European Industrial Training, 29*(3), 199–216.

Jones, T. M. (1991). Ethical decision making by individuals in organizations: An issue-contingent model. *Academy of Management. The Academy of Management Review*, 16 (2), 366. http://aom.org/AMR/

Jorna, P., & Smith, R. G. (2015). *Fraud against the Commonwealth: Report to government 2010–11 to 2012–13*. (AIC Monitoring Reports, 24). Canberra, Australia: Australian Government. Retrieved from http://aic.gov.au/publications/current%20series/mr/21-40/mr24/09_dealing.html

Kegan, R. (1994). *In over our heads: The mental demands of modern life*. Cambridge MA: Harvard University Press.

Kegan, R., & Lahey, L. L. (2009). *Immunity to change: How to overcome it and unlock potential in yourself and your organization*. Boston, MA: Harvard Business Press.

Kontominas, B. (2018, 6 September). Canterbury-Bankstown Bulldogs players charged over naked Mad Monday celebrations. Retrieved from https://www.abc.net.au/news/2018-09-06/bulldogs-fined-over-mad-monday-shenanigans/10209374

Korea News Gazette. (2016, 28 December). PyeongChang 2018 set to move on from influence-peddling scandal. Retrieved from https://www.koreanewsgazette.com/news-focus-pyeongchang-2018-set-to-move-on-from-influence-peddling-scandal/

Kühn, S., & Sherman, L. B. (2014). Curbing corruption in public procurement: A practical guide. www.transparency.org/whatwedo/publication/curbing_corruption_in_public_procurement_a_practical_guide

Lashmar, P. (1999, 23 January). Olympic Games: Murky tale of presents and prostitutes. *The Independent.* Retrieved from https://www.independent.co.uk/sport/olympic-games-murky-tale-of-presents-and-prostitutes-1075753.html

Lawrence, K. (2013). *Developing leaders in a VUCA environment.* Chapel Hill, NC: UNC Kenan-Flager Business School.

Lee, J., & Choi, H. (2018, 5 February). Samsung scion Lee walks free after jail term suspended, faces leadership challenges. Retrieved from https://www.reuters.com/article/us-samsung-lee/samsung-scion-lee-walks-free-as-south-korea-court-suspends-jail-term-idUSKBN1FO0R9

Matheson, V., Schwab, D., & Koval, P. (2018). Corruption in the bidding, construction and organisation of mega-events: An analysis of the Olympics and World Cup. In M. Breuer & D. Forrest (Eds.), *The Palgrave handbook on the economics of manipulation in professional sports* [e-book] (pp. 257–258). Cham, Switzerland: Palgrave Macmillan.

May, D. R., Chan, A. Y., Hodges, T. D. & Avolio, B. J. (2003). Developing the moral component of authentic leadership. *Organisational Dynamics*, 32(3), 247–260.

Minister for Justice. (2014). *Resource management guide no 201: Preventing, detecting and dealing with fraud.* Canberra, Australia: Australian Government.

Organisation for Economic Cooperation and Development. (2016, 19 March). Public procurement. Retrieved from www.oecd.org/gov/ethics/public-procurement.htm

Pearlstein, S. (1999, 21 January). Evidence of corruption 'irrefutable,' IOC official says Washington Post. Retrieved from https://www.washingtonpost.com/wp-srv/digest/daily/jan99/oly21.htm?noredirect=on

Petrie, N. (2011). *Future trends in leadership development.* Greenboro, NC: Centre for Creative Leadership. Retrieved from http://insights.ccl.org/wp-content/uploads/2015/04/futureTrends.pdf

Petrie, N. (2015). *The how-to of vertical leadership development – Part 2* (pp. 1–25). Colorado Springs, CO: Centre for Creative Leadership. Retrieved from http://insights.ccl.org/wp-content/uploads/2015/04/verticalLeadersPart2.pdf

PricewaterhouseCoopers. (2011). Fighting fraud in government. www.pwc.com/gx/en/psrc/global/fighting-fraud-in-government.jhtml

PricewaterhouseCoopers. (2015). Fighting fraud in the public sector III. https://pwc.docalytics.com/v/fighting-fraud-feb151

Proszenko, A. (2016, 28 January). Sydney Rooster Mitchell Pearce's career in doubt after lewd act involving dog. *Sydney Morning Herald.* Retrieved from https://www.smh.com.au/sport/nrl/roosters-captain-mitchell-pearces-lewd-act-joins-nrls-long-list-of-bad-behaviour-20160127-gmfi1d.html

Punch, M. (2000). Police corruption and its prevention. *European Journal on Criminal Policy and Research*, 8(3), 301–324. Retrieved from www.springer.com/social+sciences/criminology/journal/10610

Rooke, D., & Torbert, W. R. (2005). 7 Transformations of leadership. *Harvard Business Review* (April), 66–76.

Rutherford, P., & Shine, O. (2018, 6 November). Olympics-2018 Games chief says contracts clean, as scandal bleeds into sport. Retrieved from https://www.reuters.com/article/us-olympics-pyeongchang-politics-idUSKBN1330LE

Samsung Newsroom. (2018). Samsung Electronics unveils PyeongChang 2018 Olympic Games limited edition to celebrate the spirit of the Olympic Winter Games PyeongChang 2018. Retrieved from https://news.samsung.com/global/samsung-electronics-unveils-pyeongchang-2018-olympic-games-limited-edition-to-celebrate-the-spirit-of-the-olympic-winter-games-pyeongchang-2018

Scharmer, C. (2009). *Theory U: Leading from the future as it emerges* (1st ed.). San Francisco, CA: Berrett-Koehler Publishers.

Schmitt, J. (2010, 11 May). Complicit in corruption: How German companies bribed their way to Greek deals. *Der Spiegel*, English Edition. Retrieved from www.spiegel.de/international/europe/complicit-in-corruption-how-german-companies-bribed-their-way-to-greek-deals-a-693973.html

Senge, P. (1990). *The fifth discipline: The art and practice of the learning organization.* Milsons Point, NSW: Random House Business Books.

Sims, R. R., & Brinkmann, J. (2003). Enron ethics (Or: Culture matters more than codes). *Journal of Business Ethics*, 45(3), 243–256.

Senge, P., Scharmer, C.O., Jaworski, J., & Flowers, B.S. (2004) *Presence. Human purpose and the field of the future.* New York: Crown Business.

Spiro, J. (2018, 7 February). In South Korea, Olympic torch may shine light on track record of corruption. Retrieved from https://blogs.thomsonreuters.com/answerson/south-korea-olympic-torch-may-shine-light-track-record-corruption/

Sport Business. (2017, 17 January). Pyeongchang 2018 chief says Olympics 'clean' amid political scandal. Retrieved from https://www.sportbusiness.com/news/pyeongchang-2018-chief-says-olympics-clean-amid-political-scandal/

Talbot, A. (2016, 26 April). Rio 2016 Olympics will be a success – but just who will benefit?, *The Conversation.* Retrieved from https://theconversation.com/rio-2016-olympics-will-be-a-success-but-just-who-will-benefit-56951

The Ethics Centre. (2018). *Australian cricket: A matter of balance.* A report commissioned by the Board of Cricket Australia. Retrieved from https://www.cricket.com.au/news/cricket-australia-cultural-review-published-recommendations-ethics-players-south-africa-smith-warner/2018-10-29

Torbert, W. R. (1994). Managerial learning, organizational learning. *Management Learning*, 25(1), 57–70.

Torbert, W. R. (2003). *Personal and organizational transformation through action inquiry.* London: The Cromwell Press.

Torbert, W. R. (2010). The power of balance: Transforming self, society and scientific inquiry. *Integral Review*, 6(1), 209–235. Retrieved from https://doaj.org/article/08766fbfa0154e519884783c9a30918e

Torbert, W. R. (2013). Brief comparison of five developmental measures: the GLP, the MAP, the LDP, the SOI, and the WUSCT primarily in terms of pragmatic and transformational validity and efficacy. Action Inquiry Associates. Retrieved from https://www.gla.global/wp-content/uploads/2016/11/Developmental-Measures-Compared-1.pdf

UK National Fraud Authority. (2013). Annual fraud indicator June 2013. Retrieved from https://www.gov.uk/government/publications/annual-fraud-indicator–2

United Nations. (2019a). Sustainable development goals: Goal 12: Ensure sustainable consumption and production patterns. Retrieved from https://www.un.org/sustainabledevelopment/sustainable-consumption-production/

United Nations. (2019b). Sustainable development goals: Goal 16: Promote just, peaceful and inclusive societies. Retrieved from https://www.un.org/sustainabledevelopment/peace-justice/

Wheatley, M. J. (2006). *Leadership and the new science.* San Francisco, CA: Berrett-Koehler Publishers.

4 How sport regulations are being used to restore trust following the International Biathlon Union scandal

Erika Riedl

Introduction

The aim of this chapter is twofold. First, it will provide a brief description of the International Biathlon Union (IBU) scandal which came to light in 2018, as well as the measures put in place as an anti-corruption response. Then, an analysis of the IBU Integrity Code, and a comparison of the rules and regulations of the remaining Winter Sports Federations participating in the Olympic Winter Games[1] will be provided. Finally, some recommendations will be made on how the respective Codes of Ethics could be improved with the aim of using this mechanism to assist in restoring trust in the IBU, as envisaged by the work of Walker (2001) into 'moral repair'.

The term 'anti-corruption' in this chapter follows Miller's characterisation of corruption (Miller, 2018), and refers to off-field corruption, including fraud and bribery including, gifts and other benefits (commissions). This chapter does not look at on-field corruption, such as match-fixing (sometimes referred to as competition manipulation), or doping issues. It is important to stress that the investigations of the alleged corrupt conduct have not been finalised, and the chapter is, therefore, based on the information available at the time of writing.

IBU scandal

Background

On 12 April 2018, the Austrian Central prosecutor's office for the prosecution of economic criminal matters and corruption (*Zentrale Staatsanwaltschaft zur Verfolgung von Wirtschaftsstrafsachen und Korruption* (WKSTA)) confirmed in a press release (WKSTA, 2018) that the WKSTA was conducting preliminary proceedings (*Ermittlungsverfahren*) in connection with allegations against officials of the IBU, and officials and athletes of the Russian Biathlon team. These allegations concerned the use of prohibited substances or methods for the purpose of doping (§ 22a Abs 1 Z 1 und Z 2 Anti-Doping BuGes 2007), serious fraud in connection with doping (§§ 146, 147 Abs 1a, tw Abs 2 StGB) and the acceptance of gifts by staff (§ 309 Abs 1 u. 3 Fall 2 StGB) ('the corruption allegations'). The press release further reads that there is an accusation that suspected doping cases (which had been brought to the IBU's attention by the

World Anti-Doping Agency (WADA)) were not responded to adequately, for example through a tribunal hearing and/or sanctions. Further that bribes in the amount of USD 300,000 had been promised or accepted, and prize money was obtained through fraud via doping of around 35,000 Euros (roughly US$37,600). These allegations concern mostly the 2017 Biathlon World Championships in Hochfilzen, Austria, but some corruption allegations date back as far as 2012.

On 4 August 2018, the IBU stated that a new Code of Ethics (2018 Code of Ethics) had been approved by the Executive Board (IBU, 2018). Further, on 3–4 November 2018, the Executive Board decided to appoint and mandate an External Review Commission (ERC) (IBU, 2018) to:

i examine an internal IBU Constitution Working group proposal which was tasked with conducting a comprehensive review of the IBU Constitution, the IBU's rules of conduct (ethical, anti-doping and otherwise) and related disciplinary rules and regulations, and to make recommendations to any reforms or amendments that the Commission considered necessary or appropriate to ensure that: 'the IBU is operating in accordance with international best practice in this area, and has a strengthened ability to prevent and to respond robustly to any future breaches of its rules' …
ii conduct a full and unfettered investigation into all anti-doping, compliance, ethical and other disciplinary matters arising from the ongoing investigation by WADA and various national and international criminal authorities, as well as into any further issues of concern that arise in relation to IBU governance or ethical matters within the IBU and/or otherwise in the sport of biathlon that are identified in the course of the investigation;
iii fully cooperate with all relevant external authorities with jurisdiction over some or all of the matters, including WADA and the criminal authorities in Austria and Norway; and
iv advise the IBU whether any person or member or other body has a case to answer for breach of obligations to the IBU in relation to any of the matters.

The Terms of Reference for the IBU ERC of 6 November 2018 further includes allegations that delegates of IBU member federations at the 2016 IBU Congress had been bribed to vote in favour of the 2021 World Championships being held in Tyumen, Russia.

At the time of finalising this chapter (last revised in November 2019), the ERC had produced nine Interim Reports. However, investigations (both by the ERC and the WKSTA, as well as the Norwegian criminal authorities) are still ongoing. The Norwegian authorities are involved as the then IBU President is a Norwegian citizen, Mr Anders Besseberg (Holden, 2018).

As part of the reforms proposed, on 19 October 2019, the IBU announced that the IBU Extraordinary Congress unanimously approved a new IBU Constitution, including a new Integrity Code and Biathlon Integrity Unit (BIU), as well as a stringent vetting process for all IBU officials (IBU, 2019, 19 October; IBU, 2019, 20 October). This chapter analyses the extent to which these measures could contribute to restoring trust in response to the corruption allegations.

IBU response to the scandal

In attempting to restore trust following the scandal, the IBU has chosen, amongst other things, to put stricter anti-corruption regulations in place. It has therefore updated its Code of Ethics as a first step and introduced an Integrity Code and an Independent Integrity Unit as a second step.

According to the IBU Statutes in effect at the time:

> The President represents the IBU in all important issues, directs the Executive Board, and monitors the activities of the Secretary General and Headquarters, and The Secretary General manages the day-to-day business of the IBU in accordance with the resolutions passed by the Congress and the Executive Board, and is in charge of the IBU Headquarters. (Articles 39.1 and 42.3 of the IBU Statutes respectively)

as the corruption allegations concern the highest day-to-day decision-makers within the IBU. Following Miller's characterisation of corruption (Miller, 2018), the allegations at hand concern, at the very least, institutional personal corruption, i.e. corruption of a person *qua* institutional role occupant, but most likely also institutional corruption, as an institutional process has been undermined, such as failing to follow up on suspected doping cases, therefore breaching the organisation's obligation to engage in the fight against doping.

Those harmed by the alleged corrupt actions are therefore most and foremost the athletes competing in IBU competitions. The athletes may find themselves on an even more unlevel playing field, since the corrupt actions allowed suspected dopers to continue to compete. Should the allegation be confirmed that some delegates of IBU member federations at the 2016 IBU Congress had been bribed to vote in favour of the 2021 World Championships being held in Tyumen, Russia, corruption will have affected not only the IBU, and one of its national member federation, Russia, but the other bidding member federations and the delegates bribed also. This therefore creates a situation where outsiders may perceive that the sport in its entirety was implicated, or least the culture within the organisation was called into question. This is even more the case from a trust perspective, where the organisation could not demonstrate that it had adequate response mechanisms in place, i.e. an anti-corruption programme, including education and whistleblowing protection, and more specifically for the purpose of this chapter, a robust Code of Ethics.

Legal and regulatory environment of Winter Sports IFs in anti-corruption

Association rules and criminal liability of sports associations

The IBU has, similar to the International Luge Federation (FIL), been established as an association under Austrian Law. The other five International Federations (IFs) (the International Bobsleigh and Skeleton Federation (IBSF), the World Curling Federation (WCF), the International Ice Hockey Federation (IIHF), the

International Skating Union (ISU) and the International Ski Federation (FIS)) have been established as associations in accordance with Swiss Law.[2] Both, the Association Law (*Vereinsgesetz*) in Austria and the relevant provisions in the Swiss Civil Code (Articles 60–79), only impose a few mandatory provisions. Apart from these mandatory provisions, taking into account certain limitations (Baddeley, 1994), associations may organise themselves as they see fit, including putting rules and regulations in place.

However, it should be noted that both Switzerland and Austria have ratified the UN Convention Against Corruption (UNCAC) (UN, 2005; UNODC, n.d.). Private corruption has been included in the criminal codes of both countries concerned.[3] Individuals, and private companies, including associations, can be held criminally liable for corruption according to the laws of both countries. More specifically, in Austria, the Law on the Responsibility of Associations (*Verbandsverantwortlichkeitsgesetz* (VbVG)) (sections 3 and 4) provides that an association can be held criminally liable for criminal acts committed by their employees and decision-makers. The upper limit of fines to be imposed is 1.3 million euros (roughly US$1.4 million).[4] In Switzerland, pursuant to Article 102 of the Swiss Criminal Code, an organisation can be held criminally liable in addition to the individual(s) who committed bribery if the organisation is found responsible for having failed to take all: 'reasonable organisational measures that are required in order to prevent such an offence'. Organisations can be fined up to 5 million Swiss Francs (roughly US$5.2 million) (Hoehn et al., 2016).

Opportunity and necessity of anti-corruption efforts by IBU, and other Winter Sports IFs[5]

IFs are, therefore, mostly free to put their own 'anti-corruption' rules in place. In the past, however, it seems that IFs have only reacted and sought to improve their anti-corruption efforts as a response to 'scandals' in their sport. For example, World Athletics (formerly the International Athletics Association (IAAF)) only established the Athletics Integrity Unit (AIU) in April 2017 after a corruption scandal emerged in November 2015. Similarly, the IBU, being the first Winter Sports IF, also created an independent Integrity Unit in response to the scandal. This independent Integrity Unit may be an additional 'tool' for the IBU to regain trust, provided those units and the Integrity Codes are fit for purpose.

A comparison with the IBU Code of Ethics in force at the time of the corruption allegations (IBU n.a.), with the one approved in September 2018, shows that the previous version did not include any bribery and anti-corruption provisions; the Code merely contained a conflict of interest policy. The 2018 IBU Code of Ethics in force between 6 September 2018 to 19 October 2019 (replaced by the Integrity Code) also includes a bribery and corruption provision, as well as a gift and other benefit policy. Furthermore, a whistleblowing policy has been included, which allows for anonymous reporting, and requires reporting of persons bound by the Code. In addition, an Independent IBU Ethics and Compliance Officer position was created (but seemingly not resourced or filled). The composition of the IBU Ethics Commission included experts (three of the five) 'independent external to biathlon'. When comparing the 2018 IBU Code of Ethics with the Codes of Ethics of the other Winter Sports IFs, as set out below, the IBU rules were quite similar to the FIS Code of Ethics, and more extensive than the Codes of Ethics currently in force from the remaining Winter Sports IFs.

An analysis of the IBU Integrity Code, and a comparison with the Codes of Ethics of the remaining Winter Sports Federations

Jurisdiction

The IBU Integrity Code (2019, October 19) clearly defines who falls within the scope of the Code, and when, including office holders and National Federation members, which was not the case for the 2018 IBU Code of Ethics. Clearly establishing who is bound by the rules and including all those who might infringe the rules within the sport, is intended to prevent situations where wrongdoers cannot be sanctioned due to lack of jurisdiction, which clearly impacts on trust. For example, the IAAF Ethics Commission (now the World Athletics Ethics Board) could not sanction a former treasurer of a member association, as he was not bound by the rules applicable to his case, i.e. the 2003 IAAF Ethics Code (Ethics Board Decision Number 10/2018 Art. 51 ff.). The Ethics Code applicable in his case bound only those: 'acting in positions of trust within the IAAF and by any other person who is otherwise entitled to act for, or on behalf of, the IAAF', which was not found to be the case for that person. The rules which followed, i.e. the 2012 IAAF Ethics Code, was amended to include 'Participants', which was defined as: 'an official, as well as a member of a delegation and person accredited to attend an International Competition'; thus a broader category of persons were thereafter bound by the IAAF Ethics Code (IAAF, 2012).

The IBU Integrity Code also clarifies that the Code will be enforced after a person's retirement with respect to any matter occurring prior to retiring. In comparison, none of the other IF's rules clarify what happens when a person resigns from their position, or in case of death. This should be amended, as it would undermine both trust and the effectiveness of an anti-corruption programme, if people could simply resign and thus forgo disciplinary sanctions. It is important for an organisation to be able to demonstrate that justice is 'seen to be done', even where those people step down voluntarily. To provide an example, the provisions of the FIFA Code of Ethics in force in 2012 allowed the Adjudicatory Chamber of the FIFA Ethics Committee to ban Mohamed Bin Hammam from all football-related activity for life, even after he decided to resign (FIFA, 2018, pp. 1–26).

Furthermore, a determination of a sanction might be required for asset recovery purposes, especially in those cases where money was misappropriated. This is an important 'tool' for an IF, to allow it to carry out its core purpose; the development of the sport. While the IBU Integrity Code provides for aggravating factors for: 'a finding that the Participant received or expected to receive a significant benefit as a result of the violation' (IBU n.d. Art. 9.3.4), the Code remains silent on how potential asset recovery would be dealt with.

Clear rules for defined conduct and clear sanctions for rule breaches

The 2010 Council of Europe's revised Code of Sports Ethics (Council of Europe, 2010) requires sport organisations to publish clear guidelines on ethical behaviour, apply appropriate sanctions, and raise awareness. This was further echoed in 2019, in the Draft Conclusions of the Council of the European Union which read as follows: 'Corruption is facilitated by a lack of rules or by inadequate implementation of existing rules on conflicts of interest, or revolving doors between the public and the private sectors' (Council of the European Union, 2019).

The UNODC Conference Report of November 2019 recommends that 'Sports organizations should examine existing best practices in the public and private sectors when developing anti-corruption strategies' (UNODC 2019, Recommendation 6). Anti-Corruption organisations primarily rely on a three-pronged approach in their fight against corruption, namely: enforcement, prevention and education.[6] Within those approaches, there are of course lessons that can be learnt from different countries and different sectors to assist in developing these strategies. For example, the Australian national Department of Health has recently issued an 'Approach to Market' seeking an expert's report on: 'Sport Integrity and Corruption: Best Practice Australian and International Policy & Program Delivery Approaches' (Commonwealth of Australia, 2019).

When analysing the various rules, it becomes clear that the conduct varies greatly from IF to IF. Furthermore, while some kind of conflict of interest policy and gift policy is included in most rules, other conduct is not described precisely and definitions of, for example corruption, benefit, private gain etc., are mostly non-existent. With regard to the IBU Integrity Code, no definition of a 'fraudulent' or 'corrupt' act is provided. This omission might create, in addition to legal uncertainty, also trust issues, and a definition would be important as well when considering the cultural differences given that IFs are operating on a worldwide level. According to Graycar and Jancsics (2017, p. 1021) there is a tipping point where a normal gift turns into a bribe, and they suggest that the organisational dimension is an important explanatory factor in the analysis of gift-bribe practices two ways. Clear rules and regulations are therefore desirable.

While the various Codes of Ethics refer to 'sport ethics', 'fair play', and to principles such as 'dignity', 'integrity' 'loyalty' and 'responsibility', as well as 'good conduct', 'honesty', and 'duty of loyalty' none of those rules clearly include a 'zero-tolerance' policy. To the contrary, certain rules are weakened in this respect by allowing explanations for failures to report a conflict of interest (WCF, 2015). Even worse, FIL rules (FIL, 2019 Art. 2) allow for 'minor violations' not to be investigated and sanctioned where the alleged offender ceases the prohibited behaviour. Since 'minor violations' has not been defined, and are not documented at all, arbitrary decisions in this respect are very likely and create an unacceptable corruption risk.

The IBU Integrity Code provides for an alternative procedure for minor violations, which are referred to the Secretary General for decision. While the sanctions of those violations are outlined, it has not been defined what conduct is considered 'minor'. The absence of this transparency weakens the otherwise independent investigations (by the BIU) and adjudication mechanism (by the Disciplinary Tribunal by the CAS Ordinary Division) established under the Code. This is even more pronounced where there exists no right of appeal against those decisions.

Discovery of corrupt conduct

Even law enforcement agencies agree that corruption cases are the most difficult to prosecute, especially since in most cases both parties are happy with their 'deal', e.g. the one offering the bribe and the one taking the bribe. The need for people to come forward and 'blow the whistle' is therefore crucial in many cases (Kwok, 2018). However, research demonstrates that potential whistle-blowers cite two reasons why they prefer not to report, even confidentially or anonymously, namely the fear of retaliation, and the belief that nothing will change (see Ondráčková and Verschuuren, Chapter 8 in this volume). It is suggested that these two hurdles are best countered with a robust 'speak-up' culture (Aiolfi, 2019). Related to the foregoing, the need to protect whistle-blowers has been recognised by the European Commission which proposes a new law to strengthen whistle-blower protection across the EU (European Commission, 2018). Furthermore, the anti-doping community seems to have recognised this need also. The recently approved World Anti-Doping Code (WADC, 2021) includes sanctions for those who retaliate against whistle-blowers (WADA, 2020A, Art. 2.11).

In the past, people in the sport industry, especially those directly impacted, such as athletes and support personnel, have been hesitant to come forward. The Cycling Independent Reform Commission (CIRC) Report reads in this regard as follows: 'although the influence of the classic "omerta" has declined, riders are still reluctant to report doping or suspicious conduct to the authorities' (Marty, Nicholson, & Haas, 2015, p. 12). Recognising this reluctance, some IFs have started including: (i) reporting requirements, and (ii) 'substantial assistance' provisions, in their rules. In anti-doping for example, pursuant to Article 10.6.1 of the WADC, an otherwise applicable period of Ineligibility of an athlete or other person liable under the WADC, may be suspended for up to three-quarters of the sanction period, where this athlete or other person provides substantial assistance which leads to either discovering or bringing forward and anti-doping rule violation by another person, or results in discovering or bringing forward a criminal offence or the breach of professional rules by another person (WADA, 2015). Reporting obligations, and possible sanction reductions, can now also be found in some of IF Codes (e.g. FIS 2016 Art. 4 and 5.5).

While some rules include an obligation to report any alleged breach of the rules, as well as full cooperation with investigations and providing evidence where requested, no consequences are foreseen for non-reporting and non-cooperation. The IBU Integrity Code (Article 9) provides for a general provision that a violation of the requirements of the Constitution and of any rules constitutes a violation of the Integrity Code. However, there seems to be no specific provision outlining the sanctions and procedures to be followed for violations of non-reporting or non-cooperation. Therefore, the implementation of this general provision can be questioned. Omissions should be sanctioned, as it is already the case for match-fixing, where such cases are prosecuted and sanctions imposed (Tennis Integrity Unit (TIU), 2018). The obligation to report should include all persons covered by the Code in the same way, as well as for all potential breaches. From a trust perspective, allowing exceptions for Executive Board members and Committee members, for not reporting minor breaches, as it is the case for the new IBU Integrity Code (See comment 1 to Article 8.1.1.2), is highly questionable.

The IBU Integrity Code goes further, and includes attempted violations, as well as complicity of any violation or attempted violation of the Code. Given that IFs are private institutions, and their investigation means are limited, e.g. no phone tapping or bank account tracing is possible, IFs have to – even more than law enforcement agencies – rely on information provided by persons, either through informants or via interviews conducted during investigations. Therefore both reporting and collaboration requirements for persons bound by the rules is desirable. The challenges faced by IFs in conducting investigations, makes the attempted violation provision very useful, as the burden of proof is more easily met.

These measures are supported by the establishment and implementation of Vetting Rules, such as these put in place by the IBU, which provide for integrity checks, requests for relevant information and bi-annual conflict of interest disclosures for persons wanting to become or remain IBU officials. The implementation of such measures might also increase the trust in an organisation and the sport.

Investigations procedures and sanctioning bodies

Following Beloff's view (Beloff, 2017, pp. 3–10), self-regulation of sports organisations carries within it the seed of conflict of interest; the desire to eliminate corruption collides with the desire to present the best image of the sport to the world, and what should be a vigilant eye can become a blind eye. It is therefore crucial that the person(s): (i) deciding on whether to investigate; (ii) conducting the investigation; (iii) deciding on whether a rule violation has been committed, and (iv) handing down the appropriate sanction be independent from the IF, or at least that an oversight by an independent person or body be guaranteed. While the BIU is conducting investigations independently from the IBU and has the power to start investigations as they see fit, this possibility is currently not foreseen in any of Codes of Ethics of the other IFs.

Next to an independent person investigating alleged violations, it is highly advisable that the decision whether or not to investigate, as well the investigations themselves, are overviewed by a second body with no connection to the principal body, or the IF, so as to have checks and balances in place.[7] For example, WADA's Intelligence and Investigations Unit is undergoing audits annually (WADA, 2019), and the Hong Kong Independent Commission Against Corruption [ICAC] has an Operations Review Committee overseeing all investigations

(ICAC n.d.). The IBU Integrity Code requires that BIU investigations be fully documented. However, there seems to be no oversight envisaged, apart from potentially reporting to the Board.

Some of the rules suggest that the body investigating is also the one deciding on whether a rule violation has been committed, and ultimately deciding on the sanctions to be imposed. No rule or general principle compels federations to separate the investigating and adjudicating functions within their disciplinary bodies, and different federations currently have varying systems in place (Cornu, Cuendet, & Vidal, 2017). However, for anti-corruption purposes, a distinction is strongly recommended, which is now included for the IBU. The need for at least an independent adjudicatory body seems to have been recognised in anti-doping, as the WADA mandatory International Standard for Results Management [ISRM] coming into effect on 1 January 2021 requires an 'impartial' hearing panel and for the panel to be 'operationally independent' (See Article 8.8 of the ISRM).

Different degrees of independence seem to exist when looking at the composition of the decision-making bodies of the remaining IFs. The respective rules of the IIHF (2014) and the IBSF (2011) foresee that an organ of the IF is involved in the decision part, either at an intermediary stage, or even takes the final decision. The IIHF Council determines whether a violation has occurred and refers the case to the IIHF Disciplinary Board for further sanctions. In the case of IBSF, the Ethics Committee only issues final non-binding opinions to the Executive Committee, which is the organ with authority to issue 'its final judgement' (IBSF 2011, Art. 11 and 14). Presumably this 'final judgement' may over-ride the IBSF Ethics Committee 'opinion'.

Additional suggestions

In addition to including consequences for non-reporting and non-collaboration, as outlined above, the rules could include further requirements to facilitate investigations. Article 5.3 of the IIHF Code of Conduct allows the IIHF to make a written demand and request records, such as itemised phone bills, bank statements, computers, hard drives and other electronic information storage devices. Following this example of making a written demand, the rules should also include the possibility to request such records without advanced notice for auditing purposes, i.e. allowing for a surprise effect, and thus no time for the suspect to destroy potential evidence. For example, in accordance with Article 6.1.6 of the ICC's Minimum Standards for Players' and Match Officials' areas at international matches, the International Cricket Council (ICC) at international matches 'require any person in possession of any Mobile Device, laptop computer (or any other similar device) to immediately provide such Mobile Device, laptop computer (or any other similar device) to the ICC Anti-Corruption Manager for auditing purposes' (ICC, 2018). While the 'Demand' and 'Objection to a Demand' under the IBU Integrity Code are understandable from a procedural point of view, the likelihood that evidence might be destroyed remains high.

Furthermore, there should also be a possibility to request financial statements (not only bank statements), including from persons close to the person covered by the Code, such as family members, business partners, etc. People applying to be elected or nominated for IF bodies could be required to confidentially disclose their annual income, private interests (pecuniary and non-pecuniary). The vetting procedures and/or the Ethics Codes could then require those persons to disclose any substantial (amount or percentage to be defined) increase in wealth, or changes in yearly income. Non-disclosure thereof should be included as a violation of the Codes of Ethics. Vetting procedures should allow for a living status of vetting not only in the candidature phase, but also after election, nomination and appointment. Similarly, a 2018 audit of the Australian Government Security Vetting Agency (AGSVA), which was established within the Department of Defence in 2010, found that 'AGSVA's clearances do not provide sufficient assurance to entities about personnel security risks' (Australian National Audit Office (ANAO), 2018).

It is also helpful that the standards of proof in disciplinary proceedings are lower than in criminal proceedings. The sport rules generally vary between the standard of 'on a balance of probability', and 'beyond reasonable doubt'. However, establishing the required burden of proof has proven difficult in many cases (for example IAAF Ethics Board Decision Number 11/2018, Articles 146 to 148)). One way to partly remedy this issue, outlined above, could be by including the 'Attempted' conduct, as is already the case for the IBU.

Finally, while the IBU Integrity Code includes general 'Bidding' or procurement provisions, detailed rules in this respect can be found outside the Integrity Code, and therefore not attracting integrity sanctions in the breach. It is observed that many other Codes of Ethics remain silent with regard to 'Bidding' or 'Tenders'. Given that the amounts of those contracts can be considerable, there is a high risk of corruption, and nepotism seems to be found in this area also (see the Bayley and Egle, Chapter 3, this volume). Therefore, provisions relating to procurement and unethical conduct should also be included in the respective Codes of Ethics.

Conclusion

From the analysis of the Codes of Ethics, it can be concluded that anti-corruption measures within the Winter Sports IFs are in their infancy. Many improvements can be made to lower the corruption risks in their sports. Most concerning is that, the winter sports present a low risk and a high reward environment, including a lack of deterrence, and poor system control, which are all facilitators of corruption. The IBU on their part have put rules in place which are far more extensive than the other winter sports, even though they could be strengthened in several ways as suggested throughout this article.

The Codes of Ethics for the Winter Sports IFs currently in place, – other than for the IBU – are mostly powerless in combatting anti-corruption issues should they arise in their sports. Therefore, they need to improve their anti-corruption measures if they want to change their currently frozen status, and to stand a chance to be able to combat corrupt activities. As a starting point for improvement it is suggested that the respective Codes of Ethics be strengthened.

Walker (2001) suggests that a detailed understanding of the many facets of moral repair as they apply to concrete situations is required in order to replenish trust. Time will tell whether the IBU is able to restore trust with the measures it has put in place. In comparison, after two years of operation, the Chairman of the AIU Board, David Howman, remarked as follows: 'I suggest that the AIU has quickly established itself as an effective, transparent and engaged organisation, a global leader in sports integrity. I believe our work has brought credit to the IAAF and the sport of athletics' (Athletics Integrity Unit (AIU), 2019). Whether this means World Athletics also having regained the trust from the athletics community remains in question. Trust in sports administration, or regaining such trust, is quite a difficult exercise. As recently found in New Zealand, 60% of participants in a survey across that country indicated that they were: 'not so confident', or 'not at all confident' that the governance arrangements of their organisations mitigate the risks of corruption (Sport New Zealand & New Zealand Government, 2019).

Ultimately, along with regaining trust, IFs will also need to comply with the various criminal laws in place, given the potential for criminal prosecution. In addition, financial losses caused by corrupt activities also pose a high risk. Surprisingly, IFs seem not to have realised these additional risks. A recent survey of 1,392 companies across Germany, France, Great Britain and Switzerland confirms that one of the three main reasons why those companies have put whistleblowing systems in place for reporting illegal and unethical conduct is because they 'want to avoid financial losses' (EQS Group & HTW Chur, 2019). Depending on the corrupt conduct, financial losses can be considerable. According to media reports, FIFA is trying to recover at least US$28 million which it allegedly lost in the recent football corruption scandal (Ruiz, 2016). While the Winter Sports IFs do not experience the annual revenues enjoyed by FIFA, it remains a real risk that, unless immediate action is taken, their very existence as sports may be in jeopardy.

Questions

i *Trust loss* – In whom (or, in which group) has trust been lost in this case?

ii *Trust correction* – How, if attempted, has the restoration of trust been tried?; and;

iii *Lessons learned* – How could the lessons from this case be applied to other sports, nations, states, other districts for the same sport, or other sports to prevent a further loss of trust or at least to restore trust?

Notes

1 See International Sports Federations recognised by the IOC, https://www.olympic.org/ioc-governance-international-sports-federations
2 See the respective statutes and constitutions of the Winter Sports IFs.
3 For Austria, see Sections 309 and 153a of the Austrian Criminal Code. Strafgesetzbuch (in German), https://www.jusline.at/gesetz/stgb. See also G. Krakow and G. Götz, 'Anti-Corruption in Austria', *Global Compliance News*, Baker McKenzie Vienna, https://globalcompliancenews.com/anti-corruption/handbook/anti-corruption-in-austria/. For Switzerland, see Articles 322 *octies, novies* and *decies* of the Swiss Criminal Code. Swiss Criminal Code, https://www.admin.ch/opc/en/classified-compilation/19370083/index.html. See also R. Levy, 2015, 'Can Switzerland's new "Lex FIFA" combat corruption within international sports federations?', *LawInSport*, 25 November, https://www.lawinsport.com/topics/articles/item/can-switzerland-s-new-lex-fifa-combat-corruption-within-international-sports-federations/
4 The VbVG has been challenged, but the Austrian Constitutional Court confirmed the constitutionality of the VbVG (11 Os 10/16d). Associations are therefore advised to complement strategies to avoid criminal liability under the VbVG, for example by putting clear and efficient internal guidelines and procedures to mitigate the association's liability under the VbVG. See also M. Lindtner and K. Kiehl, 2017, 'The Austrian Law on the Responsibility of Associations: New tendency to prosecution authorities to target companies as first shot', *schönherr Newsletters*, 20 June, https://www.schoenherr.eu/publications/publication-detail/the-austrian-law-on-the-responsibility-of-associations-new-tendency-to-prosecution-authorities-to-t/
5 Transparency International (TI) confirms that there is rich opportunity for corruption in sport, https://www.transparency.org/topic/detail/sport. See also Transparency International, 2016, 'Global Corruption Report: Sport', 23 February, https://www.transparency.org/whatwedo/publication/global_corruption_report_sport/
6 By way of example also the Hong Kong Independent Commission Against Corruption (ICAC), https://www.icac.org.hk/en/about/struct/index.html/
7 This outside body could for example also conduct a yearly review/audit of the anti-corruption programme in place and recommend measures to be included in the forthcoming strategic plan according to a risk assessment conducted. Ultimately this could be a good solution for smaller IFs like the ones in question, rather than seeking to comply with for example the ISO 37001 Anti-bribery management systems standard.

References

Aiolfi, G. (2019). Protecting whistleblowers in Switzerland: Can a speak-up culture and self-reporting framework help?. Retrieved from https://www.baselgovernance.org/news/ protecting-whistleblowers-switzerland-can-speak-culture-and-self-reporting-framework-help

Athletics Integrity Unit. (2019). Athletics Integrity Unit 2018 Report. Retrieved from https://www.athleticsintegrity.org/downloads/pdfs/know-us/en/AIU-Annual-Report-2018-EN_Lite-1.pdf

Australian National Audit Office (ANAO). (2018, 11 May). Mitigating insider threats through personnel security. Retrieved from https://www.anao.gov.au/work/performance-audit/mitigating-insider-threats-through-personnel-security

Baddeley, M. (1994). *L'Association sportive face au droit: Les limites de son autonomie*. Bâle et Francfort-sur-le-Main: Collection Genevoise, Helbing & Lichtenhahn.

Beloff, M. J. (2017). Sport, ethics and the law. *Sweet & Maxwell's International Sports Law Review*, 17(1), 3–10.

Commonwealth of Australia. (2019). Approach to Market Reference ID: Health/18–19/E19–66143. Retrieved from https://law.anu.edu.au/news-and-events/news/report-dr-hall-safeguard-integrity-australian-sport

Cornu, P., Cuendet, S., & Vidal, L. (2017). Disciplinary and arbitration procedures of the sport movement: Good practice handbook – for judicial authorities. Retrieved from https://edoc.coe.int/en/sport-for-all/7434-disciplinary-and-arbitration-procedures-of-the-sport-movement.html

Council of Europe. (2010). Recommendation CM/Rec(2010)9 of the Committee of Ministers to member states on the revised Code of Sports Ethics – Adopted by the Committee of Ministers on 16 June 2010 at the 1088th meeting of the Ministers' Deputies. Retrieved from https://rm.coe.int/16805cecaa

Council of the European Union. (2019). Draft conclusions of the Council and of the representatives of the governments of the Member States meeting within the Council on combating corruption in sport – Adoption. Retrieved from https://data.consilium.europa.eu/doc/document/ST-13349-2019-INIT/en/pdf

EQS Group and HTW Chur – Hochschule für Technik und Wirtschaft – University of Applied Sciences. (2019). Whistleblowing report 2019. Retrieved from https://cdn2.hubspot.net/hubfs/4749693/White%20Paper/WhistleblowingReport2019_EN.pdf?utm_medium=email&_hsenc=p2ANqtz-9upE_sUkNvXeQU_I_lXLDvI5PkF3KJ7IGf79d09q_4IWfFXbj_OZdx5m7dDoGNfsVuqZ3KayL_tyHkGdZvqlhuADwiYA&_hsmi=72690842&utm_source=hs_automation&utm_content=72690842&hsCtaTracking=2a537f55-cf89-4bc5-aa2d-40df29d31783%7C9b263ffa-81e3-44ab-abcf-aece40b0f9d1

European Commission. (2018). Whistleblower protection: Commission sets new, EU-wide rules. Retrieved from http://europa.eu/rapid/press-release_IP-18-3441_en.htm

FIFA. (2018, 3 July). Ethics Committee milestones (2012–2018). Retrieved from https://resources.fifa.com/image/upload/ethics-committee-milestones-2012-2016-2741972.pdf?cloudid=flai7jvu5ah88alhscjd

Graycar, A., & Jancsics, D. (2017). Gift giving and corruption. *International Journal of Public Administration*, 40(12), 1013–1023. Retrieved from https://spa.sdsu.edu/documents /Gift_Giving_and_Corruption.pdf

Hoehn, J.*et al.* (2016). Swiss criminal laws on bribery: Reforms as of July 2016 – Swiss and foreign companies as well as their board members are compelled to act. Pestalozzi Attorneys at Law Ltd. Retrieved from https://pestalozzilaw.com/en/news/legal-insights/swiss-criminal-laws-bribery-reforms-july-2016/

Holden, L. (2018, 12 April). Korrupsjonsanklaget Besseberg: Trygg på at det ikke blir en dom. VG. Retrieved from https://www.vg.no/sport/i/e1XXk4/korrupsjonsanklaget-besseberg-trygg-paa-at-det-ikke-blir-en-dom (English translation by Bergen, A. E retrieved from https://antidopingworld.wordpress.com/2018/04/15/ibu-president-and-corruption-investigated-besseberg-is-sure-there-will-be-no-judgment-against-him/).

Hong Kong Independent Commission Against Corruption (ICAC). (n.d.). Checks and balances. Retrieved from https://www.icac.org.hk/en/check/advisory/orc/index.html

Hong Kong Independent Commission Against Corruption (ICAC). (n.d.). About ICAC. Retrieved from https://www.icac.org.hk/en/about/struct/index.html

International Association of Athletics Federations (IAAF). [now World Athletics]. (2012, 1 May). Code of Ethics. Retrieved from http://www.iaaf.org/download/download?filename=d89e2268-bc28-4d2e-a1c1-92c1eee26dc8.pdf&urlslug=Code%20of%20Ethics

IAAF Ethics Commission (now the World Athletics Ethics Board). (n.d.). Decisions. Retrieved from https://www.iaafethicsboard.org/decisions

International Biathlon Union (IBU). (2018). International Biathlon Union appoints external review commission. Retrieved from https://www.biathlonworld.com/news/detail/ibu-external-review-commission

International Biathlon Union (IBU). (n.d.). IBU code of ethics. Retrieved from http://res.cloudinary.com/deltatre-spa-ibu/image/upload/ccieaf75bdt8vf3vnw2g.pdf

International Biathlon Union (IBU). (2018, 5 August). IBU executive board: Code of ethics adopted amid final preparations for congress. Retrieved from https://www.biathlonworld.com/news/detail/press-release-august-5th-2018

International Biathlon Union (IBU). (2019, 19 October). IBU integrity code. Retrieved from http://res.cloudinary.com/deltatre-spa-ibu/image/upload/tziqluncgelica29obn7.pdf

International Biathlon Union (IBU). (2019, 20 October). Historic extraordinary IBU congress marks beginning of new era for IBU. Retrieved from https://www.biathlonworld.com/news/detail/historic-ibu-extraordinary-congress-marks-beginning-of-new-era-for-ibu

International Bobsleigh & Skeleton Federation (IBSF). (2011, 10 September). Code of ethics. Retrieved from www.ibsf.org/images/documents/downloads/code_of_ethics_E_120712_IBSF.pdf

International Cricket Council (ICC). (2018). ICC minimum standards for players' & match officials' areas (PMOA) at international matches – effective as from 1 December 2018. Retrieved from https://icc-static-files.s3.amazonaws.com/ICC/document/2018/12/16/f3b76dad-9668-4a64-aeb8-0e8684d8e28b/-FV-Effective-from-1-December-2018-PMOA-Minimum-Standards-CEC-approved-.pdf

International Ice Hockey Federation (IIHF). (2014, 1 June). IIHF code of conduct. Retrieved from https://iihfstorage.blob.core.windows.net/iihf-media/iihfmvc/media/downloads/regulations/2018-iihf-code-of-conduct.pdf

International Luge Federation (FIL). (2019, 1 July). FIL ethics code. Retrieved from https://www.fil-luge.org/cdn/uploads/fil-ethik-code-englisch.pdf

International Olympic Committee (IOC). (2019). International sports federations. Retrieved from https://www.olympic.org/ioc-governance-international-sports-federations

International Ski Federation (FIS). (2016, November). FIS universal code of ethics. Retrieved from https://assets.fis-ski.com/image/upload/v1536910199/fis-prod/assets/FIS_Code_of_ethics.pdf

Krakow, G., & Götz, E. (n.d.) Anti-corruption in Austria. Retrieved from https://globalcompliancenews.com/anti-corruption/handbook/anti-corruption-in-austria/

Kwok, T. (2018). EP013A, Lecture Day 9, Protection of whistle blower: Witness protection [oral presentation]. EP013A, Hong Kong: HKU Space – Hong Kong School of Professional and Continuing Education.

Levy, R. (2015). Can Switzerland's new 'Lex FIFA' combat corruption within international sports federations?. Retrieved from https://www.lawinsport.com/topics/articles/item/can-switzerland-s-new-lex-fifa-combat-corruption-within-international-sports-federations

Lindtner, M., & Kiehl, K. (2017). The Austrian law on the responsibility of associations: New tendency to prosecution authorities to target companies as first shot. Retrieved from https://www.schoenherr.eu/publications/publication-detail/the-austrian-law-on-the-responsibility-of-associations-new-tendency-to-prosecution-authorities-to-t/

Marty, D., Nicholson, P., & Haas, U. (2015). *Cycling Independent Reform Commission Report to the President of the Union Cycliste Internationale* (p. 12). Retrieved from https://www.uci.org/docs/default-source/imported-library/circreport2015_neutral.pdf?sfvrsn=7a9764d3_14

Miller, S. (2018, 21 September). Corruption. *Stanford encyclopedia of philosophy*. Retrieved from https://plato.stanford.edu/archives/win2018/entries/corruption

Ruiz, R. R. (2016, 16 March). FIFA, embracing role as victim, seeks to collect millions in U.S. case. *The New York Times*. Retrieved from https://www.nytimes.com/2016/03/17/sports/soccer/fifa-restitution-us-justice-department-bribery-case.html

Sport New Zealand, New Zealand Government. (2019). Sport integrity review – Findings and recommendations – September 2019. Retrieved from https://sportnz.org.nz/assets/Uploads/Findings-and-Recommendations-Sport-Integrity-Review-updated4.pdf

Tennis Integrity Unit (TIU). (2018). Federico Coria suspended and fined for tennis corruption offences. Retrieved from www.tennisintegrityunit.com/media-releases/federico-coria-suspended-and-fined-tennis-corruption-offences

Transparency International (TI). (2016). Global corruption report: Sport. Retrieved from https://www.transparency.org/whatwedo/publication/global_corruption_report_sport

United Nations (UN). (2005). United Nations Convention Against Corruption (UNCAC). United Nations. Retrieved from https://www.unodc.org/unodc/en/corruption/uncac.html

United Nations Office on Drugs and Crime (UNODC). (n.d.). Signature and ratification status. Retrieved from www.unodc.org/unodc/en/corruption/ratification-status.html

United Nations Office on Drugs and Crime (UNODC). (2019). *Conference report – Safeguarding sport from corruption – Towards effective implementation of resolution 7/8 on corruption in sport 3rd and 4 September 2019 (Recommendation 6)*. Retrieved from https://www.unodc.org/documents/Safeguardingsport/Meetings/2019-09_-_Safeguarding_Sport_from_Corruption/REPORT.pdf

Walker, M. U. (2001). Moral repair and its limits. Marquette University e-Publications@Marquette, 1-1-2001. Retrieved from https://epublications.marquette.edu/cgi/viewcontent.cgi?referer=&httpsredir=1&article=1151&context=phil_fac

World Anti-Doping Agency (WADA). (2015; 2019, 1 June). World Anti-Doping Code 2015 with 2019 amendments. Retrieved from https://www.wada-ama.org/sites/default/files/resources/files/wada_anti-doping_code_2019_english_final_revised_v1_linked.pdf

World Anti-Doping Agency (WADA). (2019). Intelligence and Investigations Department – Annual audit conducted by Independent Supervisor from 15–18 April 2019. Retrieved from https://www.wada-ama.org/sites/default/files/resources/files/2019_intelligenceandinvestigations_audit_conclusions_en.pdf

World Anti-Doping Agency (WADA). (2020, 15 June). World Anti-Doping Code (effective 1 January 2021). World Anti-Doping Agency. Retrieved from https://www.wada-ama.org/en/resources/the-code/2021-world-anti-doping-code

World Athletics Ethics Board. (2018). Ethics board decision – DO, JK – Decision number 10/2018 (Art. 51 ff.). Retrieved from https://www.iaafethicsboard.org/decisions

World Curling Federation (WCF). (2015, 20 March). Code of conduct polic y. Retrieved from http://worldcurling.org/governance/policies/

Zentrale Staatsanwaltschaft zur Verfolgung von Wirtschaftsstrafsachen und Korruption (WKSTA). (2018). Causa Hausdurchsuchung am IBU-Sitz in Salzburg. Retrieved from http://docs.dpaq.de/13451-biathlon_presseaussendung_12.04.2018.pdf

Legislation

Bundesrecht konsolidiert: Gesamte Rechtsvorschrift für Strafgesetzbuch, Fassung vom 24.02.2020. Austrian Criminal Code (available in German). Retrieved from https://www.ris.bka.gv.at/GeltendeFassung.wxe?Abfrage=Bundesnormen&Gesetzesnummer=10002296

Bundesrecht konsolidiert: Gesamte Rechtsvorschrift für Vereinsgesetz 2002, Fassung vom 24.02.2020. Retrieved from https://www.ris.bka.gv.at/GeltendeFassung.wxe?Abfrage=Bundesnormen&Gesetzesnummer=20001917

Gesamte Rechtsvorschrift für Anti-Doping-Bundesgesetz 2007, Fassung vom 24.02.2020. Austrian Anti-Doping Law (available in German). Retrieved from https://www.ris.bka.gv.at/GeltendeFassung/Bundesnormen/20005360/ADBG%202007%2c%20Fassung%20vom%2001.04.2019.pdf

Schweizerisches Strafgesetzbuch (Korruptionsstrafrecht), Änderung vom 25. September 2015. Retrieved from https://www.admin.ch/opc/de/official-compilation/2016/1287.pdf

Swiss Criminal Code of 21 December 1937 (Status as of 1 February 2020) (Articles 322 octies, novies and decies). Retrieved from https://www.admin.ch/opc/en/classified-compilation/19370083/index.html

5 Exercising discretion for social/recreational athletes

Case study Athlete XYZ

Victoria Jamieson and Catherine Ordway[1]

Introduction

Miller (2018) defines 'Corruption' as encapsulating a range of behaviours including 'cheating in sport by using drugs' (s.1). The World Anti-Doping Agency (WADA) mandate is to protect the 'spirit of sport' (WADA, 2015, p. 14). Leaving it to others to discuss what the 'spirit of sport' may mean (Hayes, 2016; Pielke, 2016, pp. 25–47; De Hon, 2017), 'Doping' under the World Anti-Doping Code (WADC) is broader than 'cheating to win' (Ordway & Opie, 2016). Doping refers to a violation of at least one anti-doping rule listed in the WADC including: the presence, possession, trafficking and/or administration of a banned substance or method, known as 'ADRVs' (WADA, 2015, Art 2.1–2.8). This chapter does not address the merits of the WADC's strict liability approach, particularly relating to presence cases arising from a test result (Connolly, 2005; Cox, 2014), as the issues raised here relate to the reliance on non-analytical evidence to 'prosecute' ADRVs. For the same reason, the important discussion on the balance required to achieve fairness for elite athletes in establishing 'no fault' or 'no significant fault' under the WADC (e.g. Rigozzi et al., 2015), is also not directly relevant to the issue raised by the case study here, precisely because this discretion does not apply where the person is 'at fault' in ordering a prohibited substance online. Rather, the concern which has not been addressed by the more recent re-draft of the WADC 2021 (WADA, 2020) is that the broad definition of 'athlete', combined with the lack of discretion to determine appropriate sanctions for those inadvertently captured, or otherwise clearly not attempting to 'cheat', amounts to an abuse of power and breaches the trust of the stakeholders required to maintain the Social Licence to Operate (SLO). This concern is encapsulated by the acknowledgement from Richard Young, the lead drafter of the World Anti-Doping Code: 'When the public reads ... that a nice kid gets banned for two years for a mistake in taking a cold medication, it undermines the credibility of the system' (WADA, 2012, p. 5).

The actors enforcing the WADC, primarily the national anti-doping organisations (NADOs), are not given the authority under the WADC to exercise a discretion to determine appropriate and proportionate responses to those cases clearly not involving 'cheating' or 'performance enhancement', particularly for those people falling outside the range of elite and sub-elite competitors NADOs are mandated to serve. The NADOs are usually taxpayer funded entities and have legitimacy through their SLO to protect clean sport. The publicly funded resources available to the NADOs are very limited. This chapter argues that the public confidence, or trust, in the work of NADOs under the WADC may be undermined where NADOs are perceived to be 'heavy-handed' or excessive in their treatment of social/recreational participants or those athletes clearly not attempting to 'cheat'. It may also adversely impact on the public perception of the prevalence of doping. Amending the WADC in the next round of consultations, and providing NADOs with clear guidelines on the exercise of their discretion, using an Ethics of Care (EoC) perspective, would restore trust and credibility in the anti-doping system and focus scarce resources in the areas of greatest need.

Erosion of trust in government and sporting institutions

Trust in public institutions, governments and Western democracies has been eroding for some time (Dalton, 2005, p. 135). Think tanks like the *TrustGov* project (University of Southampton n.d.), and the Australian equivalent, the *Public Trust Program* (Democracy 2025, 2020), map public perceptions of democracy, security and trust against the *World Values Survey* (WSV Association n.d.), and seek to understand how to 'Bridge the Trust Divide' (Stoker et al., 2018).

Within the sport ecosystem, the scenario is no different. In 2016, the Chief Executive of the Institute of Human Rights and Business, John Morrison, pointed to the withdrawal of bid cities from the race to host major events (e.g. Oslo from the 2022 Winter Olympics bid, and Boston and Hamburg from the Summer 2024 Olympic Games), together with: 'The fact that sports bodies such as the IAAF [athletics], FIFA [football] and IOC [Olympic Games] have lost or are losing public trust' as evidence that: 'Major sports bodies face a growing crisis of legitimacy', which he refers to as 'social licence' (Morrison, 2016, brackets added). The research by the strategic communications consultancy, The Brewery at Freuds, found in 2017 that one-third of the 2,000 people surveyed in Britain indicated that their 'trust in the sport industry has declined in the last 12 months' (Kelner, 2017). The authors of the report observed that: 'The erosion of trust, both through scandals and global forces, means that sports must adapt to rekindle and nurture their relationships or they risk losing relevance' (The Brewery, 2017, p. 67).

A recent media release by the NADO for the United Kingdom (UKAD) refers to research showing that:

> two thirds of the British public (66%) think that stories about an elite athlete or athletes doping in sport have had a negative impact on their trust in the integrity of sport. In addition, nearly half of British adults (48%) say that high-profile stories on doping in sport make them think that doping is widespread (UKAD, 2017).

This research suggests that, as 'information obesity' (Green, 2006) creates a reliance of headlines over content, combined with the increased reporting of cases that do not involve elite athletes or 'cheating to win', then the NADOs themselves are contributing to a public perception that doping is widespread. This of course needs to be balanced against the requirement for NADOs and WADA to be transparent in their decision-making, and to be reporting against the funding received. The Wood Review into Australian sport integrity also referred to the UKAD findings above and stated that: 'Bodies with responsibilities for organising sport are holders of public trust' (Wood et al., 2018, p. 164). This responsibility includes a requirement to educate athletes and others within the sport ecosystem of their obligations and responsibilities to avoid WADC Doping and make choices expected of 'good citizens' (e.g. Dalton, 2015; McCuaig & Hay, 2013).

Trust placed in anti-doping bodies

The international sporting community has demonstrated that it accepts that the behaviour encompassed by the WADC ADRVs is important to regulate. Doping erodes public trust in one of the key elements of competitive sport – the uncertainty of the outcome based on a 'level playing field' (Pielke, 2013). Leaving aside the debates about how idealistic this aim is (Healey, 2016), the public has placed their trust in WADA, the national and international sports federations, and the NADOs to regulate and implement the WADC. This trust or 'social licence' provides the anti-doping bodies with the legitimacy, or authority, to act. A 'social contract' (Nehme & Ordway, 2016) or SLO are concepts which have been applied in other industries, where public trust is required, and an SLO is extended. First used in this manner in the mining industry from 1997 (Boutilier, 2014, p. 263), the term 'SLO' has also been applied broadly in forestry (Edwards et al., 2016), medical research (Dixon-Woods & Ashcroft, 2008), marine-protected areas (Voyer et al., 2015) and similar industries including: 'oil and gas exploration and production, pipelines, renewable energy, farming, water use, ports and retailing' (Boutilier, 2014, p. 264; Hall et al., 2015).

As the term 'SLO' became more widely used, it was suggested that there were several levels, and that trust was required to bring the organisation credibility, legitimacy and 'approval' (Thomson & Joyce, 2008 cited by Boutilier, 2014, p. 264). Thomson and Boutilier (2011) proposed: 'a cumulative hierarchy model in which trust was treated as a boundary criterion that, once achieved, permitted the emergence of the highest level of social licence' (cited by Boutilier, 2014, p. 264). It is therefore suggested here that provided the public has trust in WADA and the NADOs, where people caught in the anti-doping net are treated fairly and community resources are used efficiently, the SLO will be maintained.

The concept of 'legitimacy' in anti-doping has been analysed widely, in both the social and legal sense. Legal legitimacy is: 'the type of legitimacy conferred on NADOs when they are established by a national government according to local procedures and laws' (Henning & Dimeo, 2018, p. 7), such as that found in Australia and New Zealand, but the idea of a SLO is relatively new. SLO is a valid concept to apply to anti-doping bodies in sport because, as for the industries cited above, gaining a SLO requires the NADO to be perceived as legitimate, and the loss of trust creates reputational risk and breaches the SLO (Joyce & Thomson, 2000 cited by Boutilier, 2014, p. 264).

Early research on motivations for doping athletes also included 'social legitimacy' in the sense that: an 'authority's perceived legitimacy is influenced by actual experiences with the authority's system and by others' reports of their experiences' such as 'fair and just treatment' (Donovan et al., 2002, pp. 276–7; Henning & Dimeo, 2018, p. 16). Social legitimacy influences the willingness, or moral obligation, of those affected by the rules to comply: 'Contingent compliers are prepared to, and prefer to, comply with common, fair rules as long as they believe that most others do so as well' (Føllesdal, 2011, p. 87). Fairness: in the rules, their application and decision-making is at the heart of legitimacy (McDermott et al., 2013). Going beyond the notion of 'fair play' set out in the WADC and the *Olympic Charter* (IOC, 2019), the SLO also requires accountability by those organisations charged with maintaining and restoring trust (Ronglan, 2015).

The definition of 'athlete' in the current WADC gives NADOs the discretion to extend their scope to include competitors below the international or national level (WADC, 2015, p. 131). Combined with the principle of strict liability in relation to positive test results, this broad scope creates a power imbalance in favour of NADOs. As observed in relation to the previous iteration of the WADC, the application of the strict liability principle to such a broad pool of potential athletes can be compared to seine net fishing: 'sometimes you catch dolphins when you are trawling for tuna' (Ordway, 2013). It is conceded that it is not always easy to determine whether participants are in fact 'cheating' and seeking to illegitimately enhance their performance, even if they were unaware that they could be caught by the anti-doping 'net'. The question posed here is whether, to continue this metaphor, once WADA becomes aware that 'dolphins' are being caught, the SLO demands that the fishing methods be changed.

Breaching the SLO through rule unfairness: WADC definition of 'Athlete'

Breaches of a SLO can occur in a number of ways, including procedural unfairness, excessive scope or reach and/or the unfair application of those rules. One mechanism used in regulating Doping is the extremely broad definition of 'athlete' under the WADC:

> Any Person who competes in sport at the international level (as defined by each International Federation) or the national level (as defined by each NADO). An Anti-Doping Organization [ADO] has discretion to apply anti-doping rules to an athlete who is neither an International-Level Athlete nor a National-Level Athlete, and thus to bring them within the definition of 'athlete'. In relation to athletes who are neither International-Level nor National-Level Athletes, an Anti-Doping Organization may elect to: conduct limited Testing or no Testing at all; analyse Samples for less than the full menu of

> Prohibited Substances; require limited or no whereabouts information; or not require advance Therapeutic Use Exemptions [TUEs]. However, if an Article 2.1, 2.3 or 2.5 ADRV is committed by any athlete over whom an Anti-Doping Organization has authority who competes below the international or national level, then the Consequences set forth in the Code (except Article 14.3.2) must be applied. For purposes of Article 2.8 and Article 2.9 and for purposes of antidoping information and education, any Person who participates in sport under the authority of any Signatory, government, or other sports organization accepting the Code is an athlete. (WADC, 2015, p. 131 – brackets added).

This definition fails to distinguish between competitors 'cheating in sport' as defined by Miller above, and social participants who are completely unaware that anti-doping policies apply to them. The latter category receives no anti-doping education relating to their obligations and may be unintentionally caught up in the contractual anti-doping process through this extremely wide scope. Reflecting the historical development of the WADC, which primarily relied on drug testing to detect Doping, and education for deterrence, this definition also focuses on the activities within the control of the NADO. By including in the athlete definition, the ability for NADOs to limit the scope of the testing and education pool, the WADC fails to envisage a situation where social participants are referred to NADOs by Law Enforcement Agencies (LEAs) or other agencies. These social participants might otherwise be unknown to the NADOs or the national sport federations because their participation in a sporting event may have been irregular, or even one-off (e.g. a 'Come and Try Day'). This definition demonstrates that the WADC does not adequately consider situations where non-analytical evidence, such as phone records, emails, bank statements or delivery consignments, may bring people unintentionally into the WADC contractual net. The concern then is that NADOs are, or believe themselves to be, compelled to treat these people with the full force and resources of the WADC. The key question is whether the WADC is the most appropriate mechanism to regulate the behaviour of adults who happen to play sport, as compared with elite athletes attempting to 'cheat to win', or an Athlete Support Personnel (such as a coach or team doctor) trafficking in performance-enhancing drugs.

It is argued here that the balance can be found through WADA adopting an EoC approach to allow NADOs the flexibility and discretion to create a restorative, instead of punitive, justice environment. As set out in other chapters in this book (for example Chapter 11 by Olukoya and Ogunleye-Bello, and Chapter 12 by Ordway and Lenten, this volume), Gilligan's (1982) feminist theory, expanded by Noddings (1984), promotes a view that those in positions of power have a moral duty to care. The EoC then would require WADA to take action to alleviate injustice and harm where it has been brought to its attention. It is no longer sufficient then to merely brush off social participants caught up like 'dolphins' as collateral damage for the greater good of clean sport. Instead, the 'spirit of sport' and 'fair play' elements of the WADC demand that, in the interests of both NADOs and the participants involved, NADOs are given the tools to respond proportionately and with respect. This is turn maintains trust and the SLO for both 'innocent' athletes and the public demanding a 'level playing field'.

Case study: Athlete XYZ

Mr XYZ, whose name has been supressed by the tribunal, reportedly weighed 130 kilograms and purchased weight-loss remedies online between November 2014 and January 2015. Unbeknown to Mr XYZ, these products contained ingredients which were prohibited under the 2015 WADC, and by New Zealand (NZ) Customs. The purchases were identified in a NZ Customs investigation that monitored online purchases of illegal products and medicines. The importers of products, which included WADA prohibited substances, were referred to the New Zealand NADO, Drug Free Sport NZ (DFSNZ). DFSNZ checked these referrals against lists of registered members held by national sport organisations. Mr XYZ was one of approximately 100 people thereby falling within the definition of 'athlete' referred from the NZ Customs investigation.

Athlete XYZ volunteered at, and participated in, social and master level competitions, at his local surf lifesaving club and golf club. Although Athlete XYZ had never competed in a national or international level competition, or received any anti-doping education, his community-level membership and participation in events arranged by clubs under the umbrella national organisations, automatically captured him under the DFSNZ *Sports Anti-Doping Rules* (SADR) (DFSNZ v XYZ, 2019, April, p. 15). The SADR did not distinguish between social and elite level athletes, so Athlete XYZ was classified as an athlete for the purpose of the SADR and the WADC. DFSNZ therefore sought to sanction Athlete XYZ for use or attempted use (SADR Art 2.2; WADC, 2015, Art 2.2) and possession (SADR Art 2.6; WADC, 2015, Art 2.6) of prohibited substances (clenbuterol and dianabol). DFSNZ places the responsibility on national sports organisations to ensure that all regional and club participants are aware of their obligations under the WADC and the SADR. This then allows DFSNZ to assume that all athletes captured under the SADR are aware of their anti-doping obligations.

Athlete XYZ disputed the sanction by arguing that he was not aware of his inclusion and obligations under the WADC, he did not intend to enhance his sporting performance and he had not received anti-doping education. The media statement from DFSNZ indicates a belief that Athlete XYZ was intending to cheat through using steroids to improve his performance:

> The respondent (XYZ) regularly competed in club and inter-club golf competitions. XYZ's recorded scores meant that he was in the top 3% of golfers in NZ. He also competed at a national masters surf life-saving event. The respondent purchased clenbuterol, and later purchased dianabol. Clenbuterol is an anabolic agent that acts to increase the ability of the body to burn fat, while maintaining lean muscle mass. Dianabol is an anabolic steroid, modified from testosterone. Dianabol is used by athletes to gain size and strength. (DFSNZ, 2019)

While the intention of Athlete XYZ in ordering these products may never be known, the suggestion that golfers, or surf life-savers, would benefit in their performance from the use of steroids does not seem to be borne out by the WADA testing statistics (WADA, 2018(a)). Testing in golf internationally is low, suggesting that Doping is not considered to be high risk in that sport (230 samples in total between the Professional Golf Association (192), and the International Golf Federation (38). WADA, 2018a, Table 8, p. 58; Table 2, p. 169; Table 34, p. 235). This can be compared with a sport struggling with steroid abuse, the International Weightlifting Federation, which conducted 3,238 samples, including 415 analysed for steroid profiles (51 returned Adverse Analytical Findings; WADA, 2018a, Table 9, p. 63). The International Golf Federation only referred 2 of its 38 tests for the additional steroid profile, and they came back negative. The same report indicates that of the 1,272 tests conducted by DFSNZ, four were on behalf of the International Life Saving Federation, and none in golf (WADA, 2018a, Table 6, p. 172; Table 75, p. 271).

In the decision by the Sports Tribunal of New Zealand (STNZ), the tribunal agreed that most people in the position of XYZ would be unaware that he was bound by the WADC and the SADR:

> We would expect that most sports club members engaged in recreational sport or simply club members for social and dining reasons would be extremely surprised to find that they would be subject to prosecution (using that term loosely) by DFSNZ if they were found to have used a prohibited drug for weight-loss or cholesterol reduction or menopausal hormone replacement reasons. They would be dismayed if they were to be subjected to an unannounced urine test while enjoying an after-match drink at the club and equally dismayed if told that CAS case law and/or DFSNZ's view of SADR leaves no discretion but to prosecute and the tribunal with no discretion but to impose SADR sanctions without regard to differences between them and elite and professional athletes. Such persons would certainly be aware that elite athletes are subjected to the rigours of the regime – and rightly so – but none of the media publicity around that regime would have alerted them to the possibility of their finding themselves in the position that the respondent in this case finds himself. (DFSNZ v XYZ, 2019, March 69)

The SADR did not expressly include a discretion not to sanction lower-level athletes, like Athlete XYZ, for non-analytical ADRVs (SADR n 167). Accordingly, the STNZ was unable to: 'absolve a respondent who lacks genuine culpability' and was instead required to implement the sanctions listed in the WADC (DFSNZ v XYZ, 2019, March). In the media release, the STNZ questioned the: 'utility and fairness in prosecuting recreational athletes who do not receive the educational attention on anti-doping that elite athletes do' (STNZ 2019). Notwithstanding, the STNZ acknowledged that Athlete XYZ had competed in club events, making it inevitable that he be sanctioned under the WADC and the SADR (DFSNZ v XYZ, 2019, March).

It was also not possible for the STNZ to apply the standard sanction reduction allowed by the WADC relating to 'no fault' or 'no significant fault or negligence' (WADC 2015, Art 10.4 and 10.5), or provide 'substantial assistance' relating to another person's ADRV (WADC 2015, Art 10.6). These clauses do not apply in circumstances where the person has acted alone and intentionally imported a prohibited substance but was unaware of their obligations under the WADC (DFSNZ v XYZ, 2019, 16 March). Contrary to the social utility of promoting the health benefits of exercise, particularly for the chronically obese, Athlete XYZ was banned from participation in sport for two years, as required under the WADC. The STNZ then reduced the period of the sanction to reward the athlete's timely admission, and to reflect the delay caused by the STNZ's request for legal clarification on the status of recreational athletes. As Athlete XYZ had been provisionally suspended already, the sanction was therefore backdated to the day after his last round of golf (3 October 2018) and expired one year later.

The comments from the STNZ that DFSNZ's 'potentially vast regime' (DFSNZ v XYZ, 2019, March, p. 21) had apparently made 'an executive decision' to 'police' low-level athletes without public consultation (DFSNZ v XYZ, 2019, 14 April p. 7), were echoed by the NZ Rugby Post Hearing Review Body (PHRB). In another case netted through the NZ Customs data from the same period, relating to a former lower-level rugby union athlete, the PHRB expressed its concern that:

> What seems to the PHRB to be extraordinary, is the amount of resources, money, people and time which [DFSNZ] has continued to expend on this case - a sledgehammer and the attempting to crack the tiniest of nuts (if one existed at all) comes to mind. (Johannsen, 2019)

The STNZ has continued to express frustration with the lack of discretionary powers under the anti-doping system more broadly: 'Unlike every other adjudicative body in New Zealand the tribunal is prevented from assessing a fair, reasonable and proportionate response which properly reflects what has occurred' (DFSNZ v Pouwhare-Anderson, 2019, 8, p. 3).

The Athlete XYZ case has international implications as many NADOs have implemented the WADC in a similar manner to NZ. Without guidance from WADA, social/ recreational athletes around the world could be unknowingly captured by the anti-doping movement. Not only does this impact on the SLO for NADOs but requires NADOs to divert their scarce resources away from the integrity of elite and sub-elite sport. Rewording the WADC from an EoC perspective would allow the transparent exercise of a discretion and thereby restore trust in the athletes and the public in order to focus anti-doping efforts in the areas of greatest need.

NADO responses to this scenario

As set out above, one of the major limitations of the WADC is that it has been designed around a testing detection methodology. Although Possession and Trafficking ADRVs have been in the WADC since the original 2003 version, and these violations are required to be established through evidence other than laboratory analysis, it appears that little thought has been given to how this might impact on a broader spectrum of the sport playing population. Over the last 15 years, the strategic and operational importance of intelligence and investigations to detect Doping has been increasingly appreciated. However, the amendments to the WADC to reflect that change have been cobbled together, rather than creating a streamlined document. The effect of this is that the possibility of a person being caught up in a broad fishing expedition of non-analytical evidence, as is the case for Athlete XYZ, was never envisaged. This means, despite WADA's stated intention that the implementation of the WADC should lead to standardisation and harmonisation, different NADOs can and have adopted contrary responses to lower-level athletes becoming caught in the anti-doping net. Some of the differences in approach set out below may be explained through whether there is any likelihood that evidence will be referred to the NADO from LEAs and similar bodies.

The WADC is a living document and has regularly undergone cycles of improvement in consultation with its stakeholders. In November 2017, WADA initiated a two-year review process of the WADC for implementation in 2021 (WADA n.d.). Many stakeholders recommended that WADA re-define 'athlete' to recognise non-elite athletes and to provide greater clarity as to the discretion to be exercised by NADOs when sanctioning ADRVs at the recreational level (WADA, 2018b). Of note, the DFSNZ's submission included these observations:

> With regards to the imposition of sanctions, the Code must be calibrated to strike the right balance. While the current sanction regime is appropriate for high performance athletes at the international and national level, DFSNZ has concerns about its implications for athletes at the other end of the spectrum. With the evolution of anti-doping practices expanding further into investigations and employment of intelligence, there is increased potential for greater numbers of low-level athletes, at the lower end of offending, to be exposed. Imposing the full force of the Code in such situations may lead to suboptimal outcomes. While DFSNZ strongly believes that all athletes ought to be held to the same standard of integrity, it considers that it would be beneficial for WADA to re-examine the current sanction regime to consider whether it appropriately accounts for athletes competing at a social or casual level whose breaches are comparatively minor. We recognise that it may be difficult to differentiate between athletes who compete on a social or casual basis and athletes who aspire to higher honours (and seek an unfair advantage to get there). Further research may be required in this area to understand the reasons for taking prohibited substances in such circumstances.
>
> If an alternative sanction regime was adopted for lower-level athletes, this might include an option for an ADO to issue a formal and public written warning. Alternatively, a sanction reduction mechanism might be considered for athletes who participate in a set number of educational activities during a period of ineligibility. It could be a powerful and persuasive educational tool

> to have people who have fallen foul of the rules participating, particularly at school level. Nonetheless, the Code currently operates in a broadly 'all or nothing' manner. Athletes below national level can be included or excluded at the discretion of the ADO, but where the Code is applied, they face the same penalties as high performing athletes, notwithstanding the generally lower levels of knowledge. Some better ability for the Code to respond to the situations of such athletes would greatly enhance the effectiveness and suasion of the Code (WADA, 2018b, p. 231).

A NADO can elect to address recreational athletes in their rules, but once a recreational athlete falls within the NADO's jurisdiction, there is no discretion permitted in sanctioning that athlete whether it relates to returning a test result for a prohibited substance; evasion of sample collection, or tampering with any part of doping control (WADC, 2015, Art 2.7). The WADC does not advise NADOs on how to respond to recreational athletes named in non-analytical evidence. NADOs have therefore taken divergent positions based on broader national policy considerations, and their ability to receive non-analytical data from LEAs. Examples include:

Finland: The Finnish Center for Integrity in Sports (FINCIS) make no distinction in the 'prosecution' of people falling within the definition of 'athlete' (based on analytical or non-analytical evidence) regardless of competitive level (Personal communication with Mr Petteri Lindblom, Legal Director, FINCIS, 20 June 2019).

Japan: The Results Management & Intelligence Department General Manager of the Japanese Anti-Doping Agency (JADA), Mr Akira Kataoka indicated that JADA also: 'bring[s] all the cases forward to our disciplinary process regardless of the level of the athlete, type of the prohibited substances detected, type of ADRV, and so on' and he expected that this would continue to be the case under the WADC 2021 (Personal communication with Akira Kataoka, JADA, 24 June 2019).

Norway: Anti-Doping Norway (ADNO) is also consistent in its action taken against 'athletes' of all levels. As the Chief Executive of ADNO, Mr Anders Solheim, expressed it:

> They are all bound by the rules as members and we cannot indirectly accept any kind of doping use or involvement in use. The moment we look through our fingers regarding doping, we have lost our strength and trust in society. I would turn it around and say that those who are aware of doping in organised sport and do not act should be questioned about their compliance. (Personal communication with Anders Solheim, ADNO, 20 June 2019).

Denmark: Countries including Denmark, Sweden and the Netherlands have been very concerned about how to address the problems arising from the abuse of steroids in the fitness industry and in gymnasiums (ADD, 2012; Bojsen-Moller & Christensen, 2010, p. 865; Thualagant & Pfister, 2012). The NADO for Flanders (Belgium) is also testing amateur athletes, including in fitness centres (Constandt, 2013). Anti-Doping Denmark (ADD) and the Danish national sports organisations have national anti-doping regulations in place to implement both the WADC for elite level athletes, and to create Anti-Doping Regulations for Recreational Sports for organised community-level sport. In addition, national legislation requires ADD to enter into anti-doping agreements with the private fitness industry. Under the Danish rules, recreational athletes are defined as persons who only participate in sport for the purposes of: 'training, physical activity and health, as well as social interaction', which includes members of gymnasiums (ADD, 2015, Art 1.1). A scenario similar to that of Athlete XYZ would fall under the recreational sports regulations which allows for a range of proportionate sanctions, including a warning, with a sanction of two years suspension as the starting point (ADD, 2019; Personal Communication with Jesper Frigast Larsen, Legal Manager, ADD 8 June 2020).

Canada: The Canadian Centre for Ethics in Sport (CCES) focuses its anti-doping efforts on National Athlete Pool (NAP) athletes and above. This group must be educated, and they sign agreements to confirm they are subject to the CCES Anti-Doping Program (CADP; CCES, 2017). Lower-level community sport participants, and 'student-athletes' who are going to university and college and not otherwise participating in elite level sport, are subject to the CADP, but treated with more flexibility. For example, 'student-athletes' may access a Medical Review process, instead of requiring advance TUEs. No difference is made in terms of sanctioning calculations when a violation is determined. CCES publicly reports the outcome of all cases and provides a link to the reasoned decision (for example CCES March 2019; CCES May 2019).

A decision on whether to 'prosecute' sport participants who are not 'student-athletes' or are active in sport below the NAP level, like Athlete XYZ, for non-analytical violations is based on many factors on a case by case basis. It would not be an automatic decision to proceed. (Personal communication with David Lech, General Counsel, CCES 10 June 2020). The CCES conducts a 'degree of fault analysis' to determine a proportionate sanction based on the particular circumstances. In an influential case involving a social footballer (soccer), Toor, the Sport Dispute Resolution Centre of Canada (SDRCC), noted that the CCES had considered the following in their analysis:

- Age/Level of athlete: 27 years of age playing at the elite club level.
- Level of support/education: no team doctor or trainer and no formal doping education.
- Prohibited Substance/ Method: methylhexaneamine consumed through the supplement Jack 3D, which was not listed on the label.
- Research: none (CCES 2012; paraphrased pp. 10–12).

The SDRCC reduced the CCES requested seven month ban down to two months stating that as this athlete had never received any anti-doping education he was therefore not at fault for not asking about the contents of the product from the store owner or from the CCES (CCES, 2012, pp. 13–15).

Netherlands: In a similarly pragmatic approach, the Doping Authority Netherlands also considers the resources to be allocated to each case from the fundamental position set out in the WADC that each NADO should: 'vigorously pursue all potential ADRVs within [their] jurisdiction'. Dr Olivier de Hon, Chief Operating Officer, clarified that their 'case management review' considers the following factors:

- Level of the competition involved
- Type of substance and/or method
- Indications of In Competition or Out of Competition use
- Indications of inadvertent or intentional use
- Links to other (potential) ADRVs (Personal communication with Olivier de Hon, Doping Autoriteit 13 June 2019).

USA: The United States Anti-Doping Agency (USADA) is required to act where there is evidence that a suspected ADRV has occurred, based on a documented prioritisation model (USADA, 2017, January). In prioritising the use of its resources, USADA takes into account: a) athletes who are likely to represent the USA at the international level, b) investigations that 'have the potential to involve doping by multiple athletes through the involvement of Athlete Support Personnel'; or c) the suspected use of prohibited substances or methods that are 'more difficult to detect through analytical testing' (USADA, 2017, January, p. 1, dot point 6). USADA's policy then provides guidance as to when whistleblower tips and intelligence is actionable, justifying the allocation of additional investigative resources (USADA, 2017, July).

USADA also has taken a 'health-centred strategy' (Henning, 2017) through creating a simplified TUE policy for 'recreational competitors' (USADA, 2019, 1 January). In the case that changed USADA's policy on social participants, USADA overturned the original TUE decision relating to the 58-year-old amateur cyclist, Hammond, who required a prohibited substance (testosterone) to treat hypogonadism and low bone density (Dreier, 2017). While acknowledging the delicate balance that NADOs need to walk in preventing TUEs being used to cheat (see Chapter 6 by Roberts and Ordway, this volume; Beaudin, 2013), Hammond was considered: 'unlikely to actually win one of these amateur races, in addition to proving a medical need for an illicit chemical' (Dreier, 2016). The TUE rejection had meant that Hammond had to stop participating in sport if he wanted to continue to use his lifesaving medication:

> Despite the facts that he was not seeking performance enhancement and was following his doctor's recommendations, Hammond would have been considered a doper. Sport and health become mutually exclusive when athletes are asked to ignore medical advice in deference to antidoping. In this way, anti-doping actually works against the best interests of athletes' health. (Henning, 2017, p. 6; see also Denning & Dimeo, 2015).

Henning (2017) notes that: 'While the [recreational competitor] category itself suggests a greater willingness to allow a necessary medication to be used or new standards on which to make the decision', the significant limitations with the USADA strategy means that: 'it is unclear that these will actually result in more exemptions for amateur athletes' (p. 7). This then creates an opportunity for WADA to provide that leadership and guidance to NADOs to assist in getting the balance right.

The USADA approach to apply greater leniency through application of the '*No Fault*' or '*No Significant Fault*' sanction reduction mitigation clauses under the WADC is also novel. In practice, USADA has demonstrated its discretion through extending leniency towards lower-level athletes. USADA's CEO, Travis Tygart, stated that: 'where there is no intention to cheat and no performance benefit, an athlete should not face any violation [sanction] or unnecessary public attention' (USADA, 2019, March). For example, a 90-year-old cyclist competing in a master's level competition was given only a public warning and his result disqualified after testing positive in competition for a prohibited substance. An investigation found the cyclist's positive test was likely to have been caused by a contaminated supplement taken before his race, therefore supporting a finding of *No Significant Fault* in committing the ADRV (USADA, 2019, 4 January).

WADA's response (WADC 2021)

The different WADC versions have employed a wide definition of *athlete* for deterrence and a narrower definition of *athlete* for the purposes of analytical investigations. The 2021 amendments to the WADC, which took effect on 1 January 2021, have attempted to address some of the concerns raised by the various stakeholders, including DFSNZ, by creating a new definition of 'recreational athlete' as follows:

> A natural Person who is so defined by the relevant NADO; provided, however, the term shall not include any Person who, within the five years prior to committing any ADRV, has been an International-Level Athlete (as defined by each International Federation consistent with the International Standard for Testing and Investigations) or National-Level Athlete (as defined by each NADO consistent with the International Standard for Testing and Investigations), has represented any country in an International Event in an open category or has been included within any Registered Testing Pool or other whereabouts information pool maintained by any International Federation or NADO. [Note 129: The term "open category" is meant to exclude competition that is limited to junior or age group categories.] (WADA, 2020, p. 93)

This means that, where NADOs choose to define 'recreational athlete', the definition must exclude certain categories of people, including those who have participated in an international event in recent years (WADA, 2020, p. 93).

The benefit in NADOs creating this additional national definition of recreational athletes then is that, for the first time, the WADC 2021 stipulates: 'different, but still [a] highly prescriptive range of sanctions' for recreational athletes in comparison to elite athletes (Johannse, 2020). Instead of the otherwise mandatory four-year period then, for Possession and Use violations (as applied in the Athlete XYZ case), if DFSNZ defined *recreational athlete* in the SADR, then future cases similar to XYZ may, in theory, only receive a reprimand as a minimum consequence for an ADRV, as opposed to a mandatory period of ineligibility as currently required. This discretion is set out as follows:

> Where the ADRV not involving a Substance of Abuse [defined in the 2021 WADA Prohibited List] is committed by a … Recreational Athlete, and the … Recreational Athlete can establish No Significant Fault or Negligence, then the period of Ineligibility shall be, at a minimum, a reprimand and no period of Ineligibility, and at a maximum, two years Ineligibility, depending on the … Recreational Athlete's degree of Fault. (WADA, 2020, p. 38, Art 10.6.1.3 – bracket added)

The new reduced sanction under Art 10.6.1.3 (above) refers to the defined term *No Significant Fault or Negligence* which is as follows:

> The athlete or other Person's establishing that any Fault or negligence, when viewed in the totality of the circumstances and taking into account the criteria for No Fault or Negligence, was not significant in relationship to the ADRV. (WADA, 2020, p. 92)

The term 'Fault' is also defined under the 2021 WADC as follows:

> Fault is any breach of duty or any lack of care appropriate to a particular situation. Factors to be taken into consideration in assessing an athlete's or other Person's degree of Fault include, for example, the athlete's or other Person's experience, whether the athlete or other Person is a Protected Person, special considerations such as impairment, the degree of risk that should have been perceived by the athlete and the level of care and investigation exercised by the athlete in relation to what should have been the perceived level of risk. In assessing the athlete's or other Person's degree of Fault, the circumstances considered must be specific and relevant to explain the athlete's or other Person's departure from the expected standard of behaviour. (WADA, 2020, p. 90)

In addition, the WADC 2021 has created time and resource-saving 'Results Management Agreement' mechanisms for NADOs (Art 10.8). For example, for ADRVs attracting four-year bans, the sanction may be reduced for one year for early admissions (WADA, 2020, p. 77). The 'Case Resolution Agreements' set out in Art 10.8.2 allow NADOs to reduce the sanction where there is a prompt the admission, after taking into account the type of ADRV, 'the seriousness of the violation', and the 'degree of Fault'. However, while the agreed sanction may be backdated to the date the ADRV occurred: 'one-half of the agreed-upon period of Ineligibility going forward from the earlier of the date the Athlete or other Person accepted the imposition of a sanction or a provisional suspension which was subsequently respected by the athlete or other Person' (WADA, 2020, p. 78).

This suggests that even if the delay in resolving the issue is caused by the NADO, half of the sanction must be served from the provisional suspension date (if there was one imposed by the NADO), or otherwise from the date the sanction was accepted. This Article also doesn't appear to envisage a situation where no sanction, and only a warning, is imposed.

The changes proposed in the WADC 2021 therefore go some way towards restoring trust by distinguishing social competitors from elite athletes. The new clarification allows for the prioritisation of anti-doping resources to elite level athletes, and also provides some leniency in sanctioning non-elite athletes. This, in turn, more closely aligns the focus of anti-doping efforts with the publicly perceived area of greatest need, that is, clean sport at the elite level.

Limitations of the WADC 2021 approach

While the amendments above go some way to addressing the concerns raised by NADOs, including DFSNZ, in their Code consultation submissions, there are some serious limitations in the 2021 WADC as follows:

(i) The definition of *recreational athlete* as a new class of *athlete* creates confusion. The *recreational athlete* is not a default position but requires a NADO to take positive action to incorporate a version of the definition into its national anti-doping policy or legislation. In addition, there is a new Note which attempts to clarify the definition of *athlete*. On one reading, the Note appears to create five classes of *athlete*, with people potentially falling into overlapping categories (3–5):

> Individuals who participate in sport may fall in one of five categories:
>
> 1) International-Level Athlete,
> 2) National-Level Athlete,
> 3) individuals who are not International- or National-Level Athletes but over whom the International Federation or NADO has chosen to exercise authority,
> 4) Recreational Athlete, and
> 5) individuals over whom no International Federation or NADO has, or has chosen to, exercise authority.
>
> All International- or National-Level Athletes are subject to the anti-doping rules of the Code, with the precise definitions of international and national level sport to be set forth in the anti-doping rules of the International

Federations and NADOs (WADA, 2020, Note 122 p. 89).The WADC 2021 has also added a new 'Protected Person' definition (persons lacking legal capacity; WADA, 2020, p. 93), which could also apply to people in any of the five categories of *athlete*. It is assumed that the discretion outlined for *recreational athletes* would not apply to category 5) participants above, which is exactly the situation as faced by Athlete XYZ. It is anticipated, based on the advice from the NADOs consulted with for this chapter, that many NADOs will choose not to create a separate class of *recreational athlete* in their national policies to avoid this confusion.

(ii) Instead of encouraging the creation of different national definitions, the WADC 2021 should specify that the default position is that *athletes* participating below the international level, defined by the responsible International Federation, are *recreational athletes.*

(iii) Rather than being a class of *athlete* then, it should be explicit in the WADC that the term *recreational athlete* applies to provide NADOs both with a 'prosecutorial' discretion on whether to refer the matter for a sanction beyond a documented warning, and also serves to assist a NADO or tribunal in applying a fair and proportionate sanction.

(iv) As currently drafted, the WADC 2021 changes still pose a risk of capturing unsuspecting non-elite athletes, as anti-doping education is not mandated before sanctioning *athletes.* It is suggested that any sanction, beyond a warning, for lower-level athletes should require evidence that anti-doping education had been made available to them.

(v) The 2021 WADC also misses the opportunity to address the situation presented where the person is at *fault*, as in the case of Athlete XYZ, in that they intentionally purchased a product (usually online which creates an evidentiary trail). It should be open to social participants to request a lower (or no) sanction in situations where, as distinct from a case of trafficking, the item was for personal use, the product contained a substance prohibited by the WADC (which they may or may not have been aware of), they were unaware that the anti-doping rules applied to them, and they had no intention to 'cheat' at sport (noting that this is difficult for NADOs to disprove).

Rationale for a proportionate discretion

The proportionality principle was drafted into the WADC on: 'an intentionally restrictive basis' (Niggli & Sieveking, 2006, p. 9). It is argued that in a narrow range of circumstances, the net should be carefully loosened. By allowing NADOs a discretion to determine appropriate and proportionate responses for those inadvertently captured, rather than creating a weakness in the system (or 'look[ing] through our fingers' as described by Solheim above), it assists to restore trust and reinforces the message of integrity in elite sport. Including social participants in the anti-doping policies as part of a 'blanket' or 'trawling net' rule, may discourage participation in sport at the lower levels (against public health recommendations), impact on human rights and absorb resources better spent at the elite level.

Sanctioning, including the possibility of publicly shaming, people who were never intended to have been part of the anti-doping system, and thereby cannot be said to have engaged in 'corrupt' or 'cheating' behaviour, may undermine the trust placed in these regulatory bodies. Doping cases have enormous impacts on the mental health of anyone caught in the net:

> Athletes transitioning back into the 'real world' have a difficult enough time coping with mental health issues, as exposed recently in the ABC Four Corners program After the Game. This transition is made more challenging for those athletes tarnished with a doping ban. As former pro-cyclist Joerg Jaksche, at the Crossing the Line Summit, explained, the burden of being 'googlable' for eternity adversely impacts equally on athletes who had cheated, and those who had merely been caught up by the system. (Ordway, 2017)

It also wastes the time and limited money NADOs have to focus their energy on education and detection programmes that would be far more effective in achieving their strategic goals (see Gatterer et al., 2020).

The NADOs are usually taxpayer funded entities (Chappelet & van Luijk, 2018, p. 181) and have legitimacy through their SLO to promote clean sport. The publicly funded resources available to the NADOs are finite. Absorbing the anti-doping movement's scarce resources with social athletes is a distraction and highlights where money may be better spent, including on values education in schools (Gatterer et al., 2020; e.g UNODC n.d. (a)(b)). Public confidence, or trust, in the work of NADOs under the WADC may be further undermined where NADOs are not perceived to be proportionate or are excessive in their treatment of non-elite athletes. It is therefore proposed that rewording the WADC from an EoC perspective would permit the transparent and fair exercise of discretion. This would in turn restore trust in the athletes and in the public in order to focus anti-doping efforts and resources in the areas of greatest need.

For example, Australia considers itself one of the world's leading countries on sport integrity, and the Australian Sports Anti-Doping Authority (ASADA) is one of the most generously publicly funded NADOs (as of 1 July 2020, within Sport Integrity Australia). To put the national government's spending on sport integrity into perspective, it sits within the collection titled: 'Budget 2019–20: Prioritising mental health, preventive health and sport' (Commonwealth of Australia, 2019). The national budget to: 'combat present, emerging and future threats from doping, match-fixing, illegal betting, organised crime, and corruption' is AUD '$33 million from 2019–20 to 2020–21'. Sport disputes threatening the integrity of sport in Australia are intended to be resolved: 'consistently, cost-effectively and transparently' (Australian Government, 2019). A clear direction from WADA on the discretion that NADOs can exercise would therefore assist the Australian Government to focus its resources on 'threats' to sport and achieve its aims in the most time and cost-efficient manner.

Drug testing costs have been rising, while the effectiveness of doping tests have been seriously questioned. In Australia, an individual urine full-screen in-competition test can cost up to $824.00 (ASADA, 2020). Athletes seeking to cheat are also increasingly using more sophisticated methods, requiring more expensive analytical methodology. The latest *Annual banned-substance review* has examined literature published between October 2018 and September 2019 and found that:

> The misuse of substances (and cells) that are naturally produced in humans is particularly challenging … especially concerning compounds belonging to the classes of endogenous anabolic agents and growth factors but also regarding methods of doping including autologous blood transfusion and gene doping. (Thevis et al., 2020, p. 22)

Improved analytical sensitivity, however, also means that very minimal concentrations caused by food and other non-intentional contamination can be detected, for example in the recent cases of Vincent-Lapointe, Lawson and Fuchs (Harrison, 2020; CAS, 2020; Taylor, 2020; Matthey, 2020). WADA has therefore spent a decade encouraging all NADOs in 'Coordinating Investigations and Sharing Anti-Doping Information and Evidence' (WADA, 2011), which can lead to the data dump situations that Athlete XYZ found himself caught up in.

LEAs similarly do not have the resources to investigate and prosecute every crime committed in society. To guide policing bodies in the appropriate use of resources, a range of models have been developed to assist. For example, the Australian Federal Police (AFP) currently uses the *Case Categorisation and Prioritisation Model* (CCPM). The CCPM considers the:

- incident/crime type;
- impact of the matter on Australian society;
- importance of the matter to both the client and the AFP in terms of the roles assigned to them by Government and Ministerial Direction; and
- resources required by the AFP to undertake the matter (AFP, 2016).

No single element of the CCPM is considered in isolation to determine whether a matter is accepted or rejected for investigation, but instead a combination of the Impact and Priority ratings determine the next steps. It is argued here that an adapted LEA model, appropriate for the sport (generally contractual not criminal) environment, could be developed and promoted by WADA.

Apart from financial considerations, an EoC approach places a positive moral obligation to care on those organisations designing anti doping programmes, including WADA. In cases such as Athlete XYZ, who were never intended to be captured by the anti-doping policies and did not receive any education or advice to warn them of their obligations, it is argued that a higher duty is therefore imposed. This higher duty is to be inclusive and care for members of the community who have been excluded, in this case recreational athletes. This positive moral obligation translates into an obligation to create policies and programmes to particularly ensure that 'marginalised' and 'vulnerable' people are cared for through creating a meaningful and transparent discretion to consider their cases appropriately. The case of Athlete XYZ involving the personal use of substances captured by the WADC must be distinguished from a scenario where a person is trafficking in performance-enhancing drugs.

Based on the *International Charter of Physical Education and Sport* (UNESCO, 2015 Preamble) and the *Olympic Charter* (IOC, 2019, pp. 11–12), an argument has been made that access to sport is a human right (Adi, 2009; Ordway, 2018). Policies described as 'disproportionate', 'excessively rigorous' and 'very harsh' (WADA, 2018b, pp. 22, 50, 207), by those required to sanction people who should not be captured by the WADC, effectively breaches the human rights of those people through disincentivising and/or barring them from playing sport (Rigozzi et al., 2003). The health benefits of participating in sport need to be balanced against the dire impacts of using some prohibited substances and methods under the WADC, including steroids (WADA, 2015, Art 4.3.1.2; van Amsterdam et al., 2010; Dodge & Hoagland, 2011; Montisci et al., 2012). In what some have described as a paternalistic attitude in using anti-doping violations to 'police' life decisions by adults (Brown, 1984), and athlete minors (McNamee, 2009), it is fair to observe that social athletes are equally susceptible to the health concerns linked with prohibited substances as elite athletes (European Union, 2014, s.5.3 p. 33). Social athletes may be even more susceptible as they do not have access to sophisticated medical advice and doping methods available to some elite athletes (Efverström et al., 2016). If social athletes are made aware that there is a risk of a sanction under the anti-doping rules, it may also deter them from engaging in potentially dangerous practices.

Recommendations

The implementation of an EoC perspective would realign anti-doping efforts with public expectations, namely that sport is to be encouraged and anti-doping resources in sport ought to be directed towards elite and sub-elite athletes attempting to 'cheat', and lower-level athletes or *Athlete Support Personnel* seeking to traffic in performance-enhancing drugs. Through the lens of an EoC approach, WADA could make the following additional amendments to the WADC and its broader anti-doping program to explicitly define the discretion that may be exercised by NADOs:

1 **Prioritisation Guidelines:** develop a new WADA Guideline to set out a model for assessing violations of the WADC using a matrix that rates impact and priorities based on LEA models. This should include whether the person had received anti-doping education, and whether it was a clear case of 'cheating' or corruption (such as trafficking in performance-enhancing drugs to other *Athletes*) (e.g. USADA and the Netherlands). This could clarify the Case Resolution Agreement (Art 10.8.2).

2 **Definitions:** rather than becoming a separate category to *Athlete*, the WADC could clarify that the *Recreational Athlete* creates a default position for tribunals and NADOs to apply in appropriate cases to determine whether to allocate investigations and/or 'prosecutorial' resources, and to reduce sanctions proportionately and transparently. The five categories under the Note to the definition of *Athlete* creates confusion. All participants in organised sport are *Athletes*. The anti-doping requirements on those at the elite level of high-risk sports should be expected to be more onerous and should be defined for each sport by the respective International Federation.
3 NADOs must be free to extend anti-doping measures more broadly into the fitness industry and student athlete cohorts where appropriate, applying nationally appropriate definitions (e.g. Denmark and Canada). Retired former-elite athletes should be encouraged to continue to participate in sport, and be permitted to seek classification with their NADO as *Recreational Athletes* immediately following retirement where they demonstrate that they are only competing in lower-level sports and are not permitted reinstatement as an elite athlete (subject to appeal by and to the responsible International Federation, the NADO or WADA as appropriate).
4 **Anti-Doping tools:** articulate a clear hierarchy to support NADOs in determining appropriate resourcing for the various deterrence anti-doping tools available (i.e. including testing, investigations, TUE processes and Education) for *Athletes, Athlete Support Personnel* and the types of ADRVs.
5 **Education:** support NADOs to deliver education materials to *Athletes* by designing additional examples and templates explaining the purpose for each type of anti-doping education by content and delivery methodology based on the research, such as the five approaches identified by Backhouse et al. (2014):

    1 knowledge-focused (e.g. side effects);
    2 affective-focused (e.g. targeting feelings of value and self-worth);
    3 social skills training (e.g. assertiveness, decision-making, and resistance to peer pressure);
    4 life skills training (e.g. multicomponent: social skills, personal skills, and knowledge); and
    5 ethic- and value-based (e.g. against the rules, fair play, honesty, and integrity) (p. 53).

6 The latter approach includes what John William Devine refers to as 'moral training', which is arguably the most crucial content, particularly for school and university education (Devine, 2017; UNODC. n.d.a,b).
7 **TUE Criteria:** review the TUE guidelines to clarify the criteria appropriate for *Recreational Athletes*; balancing a health-centred strategy with closing loopholes that enable cheating in sport. This review should also include any amendments to the WADA Prohibited List that adversely impact on *Recreational Athletes*.
8 **Sanctions:** specify proportionate sanctioning options available to tribunals based on the discretionary matrix above. The range of sanctions may include letters of warning, mandatory completion of online anti-doping education,

community service, and other appropriate sanctions, up to life bans for culpable cases. It should be made explicit that other than in exceptional circumstances, 'naming and shaming' is inappropriate at the *Recreational Athletes* level. Currently, the WADC's reference to a 'reprimand' does not specify whether it should be made public. This must be balanced by transparency requirements (below).

9 A sanction could also include a consideration as to whether it is appropriate for the *Athlete/Athlete Support Personnel* to reciprocate through an apology, or other appropriate reparative actions to those stakeholders impacted by their behaviour.

10 **Transparency and Reporting:** ensuring that the *Recreational Athlete* flexibility is not abused, transparency in reporting the implementation of the discretion granted to NADOs, including a central registry of all decisions and warning letters, must be included in the WADC and Guidelines. For intelligence to be collected to determine whether the status of the individual changes over time, internal records should be made available for WADA, NADOs and the relevant International Federation (including via the WADA ADAMS system).

11 **Monitoring:** establish a designated team within WADA to monitor, and in appropriate cases, approve or appeal *Recreational Athlete* discretion decisions. This team can also monitor long-term trends and identify future areas of interest for policy and educational improvements. The historical archiving for transparency, accountability and academic analysis requires enforcement by WADA to ensure consistent terminology (by ADRV, substance, type of athlete and reporting dates) in finalising cases for all reporting stakeholders, including national/ sport tribunals.

12 **Collaboration:** facilitate NADOs working collaboratively with LEAs and other agencies through Governmental relationships to encourage two-way information sharing. In some cases, it is more appropriate to refer breaches of criminal and other laws (e.g. Customs) onto other agencies for enforcement action, rather than addressing under anti-doping policies (e.g. illegal importation fines and other sanctions). Collaborations with Universities and schools for education and research purposes should also be encouraged and facilitated where-ever possible to provide students with skills and experience in anti-doping rationale and practices.

Conclusion

The WADC 2021 has made significant improvements in relation to recreational athletes through the new definition and in providing some discretion in sanctions. WADA should make further progress toward restoring trust by implementing an EoC perspective to the drafting of the WADC by extending this discretion to NADO 'prosecutorial' discretion. Rewording the WADC from an EoC perspective would allow the transparent exercise of discretion in cases that do not involve 'cheating' or corruption. This then restores trust in the athletes and the public in order to focus anti-doping efforts in the areas of greatest need.

The assessment of the current practice of major NADOs shows that there is no universally accepted method in implementing the WADC (Hanstad et al., 2010; Gatterer et al., 2020). Some sports tribunals have also expressed their discomfort in having to apply the rules rigorously, particularly where the athlete had not benefited from receiving any anti-doping education (e.g. CCES, 2012). As was observed by the STNZ in the XYZ sanction decision:

> We have much sympathy for the position of the respondent – an amateur recreational participant in sport at local or club level – who now bears the stigma of having taken drugs for what he perceived would assist him to lose weight for health reasons and not for performance enhancement. We of course acknowledge that DFSNZ is vested with the discretion to apply the Code to every person in New Zealand who is connected with any level of sporting activity that is subject to SADR. However, we question the common sense, fairness and proportionality of the approach that is being taken and the consequences which flow from an undiscriminatory and arbitrary application of the Code to persons who no reasonable person sympathetic with the aims of the Code would think appropriate. (DFSNZ v Athlete XYZ, 2019, April, paragraph 12)

The implementation of the proposed additional changes would allow the transparent exercise of a discretion and thereby restore trust, and the SLO, in the athletes and the sport ecosystem in order to focus anti-doping efforts in the areas of greatest need. Noting that while it is not always easy to distinguish between the 'dolphins' and the 'tuna' when setting the anti-doping net, articulating this discretion serves to send the message that sport is a force for good, and the benefits to health and in community-building out-weigh the need for strict adherence to rules in cases where there was no attempt to cheat or corrupt the integrity of sport.

Questions

i *Trust loss* – In whom (or, in which group) has trust been lost in this case?
ii *Trust correction* – How, if attempted, has the restoration of trust been tried?; and;
iii *Lessons learned* – How could the lessons from this case be applied to other sports, nations, states, other districts for the same sport, or other sports to prevent a further loss of trust or at least to restore trust?

Note

1 This chapter is based on the unpublished Honours thesis submitted by Victoria Jamieson to the University of Canberra in 2019 "Athlete XYZ: How should the World Anti-Doping Code apply to the recreational athlete?". The authors would like to thank many people for their feedback and ideas which further contributed to this chapter, including Shaun Star, David Lech, Jesper Frigast Larsen, Dr Olivier de Hon, Akira Kataoka, Anders Solheim, Petteri Lindblom, Nick Paterson, Kerry Knowler, Daniel Kalderimis and Scott Langham.

References

ADD. (2012). Strategy for stopping steroids report. Anti-Doping Denmark. Retrieved from https://www.west-info.eu/files/Strategy-for-Stopping-Steroids.pdf (also available from http://dopingjouren.se/pdf-material/Strategy%20for%20Stopping%20Steroids_Report_WEB.pdf).

ADD. (2015, 1 January). National anti-doping rules. Anti-Doping Denmark. Retrieved from https://antidoping.dk/media/1159/national_anti_doping_rules_denmark.pdf

ADD. (2019, 1 January). Dopingreglement for motionsidræt under Danmarks Idrætsforbund (DIF), Dansk Firmaidrætsforbund (Firmaidrætten) og DGI [translated to Doping Regulations for exercise below Danish Sports Federation (DIF), Danish Company Sports Association (Company Sports)]. Retrieved from https://www.antidoping.dk/media/1157/dopingreglement_for_motionsidraet.pdf

Adi, A. (2009). Olympic humanitarianism. *Culture*, 11(3), 13–16.

AFP. (2016, 1 July). The case categorisation and prioritisation model: Guidance for AFP clients. Australian Federal Police. Retrieved from https://www.afp.gov.au/sites/default/files/PDF/ccpm-july-2016.pdf

ASADA. (2020, 1 January). Fees. Australian Sports Anti-Doping Agency. Retrieved from https://www.asada.gov.au/about-asada/finance/fees

Australian Government. (2019, 31 March). Budget 2019–20: Implementing Sport 2030 – safeguarding the integrity of Australian sport. Fact Sheet. Department of Health. Retrieved from https://www.health.gov.au/sites/default/files/implementing-sport-2030-safeguarding-the-integrity-of-australian-sport_0.pdf

Backhouse, S. H., Collins, C., Defoort, Y., McNamee, M., Parkinson, A., Sauer, M.*et al.* (2014*). Study on doping prevention: A map of legal, regulatory, and prevention practice provisions in EU, 28.* European Commission, Luxembourg. Retrieved from http://eprints.leedsbeckett.ac.uk/753/1/doping-prevention-report_en.pdf

Beaudin, M. (2013, 21 October). Is it medicine or dope? A cat. 4 vs. the USADA. *Velo News.* Retrieved from https://www.velonews.com/news/is-this-man-a-doper/

Bojsen-Moller, J., & Christensen, A. (2010). Use of performance and image enhancing substances among recreational athletes . *Scandinavian Journal of Medicine and Science in Sports*, 20, 861. Retrieved from http://citeseerx.ist.psu.edu/viewdoc/download?doi=10.1.1.466.6735&rep=rep1&type=pdf

Boutilier, R. G. (2014). Frequently asked questions about the social licence to operate. *Impact Assessment and Project Appraisal*, 32(4), 263–272.

Brown, W. M. (1984). Paternalism, drugs, and the nature of sports. *Journal of the Philosophy of Sport*, 11(1), 14–22.

CAS. (2020, 9 March). The Court of Arbitration for Sport (CAS) annuls the suspension of Jarrion Lawson. Media Release. Court of Arbitration for Sport. Retrieved from https://www.tas-cas.org/fileadmin/user_upload/CAS_Media_Release_6313.pdf

CCES. (2012, 23 January). In the matter of an anti-doping rule violation by Jasdeep Toor (Athlete). SDRCC file no. DT 11–0165. Sport Dispute Resolution Centre of Canada. Retrieved from www.crdsc-sdrcc.ca/eng/show-decision-detail-en.action?decisionId=617

CCES. (2017, 1 September). The Canadian Anti-Doping Program [CADP] 2015 version 2.0. Canadian Centre for Ethics in Sport. Retrieved from https://cces.ca/sites/default/files/content/docs/pdf/cces-policy-cadp-2015-v2-e.pdf

CCES. (2019, 20 March). U Sports football athlete suspended for presence of Higenmine. News Centre. Canadian Centre for Ethics in Sport. Retrieved from https://cces.ca/news/u-sports-football-athlete-suspended-presence-higenamine

CCES. (2019, 1 May). U Sports football athlete not at fault for presence of dexamethasone. News Centre. Canadian Centre for Ethics in Sport. Retrieved from https://cces.ca/news/u-sports-football-athlete-not-fault-presence-dexamethasone

Chappelet, J. L., & van Luijk, N. (2018). The institutional governance of global hybrid bodies: The case of the World Anti-Doping Agency. Hybridity in the governance and delivery of public services. *Studies in Public and Non-Profit Governance*, 7.

Commonwealth of Australia. (2019). Budget 2019–20: Prioritising mental health, preventive health and sport. Department of Health. Retrieved from https://www.health.gov.au/resources/collections/budget-2019–2020-prioritising-mental-health-preventive-health-and-sport).

Connolly, R. (2005). Balancing the justices in anti-doping law: The need to ensure fair athletic competition through effective anti-doping programs vs. the protection of rights of accused athletes. *Va. Sports & Ent. LJ*, 5, 161.

Constandt, B. (2013). *De Vlaamse dopingstrijd (1965-heden). Een politiek-maatschappelijke voorgeschiedenis van het huidige antidopingdecreet* [The Flemish doping battle (1965-present). A socio-political history of the current anti-doping decree] (Unpublished master's thesis). Ghent University, Ghent, Belgium. Retrieved from https://lib.ugent.be/en/catalog/rug01:002060145?i=0&q=constandt&type=master

Cox, T. W. (2014). The international war against doping: Limiting the collateral damage from strict liability. *Vand. J. Transnat'l L.*, 47, 295.

Dalton, R. J.(2005). The social transformation of trust in government. *International Review of Sociology*, 15(1), 133–154.

Dalton, R. J. (2015). *The good citizen: How a younger generation is reshaping American politics.* Washington, DC: CQ Press.

De Hon, O. (2017). The redundancy of the concept of 'spirit of sport' in discussions on the prohibited list of doping substances. *International Journal of Sport Policy and Politics*, 9 (4), 667. doi:10.1080/19406940.2017.1348380

Democracy 2025. (2020). Public trust program. Museum of Australian Democracy Old Parliament House and the University of Canberra Institute for Governance and Policy Analysis. Retrieved from https://www.democracy2025.gov.au/programs/public-trust-p rogram.html

Denning, A., & Dimeo, P. (2015). Questions of fairness and anti-doping in US cycling: The contrasting experiences of professionals and amateurs. *Drugs*, 22(5), 400. Retrieved from www.ncbi.nlm.nih.gov/pmc/articles/PMC4659343/

Devine, J. W. (2017, 18 August). How sport can move on from a championship marked by the booing of Justin Gatlin. *The Sports Integrity Initiative.* Retrieved from https://www.sp ortsintegrityinitiative.com/sport-can-move-championships-marked-booing-justin-gatlin/

DFSNZ. (2019, 6 March). Statement on sports tribunal decision involving XYZ. Media Release. Drug Free Sport New Zealand. Retrieved from https://drugfreesport.org.nz/news/media-releases/statement-on-sports-tribunal-decision-involving-xyz

Dixon-Woods, M., & Ashcroft, R. E. (2008). Regulation and the social licence for medical research. *Medicine, Health Care and Philosophy*, 11(4), 81–391

Dodge, T., & Hoagland, M. F. (2011). The use of anabolic androgenic steroids and polypharmacy: A review of the literature. *Drug and alcohol dependence*, 114(2–3), 100–109.

Donovan, R. J., Egger, G., Kapernick, V., & Mendoza, J. (2002). A conceptual framework for achieving performance enhancing drug compliance in sport. *Sports Medicine*, 32(4), 269–284. Retrieved from www.academia.edu/download/50142794/A_Conceptual_Framework_for_Achieving_Per20161106-20122738 1rfn21h.pdf

Dreier, F. (2016, 22 April). Prescription steroids get a quiet exemption. *The Wall Street Journal*. Retrieved from https://www.wsj.com/articles/prescription-steroids-get-a-quiet-exemption-1461365753

Dreier, F. (2017, 8 February). The need for 'T'—amateur cycling and testosterone TUEs. *Velo News*. Retrieved from https://www.velonews.com/news/need-t-amateur-cycling-testosterone-tues/

Drug Free Sport New Zealand (DFSNZ). (2014). Sports Anti-Doping Rules (SADR) [updated rules as at 2020 available from https://drugfreesport.org.nz/the-rules/]

Drug Free Sport New Zealand (DFSNZ) v XYZ (ST 12/18). (2019, 4 March). Decision of Sports Tribunal. Sports Tribunal of New Zealand. Retrieved from www.sportstribunal.org.nz/assets/Uploads/ST1218-Decision-DFSNZ-v-XYZ2.pdf

Drug Free Sport New Zealand (DFSNZ) v XYZ (ST 12/18). (2019, 3 April). Decision of Sports Tribunal on sanction. Sports Tribunal of New Zealand. Retrieved from www.sportstribunal.org.nz/assets/Uploads/ST1218-Decision-DFSNZ-v-XYZ-Sanction3.pdf

Drug Free Sport New Zealand (DFSNZ) v Pouwhare-Anderson (ST 03/19). (2019, 12 July). Decision of Sports Tribunal. Sports Tribunal of New Zealand. Retrieved from www.sportstribunal.org.nz/assets/Uploads/Decision-12-July-2021.pdf

Edwards, P., Lacey, J., Wyatt, S., & Williams, K. J. (2016, 15 September). Social licence to operate and forestry–an introduction. *Forestry: An International Journal of Forest Research*, 89(5), 473–476. Retrieved from https://doi.org/10.1093/forestry/cpw036

Efverström, A., Bäckström, Å., Ahmadi, N., & Hoff, D. (2016). Contexts and conditions for a level playing field: Elite athletes' perspectives on anti-doping in practice. *Performance Enhancement & Health*, 5(2), 77–85.

European Union. (2014, 12 December). Study on doping prevention: A map of legal, regulatory and prevention practice provisions in EU 28. European Commission. Retrieved from https://ec.europa.eu/assets/eac/sport/news/2014/docs/doping-prevention-report_en.pdf

Føllesdal, A. (2011). The legitimacy challenges for new modes of governance: Trustworthy responsiveness. *Government and Opposition*, 46(1), 81–100. Retrieved from https://onlinelibrary.wiley.com/doi/pdf/10.1111/j.1477–7053.2010.01331.x?casa_token=vjkfcTE6un8AAAAA:_y3AGMP9kBymWvZ1r601MERKV53rYB6cvEqG98TxcITd1sYsNWZkohU-vGQ3CzasYjsu4WJIfJMaA7c

Gatterer, K., Gumpenberger, M., Overbye, M., Streicher, B., Schobersberger, W., & Blank, C. (2020, May). An evaluation of prevention initiatives by 53 national anti-doping organizations: Achievements and limitations. *Journal of Sport and Health Science*, 9(3) 228–239.

Gilligan, C. (1982). *In a different voice*. Cambridge, MA: Harvard University Press.

Green, A. (2006). *Hyper-availability and information obesity in effective personal communication skills for public*. London: Kogan Page Publishers.

Hall, N., Lacey, J., Carr-Cornish, S., & Dowd, A. M. (2015). Social licence to operate: Understanding how a concept has been translated into practice in energy industries. *Journal of Cleaner Production*, 86, 301–310.

Hanstad, D. V., Skille, E. Å., & Loland, S. (2010). Harmonization of anti-doping work: Myth or reality? *Sport in society*, 13(3), 418–430.

Harrison, D. (2020, 27 January). Canoe star Laurence Vincent Lapointe found not guilty of taking banned substance. *CBC Sports*. Retrieved from https://www.cbc.ca/sports/olympics/summer/canoe-kayak/laurence-vincent-lapointe-doping-verdict-1.5441395

Hayes, P. (2016). The commercial rationale of the World Anti-Doping Code. In U. Haas & D. Healey (Eds.), *Doping in sport and the law* (pp. 269–290). London: Hart Publishing Bloomsbury. doi:10.5040/9781509905911.ch-014

Healey, D. (2016). The myth of the level playing field in sport. In U. Haas & D. Healey (Eds.), *Doping in sport and the law* (pp. 3–17). London: Hart Publishing Bloomsbury. doi:10.5040/9781509905911.ch-001

Henning, A. (2017). Challenges to promoting health for amateur athletes through anti-doping policy. *Drugs: Education, Prevention and Policy*, 24(3), 306–313. Retrieved from https://www.ncbi.nlm.nih.gov/pmc/articles/PMC5515538/#

Henning, A., & Dimeo, P. (2018). Perceptions of legitimacy, attitudes and buy-in among athlete groups: A cross-national qualitative investigation providing practical solutions. World Anti-Doping Agency, Montreal. Retrieved from https://dspace.stir.ac.uk/bitstream/1893/29905/1/PL%20Final%20Report%20Henning%20Dimeo%202018%20(1).pdf.

IOC. (2019, 26 June). *Olympic charter*. International Olympic Committee. Retrieved from www.olympic.org/Documents/olympic_charter_en.pdf

Johannsen, D. (2019, 28 May). Drug Free Sport NZ dealt hefty criticism by NZ Rugby review body in latest clenbuterol ruling. *Stuff*. Retrieved from https://www.stuff.co.nz/sport/other-sports/111751470/drug-free-sport-nz-to-appeal-athlete-xyz-ruling-to-the-court-of-arbitration-for-sport?rm=a

Johannsen, D. (2020, 6 March). The bust: Athlete XYZ and the legacy of NZ's biggest steroid investigation. *Stuff*. Retrieved from https://www.stuff.co.nz/sport/other-sports/119940427/the-bust-athlete-xyz-and-the-legacy-of-nzs-biggest-steroids-investigation

Kelner, M. (2017, 5 July). General public is losing faith in scandal-ridden sports, survey claims. *The Guardian*. Retrieved from https://www.theguardian.com/sport/2017/jul/05/public-faith-sport-low-corruption-doping-sacndals-survey

Matthey, J. (2020, 12 June). Boxer cleared of doping after sex excuse keeps Olympic dream alive. *news.com.au*. Retrieved from https://www.news.com.au/sport/boxing/boxer-cleared-of-doping-after-sex-excuse-keeps-olympic-dream-alive/news-story/e16cdfdccbcde30b20725d46d442fd02

McCuaig, L., & Hay, P. J. (2013). Principled pursuits of 'the good citizen' in health and physical education. *Physical Education and Sport Pedagogy*, 18(3), 282–297.

McDermott, V., Henne, K., & Connor, J. (2013). Legitimating the fight? Questions about cross-cultural perspectives on anti-doping strategies in the Pacific. In *Proceedings of 2013 TASA conference: Reflections, intersections and aspirations 50 years of Australian sociology* (pp. 1–12). Melbourne: Monash University.

McNamee, M. (2009). Beyond consent? Paternalism and pediatric doping . *Journal of the Philosophy of Sport*, 36(2), 111–126.

Miller, S. (2018, 21 September). Corruption. *Encyclopedia of philosophy*. Stanford University. Retrieved from https://plato.stanford.edu/entries/corruption/

Montisci, M., El Mazloum, R., Cecchetto, G., Terranova, C., Ferrara, S. D., Thiene, G., & Basso, C. (2012). Anabolic androgenic steroids abuse and cardiac death in athletes: morphological and toxicological findings in four fatal cases. *Forensic Science International*, 217(1–3),e13–e18.

Morrison, J. (2016, 18 January), Restoring the social licence of mega-sporting events. Commentary. Institute of Human Rights and Business (IHRG). Retrieved from https://www.ihrb.org/focus-areas/mega-sporting-events/restoring-the-social-licence-of-mega-sporting-events

Nehme, M., & Ordway, C. (2016). Governance and anti-doping: Beyond the fox and the hen house. In U. Haas & D. Healey (Eds.), *Doping in sport and the law*. London: Hart Publishing Bloomsbury. doi:10.5040/9781509905911.ch-011.

Niggli, O., & Sieveking, J. (2006, February). Selected case law rendered under the World Anti-Doping Code. *Jusletter*. Retrieved from https://www.wada-ama.org/sites/default/files/resources/files/Jusletter_eng.pdf

Noddings, N. (1984). *Caring: A feminine approach to ethics & moral education*. Berkeley: University of California Press.

Ordway, C. (2013). *Doping Issues in Sport and the ACC Report*. Presentation, ANZSLA, Sydney, Melbourne, Brisbane, Perth and Adelaide.

Ordway, C. (2017, 31 August). Should a doping ban = a life sentence? The Sports Integrity Initiative. Retrieved from https://www.sportsintegrityinitiative.com/doping-ban-life-sentence/

Ordway, C. (2018, May). Does sex segregated sport still hold value? *World Sports Advocate* 16(5), 16–19. Retrieved from https://researchprofiles.canberra.edu.au/en/publications/does-sex-segregated-sport-still-hold-value

Ordway, C., & Opie, H. (2016). Integrity and corruption in sport. In N. Schulenkorf & S. Frawley (Eds.), *Critical issues in global sport management* (pp. 60–85). Abingdon: Routledge.

Pielke, R.Jr. (2013, 19 February). Does uncertainty of outcome define sport? *The Least Thing*. Retrieved from http://leastthing.blogspot.com.au/2013/02/does-uncertainty-of-outcome-define-sport.html

Pielke, R. A. (2016). *The edge: The war against cheating and corruption in the cutthroat world of elite sports*. Berkeley, CA: Roaring Forties Press.

Rigozzi, A., Haas, U., Wisnosky, E., & Viret, M. (2015). Breaking down the process for determining a basic sanction under the 2015 World Anti-Doping Code. *The International Sports Law Journal*, 15(1–2), 3–48.

Rigozzi, A., Kaufmann-Kohler, G., & Malinverni, G. (2003). Doping and fundamental rights of athletes: Comments in the wake of the adoption of the world anti-doping code. *International Sports Law Review*. Retrieved from https://lk-k.com/wp-content/uploads/Doping-and-fundamental-rights-of-athletes-Comments-in-the-wake-of-the-adoption-of-the-World-Anti-Doping-Code.pdf

Ronglan, L. T. (2015). Elite sport in Scandinavian welfare states: Legitimacy under pressure? *International Journal of Sport Policy and Politics*, 7(3), 345–363.

STNZ. (2019, 4 April). Sports Tribunal delivers decision on sanction in XYZ case. Media Release. Sports Tribunal of New Zealand. Retrieved from www.sportstribunal.org.nz/assets/Uploads/Media-Release-DFSNZ-v-XYZ-ST1218-Sanction.pdf

Stoker, G., Evans, M., & Hakupka, M. (2018). Bridging the trust divide: Lessons from international experience. *Democracy 2025*. Report No. 2. Retrieved from https://www.democracy2025.gov.au/documents/Democracy2025-report2.pdf

Taylor, J. (2020, 24 April). Assessing contamination and thresholds under the World Anti-Doping Code: An advocate's view on Lawson v IAAF (CAS 2019/A/6313). *LawInSport*. Retrieved from https://www.lawinsport.com/topics/item/an-advocate-s-view-on-lawson-v-iaaf-cas-2019-a-6313

The Brewery at Freuds. (2017). *Sport*. London: The Brewery (London) Ltd.

Thevis, M., Kuuranne, T., & Geyer, H. (2020). Annual banned-substance review–Analytical approaches in human sports drug testing. *Drug Testing and Analysis*, 12(1), 7–26.

Thualagant, N., & Pfister, G. (2012). The fight against fitness doping in sports clubs – Political discourses and strategies in Denmark. *Performance Enhancement & Health*, 1(2), 86–93. Retrieved from https://doi.org/10.1016/j.peh.2012.08.003

UKAD. (2017, 10 July). UKAD issues urgent wake-up. call as doping stories hit public trust in the integrity of sport. Media Release. UK Anti-Doping (UKAD). Retrieved from https://

www.ukad.org.uk/news/article/ukad-issues-urgent-wake-up-call-as-doping-stories-hit-public-trust-in-the-i

UNESCO. (2015, 17 November). *International charter of physical education and sport.* United Nations Educational, Scientific and Cultural Organization. Retrieved from http://portal.unesco.org/en/ev.php-URL_ID=13150&URL_DO=DO_TOPIC&URL_SECTION=201.html

University of Southampton. (n.d.) TrustGov: Trust in Government Project, University of Southampton and Harvard University. Retrieved from https://trustgov.net/

UNODC. (n.d.a). Education for justice. United Nations Office on Drugs and Crime. Retrieved from https://www.unodc.org/e4j/en/index.html

UNODC. (n.d.b). Line up Live up. United Nations Office on Drugs and Crime. Retrieved from https://www.unodc.org/dohadeclaration/topics/crime-prevention-through-sports.html

USADA. (2017, 1 January). USADA-led non-analytical investigations under the USADA protocol for Olympic and paralympic movement testing. US Anti-Doping Agency. Retrieved from https://www.usada.org/wp-content/uploads/USADA%E2%80%90Led-Non%E2%80%90Analytical-Investigations-Principles.pdf

USADA. (2017, 11 July). What are non-analytical anti-doping rule violations? US Anti-Doping Agency. Retrieved from https://www.usada.org/non-analytical-anti-doping-rule-violations/

USADA. (2019, 1 January). Therapeutic use exemption policy. US Anti-Doping Agency. Retrieved from https://www.usada.org/wp-content/uploads/tue-policy.pdf

USADA. (2019, 4 January). U.S. cycling athlete Carl Grove accepts public warning. Press Release. US Anti-Doping Agency. Retrieved from https://www.usada.org/carl-grove-accepts-public-warning/

USADA. (2019, 8 March). U.S. paralympic track & field athlete Chelsea McClammer accepts finding of no fault. Press Release. US Anti-Doping Agency. Retrieved from https://www.usada.org/chelsea-mcclammer-accepts-finding-of-no-fault/

van Amsterdam, J., Opperhuizen, A., & Hartgens, F. (2010). Adverse health effects of anabolic–androgenic steroids. *Regulatory Toxicology and Pharmacology*, 57(1), 117–123.

Voyer, M., Gladstone, W., & Goodall, H. (2015). Obtaining a social licence for MPAs–influences on social acceptability. *Marine Policy*, 51, 260–266.

WADA. (n.d.). 2021 Code review. World Anti-Doping Agency. Retrieved from https://www.wada-ama.org/en/what-we-do/the-code/2021-code-review

WADA. (2011, May). Coordinating investigations and sharing anti-doping information and evidence. World Anti-Doping Agency. Retrieved from https://www.wada-ama.org/sites/default/files/resources/files/WADA_Investigations_Guidelines_May2011_EN.pdf

WADA. (2015; 2019, 1 June). World Anti-Doping Code 2015 with 2019 amendments. World Anti-Doping Agency. Retrieved from https://www.wada-ama.org/sites/default/files/resources/files/wada_anti-doping_code_2019_english_final_revised_v1_linked.pdf

WADA. (2012). Code collaboration. *Play True*, 1, pp. 4–5. World Anti-Doping Agency. Retrieved from https://www.wada-ama.org/sites/default/files/resources/files/PlayTrue_2012_The_Code_in_Review_1_EN.pdf

WADA. (2018a). 2018 anti doping testing figures. World Anti-Doping Agency. Retrieved from https://www.wada-ama.org/sites/default/files/resources/files/2018_testing_figures_report.pdf

WADA. (2018b, 6 January). 2021 Code review – First consultation: Questions to discuss and consider. World Anti-Doping Agency. Retrieved from https://www.wada-ama.org/sites/default/files/2018_06_04_stakeholdercomments.pdf

WADA. (2020, 15 June). World Anti-Doping Code (effective 1 January 2021). World Anti-Doping Agency. Retrieved from https://www.wada-ama.org/en/resources/the-code/2021-world-anti-doping-code

Wood, J., Howman, D., & Murrihy, R. (2018, March). *Report of the review of Australia's sports integrity arrangements, report No 12074*. Retrieved from https://www1.health.gov.au/internet/main/publishing.nsf/Content/63F0A5D7BDA5A0B5CA2582CF0005E6F9/$File/HEALTH-RASIA-Report-Acc.pdf

WSV Association (n.d.). World values survey. World Values Survey Association. Retrieved from www.worldvaluessurvey.org

6 Dominance or deceit in professional cycling

The perceived reality of Team Sky

Samantha Roberts and Catherine Ordway[1]

Introduction

If there is one sport that has been affected by behaviour that bring into question trust and transparency, it is cycling. The three Grand Tours of road cycling, the Tour de France, Giro d'Italia, and the Vuelta a Espana, are some of the most challenging and competitive sporting events. Questions surrounding the validity of the performances of the riders, as well as the transparency and governance of the sport, continue to tarnish international cycling. Of particular focus in this chapter is Team Sky (now Team Ineos) and its role in attempting to restore trust in the sport.

The use by athletes of what the World Anti-Doping Agency (WADA) defines as prohibited substances and methods (WADA, 2019) to distort the outcome of sporting competition is defined as 'corruption' (Miller, 2018). Whether it is an athlete seeking an advantage over their rivals or, separate to the WADA programme, trainers giving substances to animals, like racehorses or greyhounds, to impede performance, 'doping' deceives everyone involved in the sport industry and results in a breach of trust. Ultimately, sport relies upon the principle of 'uncertainty of outcome' (Pielke, 2013). Activities that deliberately seek to stretch or break the rules of the sport may be deemed as a form of corruption, or cheating. Zurloni, et al. link the concepts of doping and deception, arguing that different interpretations of both terms can aid in the explanation of the relationship between the two. They state that: 'first, doping behaviour constitutes a kind of deception, intended as a form of cheating. Secondly, doping behaviour presumably leads to deceptive behaviour(s), necessary in order to avoid being exposed' (2015, p. 192). The question then becomes, 'Who is being deceived?' The contention here is that, depending on the lens through which one looks, all stakeholders in the sport industry are impacted by doping behaviour, meaning that trust relationships with each of these stakeholder groups will have been damaged in some way. For many of these stakeholders, their first point of reference, information or support may be the sport's governing body. It is to that body that the stakeholders look to in restoring trust. In the post-Lance Armstrong era of men's professional cycling, the case study of Team Sky provides an opportunity to assess how well the International Federation for cycling (UCI) has restored trust, and whether there is more work to be done.

It is also important to consider here that, in some circumstances, whether in sport, politics or business, the structure of an organisation can facilitate corruption. Other chapters in this book discuss corruption and cheating in a variety of different sports and in several different contexts. In many of these examples, the organisation, such as the sport's national or international governing body, did little to try and address the issues presented by such behaviour. Despite the fact that any corrupt behaviour is conducted by individuals (in sport, whether that be athletes, officials, or those in positions of governance), the organisational environment is such that this activity is tolerated and, in some cases, perpetuated by those in positions of power. It is here that the discussion of bad apples, bad barrels and bad orchards becomes of interest (see Chapter 3 by Bayley and Egle, this volume).

It is important to understand where and how corruption originates and the cultural or environmental issues that support it, particularly in the context of the 'Lucifer Effect' (Zimbardo, 2007) and the lure of the 'dark side' of what is deemed as acceptable behaviour. Zimbardo (2007) goes on to describe how 'situational forces and group dynamics' can work together to change decent men and women into what he calls 'monsters', which is a different conceptualisation of the 'bad orchard'. It could be argued that officials, previously regarded as 'good citizens' working inside organisations, such as International Federations, have contributed to a culture perpetuating the use of performance-enhancing drugs (PEDs), particularly where a wider doping culture exists. For example, in the International Association of Athletics Federations (IAAF), the culture of corruption, enhanced by a lack of oversight or accountability, created an environment where it became justifiable to facilitate delays in processing and/or receive bribes to cover up positive drug tests (e.g. IAAF Independent Commission, 2015; Sadoff, 2016; Leicester & Pugmire, 2020). Similarly, the former President of the International Weightlifting Federation created a pervasive culture of 'institutionalised corruption' and actively interfered in the doping control test distribution planning and results management processes (McLaren Global Sports Solutions, 2020, pp. 89; 101–13).

The Cycling Independent Reform Commission [CIRC] report into the UCI found the leadership style of the former president to be 'autocratic', that the financial and governance process lacked transparency and that the UCI frequently failed to follow its own rules, particularly in relation to Therapeutic Use Exemptions (Marty et al., 2015. p. 8). In relation to whether the UCI contributed to a doping culture, the CIRC observed that:

> The allegations and review of UCI's anti-doping programme reveal that decisions taken by UCI leadership in the past have undermined anti-doping efforts: examples range from adopting an attitude that prioritised a clean image and sought to contain the doping problem, to disregarding the rules and giving preferential status to high profile athletes, to publicly criticising whistleblowers and engaging in personal disputes with other stakeholders. These actions severely undermined the credibility of UCI and therefore the reputation of the sport. However, the CIRC is not suggesting that UCI leadership knowingly or deliberately allowed doping and high-profile dopers to

> continue within the sport knowing or suspecting them to still be doping, but rather that a lack of proper institutional checks and balances within UCI, meant that these matters were not subjected to the rigorous scrutiny and application of the rules and best practice that they should have been. (Marty et al., 2015, pp. 8–9)

In order to explore how Team Sky has navigated their way to success within an apparent culture and long-standing history of doping, particularly in men's professional road racing, the chapter is divided into four sections: part A discusses the change in the landscape of professional cycling after the release of the United States Anti-Doping Agency's (USADA) report into Lance Armstrong and the United States Postal Cycling team in 2012; part B explores the introduction and subsequent dominance of professional road cycling team, Team Sky, and highlights some of the issues and questions that have been raised as a result of this success; part C discusses the nature and structure of inter-organisational relationships in sport between sponsor and sponsored property and how cheating can lead to the breakdown and dissolution of such agreements. When the commitment between partners is potentially destroyed and trust damaged, this part discusses the impact this perceived lack of trust and integrity in the sport of cycling has on the stakeholders, particularly given that sponsors may be reluctant to speak out about integrity issues in a sport when they are able to achieve greater visibility and brand awareness as a result of such relationships (Gorse, 2014; Fotheringham, 2019). The chapter concludes in part D with potential strategies to restore trust in the sport.

A The legacy of Lance

On the 17 January 2013, a global audience watched – many in disbelief, many in anger, and some with a sense of vindication – as seven-time Tour de France champion Lance Armstrong, in an interview with TV icon Oprah Winfrey, discussed the findings of the USADA report into his US Postal cycling team. In what USADA described as: 'the most sophisticated, professionalized, and successful doping program that sport has ever seen' (USADA, 2012, para.1.), the allegations against Armstrong would forever tarnish not only his reputation but also that of the sport of professional road cycling's blue ribbon race, the Tour de France; a race he won seven times in succession between 1999 and 2005.

WINFREY: Did you ever take banned substances to enhance your cycling performance?

ARMSTRONG: Yes

WINFREY: Was one of those banned substances EPO?

ARMSTRONG: Yes

WINFREY: Did you ever blood dope or use blood transfusions to enhance your cycling performance?

ARMSTRONG: Yes

WINFREY: Did you ever use any other banned substances such as testosterone, cortisone, or Human Growth Hormone?

ARMSTRONG: Yes

WINFREY: In all of your Tour de France victories, did you ever take banned substances or blood dope?

ARMSTRONG: Yes

WINFREY: Was it humanly possible to win the Tour de France without doping seven times?

ARMSTRONG: Not in my opinion … that generation, I didn't invent the culture, but I didn't try and stop it.

(BBC, 2013)

Whilst these admissions focused much of the attention on Armstrong, the use of PEDs in cycling has long been an issue. Even as far back as the 1924 Tour de France, it was reported that the Pelissier brothers, Henri and Francis, admitted to using a range of substances to ride in the race (Woodland, 2007; Labib et al., 2013). The UCI was the first international federation to begin drug testing in the 1950s (Rofe & Ordway, 1998, p. 3). In 1955 it was reported that in one French race, 25 cyclists were tested and 5 went positive (Dr F. Newton ISAF Doping Control Rules 4th Ed 1997 in Siekmann et al., 1999). The 'Festina Affair' in 1998 (Fotheringham, A., 2016) and Operacion Puerto (Operation Mountain Pass) from 2004 (Arnold, 2016; Hardie, 2011) both involved the systemic use of PEDs to try to gain an edge in the Grand Tours. Accordingly, the doping generation didn't start or end with Armstrong (Parisotto, 2006). Another American rider, Floyd Landis, and Spaniard, Alberto Contador, were both stripped of Tour de France victories post-2005 and doping in men's cycling has of course not stopped there.

For many listening to Armstrong's admission after admission in the interview with Winfrey, there was also a huge sense of disappointment. Much like sporting icons Michael Jordan and Muhammad Ali, Lance Armstrong had transcended his sport, and sport more broadly. After fighting and beating Stage 3 metastatic testicular cancer that had spread to his lungs and brain, Armstrong founded the LiveStrong Foundation to raise funds to search for a cure for cancer. LiveStrong provided help and hope for survivors, and soon everyone was wearing the yellow wristbands supporting the fight and his cause. However, according to reports from former teammates, including the likes of American cyclists and teammates Landis and Tyler Hamilton, wife of a former teammate Betsy Andreu, and team masseuse Emma O'Reilly, Armstrong had become a bully, an aggressor on and off the bike, threatening those who sought to expose his use of PEDs during his career (Hamilton, 2012).

The UCI's role

With the release of the USADA report that highlighted Armstrong's behaviour and use of PEDs throughout his career, many, particularly in the media, began to question and investigate how Armstrong could 'get away' with cheating the sport.

Despite a somewhat questionable legacy left by previous UCI president, Hein Verbruggen, who: 'was accused of failing to confront the pervasive use of performance-enhancing drugs in the sport' (Grimes, 2017, para.1), it didn't take long for then-UCI president, Pat McQuaid, to almost 'blame' the entire doping culture in the sport in the 1990s and early 2000s on one rider. McQuaid stated in a press conference that: 'Lance Armstrong deserved to be forgotten from the sport of cycling' (Pretot, 2012). However, stories of bribes to cover up failed drug tests disguised as support for international anti-doping initiatives began to circulate and people started to question whether the UCI as an organisation was fit for purpose (Cooke, 2015; AIGCP, 2019). The resulting independent CIRC investigation found that 'there was a culture of doping in cycling, and today it is probably less pervasive and all-encompassing than it was' (Marty et al., 2015, p. 24). The CIRC also identified that the 'policy of offering favours and defending Lance Armstrong seriously harmed the UCI's image and credibility despite all the efforts and dedication of its employees to fight doping' (Marty et al., 2015, p. 198).

In this environment, McQuaid found his position as president under attack. However, controversy is not necessarily fatal for presidential candidates. Experience shows that in international and national sport organisation elections, voters tend to maintain the status quo. For example, despite very public allegations of corruption and other forms of maladministration, Sepp Blatter was elected as international football (FIFA) president five times (Hough & Heaston, 2017, p. 340). Similarly, investigations into alleged bullying (AOC, 2017), the resulting *Culture Alignment* review into 'poor organisational culture' (The Ethics Centre, 2017) and an alternate candidate offering to forgo the substantial presidential salary (ABC/AAP, 2017), were insufficient to undermine loyalty for John Coates, who has been the Australian Olympic Committee president since 1990 (Masters, 2020).

The 2013 UCI vote ended up being far closer than anyone expected (BBC, 2013), and contrary to tradition, McQuaid was unsuccessful. Incoming UCI president, Brian Cookson (2014), the former head of British Cycling, ran his election campaign on the platform of 'Restoring Trust, Leading Change', apparently recognising the need to change business practices within the UCI and the culture of the organisation more broadly. Despite the platform, his former rival, McQuaid, recently alleged that Cookson continued to operate in the 'grey area' of the rules, including for example, not enforcing the requirement that cyclists only ride commercially available bikes (Stickybottle, 2018). As was acknowledged in the CIRC Report: 'all cultures evolve, or change, and doping is no different. Doping still exists, and it is expert at changing its shape' (Marty at al., 2015, p. 24). Against this backdrop, and a very successful track cycling performance in the velodrome at the Olympic Games in Beijing in 2008, a new British professional team joined the UCI Tour – Team Sky.

B A new team with a much-needed philosophy: Case study – Team Sky

When the birth of the new British professional cycling team, Team Sky, was announced in 2009, it was on the basis of a zero-tolerance policy toward any behaviour related to, or involving the use of, performance-enhancing substances. They weren't the first to adopt this strategy. When the T-Mobile Deutsche Telekom team was taken over by Bob Stapleton in 2006 and rebranded as Team Columbia Highroad, he did so with this zero-tolerance ideal (Emmett, 2009). The Slipstream/Chipotle Cycling Team was also built with this same philosophy in mind. Addressing the issue of doping head on, Slipstream manager, Jonathan Vaughters launched the team in 2007 with a 10-minute video featuring anti-doping campaigner, David Millar, 'talking about the pressures and weakness that forced him into doping, and about his role in his new team' (Pickering, 2007). Vaughters is a controversial character, having been a member of the Armstrong US Postal team, but did not confess to his own doping journey until 2012 (Vaughters, 2012). Throughout this period, the fallout from Armstrong's revelations had wide reaching implications for professional teams, national cycling federations, administrators, riders and their entourage (e.g. Orica GreenEdge; Vance, 2013; Ordway, 2012). One key question was whether confirmed or suspected dopers deserved a second chance, or whether a clean break was required to restore trust.

Team Sky riders, trainers, team managers, administrators and medical staff, were required to sign an agreement stating that they hadn't, and wouldn't, take part in doping (Wynn, 2012). David Brailsford, the team boss, who was also at the helm of Team GB's (Great Britain) dominance at the Olympic Games in 2008, and again in 2012, proudly trumpeted this zero-tolerance policy (Cossins, 2012). Brailsford also aimed to deliver a British winner of the Tour de France, a feat never before accomplished, as part of his five-year strategy. Little did he know that his team would see two British winners of the Maillot Jaune, or yellow jersey, in four years. The iconic yellow jersey has been worn by the leader throughout the race each year since 1919. The rider wearing the yellow jersey after the final stage of the race, and therefore the person who has covered the course of the Tour in the quickest time, to its traditional finish in Paris is then declared the overall winner.

The Tour de France, as with the other Grand Tours, consists of a variety of stages: flat, hilly, mountain stages with mountain-top finishes and individual time-trials (for an example of a route of the Tour, visit https://www.letour.fr/en/overall-route). Based on the race route, team administration decide who is going to compete, building a team around one or two leaders, based on those with a realistic chance of winning the overall race (known as General Classification, or GC). The rest of the team may contain a traditional sprinter to contest the sprint stages, a climbing specialist to either win stages in the mountains of the Tour or to support the leader (or leaders) of the team, so they don't lose time to their rivals in the Alps or Pyrenees. The rest of the team, to a total of eight members, will be made up of 'domestiques', riders who work for the benefit of their team and leader(s). For example, the domestique will be the rider dropping back in the race to meet the team car to collect food and drinks for their teammates, and, in the event of a breakaway or pursuit, will lead the 'charge' or 'train', protecting as much of the energy of those who might win stages as is possible.

Wiggins' win

The year of the London 2012 Olympic Games turned out to be the launching pad for Team Sky's dominance of the Tour de France. The Tour de France is one of cycling's Grand Tours along with the Giro d'Italia (Tour of Italy) and the Vuelta a Espana (Tour of Spain). The three week event involves a total of between 176 and 198 riders in the peloton, depending on the number of members on each team (up until 2018, each team in a Grand Tour could enter nine riders; after 2018, that number was reduced to eight). The term *peloton*, originating from the French, refers to the main body of riders in the race (Merriam-Webster, 2020). After Team Sky riders finished in the top 25 places in the previous two Tours (24th in 2010 and 15th in 2011), the 2012 Team Sky was stacked with both British and international talent. The game plan for the 2012 Tour, however, was that Wiggins should be the supported lead rider (Williams, 2012). British riders Bradley Wiggins, Mark Cavendish and Chris Froome, alongside Australian Richie Porte and Norwegian rider Edvald Boasson Hagen, dominated the 2012 Tour de France for Team Sky. From the start in Liege, Belgium, to the iconic finish on the Champs-Élysées in Paris, Team Sky were competitive in each of the 21 stages, winning 6 of them (Cavendish with three stage wins, Wiggins with two, and Froome winning one). The depth of talent in Team Sky was evident: as team leader, Wiggins won both the individual time trial stages, whilst Froome won in the mountains. Cavendish was victorious in three sprint stages, including the final stage in Paris.

After an elevated third-place finish in 2009 (after Armstrong's results were expunged from the record books), and a record-filled career in the velodrome, Wiggins became the first British winner of the Tour de France (News Wires, 2012). He went on to cement his legacy when he followed up his Tour de France victory with a gold medal in the individual time trial at the London 2012 Olympic Games only few weeks after the conclusion of the Tour. Cyclists often compete in races relatively close together, so competing strongly in both those events at the time was not especially noteworthy. Wiggins winning Olympic gold, and teammate Froome, after finishing second in the Tour, earning the bronze medal in the same Olympic race, demonstrated the strength in Team Sky at that time (despite reported personal rifts between the two riders; Carr & Hussain, 2020).

It wasn't until years later that questions would be raised about Wiggins' achievements.

Four-peat for Froome

As the 2013 Tour de France occurred soon after Armstrong's interview with Winfrey, the focus of the media was firmly placed on the integrity of the race and of the performances of its competitors. Each post-stage interview was filled with questions, not about how the stage played out or how the riders felt, but about PED use in the peloton and cheating in the sport. Fans would continue this barrage as they lined the streets of France along the race route, although much of this stemmed from the

French dislike of foreigners dominating 'their' race. Against this hostile backdrop to the Tour, Team Sky again turned up to win the race. A knee injury meant that Wiggins was not able to defend his title (Fotheringham, 2013), so Team Sky were led by the 2012 runner-up, Froome (ProCyclingStats, 2012).

Froome won three stages and held the yellow jersey from stage 8 to the 21st and final stage in Paris, securing his first, and Team Sky's second, Tour de France win. His margin of victory was over four minutes from his nearest rival, and more than a minute quicker than the average margin from 2010 to 2019. This dominance reinforced the many questions he had faced throughout the race, due to the intense media focus post-Oprah interview. Froome didn't have the same kind of pedigree coming into racing at the Tour de France as Wiggins did, leading commentators, such as Harris, to suggest that Froome had: 'risen from virtual obscurity to Tour winner in three years and ousted Wiggins to become the figurehead of the richest team in cycling' (Harris, 2014, para. 2). The allegations of PED use and the questions surrounding Froome's integrity only grew after he won the Tour again in 2015.

Froome was one of the pre-race favourites heading into the 2014 Tour, along with Spaniard Alberto Contador. Contador, who had been stripped of his 2010 Tour de France victory after testing positive for banned substance clenbuterol, had served his two-year ban after unsuccessfully arguing that the anabolic agent had entered his system through contaminated meat (CAS, 2012). The hype around Team Sky and Froome was heightened further due to the decision to host the Grand Depart, the opening stage of the race, after the success of the 2007 Depart, in the United Kingdom. This represented a huge opportunity for Team Sky in particular to compete on what could be deemed as 'home soil', and to showcase the team and the riders in a positive way. An estimated 2.5 million fans from across the UK gathered in Yorkshire to see the riders of the Tour, with Team Sky very much in the forefront of attention (Jurejko & Scrivener, 2014). Members of the British Royal family, Prince William, the Duchess of Cambridge and Prince Harry attended the first stage, further heightening interest around the event. After crashing on two consecutive days, Froome was forced to abandon the Tour on the fifth stage with fractures in his right hand and left wrist, making holding the handlebars on his bike virtually impossible (Bloor, 2014).

The following year, the scrutiny of Froome and his performances intensified. It was reported that, as he was scaling some of the most challenging mountains on a Tour de France route, fans yelled 'doper' at Froome and threw cups of urine in his face (Cary, 2015). In order to try and address the concerns of the many stakeholders in cycling, Froome undertook a series of independent physiological tests soon after winning the Tour for a second time in 2015 and released the results publicly (Cycling News, 2015). It was found that he had physiological advantages over his rivals, allowing him to perform at optimal levels over longer periods of time (Moore, 2015), despite suffering from asthma.

Building on the success of 2012, 2013 and 2015, with a core group of riders including Froome, Geraint Thomas, Wout Pouls and Luke Rowe, Team Sky's dominance continued. Froome won both the 2016 and 2017 Tour de France races, the 2017 Vuelta a Espana, and the 2018 Giro d'Italia.

Success continues …

Froome was once again a pre-race favourite to win the 2018 Tour de France. However, it was his British teammate, Geraint Thomas, who ended up riding to victory and the legendary yellow jersey (Froome finished third). Thomas was dominant in the mountains, winning two stages and wearing the yellow jersey from the 11th stage to the Champs-Élysées. Team Sky ended the race with three riders in the top 20: Thomas, Froome, and the young Colombian rider, Egan Bernal, fifteenth (ProCyclingStats, 2018).

Going into the 2019 Tour, the team, now known as Team Ineos (after BSkyB decided to end their sponsorship of the team, a decision not seemingly related to doping allegations (Cycling News, 2018)), looked like it would have three team leaders – Froome, Thomas and Bernal. In a team of eight riders, having three working towards winning the race and, therefore, not necessarily supporting each other's goals, makes a team less competitive within a Grand Tour environment. Even two leaders, or co-leaders, can be problematic to start a race (Press Association, 2019). A horrific training accident led to Froome missing most of the 2019 season as he recovered in hospital and rehabilitation from his injuries, leaving Bernal to take the yellow jersey and Colombia's first Tour de France win (ProCyclingStats, 2019).

With the 2020 Tour De France postponed as a result of the COVID-19 pandemic (Law, 2020), Team Sky/Ineos had won seven of the last eight Tour de France races. The question that many have been asking is whether the victories were based on dominance or deceit?

Dominance or deceit?

In a sport industry where conditions exist for an uncertain outcome, then, in an ideal world, dominance by one athlete or team over a long period of time shouldn't occur. However, there have been many examples in sport of dominance by a team or athlete. For example, Formula One was dominated by Michael Schumacher in the 1990s (Beer, 2019); the New York Yankees were dominant in baseball from the mid-1930s for almost 20 years, which saw them win 12 World Series titles in 13 attempts (Chavez, 2020); the women's gymnastics team from the Russian Federation won every World Championship and Olympic singles title between the years of 1952 and 1992 (Sheth, 2017); Team USA women's basketball won eight gold medals at the Olympics between 1984 and 2016 (Wright, 2018); and Manchester United have had a grip on the men's football Premier League in the UK since its inception in 1993 (Gorse, 2014). Yet, the fact that Lance Armstrong had won seven-straight Tour de France races over some of the world's most difficult routes (through the Alps and the Pyrenees mountains in France) was so exceptional that any future success in cycling was going to be questioned. The previous record of five consecutive wins (1991–1995) by Spaniard Miguel Indurain wasn't without its critics either, with some suggesting his performances were 'mutant-like' (Cossins, 2013). Weight was added to the doping concerns once

Indurain's association with others connected to doping, specifically Dr Conconi, were revealed (Cycling News, 2013; Fontecchio, 2018). Drs Ferrari and Fuentes, in particular, have also been implicated in doping scandals, including working with Armstrong and the T-Mobile cycling team respectively (USADA, 2012; Arnold, 2016). Stakeholders, from within the fan groups and in the media, after the 2013 Armstrong admission were on notice for 'superhuman' achievements in cycling.

The performances of Team Sky and their riders became the focus of investigation first in 2016 when notorious hackers Fancy Bears leaked the personal medical history of 2012 Tour champion Wiggins, amongst others (WADA, 2016a; 2016b; 2016c). The leaked information included confirmation that Wiggins had been in receipt of six therapeutic use exemption certificates (TUEs) during his career to allow him to take medicine for allergies and asthma (Cycling News, 2016). These TUEs are given to an athlete if they have an illness or condition that requires them to take an otherwise prohibited substance or method (WADA, 2020). This led to an investigation by UK anti-doping authorities (UKAD) into an apparent delivery of a padded envelope (known as a 'jiffy bag') of triamcinolone, a banned corticosteroid that helps a rider lose weight but maintain power levels but is used legitimately in the treatment of severe asthma, for Wiggins to use at a race in 2011 (Fotheringham, W., 2016). A UK governmental enquiry led to major charges under the rules of sport against Wiggins in 2018 in a report entitled 'Combatting doping in sport'. In the report, it was stated that 'the application for a TUE for triamcinolone for Bradley Wiggins, ahead of the 2012 Tour de France, also meant that he benefited from the performance-enhancing properties of this drug during the race' (DCMS, 2018, p. 32). While this didn't equate to an anti-doping violation according to the WADA Code: 'it does cross the ethical line that [team boss] David Brailsford says he himself drew for Team Sky' (DCMS, 2018, p. 32) – that of zero-tolerance.

Asthma also served as the catalyst for Froome returning abnormal levels of the drug salbutamol, also used to treat asthma. According to WADA, salbutamol (2018 para.4), has: 'no known performance-enhancing properties when inhaled at a therapeutic dose. However, if used in excessive doses or by systematic routes (e.g. oral), it can be a stimulant or an anabolic agent, which is why it is on the Prohibited List with a threshold amount'. Despite battling through the health ramifications of several diseases, including bilharzia and typhoid (Harris, 2014), Froome's lung capacity astounded doctors. When he provided a urine sample in 2017 with twice the allowable limit of salbutamol in his system, having at that point won three Tour de France races, many feared that history was about to repeat itself. Again, the conversation would be focused on whether a rider, who had dominated the Tour, was about to fall from grace, just as Armstrong had done previously. More importantly to the team, under the WADA Code, Froome could face a lengthy ban from the sport if he couldn't provide an adequate explanation (De Menezes, 2017).

Again, TUEs became central to the investigation, with Froome having received exemptions for the use of salbutamol to treat his asthma in previous years. Froome argued that, when he returned the abnormal level, he was competing at the Vuelta a Espana and his asthma was causing him significant issues. Froome claimed that he followed his team doctor's advice to increase the dose (Cycling News, 2017). After months of accusation and investigation, the UCI ruled that Froome had provided enough information and justification to support his argument and dropped all charges against him (Cary, 2018). Moreover, according to WADA (2018, para 5): 'unlike most substances, given the variables that exist with salbutamol depending on conditions specific to each case, the rule is designed to afford athletes found to have exceeded the threshold with the opportunity to prove how it has occurred and justify proper therapeutic use', which Froome did.

Other people who have worked within Team Sky have also had their integrity questioned. Team doctor, Richard Freeman, was at the centre of the investigation into Wiggins and the 'jiffy bag', although the UKAD investigation into this proved to be inconclusive (Brown, 2017). Former team coaches Shane Sutton and Simon Cope were also implicated, although both denied their part in the scandal (Skelton, 2018). Jonathan Tiernan-Locke, was the first British cyclist to be found guilty of an anti-doping rule violation (ADRV), when he returned adverse biological passport results. The Athlete Biological Passport, or ABP, was introduced by the UCI in 2008 (Marty et al., 2015, p. 52) and then adopted by WADA in 2009 to provide a standardised approach to the 'profiling of individual athletes haematological variables' (WADA, 2020, para 7). The timing for this ADRV, during the UCI presidency of Cookson, caused embarrassment for his British compatriot, even though he wasn't riding for Team Sky at the time of his offence (BBC, 2014).

Throughout all of this, the media continue to pursue the story of Team Sky's dominance of road cycling over the last eight years. Team Sky took the step of allowing cameras to follow their preparation activities for the Tour de France to aid transparency. They wanted to demonstrate that Brailsford's ideology of 'marginal gains', the process of improving every small component of cycling by just 1%, can add up to massive improvement without cheating (Clear, 2014). Brailsford drilled the team on a precision lead out, that is, a: 'train of riders from the same team whose sole ambition is to deliver their sprinter to the finish line safely and in the best place possible' (Global Cycling Network, 2017). By lining up behind each other, the amount of aerodynamic drag, or resistance each rider in the train must deal with is reduced (Churazova, 2019). Conserving energy, the sprinters then have a more explosive burst of power and speed before the finish line. The ability to reduce drag 'is one of the defining aspects of most bicycle racing' (Crouch et al., 2017, p. 102).

In the absence of the titillating doping scandals, the success of Team Sky served to exacerbate the associated perverse gamesmanship of 'mudslinging', rumour mongering and lies. The traditional rivalry between France and the UK was blamed for the French media's insinuation that Team GB used wheels that were too round, or 'magic' in the velodrome at the 2008 Olympic Games in Beijing, allowing Wiggins to win two gold medals (Fotheringham, 2012). In such an environment, it could be expected that some stakeholders in the sport industry, especially sponsors, would consider walking away from any associations with a rider, team, event or with the sport as a whole, viewing the risk of association far outweighing the benefits of any type of business relationship.

C The nature of trust in sponsorship relationships in sport

The network of relationships in sport is broad and ties stakeholders together in a range of ways. Who those stakeholders are and how they are impacted by any corruption, cheating or deception, depends on the nature and extent of their relationship with the perceived guilty party. Chadwick (2009) identified some of the key groups of stakeholders, including fans; athletes and teams, competitions and events; broadcasters and the media; and commercial partners and sponsors. These relationships may be informal but, more likely, there is a contractual agreement between the parties involved. Modern sponsorship arrangements reflect concepts of relationship marketing, rather than the traditional transactional: 'X dollars from a sponsor with Y given back in return from a sponsored property (e.g. access to athletes, tickets, etc)'.

The concept of trust, the foundational concept for this book, has long been recognised as a central tenet of business and personal relationships, and, as such, relationship marketing (Theron et al., 2015). In marketing and sponsorship literature, trust is defined by Rousseau et al. (1998, p. 395) as: 'a psychological orientation comprising the intention to accept vulnerability based upon the positive expectations of the intentions, or behaviour of the other party in the sponsorship dyad'. Moorman et al. expresses it as: 'a willingness to rely on an exchange partner in whom one has confidence' (1992, p. 315). When that confidence is based on deception, then stakeholders are entitled to ask whether trust ever truly existed. This lack of trust impacts on those relationships, with Ring and Van de Ven (1994) identifying four reasons for relationship dissolution, one of which involves the conditions violating trust. These conditions might include, for example in the sport setting, a rule transgression, like doping, and even the subsequent management of that transgression by sporting authorities. Moreover, Roberts and Burton (2018) highlight the fact that the damage to trust between partners in any kind of business relationship can lead to the questioning of integrity which, in turn, further weakens trust and commitment in that relationship.

Integrity issues inevitably lead to these relationships breaking down. Professional cycling has seen a number of stakeholders withdraw from the sport due to the history of PED use in the peloton. For example, since 2006, sponsors, including Deutsche Telekom, Audi, adidas, Phonak and Rabobank, have withdrawn financial support for the race and/or the teams involved, citing the continuing threat of doping scandals as the primary reason for their withdrawal (Gorse, 2014). German television stations ZDF and ARD refused to broadcast the Tour de France for a number of years due to the perceived doping culture that surrounded the race, commenting that the sporting value of the Tour for them had been reduced by the accumulation of failed drugs tests (Fotheringham, 2007). It could be argued that deception, in this case the use of PEDs and the apparent facilitation by those in positions of leadership, prompts stakeholders to question whether their commitment to a relationship is worth the perceived risk. Any investment in sponsorship is based on an informed decision about the trustworthiness, compatibility and commitment of the sports property (Amis et al., 1997).

One of the means available to the sports property, in this case a governing body or team, to demonstrate their commitment to the sponsor's values is to deal effectively with the transgression through a range of measures (Ordway & Opie, 2016). In the case of FIFA for example, considerable pressure was exerted on sponsors by the media, and the organisation #newFIFAnow, to speak out in relation to claims of bribery and corruption, and in response to poor working conditions in preparation for the men's World Cup in Qatar (Wilson, 2015). With sponsorship contributing significantly to the ability of cycling teams to compete on the global stage, it becomes crucial to ensure that long-term relationships are maintained. The sports property, in this case Team Sky and now Ineos, receives a sustained financial commitment. The sponsor enjoys the benefits of being associated with a successful team, with the positive image spill over (Pope et al., 2009; Cliffe & Motion, 2005; Ferrand & Pages, 1999). This image can be tarnished irrevocably if that sponsor's logo is pictured on the shirt of an athlete who has failed a drugs test.

With these revenue streams being lost, and many other stakeholders questioning the integrity of the race and its riders, the focus then needs to be on the rebuilding and restoration of trust between stakeholder groups. For the UCI, the key questions are: 'How do stakeholders know if the response to corruption or act of deception is "enough"?', 'Who decides if a response is effective?' and 'Can ALL stakeholder groups ever be truly satisfied?'

D Restoring trust in cycling

In releasing independent test results, it is apparent that Froome and his team tried to address the concerns of cycling stakeholders by providing what they deemed evidence to support the fact that he was competing, in the Tour de France and other races, clean. However, the combination of questions around the appropriate salbutamol and TUE use, the perceived behaviour of Team Sky surrounding Wiggins and other riders, including for example the apparent receipt of padded envelopes, in the context of the well-established culture of doping in men's road cycling historically, it is only to be expected that stakeholders remain sceptical. As Walker suggests, sometimes: 'we are not sure if we are seeing responses (rather than reactions) to the wrong that has been done in an attempt to set things right; or, we may wonder whether we are seeing the right responses' (2001, p.116).

It is important to note here that what these 'right' responses might be, will and do vary both across and within stakeholder groups. In developing the Sponsor Response to Sporting Transgression, or SRST, model, Gorse (2014) found that how each individual sponsor interprets factors like the severity of a case of transgression (for example, doping), the amount of media coverage the incident might generate, and the frequency of such cases will impact on any decision that might be made. Important too is the nature of the relationship between sponsor and sponsored property – if each of the parties trust the other, then a sponsor might be more likely to remain associated with the property but may seek to separate themselves from the incident, renegotiate terms of a contract or limit the use of a particular athlete in any marketing activity.

There are a number of key considerations to determine what might be the 'right' responses:

1. Time – both in timeliness of response and playing the long game, noting that the restoration of trust in cycling cannot be immediately achieved. There have been too many cases of PED use in the sport for people to simply forget its history and believe that everyone in the peloton is clean, even if they are. The history of the sport very much overshadows the present. The cynicism with which the UCI and its riders is regarded can only be addressed over time. The CIRC Report also acknowledged the long-term commitment that the UCI had made to anti-doping. Changing their policy from 'containment' in 2006/2007 to 'catch the cheaters', despite the inevitable short-term pain, has contributed to an improved culture (Marty et al., 2015, pp. 159–60).

2. Transparency and Consistency: Many of the activities and decisions that occurred in the past were shrouded in a cloak of secrecy (Marty et al., 2015). Transparency in the decision-making process will build trust, even if there is disagreement in the outcome. For example, clearly communicating the reasons for applying different sanctions, including ban lengths, based on proportionality principles, flexibility and fairness by the various national tribunals and CAS ((Niggli & Sieveking, 2006), can avoid confusion and distrust in the minds of the stakeholders (Straubel, 2004; Reilly, 2012; Gorse, 2014).

3. Redress and Remorse: One challenge for cycling is how to manage the fact there are many people (riders and team staff) who were part of the doping culture of the sport who are still involved in team ownership, operations or governance today (Marty et al., 2015, p. 79). Teams, and sponsors, have managed perceptions through terminating contracts and requiring signed declarations of commitment to clean sport (Ordway, 2012; Vance, 2013; Marty et al., 2015, p. 77). The question that remains is how to assess whether these are genuine expressions of remorse and if people should be 'given' a second chance for redemption (Ordway, 2017; Chapter 11 by Olukoya and Ogunleye-Bello, this volume). Another initiative, attempting to address the reported abuse of TUEs, was to establish the Mouvement Pour un Cyclisme Credible (MPCC), or the 'Movement for Credible Cycling' in 2007. Although limited in its mandate, the MPCC aimed to address what was seen as 'gaps' in the UCI and WADA rules around the use of corticosteroids in cycling (Marty et al., 2015, p. 84; Quenet, 2016). While not everyone was convinced by the motives and efficacy of the MPCC, teams not signing up to be part of the MPCC, such as Team Sky, gave stakeholders the opportunity to ask more questions (Quenet, 2016).

4. Walking the talk: One of the most important measures for ethical culture in organisations is 'walking the talk' (Ethisphere, 2020). Whilst the common assumption is that those developing the substances that enhance performance will always be at least two steps ahead of testers in what has become a 'drug-testing arms race' (Bassindale, 2015; Choy et al., 2012), or in this case two wheels, this cannot be used as an excuse to reduce the significance of PED use. If authorities are seen as making every effort in addressing issues of PED use in sport, stakeholders, like sponsors, can

be more assured in their decisions to remain involved in the sport. As has been suggested in other chapters, punishing those who use substances and deterring others from doing the same is only part of the trust restoration process. All stakeholders need to believe in the integrity of competition. On the understanding that humans are trained, and bikes built, to maximise their success, the outcome is therefore uncertain. The ideal that is sought is confidence that the race is clean, that what they are witnessing is human and machine working together to achieve what very few do – to complete one of cycling's Grand Tours. Both the UCI and team sponsors can look at the fallout from the ongoing scandals, including in other sports, to see what lessons can be learned.

Team Sky have certainly tried to lift this veil of cynicism or scepticism that has blighted the sport since the USADA report, and the true extent of doping in the peloton in the 1990s and early-2000s began to unfold. Releasing biological data and making a five-part documentary series following their preparation activities for the Tour de France has aided in achieving transparency (British Cycling, 2012). Team Sky riders Froome, Geraint Thomas and Luke Rowe are also very active on social media channels, particularly Twitter, communicating with fans and building relationships with stakeholders in the sport (Williams & Chinn, 2010; Abeza & O'Reilly, 2014; Wang & Zhou, 2015). This has seemingly assisted in rebuilding trust that might have been broken between the team and any stakeholders. One indicator for this is that the owner of petrochemical company, Ineos, British billionaire Sir Jim Ratcliffe, replaced BSkyB as title sponsor of the team, even before Sky were due to end their official agreement (Ballinger, 2019).

Conclusion

As previously highlighted, transparency is key when it comes to restoring trust in anything, not just sport. Transparent processes and procedures are vital to ensure that everyone can see what has happened and why, taking away the element of interpretation that can be so damaging. In a world where news can spread instantaneously, the court of opinion can convene quickly to fill the vacuum if all the relevant information isn't made available.

The efforts of Team Sky and other professional teams who have adopted a similar zero-tolerance policy, need to continue to be supported by those in positions of governance in order to restore trust in cycling. International Federation leaders, including from the UCI, have continued to profess that it is important to restore trust in sporting competition, but don't specify who and what stakeholders should be trusting. The web of stakeholder relationships is so intertwined that the behaviour of one stakeholder can directly impact on levels of trust between all stakeholders.

Sponsors can and do have a role in rebuilding trust in cycling. By supporting those riders and teams who are adopting ethical practices, both in sport as well as business, and promoting the benefits of operating in this way can begin to change the culture of the sport while changing the narrative at the same time. Sponsor commitment to clean sport needs to go beyond mere access to the millions of people who line the roads across France, Italy and Spain every year for the Grand Tours. Sponsors have a responsibility to lead change, just as the athletes and the leaders do.

Questions

i *Trust loss* – In whom (or, in which group) has trust been lost in this case?
ii *Trust correction* – How, if attempted, has the restoration of trust been tried?; and;
iii *Lessons learned* – How could the lessons from this case be applied to other sports, nations, states, other districts for the same sport, or other sports to prevent a further loss of trust or at least to restore trust?

Note

1 The authors wish to thank Erika Riedl, Anne Gripper, Kerry Knowler and Steve Jones for their review of the chapter and their helpful advice.

References

ABC/AAP. (2017, 7 May). John Coates remains as AOC president, beating challenger Danni Roche. *ABC News.* Australian Broadcasting Commission. Retrieved from https://www.abc.net.au/news/2017-05-06/john-coates-retains-australian-olympic-committee-presidency/8502672

Abeza, G., & O'Reilly, N. (2014). Social media platforms' use in building stakeholder relationships. *Journal of Applied Sport Management*, 6(3).

AIGCP. (2019, 29 October). An open letter to the UCI from AIGCP. Association Internationale des Groupes Cyclistes Professionels (member teams also individually released this statement). Retrieved from https://www.teamineos.com/article/an-open-letter-to-the-uci-from-aigcp

Amis, J., Pant, N., & Slack, T. (1997). Achieving a sustainable competitive advantage: A resource-based view of sport sponsorship. *Journal of Sport Management*, 11, 80–96.

AOC. (2017, 1 September). Statement by the AOC executive on Mike Tancred. Australian Olympic Committee. Retrieved from https://www.olympics.com.au/news/statement-by-the-aoc-executive-on-mike-tancred/

Arnold, R. (2016, 5 November). Jaksche Explains his perspective of Operacion Puerto. *Ride Media.* Retrieved from https://www.ridemedia.com.au/interviews/jaksche-explains-his-perspective-of-operacion-puerto/

Ballinger, A. (2019, 19 March). Team Sky officially confirm takeover by new sponsor Ineos. *Cycling Weekly.* Retrieved from https://www.cyclingweekly.com/news/latest-news/team-sky-officially-confirms-takeover-new-sponsor-ineos-411073

Bassindale, T. (2015, 15 June). In sport's drug-testing arms race, the cheats are usually a step ahead. *Medical Express* (*The Conversation*). Retrieved from https://medicalxpress.com/news/2015-06-sport-drug-testing-arms.html

BBC. (2014, 17 July). Team Sky's Jonathan Tiernan-Locke gets two-year doping ban. *BBC.* Retrieved from https://www.bbc.com/sport/cycling/28354686

BBC. (2013, 27 September). Brian Cookson elected as UCI president, defeating Pat McQuaid. *BBC.* Retrieved from https://www.bbc.com/sport/cycling/24300072

Beer, M. (2019, 3 January). Mercedes: 'Founding father' Schumacher key to F1 dominance. *Motorsport.com.* Retrieved from https://www.motorsport.com/f1/news/schumacher-founding-father-mercedes-wolff/4318884/?nrt=54

Bloor, S. (2014, 9 July) Tour de France 2014: Chris Froome crashes out – in pictures. *The Guardian.* Retrieved from https://www.theguardian.com/sport/gallery/2014/jul/09/tour-de-france-2014-chris-froome-crashes-out

British Cycling. (2012, 30 August). Watch 'British cycling: A road to glory' tonight on Sky. Retrieved from https://www.britishcycling.org.uk/road/article/bc20120830-Watch-%e2%80%9cBritish-Cycling–A-Road-to-Glory%e2%80%9d-tonight-on-Sky-0

Brown, G. (2017, 16 November). Explainer: Sky's mysterious jiffy bag. *VeloNews.* Retrieved from https://www.velonews.com/news/explainer-skys-mysterious-jiffy-bag/

Carr, J., & Hussain, D. (2020, 20 May). Olympic cycling legend Sir Bradley Wiggins and his wife Cath announce they are separating. *Mailonline.* Daily Mail Australia, Associated Newspapers Ltd. Retrieved from https://www.dailymail.co.uk/news/article-8333427/Olympic-cycling-legend-Sir-Bradley-Wiggins-wife-Cath-announce-separating.html

Cary, T. (2018, 2 July). Chris Froome cleared to defend Tour de France after doping case dropped. *The Telegraph.* Retrieved from https://www.telegraph.co.uk/cycling/2018/07/02/chris-froome-salbutamol-case-dropped-uci-freeing-team-sky-rider/

Cary, T. (2015, 18 July). Tour de France 2015: Chris Froome has urine thrown in face and branded 'doped' by roadside spectator. *The Telegraph.* Retrieved from https://www.telegraph.co.uk/sport/othersports/cycling/tour-de-france/11748812/Tour-de-France-2015-Chris-Froome-has-urine-thrown-in-face-and-branded-doped-by-roadside-spectator.html

CAS. (2012, 6 February). Alberto Contador found guilty of an anti-doping rule violation by the Court of Arbitration for Sport (CAS): Suspension of two years. Media Release. Court of Arbitration for Sport. Lausanne. Retrieved from https://www.tas-cas.org/en/general-information/news-detail/article/alberto-contador-found-guilty-of-an-anti-doping-rule-violation-by-the-cas-suspension-of-two-years.html

Chadwick, S. (2009). From outside lane to inside track: sport management research in the twenty-first century. *Management Decision*, 47(1), 191–203.

Chavez, A. (2020, 9 June). Ranking the best Yankees dynasties in history. *Pinstripe Alley.* Retrieved from https://www.pinstripealley.com/2020/6/9/21284693/yankees-ranking-best-dominant-dynasties

Choy, S., & Ravichandiran, M. (2012). The sports doping race. *Medicine and Technology*, 79, 1–23. Retrieved from www.uwomj.com/wp-content/uploads/2012/11/v79n1_8.pdf

Churazova, A. (2019). Aerodynamics of cycling explained through CFD. *SimScale Blog.* Retrieved from https://www.simscale.com/blog/2017/07/cycling-aerodynamics/

Clear, J. (2014,2 March). The value of marginal gains. *Life Hacker.* Retrieved from https://lifehacker.com/the-value-of-marginal-gains-1514453003

Cliffe, S. J., & Motion, J. (2005). Building contemporary brands: A sponsorship-based strategy. *Journal of Business Research*, 58, 1068–1077.

Cooke, N. (2015, 11 March). Nicole Cooke: CIRC report is admirable but authorities must do more on drugs. *The Guardian*. Retrieved from https://www.theguardian.com/sport/2015/mar/11/circ-report-anti-doping-cycling-nicole-cooke

Cookson, B. (2014). Restoring trust, leading change. Retrieved from www.verocom.co.uk/wp-content/uploads/2014/01/Brian-Cookson-Manifesto.pdf

Cossins, P. (2012, 21 July). Wiggins wins Tour's final time trial in Chartres. *Cycling News*. Retrieved from https://www.cyclingnews.com/races/tour-de-france-2012/stage-19/results/

Cossins, P. (2013, 12 June). Vayer casts doubt over performances of Indurain and Jalabert. *Cycling News*. Retrieved from https://www.cyclingnews.com/news/vayer-casts-doubt-over-performances-of-indurain-and-jalabert/

Crouch, T., Burton, D., LaBry, Z. A., Blair, K. B. (2017). Riding against the wind: A review of competition cycling aerodynamics. *Sports Engineering*, 20, 81–110.

Cycling News. (2013, 26 February). Report: Indurain and Banesto were Conconi clients. *Cycling News*. Retrieved from https://www.cyclingnews.com/news/report-indurain-and-banesto-were-conconi-clients/

Cycling News. (2015, 3 December). Chris Froome's physiological test data released. *Cycling News*. Retrieved from https://www.cyclingnews.com/news/chris-froomes-physiological-test-data-released/

Cycling News. (2016, 30 September). Bradley Wiggins explains TUE use, asthma and allergies. *Cycling News*. Retrieved from https://www.cyclingnews.com/news/bradley-wiggins-explains-tue-use-asthma-and-allergies/

Cycling News. (2017, 13 December). Chris Froome returns adverse analytical finding for salbutamol. *Cycling News*. Retrieved from https://www.cyclingnews.com/news/chris-froome-returns-adverse-analytical-finding-for-salbutamol/

Cycling News. (2018, 12 December). Sky to end sponsorship after 2019. *Cycling News*. Retrieved from https://www.cyclingnews.com/news/sky-to-end-sponsorship-after-2019/

DCMS. (2018). *Combatting doping in sport. Fourth report of session 2017–2019*. Digital, Culture, Media and Sport Committee, House of Commons, UK Parliament. London. Retrieved from https://publications.parliament.uk/pa/cm201719/cmselect/cmcumeds/366/366.pdf

de Menezes, J. (2017, 13 December). Salbutamol: What is the drug Chris Froome took to treat his asthma that could lead to Tour de France ban? *The Independent*. Retrieved from https://www.independent.co.uk/sport/cycling/salbutamol-what-is-drug-chris-froome-ban-team-sky-tour-de-france-vuelta-a-espana-a8107446.html

Emmett, J. (2009, 11 August). Bob Stapleton is cycling's new dynamo. *SportsPro Media Ltd*. Retrieved from https://www.sportspromedia.com/analysis/cyclings_new_dynamo

Ethisphere. (2020). Measuring ethical culture. Ethisphere's 2020 Culture Benchmark Data Set. Retrieved from https://ethisphere.com/wp-content/uploads/Ethical_Culture_Infographic_2020-f.pdf

Ferrand, A., & Pages, M. (1999). Image management in sport organisations: The creation of value. *European Journal of Marketing*, 33(3/4), 387–401.

Fontecchio, C. (2018). Indurain: I think maybe it's time. *Podium Café*. Retrieved from https://www.podiumcafe.com/2018/6/22/17488590/indurain-i-think-maybe-its-time

Fotheringham, W.(2007, 19 July). German TV pulls coverage after T-Mobile rider fails test. *The Guardian*. Retrieved fromhttps://www.theguardian.com/sport/2007/jul/19/cycling.tourdefrance

Fotheringham, A. (2016). *The end of the road: The Festina affair and the tour that almost wrecked cycling*. London: Bloomsbury Publishing.

Fotheringham, W. (2012, 6 August). London 2012: Are 'magic wheels' the secret to GB cycling dominance? *The Guardian*. Retrieved from https://www.theguardian.com/sport/2012/aug/05/london-2012-wheels-gb-cycling

Fotheringham, W. (2013, 1 June). Bradley Wiggins out of Tour de France because of knee injury. *The Guardian*. Retrieved from https://www.theguardian.com/sport/2013/may/31/bradley-wiggins-tour-de-france-knee-injury1

Fotheringham, W. (2016, 30 September). Bradley Wiggins opens up with full story on asthma, allergies and TUEs. *The Guardian*. Retrieved from https://www.theguardian.com/sport/2016/sep/30/bradley-wiggins-full-story-asthma-allergies-tues

Fotheringham, W. (2019, 20 March). Team Sky's Ineos deal will prompt mixed emotions in the peloton. *The Guardian*. Retrieved from https://www.theguardian.com/sport/2019/mar/19/team-sky-ineos-mixed-emotions-peloton-cycling

Fry, C. (2015, 15 July). Is the Tour de France more dangerous these days? *The Conversation*. Retrieved from https://theconversation.com/is-the-tour-de-france-more-dangerous-these-days-44526

Fry, C., & Hemphill, D. (2014, 10 July). Unofficial rules of the Tour de France matter most. *The Conversation*. Retrieved from https://theconversation.com/unofficial-rules-of-the-tour-de-france-matter-most-28841

Global Cycling Network. (2017, 6 May). The leadout train: Road cycling explained. *Global Cycling Network*. Retrieved from https://www.youtube.com/watch?v=v3xbxtBtJvs

Gorse, S. (2014). *Corruption in international sport: Implications for sponsorship management*. Unpublished doctoral thesis. Coventry University, UK.

Grimes, W. (2017, 15 June). Hein Verbruggen, Who raised cycling's profile, dies at 75. *The New York Times*. Retrieved from https://www.nytimes.com/2017/06/15/sports/cycling/obituary-hein-verbruggen-dead-international-cycling-union.html#:~:text=Hein%20Verbruggen%2C%20who%20brought%20the,He%20was%

Hamilton, T., & Coyle, D.(2012). The secret race: Inside the hidden world of the Tour de France. New York:Bantam.

Hardie, M.(2011). It's Not about the Blood: Operacion Puerto and the End of Modernity. In M.McNamee & V.Møller (Eds.), *Doping and anti-doping policy in sport: Ethical and legal perspectives*. Abingdon:Routledge.

Harris, N. (2014, 28 June). Chris Froome's secret battle: Eight doctors, six clinics, four countries and five different illnesses … the remarkable personal struggle of Great Britain's Tour de France champion. *Daily Mail*. Retrieved from https://www.dailymail.co.uk/sport/othersports/article-2673588/Chris-Froomes-secret-battle-Eight-doctors-six-clinics-four-countries-five-different-illnesses-remarkable-personal-struggle-Great-Britains-Tour-France-champion.html

Hough, D., & Heaston, W. R. (2017). The art of missing the point: FIFA and the control of corruption. In I … Kubbe & A. Engelbert (Eds.), *Corruption and norms: Why informal rules matter* (pp. 329–346). Cham: Palgrave Macmillan.

IAAF Independent Commission. (2005). *The Independent Commission report # 1 (Final report, 9 November 2015)10*. Retrieved from https://www.wada-ama.org/en/resources/world-anti-doping-program/independent-commissionreport-1

Jurejko, J., & Scriverner, P. (2014). Tour de France 2014: The 'grandest' of grand departs. Retrieved from https://www.bbc.com/sport/cycling/28188083

Labib, J, Labro, A., & Rose, J-C. (2013). *The tour: The legend of the race* (Part 1) [Motion Picture].

Law, J. (2020, 17 April). Tour De France 2020 still in doubt after team managers and health expert question plans for rescheduled race. *Forbes*. Retrieved from https://www.forbes.

com/sites/joshualaw/2020/04/17/tour-de-france-2020-still-in-doubt-after-team-managers-and-health-expert-question-plans-for-rescheduled-race/#7b87db5ea839

Leicester, J, & Pugmire, J. (2020, 18 June). Prosecutors call for jail terms as ex-IAAF chief Lamine Diack goes on trial for corruption. *The Scotsman*. Retrieved from https://www.scotsman.com/sport/prosecutors-call-jail-terms-ex-iaaf-chief-lamine-diack-goes-trial-corruption-2888809

Marty, D., Nicholson, P., & Haas, U. (2015). *Cycling Independent Reform Commission [CIRC]: Report to the president of the Union Cycliste Internationale*. Retrieved from https://www.uci.org/docs/default-source/imported-library/circreport2015_neutral.pdf?sfvrsn=7a9764d3_14

Masters, R. (2020, 17 April). Reign Coates: Extension could become life term for AOC president. *Sydney Morning Herald*. Retrieved from https://www.smh.com.au/sport/reign-coates-extension-could-become-life-term-for-aoc-president-20200417-p54ks5.html#:~:text=Coates%20will%20have%20served%2032,as%20boss%20of%20world%20swimming

McLaren Global Sports Solutions. (2020, 4 June) *Independent investigator report to the oversight and Integrity Commission of International Weightlifting Federation*. Retrieved from https://mclarenweightliftingenquiry.com/wp-content/themes/mclarenweightliftingenquiry/assets/mclaren-independent-investigator-report-iwf-final.pdf?mc_cid=e5107aee00&mc_eid=8a63af19bd

Merriam-Webster. (2020). Peloton. *Dictionary*. Merriam-Webster, Incorporated. Retrieved from https://www.merriam-webster.com/dictionary/peloton

Miller, S. (2018, 21 September). Corruption. *Encyclopedia of philosophy*. The Metaphysics Research Lab, Center for the Study of Language and Information, Stanford University. Retrieved from https://plato.stanford.edu/entries/corruption/

Moore, R.(2015, 7 December). The Hardest Road. *Esquire*. Retrieved fromhttps://www.esquire.com/uk/life/a19053974/chris-froome-interview/

Moorman, C., Zaltman, G., & Deshpande, R. (1992). Relationships between providers and users of market research: The dynamics of trust within and between organisations, *Journal of Marketing Research*, 29, 314–328.

News Wires. (2012, 22 July). Britain's Bradley Wiggins wins historic Tour de France. *France 24*. Retrieved from https://www.france24.com/en/20120722-cycling-britain-bradley-wiggins-wins-2012-tour-de-france-cavendish

Niggli, O., & Sieveking, J. (2006, February). Selected case law rendered under the World Anti-Doping Code. *Jusletter*. Retrieved from https://www.wada-ama.org/sites/default/files/resources/files/Jusletter_eng.pdf

Ordway, C. (2012, 18 October). On your bikes: Why Cycling Australia's chiefs should exit over Armstrong and White drugs revelations. *Sports Business Insider*. Retrieved from https://www.researchgate.net/publication/340477205_On_your_bikes_Why_Cycling_Australia's_chiefs_should_exit_over_Armstrong_and_White_drugs_revelations

Ordway, C. (2017, 31 August). Should a doping ban = a life sentence? The Sports Integrity Initiative. Retrieved from https://www.sportsintegrityinitiative.com/doping-ban-life-sentence/

Ordway, C., & Opie, H. (2016). Integrity and corruption in sport. In N. Schulenkorf & S. Frawley (Eds.), *Critical issues in global sport management* (pp. 60–85). Abingdon: Routledge.

Parisotto, R. (2006). *Blood sports: The inside dope on drugs in sport*. Melbourne, Australia: Hardie Grant Books.

Pickering, E. (2007, 15 November). Slipstream launch team. *Cycling Weekly*. Retrieved from https://www.cyclingweekly.com/news/latest-news/slipstream-launch-team-88041

Pielke, R.Jr. (2013, 19 February). Does uncertainty of outcome define sport? *The Least Thing*. Retrieved from http://leastthing.blogspot.com.au/2013/02/does-uncertainty-of-outcome-define-sport.html

Pope, N., Voges, K. E., & Brown, M. (2009). Winning ways: Immediate and long-term effects of sponsorship on perceptions of brand quality and corporate image. *Journal of Advertising*, 38(2), 5–20.

Press Association. (2019, 29 June). Tour de France: Ineos name Thomas and Bernal as joint team leaders. *The Guardian*. Retrieved from https://www.theguardian.com/sport/2019/jun/28/tour-de-france-ineos-name-thomas-and-bernal-as-joint-team-leaders

Pretot, J. (2012, 22 October). Lance Armstrong stripped of seven Tour de France titles: He 'deserves to be forgotten'. *The Star*. Retrieved from https://www.thestar.com/sports/2012/10/22/lance_armstrong_stripped_of_seven_tour_de_france_titles_he_deserves_to_be_forgotten.html

ProCyclingStats. (2012). 2012: 99th Tour de France (WT) General classification. Retrieved from https://www.procyclingstats.com/race/tour-de-france/2012/gc

ProCyclingStats. (2018). 2018: 105th Tour de France (WT) General classification. Retrieved from https://www.procyclingstats.com/race/tour-de-france/2018/gc

ProCyclingStats. (2019). 2019: 106th Tour de France (WT) General classification. Retrieved from https://www.procyclingstats.com/race/tour-de-france/2019//results

Quenet, J.-F. (2016, 29 September). 'Now we understand why Team Sky never joined' says MPCC doctor. *Cycling News*. Retrieved from https://www.cyclingnews.com/news/now-we-understand-why-team-sky-never-joined-says-mpcc-doctor/

Reilly, L. (2012). Introduction to the Court of Arbitration for Sport (CAS) & the role of national courts in international sports disputes: A symposium. *Journal of Dispute Resolution*, 1(5), 1–19.

Ring, P. S., & Van Den Ven, A. H. (1994). Developmental processes of cooperative interorganisational relationships. *Academy of Management Review*, 19(1), 90–118.

Roberts, S., & Burton, N. (2018). Should I stay or should I go? Managing sponsor relations through athlete transgression. *Journal of Global Sport Management*, 3(2), 170–188.

Rofe, S., & Ordway, C. (1998, 26 June). *Anti-Doping Policies* in Big Bucks in Sports Law Seminar, Continuing Legal Education Department of the College of Law, St Leonards, NSW. Retrieved from https://researchprofiles.canberra.edu.au/en/publications/anti-doping-policies

Rousseau, D. M., Sitkin, S. B., Burt, R. S., & Camerer, C. (1998). Not so different after all: A cross discipline view of trust (Introduction to special topic forum). *Academy of Management Review*, 23(3) 393–404.

Sadoff, D. A. (2016). Senegal unwilling to extradite to France former IAAF official on doping cover-up-related charges. *International Enforcement Law Reporter*, 32(2), 45–47.

Sheth, K. (2017). Countries with the most female Olympic gymnastics gold medals. *World Atlas*. Retrieved from https://www.worldatlas.com/articles/countries-with-the-most-female-olympic-gymnastic-gold-medals.html

Siekmann, R. C., Soek, J., & Bellani, A. (Eds.). (1999). *Doping rules of international sporting organisations*. Cambridge: Cambridge University Press.

Skelton, J. (2018). Sir Bradley Wiggins & Team Sky 'crossed ethical line' – doping in sport report. *BBC*. Retrieved from https://www.bbc.com/sport/cycling/43280081

Stickybottle. (2018). Pat McQuaid says British cycling moved into 'grey area' years ago. *Stickybottle*. Retrieved from www.stickybottle.com/latest-news/pat-mcquaid-british-cycling-grey-areas/

Straubel, M. (2004). Enhancing the performance of the doping court: how the court of arbitration for sport can do its job better. *Loy. U. Chi. LJ*, 36, 1203.

The Ethics Centre. (2017). Culture alignment. Sydney. Retrieved from http://aoc-cdn.s3.amazonaws.com/corporate/live/files/dmfile/Independent-Review-of-the-AOCs-workplace-culture.pdf

Theron, E., Terblanche, N., Boshoff, C., & Spyropoulou, S. (2015). The role of trust in relationship marketing in business-to-business financial services. In *Proceedings of the 2008 Academy of Marketing Science (AMS) Annual Conference* (pp. 209–213).

USADA. (2012, 10 October). Statement from USADA CEO Travis T. Tygart regarding the U.S. Postal Service Pro Cycling Team doping conspiracy. USADA Press Release. Retrieved from http://cyclinginvestigation.usada.org/

Vance, N. (2013, 15 May). Orica-Greenedge Anti-Doping Review Report. Nicki Vance Consulting. Retrieved from https://cdn-cyclingtips.pressidium.com/wp-content/uploads/2013/05/nicki-vance-report.pdf

Vaughters, J. (2012, 11 August). How to get doping out of sports. Opinion. *The New York Times*. Retrieved from https://www.nytimes.com/2012/08/12/opinion/sunday/how-to-get-doping-out-of-sports.html?_r=1&ref=opinion&pagewanted=all

WADA. (2016a). WADA confirms attack by Russian cyber espionage group. World Anti-Doping Agency. Retrieved from https://www.wada-ama.org/en/media/news/2016-09/wada-confirms-attack-by-russian-cyber-espionage-group

WADA. (2016b). WADA confirms another batch of athlete data leaked by Russian cyber hackers 'Fancy Bear'. World Anti-Doping Agency. Retrieved from https://www.wada-ama.org/en/media/news/2016-09/wada-confirms-another-batch-of-athlete-data-leaked-by-russian-cyber-hackers-fancy

WADA. (2016c). Cyber hack update: Data leak concerning 41 athletes from 13 countries and 17 sports. World Anti-Doping Agency. Retrieved from https://www.wada-ama.org/en/media/news/2016-09/cyber-hack-update-data-leak-concerning-41-athletes-from-13-countries-and-17

WADA. (2018, 11 July). WADA clarifies facts regarding UCI decision on Christopher Froome. World Anti-Doping Agency. Retrieved from https://www.wada-ama.org/en/media/news/2018-07/wada-clarifies-facts-regarding-uci-decision-on-christopher-froome

WADA. (2019, 1 June). World Anti-Doping Code 2015 (with 2019 amendments). World Anti-Doping Agency. Retrieved from https://www.wada-ama.org/en/resources/the-code/world-anti-doping-code

WADA. (2020). Athlete biological passport. World Anti-Doping Agency. Retrieved from https://www.wada-ama.org/en/athlete-biological-passport

WADA. (2020). Therapeutic use exemptions. World Anti-Doping Agency. Retrieved from https://www.wada-ama.org/en/what-we-do/science-medical/therapeutic-use-exemptions

Walker, M. U. (2001). Moral repair and its limits. *Marquette University e-Publications@Marquette*, Milwaukee, WI. 1-1-2001. Retrieved from https://epublications.marquette.edu/cgi/viewcontent.cgi?referer=&httpsredir=1&article=1151&context=phil_fac

Wang, Y., & Zhou, S. (2015). How do sports organizations use social media to build relationships? A content analysis of NBA clubs' Twitter use. *International Journal of Sport Communication*, 8(2), 133–148.

Williams, R. (2012, 18 July). Tour de France: Mark Cavendish puts yellow jersey before green glory. *The Guardian*. Retrieved from https://amp.theguardian.com/sport/2012/jul/17/tour-de-france-mark-cavendish

Williams, J., & Chinn, S. J. (2010). Meeting relationship-marketing goals through social media: A conceptual model for sport marketers. *International Journal of Sport Communication*, 3(4), 422–437.

Wilson, B. (2015, 18 May). FIFA World Cup sponsors urged to speak out over Qatar. *BBC*. Retrieved from https://www.bbc.com/news/business-32777320

Woodland, L. (2007). *Yellow jersey guide to the Tour de France*. London: Yellow Jersey.

Wright, C. (2018, 2 October). The dominance of the USA basketball women's national team is more than a 100–1 record. *Swishappeal.com*. Retrieved from https://www.swishappeal.com/2018/10/2/17926696/usa-basketball-womens-national-team-dominant-at-fiba-world-cup

Wynn, N. (2012, 18 October). Team Sky riders and staff must sign anti-doping policy. *Cycling Weekly*. Retrieved from https://www.cyclingweekly.com/news/team-sky-riders-and-staff-must-sign-anti-doping-policy-37869

Zimbardo, P. (2007). *The Lucifer effect: Understanding how good people turn evil*. New York: Random House Publishing.

Zurloni, V., Diana, B., Cavalera, C., Argenton, L., Elia, M., & Mantovani, F. (2015). Deceptive behavior in doping related interviews: The case of Lance Armstrong. *Psychology of Sport and Exercise*, 16 (2015), 191–200.

Part II

National responses

7 Integrity and corruption in sport

Lessons from Japan and match-fixing in *sumo*

Matt Nichol, Elisa Solomon and Keiji Kawai

Introduction

Corruption can be constructed broadly to include a range of behaviours in the public and private spheres. Traditionally, corruption was viewed as involving a legal offence that was linked to economics. Yet corruption does not always involve law and economics and therefore Miller extends the concept to include morality (Miller, 2018, p. 5). In the domain of sport, corruption can similarly be constructed as involving a mix of a breach of law, economics and morals, depending on the corrupt behaviour. Corruption in sport is now frequently framed as 'integrity' and the maintenance of a sport's integrity allows fans to rely on the uncertainty of the outcome of a sporting contest that was played according to the game's rules (Ordway & Opie, 2016, p. 40). A long-standing threat to integrity in sport is match-fixing (see Higgins, 2018) in that it corrupts the two key assumptions essential to sport: uncertainty and participants trying to win. Match-fixing generally takes three forms: attempting to alter the outcome of a sporting contest for financial gain resulting from betting, strategically losing (for example, to secure promotion, prevent relegation or to obtain future draft picks) and the 'spot-fixing' of events within a game (Higgins, 2018, pp. 124–5).

Match-fixing has had a historical presence in professional *sumo* in Japan. The most recent research into *sumo* tournaments in 2013 concluded that fixing was problematic in the two highest divisions: *makuuchi* ('grand sumo') and *jûryô* (Hori & Iwamoto, 2013). Known as *sekitori*, these two divisions comprise the highest pay and status in *sumo* and thus provide the greatest incentive to fix. Match-fixing in *sumo* can be categorised as strategic losing as it occurs at the end of a tournament in order to give a *rikishi* ('wrestler') a winning record, in turn avoiding demotion from *makuuchi* to *jûryô* or from *jûryô* to lower divisions. While fixing in many other sports is connected to gambling (Tak, 2018, p. 789), Kawai observes that in *sumo* the practice exists independent of gambling (which is generally prohibited in sport by Japan's Criminal Code) and has a long cultural significance (Kawai, 2018, p. 49).

When corruption in sport occurs, as was the case in *sumo* in 2011 after an investigation by the *Nihon Sumô Kyôkai* ('Japan Sumo Association') officially recognised match-fixing in *sumo* for the first time, there was a significant breakdown in trust between professional *sumo*, fans and the public. Trust between wrestlers was not affected as match-fixing was widely accepted inside *sumo* at the time. According to Walker, responses to corrupt misconduct typically focus on blame and punishment through penalties that provide retribution, deterrence or rehabilitation. Restoring trust after corruption also involves what Walker described as 'moral repair', where responsibility is placed on the participants in the corruption through restorative justice (Walker, 2001, pp. 114–15). This chapter will examine match-fixing in *sumo* and how trust was restored after the fixing scandal in 2011.

This chapter is divided into three parts. Part A begins by providing an overview of the structure and governance of professional *sumo* in order to allow the reader to understand the conditions that give rise to match-fixing. Next, Part B will explore the phenomenon of match-fixing in *sumo*. This chapter will conclude by examining the impact of the match-fixing in *sumo* in 2011 on trust, the measures the Japan Sumo Association took to restore trust and the role that *sumo* stables and the wrestlers could have played in the process of restorative justice.

A What is professional *sumo*?

Overview of sumo

Sumo has a 2,000-year history that is connected to the *shinto* religion, agrarian rites, the Imperial family, and during feudalism, was training for *samurai*. Modern *sumo* can be traced to the late 18th century and it is now considered Japan's national sport. The cultural significance of *sumo* is demonstrated by its description as *kokugi* ('national skill' or 'national technique'), which differentiates it from other martial arts and sports (Gilbert & Watts, 2014, p. 159). Due to the cultural, religious and historical importance of *sumo*, many Japanese do not see *sumo* in terms of the western concept of sport but instead view *sumo* as *dentô bunka* ('traditional culture') or a religious 'service' or 'performance'.

Sumo can be distinguished from most other sports due to the role of *shinto* customs and culture on the operation of a tournament and the conduct of individual bouts. A bout begins when an announcer calls the names of the two *rikishi*, a process that is repeated when they enter the *dohyo* ('ring') that is 4.5 metres in diameter. Prior to the bout, wrestlers perform a number of rituals, including lifting and stamping their feet to banish evil spirits, rinsing their mouth with water for strength, throwing salt to purify the ring and clapping their hands to demonstrate they possess no weapons. At the end of the bout the *gyôji* ('referee') points to the winner and states his name. After bowing to each other, the losing wrestler exits the ring. The winner then squats, makes a slicing hand gesture to thank the three gods of creation and receives an envelope of prize money (donated by a wrestler's sponsors) from the referee. Historically, women have been excluded from professional *sumo*. Women are prohibited from entering a ring, let alone competing as a professional wrestler.

Once the customs are completed, a *sumo* bout begins when the two wrestlers meet at the *shikari-sen* (two white lines in the middle of the *dohyo*) and perform the *tachiai* ('initial charge'). Most bouts last five to ten seconds but can sometimes take up to several minutes. To win a contest, a wrestler must either force his opponent out of the ring or to touch the ground with anything other than the sole of his foot by using one of the 82 official *kimarite* ('winning technique'). Bouts are sometimes decided if a *rikishi* uses one of the five 'non-techniques' or ways to lose, for example, slipping over. *Kimarite* techniques are categorised as pushing, thrusting, throwing or grappling (using an opponent's *mawashi* ('belt')). *Rikishi* tend to specialise in either pushing/thrusting or grappling but nearly half of all bouts are won by *yorikiri* (frontal force-out) or *oshidashi* (frontal push-out). Wrestlers are occasionally disqualified for using a 'prohibited technique', which include kicking or pulling an opponent's hair. While the importance of power to the *kimarite* is reflected in the average weight of a *sekitori* wrestler being approximately 160 kilograms (a few *rikishi* weigh less and some even up to or over 200 kilograms), *rikishi* are strong, surprisingly agile and can move quickly considering their size.

The structure of professional sumo

Professional *rikishi* compete in one of six hierarchically structured divisions. The highest division is *makuuchi*, followed in descending order by *jûryô*, *makushita*, *sandanme*, *jonidan* and *jonokuchi*. Most wrestlers begin their career in *maezum* ('pre-*sumo*') and gain automatic promotion to *jonokuchi* after one tournament. A wrestler must then obtain a *kachi koshi* ('winning record') in a tournament to maintain their rank, gain promotion and avoid demotion. There are six *honbasho* ('tournament') each year and the *banzuke* (official rankings) are released prior to the 15-day tournament. The number of bouts varies in the lower divisions but *rikishi* in *makuuchi* and *jûryô* compete each day. The wrestler with the most wins is the tournament champion and a tie results in a 'play-off' for the championship.

Most of the over 600 professional wrestlers do not progress past *makushita*. *Makuuchi* only had 43 wrestlers in March 2020. *Makuuchi* comprises five ranks: the highest rank is *yokozuna*, followed by *ozeki, sekiwake, komusubi* and *maegashira*. *Ozeki, sekiwake* and *komusubi* are collectively called *san-yaku* ('the three ranks') and most professional wrestlers aspire to this rank due to the associated status. At the spring tournament in March 2020, the division of *makuuchi* wrestlers into the traditional east and west camps consisted of two *yokozuna*, one *ozeki* for the first time since 1982, two *komusubi*, two *sekiwake* and 35 *maegashira* (ranked one to 18) (Japan Sumo Association, 2020). Except *yokozuna*, demotion applies to all other ranks and divisions. A wrestler receives the title of *yokozuna* for life, is required to retire if he performs poorly over several tournaments and cannot obtain a losing record in a *honbasho*. Consequently, *yokozuna* who incur several defeats early in a tournament frequently retire due to 'injury', a practice that may challenge the integrity of *sumo*. The Japan Sumo Association provides information in English on a *rikishi*'s recent *kimarite* ('winning technique'), tournament record, stable and other personal information (Japan Sumo Association, 2020 Find Rikishi – Banzuke).

The majority of professional *rikishi* are Japanese who are recruited from the amateur ranks of high school and university, though there have been a small but growing number of foreign *rikishi* since the 1990s (the first foreigners entered professional *sumo* in the 1960s) and the rank of *yokozuna* in recent years has been dominated by Mongolian *rikishi*. Wrestlers live and train in a *sumo heya* ('stable'), where the *oyakata* ('stable master') is an 'elder': a retired wrestler who either competed in at least 20 *jûryô* tournaments or one *makuuchi* tournament. The 48 stables vary in size from three or four wrestlers up to 40 *rikishi*. West described the stable as being similar to both a family home and paramilitary organisation (West, 1997, pp. 170–1). While no experience in *sumo* is needed to enter a *heya*, wrestlers must be between the ages of 15 and 23 years, have a height of at least 167 centimetres and weigh a minimum of 67 kilograms. The stable master gives a wrestler his '*sumo* name' and provides coaching in gruelling daily training sessions. A wrestler can leave the stable at any time but cannot return to *sumo*. Stables are hierarchically structured based on rank. Unlike individual sports such as tennis where players have the same coach, wrestlers from the same stable do not compete against one another in a tournament.

The status of sekitori *wrestlers*

The *makuuchi* and *jûryô* divisions represent the pinnacle of *sumo* and while these ranks involve greater financial compensation than the lower divisions, more importantly, they attract much higher status in *sumo* and Japanese society and involve various benefits. Prestige attaches to *sekitori* ranks and *rikishi* receive a number of associated benefits, including wearing a coloured *mawashi*, sporting the *ôichô* hair style, living in their own quarters in a stable and having private attendants (lower ranked wrestlers in their stable). In contrast, wrestlers in the other divisions wear their hair in the *chonmage* style, share rooms in the stable, prepare the meals for higher ranked *rikishi* and perform daily chores.

Promotion to *jûryô* is also notable as these wrestlers begin to earn a salary. In *makuuchi* wrestlers earn monthly wages ranging from approximately 1.1 million yen (AUD 15,714 based on an exchange rate of 70 yen for AUD 1.00) for *maegashira* to approximately 3 million yen (AUD 42,857) for *yokozuna*. Also, *rikishi* receive bonuses from sponsors for winning a bout, prize money of approximately 10 million yen (AUD 142,857) for winning a *makuuchi* tournament and approximately 2 million yen (AUD 28,571) for a *jûryô* tournament, tournament awards of approximately 2 million yen for outstanding performance, fighting spirit and technique and annual performance bonuses. As will now be seen, these factors collectively create motivation for some wrestlers (and their stables) to fix matches in order to preserve their rank.

B Match-fixing in *sumo*

Match-fixing and ninjô zumô

Intentionally losing in *sumo* to prevent a wrestler incurring a losing record is known as *ninjô zumô* ('compassionate *sumo*'), a term that differentiates match-fixing in *sumo* from the negative descriptions often associated with fixing in sport. Kawai notes that while *ninjô zumô* was rarely referred to within *sumo*, it was known to exist as early as during the *Edo* period (1603–1868). Until recently match-fixing was widely accepted by fans and the public. Wrestlers have even on occasion received ovations for such conduct. Kawai argues that this acceptance was based on *sumo* not being seen as a sport in Japan but as traditional culture that accepted fixing if both wrestlers agree to the outcome (Kawai, 2018, p. 50).

Incentives to fix sumo

Financial incentives typically play a role in an athlete's decision to match-fix (McLaren, 2011, p. 565), particularly when they are paid poorly and have limited financial security (Higgins, 2018, p. 125). However, money is only part of the reason why a *sumo* bout may be fixed. The root of the problem in *sumo* are the promotion rules. Two *makuuchi* wrestlers may agree to fix a match in order for a wrestler to avoid a losing tournament record and potential demotion to *jûryô*. The incentive to deliberately lose a bout arises in the final days of a tournament for wrestlers who face a losing record (Duggan & Levitt, 2002, p. 1595). *Rikishi* who achieve a winning or losing record before the final day of the tournament may be prepared to lose by wrestling with less energy for the remainder of the tournament as their promotion or demotion has been secured (West, 1997, p. 171). Fixing may also result from concerns over suffering injury during a tournament (Kawai, 2018, pp. 50–1). In exchange for losing a bout, a wrestler may 'trade' for a win in the next tournament against the fixer, receive financial compensation or both (Duggan & Levitt, 2002, pp. 1602–03). Kawai estimates payment to fixers are approximately 2,000 yen (AUD 30) per bout (Kawai, 2018, p. 51).

The decision to trade wins or receive financial compensation varies among the divisions and ranks. Hori and Iwamoto's research in 2013 concluded that the incentives for fixing is most prominent in *sekitori*, specifically *jûryô* and the rank of *maegashira* in *makuuchi*. For these wrestlers the monetary value of a win is considerable and they can also win a number of special cash prizes. As *rikishi* who are *san yaku* and *yokozuna* tend to face the lower ranked *maegashira* wrestlers, there is less likelihood of these *rikishi* losing future bouts, so they generally 'buy' a win rather than trading for one. Fixing for *jûryô* and *maegashira* wrestlers tends to involve trading for a future win as the ranking value associated with an eighth win is higher than the other *makuuchi* ranks and the chances of winning a 'truly fought' bout against a marquee wrestler are low. In contrast, Hori and Iwamoto found that fixing for trainee wrestlers at or below *makushita* is rare due to the absence of incentives. Prize money at these levels is minimal and wrestlers cannot afford to pay for wins as they earn stipends and not a salary. Low ranked wrestlers frequently move divisions and therefore may not face the other fixer at the next tournament to trade wins. Another factor is that on the last day of tournaments in *makushita* and lower divisions, *rikishi* compete against wrestlers with *aiboshi* ('identical records') (Hori & Iwamoto, 2013, pp. 7–10), so fixing is not an option.

Institutional support of match-fixing

The custom of match-fixing in *sumo* may be the product of its governance and institutionalism. Professional *sumo* is governed by the Japan Sumo Association, whose 1,200 members are composed of elders, wrestlers, hairdressers, announcers, referees and clerical workers. Important decisions are made by the holders of the 105 shares of elder stock, who are retired wrestlers that were *sekitori*. The Association's membership has 48 stables, half of which are located in Tokyo within two kilometres of the *Ryogoku Kokugikan*, the 'home' of *sumo*. The other stables are in various prefectures. Ownership of a stable is limited to elders. In contrast to professional sports leagues, *sumo* is therefore owned and managed by former athletes, who govern what West described as a 'secret world'. This world is predominantly regulated by informal rules and norms that promote group welfare and wealth maximisation (West, 1997, pp. 165–9, 176).

The closed institutional and cultural nature of *sumo* may accept and facilitate match-fixing as these practices were embedded in the elders during their wrestling careers. Within the governance of *sumo*, fixing is not subjected to scrutiny by 'outsiders', in turn creating a regulatory environment where match-rigging is likely to be organised by stables and endorsed by the elders' control of the Japan Sumo Association. Stables benefit from having high ranked wrestlers and are divided into five affiliated camps. Some stables even enter reciprocal agreements to fix bouts between their wrestlers (Duggan & Levitt, 2002, p. 1599), a practice that is likely to occur among stables within a camp due to the strong social relationships within a camp that is the product of a retired wrestler requiring permission from his stable master to open a new stable (Dietl et al., 2010, p. 391).

Allegations of match-fixing

Match-fixing in *sumo* began to gain public attention in the 1990s. Unlike sports where gambling is legal and leagues work with betting agencies to identify 'suspicious' or anomalous bets that may be connected to fixing, evidence of match-fixing in *sumo* can largely be ascertained from statistical analysis of the public results of tournaments. In 1996 West reviewed the results of 12 tournaments in 1994 and 1995 and found that 82.8% of wrestlers with a 7–7 record (excluding bouts between wrestlers with a 7–7 record) won their match on the final day of the tournament (West 1997, p. 172). Such a high percentage does not reflect the probable results between two wrestlers exerting the effort of a competitive bout.

After three retired *rikishi* made allegations of fixing in 1996, 1999 and 2000, Duggan and Levitt in 2002 reviewed the results of 32,000 *sumo* bouts between 1989 and 2000 that involved 281 wrestlers. Duggan and Levitt concluded that match-fixing was prevalent due to the disproportionate number of wrestlers who finished with eight wins on the final four days of a tournament (Duggan & Levitt, 2002). Then, in 2008, the Shûkan Gendai weekly magazine published an article on match-fixing in *sumo*, as did the Shûkan Post, who also named a number of retired wrestlers alleged to have participated in fixing. As is its usual practice in such circumstances, the Japan Sumo Association denied the allegations and a number of its members successfully sued the media for defamation (Kawai, 2018, pp. 50–1). Duggan and Levitt's findings were confirmed by Dietl et al. in 2010, whose analysis of *sumo* tournaments from 1995 to 2006 found that the abnormalities in the winning probabilities of wrestlers with a 7–7 record disappeared between March 2000 and May 2003, only to resurface from July 2003 to November 2006. Dietl et al. attributed the temporary decline in match-fixing to the increased public scrutiny resulting from earlier allegations of fixing (Dietl et al., 2010, pp. 384–5, 393).

Official recognition of match-fixing in sumo *in 2011*

A Japanese police investigation into illegal gambling in professional baseball in 2011 led to the police obtaining evidence of match-fixing in *sumo* from the mobile phones of coaches, trainers, match organisers and some *rikishi* (Humphreys & Watanabe, 2015, p. 12). A subsequent inquiry by the Japan Sumo Association concluded that a number of bouts were lost to prevent *rikishi* from being demoted to *jûryô*. This case was the Association's first official recognition of *kôi ni yoru mukiyokuzumô* ('intentionally lethargic bout') for the purpose of fixing and in response a journalist from the Shûkan Gendai initiated a lawsuit to recover 10 million yen (AUD 142,857) from the Japan Sumo Association as compensation for the wrongful defamation action. However, as no court decision is available it is likely that the action was settled.

Of the 23 people identified as involved in the fixing, the Japan Sumo Association forced the retirement of 19 active wrestlers (a number denied wrongdoing and some initiated legal action), one stable master was required to retire and three wrestlers and stable masters were suspended from tournaments for two years. By stating that match-fixing was a new problem and the culprits were only ranked *maegashira* (and not the more prestigious higher ranks) (Hori & Iwamoto, 2013, pp. 13–14), the Japan Sumo Association attempted to diminish the extent of the fixing, perhaps to minimise the damage in the public's trust. Yet wrestlers ranked *komusubi* and higher may have engaged in fixing earlier in their careers. Also, denying the history of match-fixing may have caused greater damage to the public's trust as earlier action against the practice of fixing could have prevented the 2011 scandal.

C Restoring trust in *sumo* after the 2011 match-fixing scandal

The impact of the 2011 match-fixing scandal on trust

At the time the match-fixing scandal broke in 2011, it was described in the media as a 'massive betrayal of trust' (see e.g. Johnson, 2011). The scale of this breach of trust was because match-fixing attacks the heart of professional *sumo*: performance-based rank. *Sumo* fans, the public and sponsors believed that wrestlers had earned their rank through hard work, training, rising through the pyramid of divisions and consistent high level performance. That this assumption was violated struck the ethics and morals of *rikishi* in *makuuchi*, and perhaps, is a reason why public tolerance for match-fixing in *sumo* has since declined. Another factor shifting public support for *ninjô zumô* may be that *sumo* fans were influenced by the recent rise in the importance of integrity and anti-corruption measures in western professional sports in Japan.

The breakdown in trust between *sumo* and the public was also the product of the Japan Sumo Association. Despite claims by several retired wrestlers and independent statistical analysis of tournament results, the Association always vehemently denied previous allegations of match-fixing. Proof of fixing in 2011 was likely to have had a greater negative impact on trust as the public and other stakeholders such as the Japanese government may have believed that the Association could have stopped the institutional practice of fixing earlier. The breach of trust between the *rikishi*, stables, elders, the Association and the public can be differentiated from the relationships of trust between *rikishi* and stables that facilitated the match-fixing, as the later relationships are governed by the secretive system of *sumo*'s self-regulation that requires strict adherence to its' customs, traditions and practices.

The Japan Sumo Association and restoring trust

Chairman Hanregoma of the Japan Sumo Association in 2011 called the fixing 'the darkest chapter' in *sumo* (The Japan Times, 2011). A strong response was required to restore trust with fans, the broader public, sponsors and government. In addition to the ritual bowing and apologies from senior administrators that is created by revelations of corporate wrongdoing in Japan, the exclusion of 19 wrestlers and a stable master from *sumo* helped to restore trust through Walker's 'restorative justice' in several ways. First, the fixers (or the majority of them) were effectively banned from *sumo*, in turn, decreasing the prospect of future fixing. Second, the penalty of forced retirement acted as a strong deterrent for current and future wrestlers. Retirement in *sumo* marks a key moment in the career and life of a *rikishi*. It involves a special ceremony, where the wrestler's traditional 'top-knot' hair style is cut, formally ending his life as a *rikishi*. This penalty was therefore a severe punishment that carried with it the indignity of not retiring at the natural conclusion of one's career. Third, stable masters were held accountable for match-fixing and strongly disincentivised to allow, encourage or facilitate future fixing.

The other key way the Japan Sumo Association attempted to restore trust was to cancel the spring tournament in 2011 (Humphreys & Watanabe, 2015, p. 13). A *honbasho* is rarely cancelled. Even during World War II, a *sumo* tournament proceeded in June 1945 after aerial bombing in Tokyo. The 2011 tournament was the first tournament cancelled since 1946 (Gunning, 2019). Calling off the spring tournament was central to restoring trust as the technical examination of wrestlers which determines rankings recommenced at the next tournament in May 2011. However, commercial interests may have also contributed to the Association's decision, as NHK and Fuji TV were believed to have been unlikely to broadcast the spring tournament (Gunning, 2019). Interestingly, the Japanese government did intervene in the self-regulation of *sumo* in response to the outbreak of the coronavirus in Japan in early 2020. The Japan Sports Agency requested the Japan Sumo Association consider cancelling or rescheduling the spring tournament in March in Osaka. Despite the financial implications of a sold out tournament that was expected to attract over 7,000 spectators a day, an extraordinary meeting of the directors of the Association decided to close the spring *honbasho* to the public for the first time. This decision was taken, in part, due to the difficulties in relocating or rescheduling a tournament and the significance of cancelling a tournament (The Japan Times, March, 2020). However, the severity of the coronavirus pandemic forced the Japan Sumo Association to take the historic step of cancelling the summer tournament in May 2020, and the July tournament was moved from Nagoya to Tokyo to reduce the travel required by the majority of Tokyo-based stables (The Japan Times, May, 2020).

Punishing the people involved in the match-fixing and deterring others from engaging in similar conduct is only part of the process of restoring trust. External stakeholders in *sumo* needed to be assured that the prospect of future fixing was minimised. To achieve this aim, Miller identifies the need for an anti-corruption or integrity system that both promotes ethical behaviour and decreases the risk of institutional corruption (Miller, 2018, p. 38). Higgins recognises that such systems in sport involving match-fixing focus on deterrence, prevention, detection and prosecution (Higgins, 2018, p. 126), which also form part of Walker's restorative justice. The forced retirements of a number of *rikishi* achieved the aim of deterrence (and to some degree prevention). Preventing match-fixing was primarily achieved through the prohibition on wrestlers using mobile phones during tournaments and banning attendants from entering dressing rooms at a *honbasho* (Kawai, 2018, pp. 50–1). It should be noted that the Association did not implement any methods for the detection of match-fixing, a significantly more difficult task than in sports where betting is legal and monitored. While these preventative measures may make fixing more difficult, several other approaches were not adopted by the Association.

Integrity systems in sport commonly involve athlete education (Higgins, 2018, p. 126). The Japan Sumo Association needed to introduce ethics training for new *sumo* and implement a code of conduct for wrestlers and stable masters. While ethics training and codes of conduct are useful tools to prevent match-fixing in the long-term, the best method to quickly restore trust was to ensure there was little risk of future fixing. A possible solution stated by West in 1997 was reforming the promotion rules to remove the incentive to fix by replacing the decision to demote a wrestler based on a tournament win/loss record with an overall win/loss record (West 1997, p. 172). West recognised the resistance to such a major reform from within *sumo* and by its fans, and nearly 30 years later, no such reform has been suggested by the Association. Perhaps a more acceptable reform for elders and wrestlers would be to reduce the ranking value of an 8–7 tournament result, a change that would largely remove the incentive to fix.

Stable masters and restoring trust

A stable is the centre of the life of a *rikishi*. Based on the limited literature and media reports, it appears that *heya* had little role in restoring trust following the 2011 fixing scandal. This is not surprising given the closed nature of professional *sumo* and the traditional role of elders as stable masters. Due to the close familial relationship between stable master and wrestler, the strict control exercised by the master over conduct within the stable, the status of elders in *sumo* and the long-standing relationships between many stable masters, it is clear that stable masters have the most influence in preventing, discouraging and punishing match-fixing. While stable masters have some self-interest in their wrestlers fixing bouts to maintain rank and thereby enhance the reputation and status of the stable, match-fixing scandals involving a stable's *rikishi* are now likely to damage the stable's public standing and may result in less financial assistance from supporter groups who help fund the cost of operating a stable. The stable master even faces the prospect of being banished from *sumo*. Stables that formally ban fixing are not likely to see *rikishi* break the strong relationship with his master by fixing matches without the stable's endorsement and if there is no benefit to the stable.

The Wrestler's Association and restoring trust

Trust after the match-fixing scandal could have been restored by the wrestlers themselves. The *rikishi-kai* is the Wrestler's Association, which holds annual meetings, lobbies for improved working conditions and makes proposals that will benefit *sumo* to the Association. Members agreeing to not fix bouts falls into both activities. While it is clear that a public announcement of an agreement among *rikishi-kai* members not to fix would have assisted in restoring trust, a number of factors prevented such action. An obvious barrier was the collective self-interest of wrestlers, any one of whom may need an opponent to lose to prevent demotion. Also, wrestlers may have been reluctant to depart from customary practices as culture and tradition occupy such a prominent position in all aspects of *sumo*. Perhaps the biggest obstacle was the status and position of elders. Due to match-fixing in *sumo* being an embedded cultural and institutional practice, its prohibition is likely to require the approval of elders. Even if wrestlers decided to stop fixing bouts, they may have been overruled by the custodians of *sumo*, the elders.

Conclusion

It is nearly ten years since match-fixing officially surfaced from the secretive shadows of *sumo*. The resulting breakdown in trust between *sumo* and fans, the public and sponsors was significant at the time but the question that arises is whether *sumo*'s key stakeholders were able to restore trust? In the years immediately after the scandal, Hori and Iwamoto's analysis of bouts between 2011 and 2013 found that match-fixing involving *jûryô* and *maegashira* had stopped (Hori & Iwamoto, 2013, p. 13). However, the absence of fixing during this time may have been due to the increased public scrutiny arising from the 2011 scandal, as Dietl et al. identified occurred in the early 2000s after allegations of fixing, only for the fixing to return. It is unclear whether this trend repeated itself as there has been no statistical analysis of tournaments since Hori & Iwamoto's, 2013 research, nor have there been any recent whistleblowers. Johnson argued that the insular nature of professional *sumo* necessitated that effective reform needed to emanate from external regulatory actors, such as government, a more critical media and fans (Johnson, 2011). Yet these regulators did little to eradicate *sumo*'s institutional match-fixing. The restoration of trust was primarily achieved through punishing the wrestlers and stable masters, penalties that may have had a lasting deterrence effect that led to fixing now being less prevalent. But wrestlers may equally be acutely aware that fixing can be identified by members of the public with the skills to statistically analyse the results of tournaments. Some may point to *sumo*'s popularity in 2020 as evidence of the restoration of trust between *sumo* and the public. Yet trust may not have been completely restored. Some Japanese attribute the recent increase in wrestlers withdrawing during a tournament due to injury to the absence of fixing, not as some commentators argue, due to injury associated with bigger and stronger wrestlers and higher workloads (see Gunning, 2017). The public's trust in *sumo* may have forever been damaged by the events of 2011. Match-fixing was one of the embedded cultural practices in *sumo* that was for a long time accepted by *rikishi*, stable masters and the governing body, and tolerated by the public. A key lesson from the 2011 *sumo* match-fixing scandal for other sports, countries and governments is that integrity standards in sport and the community in general are not stagnant and that corrupt practices that may be accepted within a sport may be repugnant to the standards and expectations of governments and the public.

Questions

i *Trust loss* – In whom (or, in which group) has trust been lost in this case?
ii *Trust correction* – How, if attempted, has the restoration of trust been tried?; and;
iii *Lessons learned* – How could the lessons from this case be applied to other sports, nations, states, other districts for the same sport, or other sports to prevent a further loss of trust or at least to restore trust?

References

Dietl, H. M., Lang, M., & Werner, S. (2010). Corruption in professional sumo: An update on the study of Duggan and Levitt. *Journal of Sports Economics*, 11(4), 383–396.

Duggan, M., & Levitt, S. D. (2002). Winning isn't everything: Corruption in sumo wrestling. *The American Economic Review*, 92(5), 1594–1605.

Gardiner, S., Parry, J., & Robinson, S. (2016). Integrity and the corruption debate in sport: Where is the integrity?. *European Sport Management Quarterly*, 1–18.

Gilbert, H., & Watts, K. (2014). Internationalising sumo: From viewing to doing Japan's national sport. In J. Breaden, S. Steele, & C. Stevens (Eds.), *Internationalising Japan: Discourse and practice* (pp. 158–179). Abingdon: Routledge.

Gunning, J. (2017, 1 November). Sumo needs to tackle rising cause of injury. *The Japan Times.* Retrieved from https://www.japantimes.co.jp/sports/2017/11/01/sumo/sumo-needs-tackle-cause-rising-injuries/#.XiT2iS9L3Jw

Gunning, J. (2019, 20 May). Sumo 101: Cancellations. *The Japan Times.* Retrieved from https://www.japantimes.co.jp/sports/2019/05/20/sumo/sumo-101-cancellations/#.XiTg8S9L3Jw

Gunning, J. (2017, 1 November). Sumo needs to tackle rising cause of injury. *The Japan Times.* Retrieved from https://www.japantimes.co.jp/sports/2017/11/01/sumo/sumo-needs-tackle-cause-rising-injuries/#.XiT2iS9L3Jw

Higgins, M. (2018).Match-fixing: A historical perspective. *The International Journal of the History of Sport*, 35(2–3), 123–140.

Hori, M., & Iwamoto, K. (2013). Match-rigging in professional sumo: Elucidation of incentive structures and empirical analysis. Hitotsubashi University Repository. Retrieved from http://hdl.handle.net/10086/25431

Humphreys, B., & Watanabe, N. M. (2015). The history and formation of East Asian sports leagues. In Y. H. Lee & R. Fort (Eds.), *The sports business in the Pacific rim* (pp. 3–24). Switzerland: Springer International Publishing.

Japan Sumo Association. (English). (2020). March grand sumo tournament Banzuke. Retrieved from www.sumo.or.jp

Japan Sumo Association. (English). (2020). Find Rikishi – Banzuke. Retrieved from www.sumo.or.jp/EnSumoDataRikishi/search/search

Johnson, D. D. (2011, 17 February). Sumo will change or die. *The Japan Times.* Retrieved from https://www.japantimes.co.jp/opinion/2011/02/17/commentary/world-commentary/sumo-will-change-or-die/#.XhZcti9L1cA

Kawai, K. (2018). Match-fixing and illegal gambling in Japan: Cultural interpretations of integrity. In J. Breaden, S. Steele, & C. Stevens (Eds.), *Internationalising Japan: Discourse and practice* (pp. 43–58). Abingdon and New York: Routledge.

McLaren, R. H. (2011). Is sport losing its integrity?. *Marquette Sports Law Review*, 21(2), 551–573.

Miller, S. (2018, 21 September). *Encyclopedia of philosophy.* The Metaphysics Research Lab, Center for the Study of Language and Information, Stanford University. Retrieved from https://plato.stanford.edu/entries/corruption/

Ordway, C., & Opie, H. (2016). Integrity and corruption in sport. In N. Schulenkorf & S. Frawley (Eds.), *Critical issues in global sport management* (pp. 38–63). London and New York: Routledge.

Tak, M. (2018). Too big to jail: Match-fixing, institutional failure and the shifting of responsibility. *International review for the Sociology of Sport*, 53(7), 788–806.

The Japan Times. (2020, 4 May). Coronavirus forces cancellation of summer Grand Sumo Tournament. Retrieved from https://www.japantimes.co.jp/sports/2020/05/04/sumo/summer-grand-sumo-tournament-canceled-coronavirus/#.Xryr9FIzZao

The Japan Times. (2020, 1 March). Spring Basho to be held behind closed doors for the first time. Retrieved from https://www.japantimes.co.jp/sports/2020/03/01/sumo/spring-basho-sumo-coronavirus/#.XmA_LVIzZao

The Japan Times. (2011, 8 February). Sumo world reacts to canceled tourney. Retrieved from https://www.japantimes.co.jp/news/2011/02/08/national/sumo-world-reacts-to-canceled-tourney/#.XiTmkS9L3Jw

Walker, M. U. (2001). Moral repair and its limits. Marquette University e-Publications@Marquette, 1–1-2001. Retrieved from https://epublications.marquette.edu/cgi/viewcontent.cgi?referer=&httpsredir=1&article=1151&context=phil_fac

West, M. D. (1997). Legal rules and social norms in Japan's secret world of Sumo. *Journal of Legal Studies*, 26, 165–201.

8 Whistleblowing platforms as a solution to fight corruption

A model from the Czech Republic

Apolena Ondráčková and Pim Verschuuren

Introduction

Through the example of a strategic initiative taken at a national level, this chapter outlines how the implementation of whistleblowing and compliance processes can contribute to restoring trust and protect sports integrity. It entails the involvement of external, neutral and trustworthy actors to assist official sport authorities and/or individual clubs. The chapter will also define what are whistleblowing or reporting mechanisms, and how they were imported from the corporate and business sectors in sports organisations. It will conclude with concrete recommendations to consider and adapt such solutions in other national or international sport contexts.

The original scandal

Ice hockey is amongst the most popular sports in the Czech Republic in terms of supporters (fans) and active players.[1] As a result, the Czech Ice Hockey Federation benefits from a broad membership base. This popularity then attracts significant financial support from numerous public and private resources, including donations/grants from the Czech Ministry of Education, Youth and Sport, from municipalities and from companies through sponsorship. In connection with this growing financial support, ice hockey in the Czech Republic has, over the past several years, professionalised and partially transformed into a business, with a considerable tangible and intangible asset.

The level of financial support for a club is directly linked to, and dependent on, the on-field success of the team, and consequently on the performance of individual players. The internal and external pressure for results creates a heightened risk environment for malpractice by various stakeholders, including parents or coaches. One of the largest and most successful ice hockey clubs in the Czech Republic, Hockey Club Slavia Praha (Club), demonstrated the level of risk in 2015. Mr Vladimír Růžička, who was a former Czech ice hockey representative (medallist from the 1998 Nagano Winter Olympic Games), a former coach of the Czech Ice Hockey National team and one of the main coaches and general manager of Slavia Praha, was recorded accepting a 'sponsorship' totalling 400,000 Czech crowns (approx. US$17,500). Paid by players' parents, it was understood that the money was intended to support the functioning of the club (ČT sport, 2015). According to the testimonies provided by parents involved, Růžička demanded not only that the athletes had to meet performance criteria but also 'show their loyalty' to the club in the form of a 'sponsorship'. Initially, Růžička was charged by law enforcement authorities with the criminal offence of accepting a bribe. However, these charges were later reclassified, as it could not be proven that the 'sponsorship' was intended as a bribe. Instead, Růžička was found guilty of the criminal offence of embezzlement as he did not pass the funds collected onto the club as promised.

The case study described above severely undermined the credibility of the national ice hockey framework, and it can be expected, the trust in the federation as well as the clubs, officials and coaches. This led to a twofold discussion within the Czech Republic: to what extent did the financial background of some players provide a 'golden ticket' to a successful ice hockey career ahead of more deserving players, and, more generally, whether minimal standards of ethics should be imposed within the sport to overcome malpractice and restore trust.

The case also highlights the vulnerability of athletes when they become victims of, or witnesses to, corruption within their sport environment, especially when ethical guidelines or reporting mechanisms are absent or unenforced. Athletes who find themselves in a reportable situation need to be assured that, before they decide to step forward, they do not have to fear (i) retaliation measures; (ii) that their report will not be properly investigated; or (iii) disclosure of their identity. These fears are heightened in a sport environment often characterised by close, interwoven personal and professional relationships. Without such guarantees, the bystander is likely to remain silent. Therefore, the reliability and effectiveness of a reporting platform depends on the trust that potential reporters place in the system and the responsible organisations.

Following the events in the Czech ice hockey environment, a cooperative arrangement was initiated between the Czech Ice Hockey Federation, Transparency International – Czech Republic (TI-CZ),[2] a non-governmental, non-profit organisation specialising in the fight against corruption and providing legal assistance to whistleblowers, and *Lovec Korupčníků* (translated literally as 'Hunter of Corruption'), an anti-corruption non-governmental, non-profit organisation. This included the establishment of an ice hockey whistleblowing line in 2015 called the 'Ethical Ice Hockey Line' (Transparency International, 2017). *Lovec Korupčníků* provides the independent contact for the whistleblowing line (email and telephone) for the collection and referral of reports to TI-CZ. TI-CZ is responsible for assessing and addressing reports, providing legal evaluation and qualified advice.

What is a whistleblowing or reporting mechanism?

Reporting mechanisms, such as implemented for the Czech Ice Hockey Federation, are also now increasingly being utilised throughout the national and international sport sectors (Verschuuren, 2019, 2020). For multinationals and public authorities though, whistleblowing facilities are well established within their compliance frameworks. The USA was the first country to explicitly promote whistleblowing from as early as last century.[3] In recent decades, other countries have also started to protect whistleblowers. This legislative trend is fuelled by a string of environmental, tax, corruption or health scandals that have been revealed by organisational insiders, who often suffered from victimisation and retaliation (such as the Enron financial fraud revealed in 2001 or the NSA global surveillance disclosures in 2013). Supranational entities like the Council of Europe (COE, 2014), the Organisation for Economic Co-operation and Development (OECD, 2011), the United Nations Office on Drugs and Crime (UNODC, 2004), are actively encouraging states to enhance national whistleblower protection. The Netherlands (2016), France and Italy (2017) are among the countries to have recently enacted whistleblowing laws. An EU-wide Directive for whistleblower protection will also come into force in 2021 (Council of the European Union, 2019). In Australia, whistleblower protections provided by 2004 amendments to the Corporations Act were expanded from 1 July 2019 to provide greater protections for whistleblowers. Public and private bodies, including national sporting organisations and professional clubs, are now required to adopt a compliant whistleblower policy under these amendments (ASIC, n.d.).

Internal reporting mechanisms are now considered as a leading fraud detection mechanism. The yearly 'Report to the Nations' published by the Association of Certified Fraud Examiners (ACFE, 2018) highlights internal tips as the most common tool to detect fraud. It also establishes that organisations that possess an internal hotline are more likely to detect fraud and suffer less losses from cases. Fifty per cent of corruption cases are now detected by tip offs, according to the 2018 ACFE report. Other research programmes have underlined that whistleblowing tools can represent effective tools of self-regulation, risk management and organisational efficiency (Stubben & Welch, 2020; Brown et al., 2008; Miceli et al., 2008; Vandekerckhove, 2006). They also help organisations to correct wrongdoing before they become public scandals that undermine the reputation and credibility of the organisation. Research in public administration has also shown that reporting mechanisms can contribute to increase transparency and accountability, both of which are factors of trust (Rose & Peiffer, 2019). Within sport organisations, where the management mostly follow vertical and top-down approaches, reporting mechanisms can also serve as a form of communication between athletes and authorities. By inviting and supporting whistleblowing, sport organisations can engage with athletes and contribute to develop transparency, accountability, ethical reasoning and trust.

Scandals seem to have had a critical influence on the decision of national and international sport organisations to set up reporting mechanisms, as seen in the Czech example. The first identified whistleblower mechanisms in sport were at the national level. In the aftermath of an abuse scandal (the Sheldon Kennedy–Graham James case), Hockey Canada in 1997 established their Speak Out programme in association with the Canadian Red Cross to encourage the reporting of athlete safety issues (Vertommen et al., 2015). One year later, after a similar case in the judo discipline (the Peter Ooms abuse scandal), the Dutch NOC*NSF opened a general telephone support services for sexual harassment in sport (Vertommen et al.,

2015). More recently, international and national sport authorities have also added new mechanisms to recognise the issues related to physical abuse, or harassment (the 'safeguarding' issue). This new managerial concern developed partly following the Larry Nassar abuse scandal in the US gymnastics (Edelman & Pacella, 2019).

In anti-doping too, reporting lines have multiplied within national anti-doping agencies and sport federations (Leeds Beckett University, n.d.), as the anti-doping community increasingly realised the limits of testing as an anti-doping tool. One of the first hotlines was called Stamp Out Doping established by the Australian Sports Anti-Doping Authority in 2006 (cited by Ordway & Opie, 2016, p. 51). Other early examples are the UK Anti-Doping *Report Doping in Sport* mechanism opened in 2010 (UKAD, n.d.) and the Union Cycliste Internationale (UCI)'s helpline in 2013 (ABC, 2013). Reacting to the Russian national doping scandal, which had been unfolding since the end of 2014, the World Anti-Doping Agency (WADA) launched a worldwide Speak-Up hotline in 2017 (WADA, 2017). WADA's tool was accompanied by a fully fledged whistleblowing policy to attract inside information on doping practices. This has now also been supported under the WADA Code through the addition of a new anti-doping rule violation that will come into effect on 1 January 2021: 'Acts by an Athlete or Other Person to Discourage or Retaliate Against Reporting to Authorities' (WADA, 2019).

At the international level, the rise of match-fixing threats has triggered a wave of additional reporting mechanisms to be established. The exponential growth of the online sports betting market has provided opportunities for criminals to earn massive profits, particularly where they are able to manipulate sporting competitions. After a succession of high-profile cases, the International Cricket Council (from 2001), the tennis authorities (in 2008; Gunn & Rees, 2008), Fédération Internationale de Football Association (FIFA in 2013), the Union Européenne des Football Association (UEFA in 2014), and the International Olympic Committee (IOC in 2015) set up their system to report corrupt behaviour. A review of the websites shows that about half of the Olympic International Federations have one reporting mechanism in place, either for one issue (such as match-fixing, harassment and abuse or doping), or for any disciplinary violation. Again, the need to restore legitimacy and trust may be one of the organisational objectives behind these mechanisms, alongside the (genuine) willingness to detect and address wrongdoing.

Reporting mechanisms can take different forms (UNODC-IOC, 2019). The first main feature is the available reporting channel(s). It can include any or all of: a phone hotline, an email address, a mobile phone application, an Internet platform or a dedicated person who collects vocal reports. Ideally, as in the Czech example, the system includes several options. A second feature relates to the organisational position and capacities of the report recipient. The mandated person can be either within the structure of the formal organisational chart (e.g. an integrity officer at a federation, league or club level, or a compliance unit) or outside the organisation (e.g. an ombudsman, a lawyer or a syndicate, that is more or less independent from the sport organisation and is tasked to collect, assess, transfer and/or treat the reports). In the Czech case, TI-CZ is completely external to the daily management of the sport federation. The third feature is the scope of the disclosed topics. They can be limited to 'private interest', where the wrongdoing affects one individual only (also called 'grievance claims'), or 'public interest', where it is may affect groups within a community, or potentially society as a whole. Within sport, reporting mechanisms target wrongdoing that jeopardise the integrity and credibility of sport. Such issues can include: institutional corruption, fraud or bribery, match-fixing, doping, harassment, physical abuse and violence.

How does this national reporting mechanism work?

The Czech Ice Hockey Federation cooperation arrangement example involved the creation of both a phone and email hotline, as well as an Internet platform, which is accessible both through the official websites of the Czech Ice Hockey Federation and the providing organisations. The terms of the agreement also extended to the provision of face-to-face training of the official ice hockey coaches, covering the legal framework of anti-corruption laws, ethical standards in sport (and in ice hockey), examples of risk scenarios, such as conflict of interest, and guidance on how to eliminate/minimise these risks.

However, for this arrangement to be both functional, and assist to restore trust in relevant stakeholders, an integral and crucial part of the cooperation depended on the following three factors: (i) independence of the TI-CZ to handle potential whistleblowing reports without unjustifiable interference of the Czech Ice Hockey Federation; (ii) close cooperation between the Czech Ice Hockey Federation and the TI-CZ; and (iii) governance measures, including 'tone from the top' consistent communication and follow-up actions from the Czech Ice Hockey Federation. First, the independence of TI-CZ enables TI-CZ to assess any report without interference of the involved stakeholders, i.e. ice hockey clubs, ice hockey federation, etc., to create its own legal and ethical viewpoint on the escalated matter and thus to ensure credibility of its judgement while increasing its trustworthiness. Second, a close cooperation allows TI-CZ to secure essential internal information from the Czech Ice Hockey Federation. For example, in relation to transfers and player contracts, this close cooperation provides TI-CZ the understanding to provide advice and guidelines which are not only legally correct but is relevant in the context. Third, a clearly documented process within the Czech Ice Hockey Federation on how to approach reports based on the preliminary analysis and recommendation from TI-CZ provides consistency. The actions from the Czech Ice Hockey Federation can include initiating dialogue between involved stakeholders or bringing forward disciplinary action. In other words, reporting channels cannot be created simply as 'window dressing'. It takes dedication from the Czech Ice Hockey Federation to uphold the purpose of the whistleblowing line by agreeing to the terms and conditions that it will not intervene, will cooperate when asked, and take appropriate measures in order to solve the reported matter.

The appropriate methods of dealing with a whistleblowing report/complaint from a sport environment must take into account the legal, political and historical particularities of the country. In the Czech Republic, as in many other countries, sport clubs and federations are private legal entities (under the Czech Civil Code). They are nonetheless entitled to be the recipients of state funding, either from the Ministry of Education, Youth and Sport or from municipalities and regions. Although they receive public subsidies and serve a public interest, sport organisations are autonomous from the state. This means that public institutions do not interfere with the internal functioning of a sport club or federation, unless it involves misuse of the funds that they have provided. Having been granted this independence, the highest standards of honesty and integrity are expected from sport organisations in their response to internal wrongdoings, whether they should internally address disciplinary violations or transfer criminal cases to the relevant law enforcement authority. This expectation is the basis of trust.

For this reason, the implementation of a reporting platform can contribute to restoring trust, where it has been breached. Objective, independent procedures and responsibilities can convince stakeholders that future cases will be handled effectively. In our Czech example, the fact that reports are collected by an external and neutral recipient, TI-CZ, can help to gain the confidence of potential whistleblowers. These people can expect to be protected and that no conflict of interest will undermine the assessment, investigation and adjudication process following their report, while giving the sport organisation sufficient room for manoeuvre in seeking appropriate ways to enhance trust. After preliminary analysis, TI-CZ will direct cases to the relevant and competent authorities, which could be law enforcement (for potential criminal cases), or the sport organisations (for potential disciplinary cases). The whistleblowing line is one tool, among others, to detect wrongdoing within national sports. Its credibility and success, however, depends solely on the willingness of the federation to set it up and to facilitate its effectiveness.

Communication and promotion strategies are other crucial elements to engage and empower stakeholders. Alongside the whistleblowing channel, in 2017 TI-CZ launched a sport campaign named 'Korupční víceboj' ('Corruption track and field') (Transparency International, 2017). This campaign raised awareness about what is considered malpractice in the Czech sport environment (i.e. misuse of public sport funds, non-systematic allocation of public funds to sport organisations, etc.) and promoted the TI-CZ free whistleblowing helpline to victims or witnesses of such malpractice. The Advocacy and Legal Advice Centre of TI-CZ also provides legal assistance in the area of sport.

This initiative has led to some tangible results. A recent case from 2017 involved a whistleblower reporting serious malpractice by a number of Prague's City Hall representatives, who are responsible for the distribution of sport funding. According to the whistleblower, responsible representatives deliberately changed the funding criteria to allow pre chosen sport clubs to acquire funding without merit. Thanks to the information and documentation provided by the whistleblower, TI-CZ was able to file a criminal complaint, which was followed up by police investigations.[4] In early November 2019, the police pressed criminal charges against nine employees of the Prague City Hall, including local politicians.[5] Despite the fact that reports from the sport environment are difficult to evaluate and to address (especially those that do not constitute illicit, but rather improper behaviour, which is subject to disciplinary rather than civil or criminal regulation), TI-CZ has continued to promote its whistleblowing channels amongst relevant stakeholders such as the Czech Olympic Committee, Czech Union of Sport, the Czech Football Associations and the Ministry of Education, Youth and Sport. TI-CZ provides the mechanism to promote a dialogue regarding the need for transparency, openness and fairness within the Czech sport culture, starting from the creation of reliable whistleblowing channels, aiming at restoring trust through transparent and accountable actions.

What makes a reporting mechanism effective?

Reporting mechanisms are not automatically effective in restoring trust and addressing integrity concerns. It is difficult to define and measure what constitutes an effective mechanism. For example, is it by the number of alerts (and if so, which threshold?)? The quality of alerts? The number of investigations and proceedings conducted? The number of investigations concluded? The evolution of integrity breaches detected in the long term? If so, how is this measured? As of today, no theoretical model for measuring the effectiveness, or trustworthiness of a reporting mechanism has been proposed by the scientific literature, or by practitioners.[6] It is very likely that these avenues will soon be explored by organisational behaviour researchers. However, some experience can already be drawn from the existing research on whistleblowing behaviour and on compliance and ethics management.

When confronted with the choice of blowing the whistle or not, individuals in fact face conflicting values, or conflicting loyalties (loyalty to the group, the organisation, society and to personal values and principles), which often leads them to remain silent (Jensen, 1987). Passive loyalty to the social group can be interpreted as a form of apathetic or silent support, in 'acquiescence' (Hoffmann, 2006) with the group values. This can lead to a 'spiral of silence', where agents interpret the silence of colleagues as signs of collective support for the organisation, reinforcing the social pressure not to rise against organisational wrongdoing (Noelle-Neumann, 1991). Literature has shown that such forms of 'omerta' can be strong in the sport context (Verschuuren, 2019, 2020), where the culture of obedience and team loyalty inhibits dissent (Adler & Adler, 1988). Some authors have noticed that sport is prone to 'hypermasculinity' fan involvement, which serves as another strong inhibitor to (potential) whistleblowers (Richardson & McGlynn, 2015). The work conducted by Erickson et al. (2017) and Whitaker et al. (2014) showed that many athletes were unaware of reporting mechanisms at international and/or national levels. They suggest that improved information for athletes is required to promote the whistleblowing systems. This lack of awareness can partly explain why some athletes may be more willing to directly confront wrongdoers instead of reporting them (Erickson et al., 2017). Also, the experience of some whistleblowers in sport demonstrates that coming forward is a difficult and risky process (Charreire-Petit & Cusin, 2013; Erickson et al., 2018; Richardson & McGlynn, 2015; Kimmage, 2007). Within such negative ethical climates, sports organisations need to enhance their trustworthiness if they want individuals to come forward and speak up. Research outside sport has shown that trust counts as one of the factors that determines whistleblowing (Wilson et al., 2018; Binikos, 2008). At the same time, under the conditions that they represent safe and reliable tools, reporting mechanisms can help increase accountability and transparency and, therefore, enhance trust. Hence, whistleblowing systems symbolise this intricate relationship between trust and good governance: trust is necessary to establish good governance and better governance enhances trust (Bouckaert & Van de Walle, 2003).

Consequently, hotlines or email addresses alone are not enough to convince sport actors to report wrongdoing they come across. To inspire trust and confidence, several complimentary elements are necessary:

- Support services need to be provided. This includes a two-way channel of communication. Potential whistleblowers may be torn by important questions such as: 'Am I sure about what I saw? Is it my responsibility to report? What are my options? What are my rights and responsibilities?' Before officially raising a complaint, a whistleblower will want to be informed about the process. If the process is engaged, psychological or legal advice should also be offered, where appropriate. Recent research has underlined the difficult psychological process that whistleblowers encounter in sport (Erickson et al., 2018). The TI-CZ allows such discussion to take place throughout the call as it is a helpline, as much as a hotline. By adopting a proactive stance and engaging stakeholders, the TI-CZ model may be a better approach than a sports federation who passively waits for alerts.
- A clear, predefined procedural frame needs to be in place to know how the information and the whistleblower will be handled (UNODC-IOC, 2019). The report recipient needs to have sufficient resources and independence to treat any incoming information, even if it directly targets the top level of the organisation. A regular and independent evaluation of the policy is also important. One way, for example, is to survey its trustworthiness from the perspective of the potential end-users.
- Communication and awareness-raising mechanisms are necessary to publicise the tool and show that the organisation values whistleblowing as a normal and expected behaviour (WHISTLE, 2019). The organisation's senior managers should participate in and promote the whistleblowing policy. As behaviours are embedded within the organisational culture, it takes time to change the ethical climate and build trust within an organisation, and ensure it touches every level. In this case study, the fact that the national federation chose to externalise its reporting process and support TI-CZ in its work immediately sends a positive message to internal and external stakeholders.

Conclusion

The Czech Ice Hockey Federation has taken a bold decision by entrusting an external and neutral partner to collect reports and conduct awareness-raising programmes within its jurisdiction. To restore credibility and trust following a widespread scandal, the Federation had to demonstrate impartiality through its procedures. If whistleblowing systems are well designed, actively promoted and accompanied by follow-up actions, they can be a valuable tool to restore trust within organisations.

Although the promotion of whistleblowing is becoming a global issue, political recognition and legal protection of whistleblowers are still lacking. Where the sensitivity of whistleblowing is regularly underlined by major scandals revealed by insiders of the economic, financial or political sectors, the sport environment can be expected to be no exception. Recent prominent corruption cases in international sports have highlighted the strong organisational silence (or *omerta*) that can prevail in some sport settings, and the high level of retaliation that whistleblowers face as official dissenters. In response to public outcry and political pressure, sports organisations have therefore started to set up whistleblowing (or reporting) mechanisms to enable sport actors to signal corruptive behaviours occurring on or off the field relating to match-fixing, misuse of public funds or, for example, bids in event hosting. Some sport organisations have started by opening a dialogue and admitted that the lack of internal whistleblowing mechanisms undermines the trust, credibility and fairness of sport institutions, and of sport as a whole. Whistleblowing systems may enhance trust, but their effectiveness is also conditioned by trust. It still has to be demonstrated to what extent these tools are trusted and can be securely used by sport actors, and if the authorities effectively handle the reports.

The example of the TI-CZ/CZ Ice Hockey Federation cooperation is also a relatively new model, and still being publicised at the national level. Its results and effectiveness have not been fully evaluated. However, it represents a positive case study for several reasons:

1 It resulted from a mutual agreement with the sport federation itself, which agreed that an external actor, Transparency International, serve as an 'ombudsman';
2 The clear and balanced frame of cooperation, with independence of the report recipient and clear procedures on the handling of cases; and
3 The engagement of the Federation to participate in the promotion of the policy within the sport.

The original scandal within the Czech Ice Hockey Federation showed that the lack of preventive and proactive measures created misconduct and distrust. It is unfortunate that it has taken a scandal to improve the functioning of this sport institution. Whether at the international or national levels, major breakthroughs in sports governance and integrity have usually arisen in the aftermath of scandals, with the scale of the reforms often closely proportionate to the amplitude of the public outcry. Even rapidly implemented to restore external reputation and legitimacy, new governance procedures and managerial decisions cannot meet expectations instantly. Trust, integrity values and ethical behaviour can only infuse an organisation over time. It requires 'tone from the top' consistent communications, promoted by both role models and staff throughout the mid- and local hierarchical structure. The power of sport to engage and mobilise societies behind a team or a discipline is shattered when widespread cheating, abuse or deception is revealed. It then takes years to rebuild organisational trust. Mechanisms like independent reporting lines are one element (among others) that need to be considered by sport organisations willing to rebuild legitimacy.

Questions

i *Trust loss* – In whom (or, in which group) has trust been lost in this case?
ii *Trust correction* – How, if attempted, has the restoration of trust been tried?; and;
iii *Lessons learned* – How could the lessons from this case be applied to other sports, nations, states, other districts for the same sport, or other sports to prevent a further loss of trust or at least to restore trust?

Notes

1 See: https://www.ceskenoviny.cz/zpravy/hokejove-ctvrtfinale-ve-sledovanosti-prevalcova lo-volebni-debatu/1759755 and https://www.czso.cz/csu/czso/statistika-sportu-zakla dni-ukazatele-2017
2 See: https://www.transparency.cz/spoluprace-s-cslh-s-transparency-international-cr-a-inicia tivou-loveckorupcniku-cz-se-rozsiruje-i-na-oblast-prevence/
3 Notably through the 1863 False Claim Act and the 1989 Whistleblower Protection Act.
4 Please note that in the time of writing (March 2020), the investigations of the case are ongoing. Also TI-CZ may not provide further details surrounding the case, so as not to endanger identity of the whistleblower or the proper investigation.
5 See: https://www.irozhlas.cz/zpravy-domov/praha-obvineni-magistrat-prahy-mestske-sta tni-zastupitelstvi-dotace-sport_1911111611_vtk
6 One noteworthy exception may be the 'Whistle while they work' programme run by the University of Griffith. See: http://www.whistlingwhiletheywork.edu.au/

References

ABC. (2013). UCI launches rider anti-doping hotline. 16 January 2013. https://www.abc.net.au/news/2013-01-17/uci-launches-rider-anti doping hotline/4468400

ACFE. (2018). Report to the nations. 2018 global study on occupational fraud and abuse. Retrieved from https://s3-us-west-2.amazonaws.com/acfepublic/2018-report-to-the-na tions.pdf

Adler, P. A., & Adler, P. (1988). Intense loyalty in organisations: A case study of college athletics. *Administrative Science Quarterly*, 33(3), 401–417. https://doi.org/10.2307/2392716

ASIC. (n.d.). Whistleblower protections for not-for-profit organisations. Retrieved from https://asic.gov.au/about-asic/asic-investigations-and-enforcement/whistleblowing/whistleblower-protections-for-not-for-profit-organisations/

Binikos, E. (2008). Sounds of silence: Organisational trust and decisions to blow the whistle. *SA Journal of Industrial Psychology*, 34(3). https://doi.org/10.4102/sajip.v34i3.728

Bouckaert, G., & Van de Walle, S. (2003). Comparing measures of citizen trust and user satisfaction as indicators of 'good governance': Difficulties in linking trust and satisfaction indicators. *International Review of Administrative Sciences*, 69(3), 329–343.

Brown, A., Lewis, D., Moberly, R., & Vandekerckhove, W. (Eds.). (2014). *International handbook on whistleblowing research*. Cheltenham, UK: Edward Elgar Publishing.

Brown, A., Mazurski, E., & Olsen, J. (2008). The incidence and significance of whistle blowing. In A. Brown (Ed.), *Whistle blowing in the Australian public sector* (pp. 25–53). Canberra: ANU E Press.

Charreire-Petit, S., & Cusin, J. (2013). Whistleblowing et résilience : Analyse d'une trajectoire individuelle. *Management*, 16(2), 142–175. https://doi.org/10.3917/mana.162.0142

Council of Europe. (2014). Recommendation CM/Rec (2014) 7 and explanatory memorandum (October 2014). Retrieved from: https://rm.coe.int/16807096c7

Council of the European Union. (2019). Better protection of whistleblowers: New EU-wide rules to kick in in 2021. Press release. Retrieved from https://www.consilium.europa.eu/en/press/press-releases/2019/10/07/better-p
rotection-of-whistle-blowers-new-eu-wide-rules-to-kick-in-in-2021/

ČT sport. (2015). Růžička čelí trestnímu oznámení kvůli podezření z korupce. Retrieved from https://sport.ceskatelevize.cz/clanek/hokej/ruzicka-celi-trestnimu-oznameni-kvuli-podezreni-z-korupce/5bde6f530d663b6fe8d6e7bd

Edelman, M., & Pacella, J. M. (2019). Vaulted into victims: Preventing further sexual abuse in US Olympic sports through unionized and improved governance. *Arizona Law Review*, 61, 463. http://dx.doi.org/10.2139/ssrn.3234438

Erickson, K., Backhouse, S. H., & Carless, D. (2017). I don't know if I would report them: Student-athletes thoughts, feelings and anticipated behaviours on blowing the whistle on doping in sport. *Psychology of Sport and Exercise*, 30, 45–54. https://doi.org/10.1016/j.psychsport.2017.01.005

Erickson, K., Patterson, L. B., & Backhouse, S. H. (2018). 'The process isn't a case of report it and stop': Athletes' lived experience of whistleblowing on doping in sport. *Sport Management Review*. https://doi.org/10.1016/j.smr.2018.12.001

European Commission. (2018, 23 April). Whistleblower protection: Commission sets new, EU-wide rules. Press release. Retrieved from http://europa.eu/rapid/press-release_IP-18-3441_en.htm

FIFA. (2013). FIFA launches new reporting mechanism. Retrieved from www.fifa.com/governance/news/y=2013/m=2/news=fifa-launches- new-reporting-mechanism-2002097.html

Gunn, B. & Rees, J. (2008, May). Environmental review of integrity in professional tennis. Retrieved from www.sportingintelligence.com/wp-content/uploads/2011/01/Integrity-in-tennis.pdf

Hoffmann, E. A. (2006). The ironic value of loyalty: Dispute resolution strategies in worker cooperatives and conventional organisations. *Nonprofit Management and Leadership*, 17(2), 163–177. https://doi.org/10.1002/nml.141

IAAF. (2017). Independent Athletics Integrity Unit is operational. Retrieved from https://www.iaaf.org/news/press-release/independent-athletics-integrity-unit

IOC. (2015). New IOC integrity and compliance hotline fully operational. Retrieved from https://www.olympic.org/news/new-ioc-integrity-and-compliance-hotline-fully-operational

Jensen, J. V. (1987). Ethical tension points in whistleblowing. *Journal of Business Ethics*, 6 (4), 321–328. https://doi.org/10.1007/BF00382941

Joint Inspection Unit. (2018). Review of whistleblower policies and practices in United Nations system organizations. Retrieved from https://www.unjiu.org/content/review-whistle-blower-policies-and-practices-united-nations-system-organizations

Kimmage, P. (2007). *Rough ride: Behind the wheel with a pro cyclist*. London: Random House.

Leeds Beckett University. (n.d.) Global whistleblowing landscape for reporting doping in sport. Report prepared for the World Anti-Doping Agency. Retrieved from https://www.wada-ama.org/sites/default/files/resources/files/leeds_beckett_wada_report_on_whistleblowing_platforms_july_2018.pdf

Miceli, M. P., Near, J. P., & Dworkin, T. M. (2008). *Whistle-blowing in organizations*. New York: Routledge.

Milliken, F. J., Morrison, E. W., & Hewlin, P. F. (2003). An exploratory study of employee silence: Issues that employees don't communicate upward and why. *Journal of Management Studies*, 40(6), 1453–1476. https://doi.org/10.1111/1467-6486.00387

Morrison E. W., & Milliken F. J. (2000). Organisational silence: A barrier to change and development in a pluralistic world. *Academy of Management Review*, 25(4), 706–725. https://doi.org/10.2307/259200

Noelle-Neumann, E. (1991). The theory of public opinion: The concept of the spiral of silence. *Annals of the International Communication Association*, 14(1), 256–287. https://doi.org/10.1080/23808985.1991.11678790

OECD. (2011). Convention on combating bribery of foreign public officials in international business transactions and related documents. Retrieved from www.oecd.org/corruption/oecdantibriberyconvention.htm

Ordway, C. & Opie, H. (2016). Integrity and corruption in sport. In N. Schulenkorf and S. Frawley (Eds.), *Critical issues in global sport management* (pp. 38–63). London and New York: Routledge.

Richardson, B. K., & McGlynn J. (2015). Blowing the whistle off the field of play: An empirical model of whistleblower experiences in the intercollegiate sport industry. *Communication and Sport*, 3(1), 57–80. https://doi.org/10.1177/2167479513517490

Rose, R, & Peiffer, C. (2019). *Bad governance and corruption*. Cham: Palgrave Macmillan.

Stubben, S., & Welch, K. (2020). Evidence on the use and efficacy of internal whistleblowing systems (SSRN Scholarly Paper ID 3273589). Social Science Research Network. https://doi.org/10.2139/ssrn.3273589

Transparency International Czech Republic. (2017, 1 September). The non-functioning system of sports financing contributes to manipulation. TI wants to change that. Transparency International. Retrieved from https://www.korupcnivicebojcz/the-non-functioning-system-of-sports-financing-contributes-to-manipulation-ti-wants-to-change-that/

UEFA. (2014). New UEFA match-fixing initiatives. Retrieved from https://www.uefa.com/insideuefa/news/newsid=2185621.html

UKAD. (n.d.). Story of anti-doping. Retrieved from https://www.ukad.org.uk/about/story-anti-doping

UNODC. (2004). United Nations Convention against corruption. United Nations Office on Drugs and Crime. Retrieved from https://www.unodc.org/documents/brussels/UN_Convention_Against_Corruption.pdf

UNODC-IOC. (2019). Reporting mechanisms in sport. United Nations Office on Drugs and Crime. Retrieved from https://www.unodc.org/documents/corruption/Publications/2019/19-09580_Reporting_Mechanisms_in_Sport_ebook.pdf

Vandekerckhove, W. (2006). *Whistleblowing and organisational social responsibility: A global assessment*. Aldershot: Ashgate.

Verschuuren, P. (2019). Whistleblowing determinants and the effectiveness of reporting channels in the international sports sector. *Sport Management Review*. https://doi.org/10.1016/j.smr.2019.07.002

Vertommen, T., Schipper-van Veldhoven, N. H., Hartill, M. J., & Van Den Eede, F. (2015). Sexual harassment and abuse in sport: The NOC* NSF helpline. *International Review for the Sociology of Sport*, 50(7), 822–839.

WADA. (2017). WADA launches 'Speak p!' – A secure digital platform to report doping violation *s*. Retrieved from https://www.wada-ama.org/en/media/news/2017-03/wada-launches-speak-up-a-secure-digital-platform-to-report-doping-violations

WADA. (2019, 25 November). World Anti-Doping Code (effective 1 January 2021). World Anti-Doping Agency. Retrieved from https://www.wada-ama.org/en/media/news/2019–2011/wada-publishes-approved-2021-world-anti-doping-code-and-international-standards

WHISTLE. (2019). Implementation of whistleblowing policies by sports organizations in the EU. Retrieved from https://sportwhistle.eu/wp-content/uploads/2019/06/Policy-recommendations-report_WHISTLE.pdf

Whitaker, L., Backhouse, S., & Long, J. (2014). Reporting doping in sport: National level athletes' perceptions of their role in doping prevention. *Scandinavian Journal of Medicine and Science in Sports*, 24(6), 515–521. https://doi.org/10.1111/sms.12222

Wilson, A. B., McNellis, C., & Latham, C. K. (2018). Audit firm tenure, auditor familiarity, and trust: Effect on auditee whistleblowing reporting intentions. *International Journal of Auditing*, 22(2), 113–130. https://doi.org/10.1111/ijau.12108

9 Collaborative tennis investigations in Australia

Rhys Harrison and James Moller[1]

Introduction

Much has been written about the love Australians have for sport: its ability to connect with people, the associated health benefits, the community status and potential financial gain are just some of the appealing factors. Tennis Australia is one of seven members in the Coalition of Major Professional and Participation Sports (COMPPS) in Australia (https://www.compps.com.au/). The challenge for Tennis Australia is that it is these same appealing factors, combined with the structure of the game of tennis itself, which opens the sport up to corruptors through match-fixing.

Professional tennis internationally is extremely vulnerable to this corruption threat. For a potential corruptor to fix an outcome, or an element of a match, it only requires collaboration with one participant, even in doubles tennis. In a team sport such as football, beyond the referee or umpire, the corruptor would be required to influence several players to achieve the desired outcome. Between 2005 and 2018, international tennis commissioned two major integrity reviews (Gunn & Rees, 2008; Lewis et al. 2018). At the conclusion of each review, the tennis world was confronted with observations such as tennis is at a 'crossroads of credibility' and the risk is 'real and cannot be taken lightly' (Lewis et al. 2018, p. 2). Significant global interest in the sport of tennis contributes to the importance of protecting the integrity of tournaments. Unfortunately, it appears the concerns raised were not taken seriously enough, and the problems intensified.

Favourable time zones to Asian-based gamblers, and an increase in viewers generally, correlates with an increase in global gambling as gamblers are more likely to bet on events that they can watch. In addition, unlike Australian and European bookmakers, Asian-based bookmakers allow customers to continuously place bets meaning there is effectively no limit to the amount that can be wagered, leading to much larger betting pools. Whilst the majority of this gambling is conducted by customers attempting to place a legitimate wager, the size of these gambling pools attract match-fixers due to the significant profits that can be achieved from a corrupted match, or event (such as a particular game or set) within a match (known as a 'spot fix'). As set out by Ordway & Opie (2016):

> Match-fixing can involve deciding not only who wins and loses, but the winning margin too. Spot fixing entails the improper influencing of an event or contingency within a sporting competition. That might include the time and rate of scoring, the score at certain times, the occurrence of particular events such as who scores first, the number of penalties awarded and so on. (p. 64)

and, in the case of tennis, when double faults or foot faults are served.

These factors have directly attributed to the increased threat to Australian sport, an industry that now generates over US$141 billion annually (Masters, 2015, p. 111). As a direct result of these changes, National Sporting Organisations (NSOs), including Tennis Australia, now have access to significant financial opportunities through partnering with the gambling industry, but these opportunities also come with the inevitable threat of associated corruption. This chapter will first examine the importance of establishing an integrity framework within the sport, and then outline the benefits of adopting a collaborative approach with law enforcement agencies to compliment that framework through reviewing the case study 'Operation Wildcard'.

Match-fixing risk to Australian sport

In recent years, Australian sporting organisations have become a target for international crime syndicates. As a result of these attacks, the integrity of sporting competitions has been forever tarnished. NSOs and law enforcement have both identified: 'the inevitable infiltration of international syndicates into Australian sport' as the greatest risk to sport in Australia (AIC, 2015). Several key factors have caused match-fixing to become more popular and, combined, they could be described as a 'perfect storm'.

Factor #1: Technological advancements in betting online and via mobile devices

The technological developments seen in the 21st century have assisted the gambling industry more than any other because it facilitates an impulse which few can resist. In the study by Bernhard et al. they identified that: 'At no other time in human history have more of us had more access, in more diverse ways, to more gambling than we do today' (Bernhard et al. 2009, p. 616). The significant technological advances in Internet speeds and mobile phones have provided the end user with the ability to watch sport on their mobile device while placing bets on that same device.

Factor #2: Globalisation of the Australian sport betting market

Prior to a challenge by Betfair, an Australian based online betting exchange, betting operators were legally prevented from accepting customers outside their State or Territory of registration (Australasian Legal Information Institute, 2008). Betfair's argument was that the Western Australian legislation restricting trade between two states and preventing online wagering companies from operating across State boundaries was in contravention of the Australian Constitution. The 2008 decision handed down by the High Court of Australia effectively opened the doors for all international online wagering operators to capitalise on Australia's passion for sport and gambling. A clear demonstration of the growth within this industry is provided by Craig Nugent, then head of the Australian Stock Exchange listed Tabcorp Holdings Ltd (TAB) Wagering and Media business, who observed that the TAB has: 'grown from a $42 million business in our first year to $4.2 billion in 16 years' (Rothfield, 2014). The challenge for Australian sport organisations and law enforcement agencies is that it is not possible to have information-sharing arrangements in place with all international wagering operators, particularly when many of operators in Asia are in unregulated (black) and under-regulated (grey) legal jurisdictions (Forrest, 2013; Kerr, 2017b).

Factor #3: Australian NSOs engaging with betting operators

The third contributing factor is the decision by the Australian NSOs to directly engage with betting operators, and to make their products available to an international audience. This exposure increases the risk of match-fixing.

For example, Tennis Australia has recently adopted an international strategy designed to drive the exposure of the Grand Slam event, the Australian Open and its lead-in tournaments, to a wider market. To implement this strategy, Tennis Australia decided to live stream the Australian Open Wildcard Playoff tournaments (https://www.tennis.com.au/tournaments/pro-tournaments/australian-open-play-off). The primary justification for this decision is to promote the sport of tennis to the wider community. However, a by-product of this strategy is that it creates the ability for the gambler to watch the matches from their devices whilst placing bets. These matches would not otherwise have been available for betting, unless the wagering service provider was obtaining a live data feed via a 'data scout' physically present at the match and relaying information back to the wagering operator (Kerr, 2017a).

'Data scouts' send live data of match action which is used to create a betting market on the match and to continually update the odds offered based on the way the match progresses. Bookmakers require live data in order to accurately update the odds they are offering. Without a live data feed, bookmakers are susceptible to accepting wagers from those with more information than they have. 'Data scouts' should not be confused with 'courtsiders', whose activities relate to placing a number of bets throughout a match in an attempt to profit from the time delays between the match action and the television broadcast (e.g. Kerr, 2016).

Factor #4: Australia's geographic and time zone proximity to Asia

The final contributing factor to the risk of match-fixing, is Australia's time zone and the fact that it is closely aligned with the time zones in Asia. As a result, and as predicted by Declan Hill in his keynote address at the 2009 Australian & New

Zealand Sports Law Association (ANZSLA) Conference (Australasian Leisure Management, 2009), Asian bookmakers have targeted Australian sports. The case involving the Southern Stars Football Club is a prime example. Figures released by Football Federation Australia (FFA) highlighted that the Asia-Pacific region preferred to place bets on A League [men's football/ soccer] matches rather than the English Premier League due to Australia's close proximity (Davutovic & Bendall, 2013). Chris Eaton, FIFA's former Head of Security stated that: 'Australia is not in a bubble, Australia is in the right time zone … the vast majority of the betting fraud is committed in south-east Asia, Manila, Hong Kong, Singapore, Thailand, et cetera. They are transacting billions of dollars on a weekly basis on sport, including on Australian sports' (Alberici, 2013).

As Eaton touches upon, the related challenge for Australian regulators is the size of the betting markets in Asia. Asian-based bookmakers adopt a model of balancing their books by accepting wagers on all possible outcomes of the event (and hedging with other bookmakers), thus profiting from a commission built into the odds on offer. In contrast to this model, traditional European bookmakers take a position on the event and are therefore exposed, dependent on the result. Due to the balanced books style of bookmaking, and because Asian gambling pools are much larger than those in Europe and Australia, Asian-based bookmakers are essentially able to accept an unlimited number of wagers from their customers as their model relies on turnover rather than the result, limiting their exposure to excessive payouts, even where a match has been fixed (Forrest & McHale, 2015, pp. 14, 29).

International challenges

The international reach of match-fixing is primarily due to its close ties with organised criminals who are extremely well resourced. The unfortunate advantage for organised crime syndicates is that match-fixing is categorised as low risk and high reward. According to the United Nations Office on Drugs and Crime, there has not been a significant appetite from law enforcement agencies to investigate crimes of this nature (UNODC, 2013). There are also challenges in predicting, identifying and proving match-fixing in tennis (Rodenberg & Feustel, 2014; Rodenberg et al. 2016; Paulden, 2016). Moreover, when law enforcement agencies have successfully prosecuted an offence, courts have given leniency to those involved. In a recent example, an Australian court found tennis player Oliver Anderson guilty of match-fixing in May 2017 but he escaped conviction (Bucci, 2017; Murnane & Moller, 2018). In May 2018, detectives from the SIIU arrested two men in relation to the use of corrupt conduct information for betting purposes. The charges relate to an investigation into alleged practices linked to a number of international tennis matches in Brazil and Egypt in 2018 (Vedelago, 2020).

International tennis response to the match-fixing risk

On 18 January 2016, with the international tennis community's attention on the Australian Open, the BBC News released a report alleging 'secret files exposing evidence of widespread suspected match-fixing at the top level of world tennis, including at Wimbledon' (Cox, 2016). Amid these revelations, Novak Djokovic disclosed that, in 2007, he had been offered: '$200,000 to lose a first-round match at a tournament in St. Petersburg, Russia' (Caple, 2016). Shortly after these revelations, the International Governing Bodies (IGBs) of tennis[2] announced that an Independent Review Panel (IRP), headed by Mr Adam Lewis QC, would 'review and report on the appropriateness and effectiveness of the Tennis Anti-Corruption Programme and make recommendations for change' (TIU, 2016). During the announcement of the review, the then Chairman of the Association of Tennis Professionals (ATP), Chris Kermode, stated that: 'It is unprecedented that the seven stakeholders of tennis have come together so quickly with one purpose, and that is with the sole aim to restore public confidence in our sport' (Clarey, 2016).

Moral repair in professional tennis

In announcing the formation of the Review, the IGBs effectively started tennis on a 'moral repair' journey. Margaret Urban Walker, an expert in ethical theory, defines moral repair as the process of: 'restoring or creating trust and hope in a shared sense of value and responsibility' (Walker, 2006, p. 28). Walker argues that the process of moral repair: 'confirms the agency, responsibility, and dignity of the participants, victims, perpetrators, and bystanders. It asserts standards of human rights, while it publicly models compassion toward both perpetrators and victims, "humanizing" the former and consoling the latter' (Walker, 2006, p. 117). Perhaps more importantly, the long-term by-product of such an approach is that eventually the community regains their trust with the sporting organisation.

This concept of moral repair has been used in numerous contexts, in both the criminal and sporting environments. One of the often-cited demonstrations is that of former South African President Nelson Mandela in 1995:

> Mandela, in one of the most audacious political gambles of his career, appeared before the mostly white crowd of 62,000 wearing a Springbok jersey to shake the players' hands before kick-off. The then All Blacks coach Laurie Mains said the entire stadium was electrified at the sight of South Africa's first black president sporting a garment that was indelibly associated with the apartheid regime. (Muhsin, 2013, para 4)

More recently, the International Cricket Council's (ICC) decision to provide a 15-day amnesty to the Sri Lankan Cricket team (ICC, 2019; BBC, 2019), was an attempt to address a systemic problem with match-fixing within that region. However, as the international cycling federation (UCI) discovered when it originally proposed to offer an amnesty period for corruption related offences (in that case, doping), a challenge arises as to how to ensure that individuals provide truthful accounts, and whether it is appropriate for any disclosure to be made publicly available (Canadian Cycling Magazine, 2013). Importantly, Walker notes that any amnesty period should be preceded by a publicly available report that provides specific details of the offences which in turn allows the organisation: 'to frame the events in a new national narrative of acknowledgment, accountability, and civic values' (Walker, 2006, p. 123). While the ICC should be applauded in attempting to restore trust, these efforts may also be counter-productive where the organisation fails to fully disclose the reported information in a timely manner. Acknowledging the need to also protect the safety of whistleblowers (see Chapter 8 Ondráčková and Verschuuren, this volume), the requirement for timeliness should also have been a lesson for international tennis.

Although the IGBs demonstrated a willingness to address the potential integrity concerns, the delay in delivering a report within a timely manner meant the integrity review lost its forward motion. In comparison, in 2000 the ICC appointed Sir Paul Condon to conduct an integrity review at the height of the match-fixing allegations in cricket. This review was concluded ten months later (Condon, 2001; Nichols, 2001). It was not until late 2018 that the IRP released their comprehensive report, *Independent Review of Integrity in Tennis*, detailing numerous integrity concerns. It concluded that:

> tennis faces a serious integrity problem … The nature of the game lends itself to manipulation for betting purposes … detection is difficult … under-performance is often attributed to 'tanking', which too often has been tolerated … The player incentive structure creates a fertile breeding ground for breaches of integrity. (Lewis et al, 2018, p. 2)

The report attributed these concerns primarily to the explosion of sports betting and the associated sale of official data. The fact that the final report took two years to complete meant that it was not possible to attract the level of media attention needed to promote the efforts to safeguard the sport. The IRP failed to capitalise on the momentum, thus poorly impacting on the moral repair process.

Australian response to the international tennis report

Although the risks posed to tennis in Australia have not gone unnoticed by Tennis Australia or the law enforcement agencies, it is clear the sport is still at risk from corruption. The nature and extent of these problems were not fully comprehended until the publication of the *Independent Review* in December 2018. The review concluded that: 'while no level of professional tennis is immune from betting-related and other breaches of integrity, the problem is particularly acute and pervasive at the lowest level of the sport' (Lewis et al. 2018, p. 2). In Australia, this was evident given the recent incidents of match-fixing which had occurred at these lower levels. The number of cases that have presented in Australia in the last five years is cause for concern. Australia is not immune from organised crime and corruption in sport is fast becoming the crime of choice for criminal organisations due to its perceived low risk versus high reward. The enthusiasm is further intensified due to the lack of interest shown by law enforcement agencies, with only Victoria Police having established a specialist unit directly charged with investigating corruption in sport, as set out below.

The review of Australia's sporting integrity framework commissioned in August 2017 (Australian Government, 2018b, 3 September), resulted in a number of innovative solutions, including the creation of a National Sports Integrity Commission (Wood et al. 2018). The proposed approach provides for a national agency (Sport Integrity Australia) charged with investigating sporting corruption offences (Australian Government, 2019b, 12 February). A crucial element in the success of this newly proposed unit will be how well it cooperates with sporting organisations. The importance of this strategy was highlighted by the United Nations Office on Drugs and Crime: 'law enforcement agencies are unlikely to have a full understanding of either the rules and nuances of the sport in question or the betting markets, and will require specialist assistance in both areas' (UNODC, 2016, p. 27). This position is supported by a recent case in the United Kingdom involving a prominent horse racing jockey Kieran Fallon who was alleged to have corrupted the outcome of 27 horse races. The case was subsequently dismissed due to a lack of evidence and, more importantly, that the case relied heavily on a witness who was not an expert in UK horse racing rules (Ingle, 2007).

Tennis Australia's Integrity Unit

Sports administrator Ann West was in an integrity and compliance role at Tennis Australia from 2001 (Walsh, 2016), before the increasing reports of integrity issues within the sport of tennis internationally and the potential ramifications on the sport in Australia led Tennis Australia to formalise a specialist integrity unit (Tennis Australia, 2016). Tennis Australia remains the only national tennis federation to have a dedicated national integrity unit within its structure. Wimbledon, Fédération Française de Tennis (FFT) and United States Tennis Association (USTA) have personnel who undertake integrity functions, but they have not employed dedicated investigators.

As Ordway identified, in the early 2000s, integrity in sport was primarily defined by anti-doping efforts (2013), but soon the types of 'wrong-doing' encapsulated by the term 'sport integrity' came to vary widely (Ordway & Opie, 2016). Many of the topics now coming within the scope of NSO integrity units, such as salary cap breaches, member protection, child safety and code of conduct issues, were already being dealt with through legal teams or in other roles. The choice to amplify the word 'integrity' into the title of roles and units in Australia gained momentum after the Australian Football League (AFL) created the first specific Integrity Manager role in 2008. Brett Clothier went to the AFL: 'which he positioned as one of the first organisations in the world to monitor integrity issues such as doping and match-fixing. Before that, he was legal counsel at Racing Victoria's integrity services department' (Ford, 2018). Following Hill's 2009 presentation at ANZSLA, the COMPPS members recognised that match-fixing challenges were becoming increasingly pressing:

In late 2010 in recognition of:

- the growing volume of sports betting (regulated and unregulated, onshore and offshore),
- the growing incidence of match-fixing globally and
- the potential for the threat of match fixing to strike at the core of sport's integrity and the perception of sports integrity in Australia,

COMPPS seized the initiative and formed an anti-corruption working party. This comprised representatives of each of the COMPPS sports, the major betting operators, players' associations and the Australian Sports Commission [now Sport Australia]. (COMPPS, 2015)

The 2011 Anti-Corruption Working Party Report to the CEOs of the COMPPS sports recommended the COMPPS Betting Integrity Group (BIG) be formed: 'comprising one member from each of the sports to coordinate joint activities between the COMPPS members and to maximise opportunities to use the collective power of the seven sports to combat corruption' (COMPPS, 2015). The BIG ultimately became the COMPPS Integrity and Security Committee (CISC), and Tennis Australia, through West, was represented on these committees.

After the *National Policy on Match-Fixing in Sport* was endorsed in 2011 (Australian Government, 2018, 27 February), the Commonwealth Government National Sport Integrity Unit (NISU) was established inside the Department of Health in 2012. NISU further expanded the definition of 'sport integrity':

> Going beyond ASADA's [the Australian Sports Anti-Doping Authority] remit in performance enhancing drugs, NISU plans to review the use of alcohol and illicit drugs in sport, as well as drugs not yet approved by the Therapeutic Goods Administration for human use, and other integrity challenges around ethical behaviour, including corruption and fraud. This will obviously require close collaboration with other State and Commonwealth agencies, NGOs and academics to achieve these outcomes. (Ordway, 2013 – brackets added)

In line with Cricket Australia and the National Rugby League who moved their legal advisers to head up separate integrity units in 2013[3] and 2014[4] respectively, in May 2016, Tennis Australia announced the appointment of West in a newly created role – Head of Integrity and Compliance. Throughout West's career, she has been instrumental in the development of the tennis anti-corruption, anti-doping and member protection policies. To support the first Tennis Anti-Corruption Policy developed in the lead up to the 2008 Australian Open, Tennis Australia signed a Memorandum of Understanding with the Victoria Police (Tennis Australia, 2007). West also played a 'liaison [role] between Tennis Australia and police investigating the matters that led to convictions in Victoria and NSW' in 2014 (Walsh, 2016; Murnane & Moller, 2018).

From 2016, West was provided the resources and given a mandate to build a team of investigators and sports compliance experts to assist with the development of Tennis Australia's integrity framework. To effectively protect tennis from this increased threat, Tennis Australia understood that the Integrity Unit would require a multi-jurisdictional approach including State/Territory and Federal governments and law enforcement agencies, licensed sports betting operators and NSOs to stand together and address this concern.

The establishment of the Sporting Integrity Intelligence Unit

In late January 2013, Victoria Police was provided with a report from Australia's national criminal intelligence agency, the Australian Crime Commission [now the Australian Criminal Intelligence Commission (ACIC)], which included: 'the findings of a 12-month investigation into the integrity of Australian sport and the relationship between professional sporting bodies, prohibited substances and organised crime' (ASADA, 2013). The report, released to the public on 7 February 2013, 'Organised Crime and Drugs in Sport: new generation performance and image enhancing drugs and organised criminal involvement in their use in professional sport', highlighted the need for law enforcement agencies to provide a greater focus and commitment to investigate issues and concerns with integrity in the sport industry due to the risk of infiltration by organised crime and money laundering via gambling markets (ACC, 2013).

On the same day, the Premier of Victoria informed the State Parliament that the Victoria Police was establishing the Sporting Integrity Intelligence Unit (SIIU) (Parliament of Victoria, 2013). The SIIU was located within Victoria Police's Intelligence and Covert Support Command and began operations on 11 February 2013. The establishment of the SIIU was underpinned by legislation that would outlaw a new and emerging crime type, more generally referred to as match-fixing. On 24 April 2013, the Crimes Amendment (Integrity in Sports) Act 2013 (Vic) received Royal Assent. The amendment introduced four offences to the *Crimes Act* 1958 (Vic) directly related to corrupting the betting outcome of an event or event contingency. The SIIU is the only dedicated sporting integrity unit with multidisciplinary resources embedded in a law enforcement agency, not only in Australia, but anywhere in the world (Murnane & Moller, 2018).

In its submission to the 'The Review of Australia's Sports Integrity Arrangements' (Australian Government, 2018b, 3 September), the SIIU identified the need for a national approach to coordinating the collection and analysis of information relating to sports betting and integrity issues from Australian law enforcement agencies, sporting bodies and the betting industry. Such an organisation would be required to be able to store protected law enforcement data, commercial in confidence betting records, as well as intelligence from various Commonwealth Government departments. The SIIU recommended the most appropriate organisation to incorporate a national sports intelligence unit as the ACIC, given its national and international networks, developed research abilities, information delivery capabilities and services to front-line policing and law enforcement. The ACIC's coercive powers also provide the organisation with a unique intelligence collection capability allowing them to inform and provide critical contributions to national strategies to combat serious and organised crime, cybercrime and national security threats (ACIC, 2019).

In the 'Report of the Review of Australia's Sports Integrity Arrangements' (known as the Wood Review; Wood et al., 2018), the panel noted that the National Integrity of Sport Unit (NISU) and the ACIC had established a Sports Betting Integrity Unit (SBIU) as a joint initiative in November 2017. The Wood Review recommended that an ongoing SBIU be established to allow for the receipt, assessment and dissemination of information regarding suspicious betting activity (Wood et al., 2018). The SIIU continues to work closely with the ACIC SBIU, sporting and racing codes and wagering service providers to strengthen these partnerships in response to match-fixing in sport.

Whilst the SIIU and Tennis Australia maintain strong relationships with Australian wagering service providers and can access information regarding suspicious betting activity, these relationships don't always exist with international bookmakers. Globally, the TIU has established relationships with a number of international bookmakers, however, too often it is clear that suspicious betting activity is associated with those bookmakers who refuse to cooperate with tennis authorities and law enforcement agencies. This remains an ongoing challenge.

Case study 'Operation Wildcard'

Following a suspicious betting alert identified on 24 October 2016 by Australian betting agency, CrownBet (now BetEasy) reported to the SIIU, the SIIU commenced 'Operation Wildcard'. The betting alert related to a first-round match at the Traralgon ATP Challenger between Australian based players Oliver Anderson and Harrison Lombe (ATP Tour Inc, 2020). The alert identified an attempted bet of A$10,000 for the much lower ranked player Lombe to win the first set against his much higher ranked opposition, Anderson. CrownBet accepted the bet for a reduced stake of A$2,000. A further bet was then attempted predicting that the match would last the full three sets. The A$2,000 bet was successful when Oliver Anderson lost the first set, and went on to win the match 4–6, 6–0, 6–2.

Anderson stated before the courts that he had been approached a few days before the match while on a trip to Cairns, Queensland by a friend and former fellow tennis player, Isaac Frost, who had asked him if he would be willing to lose the first set of his first-round match. Anderson claimed in his defence that he needed the money because he had signed a contract with an international sponsor but feared that his injury would leave him unable to satisfy his playing obligations and ultimately unable to repay his sponsorship debts.

This successful investigation highlights the importance of law enforcement involvement in combatting match-fixing. Whilst Tennis Australia may have been able to access the suspicious betting records related to the match through their agreement with CrownBet, police powers to interview and arrest Anderson were required to obtain the additional evidence needed for prosecution and subsequent punishment by tennis authorities.

The disciplinary case was heard by an independent Anti-Corruption Hearing Officer appointed by Tennis Integrity Unit [TIU]. In September 2018 the Officer ruled that the 19-month provisional sentence served by Anderson, having been suspended in February 2017, was sufficient as a full and final sanction for breaches of the Tennis Anti-Corruption Program (TACP). The appointment and independence of Anti-Corruption Hearing Officers is in line with the international process adopted by the TIU (2020a).

As Frost was working as a tennis coach, on 2 July 2017, Frost was issued with a provisional suspension excluding him from: 'competing in, or attending, any tournament or event organised or sanctioned by the governing bodies of tennis … until the conclusion of TIU investigations into alleged breaches of the Tennis Anti-Corruption Program'. This was the second suspension for Frost as he had previously been sanctioned by the TIU between 3 October 2013 and 4 September 2014 for not co-operating with a separate TIU investigation (TIU, 2017, 2 July; Murnane & Moller, 2018). As the betting-related offence occurred in the Queensland State jurisdiction, the SIIU referred the investigation to the Queensland Police Service. Frost was then sentenced without conviction to 220 hours community service (to be completed within 12 months) by the Brisbane Magistrates Court after pleading guilty to match-fixing and drug-related offences (ABC/AAP, 2018).

Importance of working collaboratively

In Australia, sporting organisations, such as Tennis Australia, are required to 'promote and oversee' the values of integrity, which includes the collection, analysis and dissemination of integrity issues to relevant stakeholders (Australian Sports Commission, n.d. 1). These guidelines have been carefully crafted to promote a 'top-down' approach; integrity values must resonate from the Board and senior leadership and they are responsible for establishing best practice integrity measures.

It is therefore incumbent on sporting organisations to ensure effective oversight of their integrity policies, which includes understanding the vulnerabilities within their sport. This involves conducting risk assessments of competitions, tournaments and athlete development to place effective controls in place. However, the notion that sporting organisations are solely responsible for protecting the integrity of a sport is no longer the case. A consistent theme emerging within the sporting community is that this responsibility has evolved, and now includes multiple stakeholders such as government departments, law enforcement agencies, athletes and support staff; all sharing the moral responsibility to work in conjunction to protect the integrity of sport. This is a view shared by David Sharpe, ASADA's Chief Executive, who stated in January 2019, that in order to safeguard sport, all stakeholders: 'need to come together' (Helmers, 2019).

In July 2016, Tennis Australia's Integrity Unit commenced operation and with this came an increased capability designed to safeguard tennis in Australia. Tennis Australia's Integrity Unit sought to implement an intelligence-led risk-based integrity programme. The concept behind establishing this strategy was twofold; the first was aimed at increasing visibility of the potential risks within the sport of tennis, both domestically and internationally. Identifying these risks and having a collective understanding within the organisation was an integral process. The second was increasing Tennis Australia's information-sharing arrangements with all stakeholders.

Tennis Australia's Integrity Unit was given the mandate of enforcing all of Tennis Australia's national policies. This included the international Tennis Anti-Corruption Program (TIU, 2020a,b), Tennis Anti-Doping Policy (Tennis Australia, 2015), Disciplinary Policy (Tennis Australia, 2019a) and Member Protection Policy (Tennis Australia, 2019b). These policies have been developed and implemented as a safeguard to protect the integrity of the sport. Tennis Australia's Integrity Unit mandate is further articulated and supported in Tennis Australia's 2017/18 Annual Report, where it is detailed in both short and long-term strategic goals (Tennis Australia, 2018, p. 57).

A key aspect to the success of Tennis Australia's Integrity Unit is the cooperation and information-sharing arrangements between with law enforcement agencies, in particular, with the SIIU. The partnership with SIIU has provided valuable insight and learnings since the creation of Tennis Australia's Integrity Unit. Having a resource such as the SIIU, staffed with expert investigators and analysts, has been crucial and has led to successful tennis corruption prosecutions.

Tennis Australia and the Victoria Police have worked closely for a number of years sharing information and providing critical assessments to potential integrity incidents. This strategy becomes more evident during the lead up to the Australian summer of tennis each year. The success of this partnership is the shared understanding towards a common goal.

Another element to the success of Tennis Australia's Integrity Unit was the early recognition of the importance of information-sharing arrangements with sports wagering providers, both nationally and internationally. As part of this process, Tennis Australia undertook a risk assessment of the various betting markets currently available within Australia as they related to tennis. Working with sports wagering providers, Tennis Australia mapped associated risks to the contingencies and assessed the appropriate internal and external controls. These controls have allowed betting agencies to more effectively monitor and report suspicious betting to Tennis Australia and the SIIU.

Given the sport of tennis is played internationally, cooperation and information-sharing arrangements needed to be formed with sports betting operators outside Australia. This view is shared by Victoria Police, and has added further protection to the sport. The engagement of companies who monitor betting markets has also been a key pillar of Tennis Australia's integrity strategic plan. This approach was recognised during the Wood Review. The Wood Review recommended establishing a Suspicious Activity Alert System which would provide real time analysis of betting alerts (Wood et al. 2018 recommendation 4; Australian Government, 2019a, 12 February, 23).

Tennis Australia's education strategy

There is little doubt that the best strategy towards preventing corruption is adopting a proactive education strategy. Any educational programme addressing the issue of match-fixing at a minimum must address the four main areas: what is match-fixing; its causes; how to recognise it and how to report it. It is vital to understand that sports corruption is not a problem which can be resolved by only implementing and enforcing laws and codes of conduct. Sporting organisations, including Tennis Australia, should look holistically at the issue and recognise the importance of values and ethics (Jones, 2012, p. 57). Andy Harvey wrote of the need to develop an: 'ethical opposition to match-fixing' (Harvey, 2015) which in so doing provides an organisation with substantive values which encompass the sport holistically.

In Australia, this position of complimenting codes of conduct and laws within the sport has been supported by Sport Australia [formerly the Australian Sports Commission]. Ordway & Opie have also identified the added benefit of this approach, in that the athlete is provided with greater situational awareness (Ordway & Opie, 2016, pp. 73–4). Understanding the need to create an ethical framework is critical to integrity management. A sports integrity framework should include a rules-based approach which provides a regulatory framework combined with a values-based approach (Maesschalck & Auweele, 2010, p. 2). Such a framework will not only proactively address serious integrity concerns but provides the necessary education around what is often a complicated ethical dilemma, where perhaps the answer is not immediately clear to the athlete (Maesschalck & Auweele, 2010, p. 8).

Tennis Australia's education framework is well established and focuses on improving an athlete's understanding of sports corruption, providing practical examples through a blended learning experience, including online and face-to-face workshops. As part of Tennis Australia's approach towards anti-corruption education, Tennis Australia has sourced assistance from the SIIU and ASADA to present at Tennis Australia's national underage championships, an information session delivered to both athlete and parent(s). To compliment this approach, in 2017, Tennis Australia launched an independent reporting service where anyone could make a confidential disclosure and be afforded the protections under Tennis Australia's Whistleblower policy.

Tennis Australia's educational strategy extends to support personnel, officials and staff attending or participating in sanctioned tournaments (including parents of 'ballkids'). At the Australian Open, and the Australian Open lead-in events, all staff and volunteers undertake an online learning course which explains their role in protecting the integrity of the sport. This approach is recognised as best practice ensuring that sporting organisations and law enforcement work together: 'to ensure the integrity of Australian sport is protected from the threat of match-fixing and the corruption that flows from it' (Australian Government, 2011, 6; Australian Government, 2018, 27 February).

Conclusion

Overall, the integrity of tennis in Australia has improved significantly over recent years due to increased collaboration between the SIIU, Tennis Australia and the TIU. This collaborative approach has resulted in the successful investigation and prosecution of match-fixing offences, sending a clear message to those attempting to corrupt matches that this will not be tolerated by either sporting bodies or law enforcement agencies. Whilst this is positive news for Australian tennis, it may simply displace the problem whereby match-fixers may choose to corrupt matches in countries where such activity is not treated as a serious offence. As such, the Australian model provides a template for other governing bodies of tennis and law enforcement agencies overseas to replicate, in an effort to protect the entire international tennis tour from those seeking to corrupt it.

Questions

- i *Trust loss* – In whom (or, in which group) has trust been lost in this case?
- ii *Trust correction* – How, if attempted, has the restoration of trust been tried?; and;
- iii *Lessons learned* – How could the lessons from this case be applied to other sports, nations, states, other districts for the same sport, or other sports to prevent a further loss of trust or at least to restore trust?

Notes

1 Thank you to Ann West and Jo Setright for providing background information.
2 Association of Tennis Professionals (ATP), Women's Tennis Association (WTA) International Tennis Federations (ITF), and the Grand Slam Board (Australian Open, French Open, Championships at Wimbledon and US Open, ITF, WTA and ATP).
3 Iain Roy was appointed Head of Integrity at Cricket Australia in December 2013: https://www.linkedin.com/in/iain-roy-9b5121/
4 Nick Weeks was appointed Head of Integrity at the National Rugby League in August 2014 (but was 'General Manager, Integrity and General Counsel' from July 2013): https://www.linkedin.com/in/nick-weeks-0280b483/

References

ABC/AAP. (2018, 16 August). Match-fixing former pro tennis player gets community service after guilty plea. *ABC News*. Australian Broadcasting Commission. Retrieved from https://www.abc.net.au/news/2018-08-16/match-fixing-former-tennis-pro-isaac-frost-community-service/10127914

ACC. (2013). Organised crime and drugs in sport: New generation performance and image enhancing drugs and organised criminal involvement in their use in professional sport. Australian Crime Commission. Canberra. Retrieved from https://trove.nla.gov.au/version/192142762

ACIC. (2019, 17 May). About Us. Australian Criminal Intelligence Commission. Australian Government. Retrieved from https://www.acic.gov.au/about-us

AIC. (2015, 14 May). Corruption in Australian sport: Trends & issues in crime and criminal justice. Australian Institute of Criminology. Retrieved from www.aic.gov.au/publications/current%20series/tandi/481-500/tandi490.html

Alberici, E. (2013, 8 February). Global gambling market a threat to sport. *ABC Lateline*. Retrieved from www.abc.net.au/lateline/content/2013/s3686776.htm

ASADA. (2013, 7 February). Ministerial statement: Organised crime and drugs in sport. Australian Sports Anti-Doping Agency, Australian Government. Canberra. Retrieved from https://www.asada.gov.au/news/ministerial-statement-organised-crime-and-drugs-sport

ATP Tour Inc. (2020). Oliver Anderson vs Harrison Lombe. ATP Head2Head. ATP Tour. Retrieved from https://www.atptour.com/en/players/fedex-head-2-head/oliver-anderson-vs-harrison-lombe/AD23/LE15

Australian Government. (2011). *National policy on match-fixing in sport*. Canberra: Australian Federal Government.

Australian Government. (2018, 27 February) National policy on match-fixing in sport. Department of Health. Retrieved from https://www1.health.gov.au/internet/main/publishing.nsf/Content/match-fixing

Australian Government. (2018a, 3 September). An Australian sports wagering scheme: The review of Australia's sports integrity arrangements. Department of Health. Retrieved from www.health.gov.au/internet/main/publishing.nsf/Content/the-review-of-australias-sports-integrity-arrangements

Australian Government. (2018b, 3 September). The review of Australia's sports integrity arrangements: A stronger national response to match-fixing. Department of Health. Retrieved from www.health.gov.au/internet/main/publishing.nsf/Content/the-review-of-australias-sports-integrity-arrangements

Australian Government. (2019a, 12 February). Safeguarding the integrity of sport – the government response to the Wood Review. Retrieved from https://www1.health.gov.au/internet/main/publishing.nsf/Content/D78723EDC196645DCA2583910001AEA2/$File/Final%20Government%20Response%20-%2011%20February%202019.pdf

Australian Government. (2019b, 12 February). The government's response to the Wood Review. Department of Health. Retrieved from https://www1.health.gov.au/internet/main/publishing.nsf/Content/the-government-response-to-the-wood-review

Australasian Legal Information Institute. (2008, 27 March). *Betfair Pty Limited v Western Australia [2008] HCA 11 (27 March 2008)*. Austlii. Retrieved from www.austlii.edu.au/cgi-bin/sinodisp/au/cases/cth/HCA/2008/11.html?stem=0&synonyms=0&query=title(betfair%20and%20western%20australia%20).

Australasian Leisure Management. (2009, 9 October). Australia a target for match-fixing. Retrieved from https://www.ausleisure.com.au/news/australia-a-target-for-match-fixing/

Australian Sports Commission. (n.d.). *Integrity guidelines for directors and leaders of sporting organisations*. Canberra: Australian Government.

BBC. (2019, 9 January). Sri Lanka corruption: ICC launches 15-day amnesty as investigation widens. *BBC*. Retrieved from https://www.bbc.com/sport/cricket/46815165

Bernhard, B., Futrell, R., & Harper, A. (2009). Gambling and globalization: Sociological perspectives on 'the House' and 'the Players'. *Sociology Compass*, 3(4), 616–629.

Bucci, N. (2017, 23 May). Former junior tennis champion Oliver Anderson avoids conviction after pleading guilty to match-fixing. *The Sydney Morning Herald*. Retrieved from https://www.smh.com.au/national/former-junior-tennis-champion-oliver-anderson-avoids-conviction-after-pleading-guilty-to-matchfixing-20170523-gwavu5.html

Canadian Cycling Magazine. (2013, 25 January). Confessed cycling cheats could get amnesty: Truth and reconciliation process emerges. *Canadian Cycling Magazine*. Retrieved from https://cyclingmagazine.ca/sections/news/confessed-cycling-cheats-could-get-amnesty/

Caple, J. (2016, 27 January). Novak Djokovic's people offered $200K for star to lose match. *ESPN*. Retrieved from www.espn.com/tennis/story/_/id/14594431/novak-djokovic-says-was-offered-200000-lose-match-2007

Clarey, C. (2016, 26 January). Tennis announces review of anticorruption efforts. *The New York Times*. Retrieved from https://www.nytimes.com/2016/01/27/sports/tennis/tennis-plans-new-measures-to-fight-match-fixing.html

COMPPS. (2015, 17 September). COMPPS integrity committee's statement on match fixing in sport. Coalition of Major Professional and Participation Sports. Retrieved from https://compps.com.au/submissions/COMPPS-2015-09-17-Statement-Match-Fixing-Case.pdf

Condon, P. (2001, April). Report on corruption in international cricket. Anti Corruption Unit, International Cricket Council. Retrieved from https://www.scoop.co.nz/stories/WO0105/S00039/report-on-corruption-in-international-cricket.htm

Cox, S. (2016, 18 January). Tennis match-fixing: Evidence of suspected match-fixing revealed. *BBC Sport*. Retrieved from https://www.bbc.com/sport/tennis/35319202

Davutovic, D., & Bendall, J. (2013, 9 February). Asian gamblers reportedly bet almost $50 million on an A-League match in December. *News.com.au*. Retrieved from www.news.com.au/sport/football/asian-gamblers-reportedly-bet-almost-50-million-on-an-a-league-match-in-december/news-story/9f4f99cb01935f821c3c82fdb161dc9b

Ford, C. (2018, 3 April). Guardians of the world of sport. *Law Institute Journal*. Law Institute Victoria. Retrieved from https://www.liv.asn.au/Staying-Informed/LIJ/LIJ/April/Guardians-of-the-world-of-sport

Forrest, D. (2013). Match fixing: An economic perspective. In M. R. Haberfeld & D. Sheehan (Eds.), *Match-fixing in international sports* (pp. 177–197). New York:Springer.

Forrest, D. & McHale, I. (2015). An evaluation of Sportradar's fraud detection system. University of Liverpool & University of Salford, Manchester.

Gunn, B., & Rees, J. (2008). *Environmental review of integrity in professional tennis*. London: International Tennis Federation.

Harvey, A. (2015). Match-fixing: Working towards an ethical framework. *Journal of the Philosophy of Sport*, 42(3). Retrieved from https://www.tandfonline.com/doi/abs/10.1080/00948705.2015.1037767

Helmers, C. (2019, 17 January). ASADA set to build barriers to protect sport. *The Canberra Times*. Retrieved from https://www.canberratimes.com.au/topic/act-sport-5u2/asada-set-to-build-barriers-to-protect-sport-20190117-p50rvc.html

ICC. (2019, 9 January). ICC announces amnesty. International Cricket Council – media release. Retrieved from https://www.icc-cricket.com/media-releases/970385

Ingle, S. (2007, 8 December). Fallon race-fixing case collapses. *The Guardian*. https://www.theguardian.com/uk/2007/dec/07/sport.ukcrime

Jones, K. (2012). The applicability of the 'United Nations convention against corruption' to the area of sports corruption (match-fixing). *The International Sports Law Journal*, 3–4, 57.

Kerr, J. (2016, 7 January). The dark side of sports data. The Drum, ABC News. Retrieved from https://www.abc.net.au/news/2016-01-07/kerr-the-darkside-of-sports-data/7072988

Kerr, J. (2017a, 18 June). Under the radar: how the global gambling industry is encroaching on amateur sport. Background briefing. *ABC*. Retrieved from https://www.abc.net.au/radionational/programs/backgroundbriefing/8612644

Kerr, J. (2017b). How to build an 'open' match-fixing alert system. *The International Sports Law Journal*, 17(1–2), 49–67.

Lewis, A., Wilkinson, B., & Hezelin, M. (2018). *Independent review of integrity in tennis – Final report.* London: Independent Review Panel.

Maesschalck, J., & Auweele, Y. (2010). Integrity management in sport. *The Journal of Community and Health Sciences*, 5(1), 1–9.

Masters, A. (2015). Corruption in sport: From the playing field to the field of policy. *Policy and Society*, 34(2), 111–123.

Muhsin, M. V. (2013, 8 December). Mandela the secret weapon in 1995 World Cup Rugby final. *The Sunday Observer*. Retrieved from www.sundayobserver.lk/

Murnane, K., & Moller, J. (2018). On the frontline: The role and operations of the Victoria Police Sporting Integrity Intelligence Unit ('SIIU'). In S. Steele and H. Opie (Eds.), *Match-fixing in sport: Comparative studies from Australia, Japan, Korea and Beyond* (pp. 187–203). Abingdon: Routledge.

Nichols, P. (2001, 20 May). Condon wades into swamp of corruption. *The Guardian*. Retrieved from https://www.theguardian.com/sport/2001/may/19/cricket.theguardian

Ordway, C. (2013, 23 September). Sports governance: Doping and integrity measures. UNSW Centre for Law, Markets & Regulation, University of New South Wales. Retrieved from https://clmr.unsw.edu.au/article/sport/sports-governance%3A-doping-and-integrity-measures (also presented at the ANZSLA Annual Conference on 17 Oct 2013 as 'Integrity for Administrators').

Ordway, C., & Opie, H. (2016). Integrity and corruption in sport. In N. Schulenkorf & S. Frawley (Eds.), *Critical issues in global sport management* (pp. 38–65). Abingdon: Routledge.

Parliament of Victoria. (2013, 7 February). *Parliamentary debates: Legislative assembly*, pp. 239–240.

Paulden, T. (2016, June). Smashing the racket. Significance. The Royal Statistical Society. Retrieved from https://rss.onlinelibrary.wiley.com/doi/epdf/10.1111/j.1740-9713.2016.00914.x

Rodenberg, R. M., & Feustel, E. D. (2014). Forensic sports analytics: Detecting and predicting match-fixing in tennis. *Journal of Prediction Markets*, 8(1), 77–95.

Rodenberg, R. M., Sackmann, J., & Groer, C. (2016). Tennis integrity: A sports law analytics review. *The International Sports Law Journal*, 16(1–2), 67–81.

Rothfield, P. (2014, 25 October). Betting boom: Australians punt $26 billion this year on sports like NRL, AFL and basketball. *The Daily Telegraph*. Retrieved from www.dailytelegraph.com.au/news/nsw/betting-boom-australians-punt-26-billion-this-year-on-sports-like-nrl-afl-and-basketball/news-story/c660220ae976cb5879cd9a547a2519d0

Tennis Australia. (2007). *Annual report 2006–2007.* Melbourne: Tennis Australia.

Tennis Australia. (2015a). *Annual report 2014–2015.* Melbourne: Tennis Australia. Retrieved from https://www.tennis.com.au/about-tennis-australia/reports-and-policies/annual-report

Tennis Australia. (2015b). Tennis anti-doping policy. Retrieved from https://www.tennis.com.au/wp-content/uploads/2016/03/Tennis-Australia-anti-doping-policy-v10-ASADA-approved-FINAL MN231214.pdf

Tennis Australia. (2016, 5 May). All news. *Tennis.com.au*. Retrieved from https://www.tennis.com.au/news/2016/05/05/tennis-australia-appoints-integrity-head

Tennis Australia. (2018). *Annual report 2017–2018.* Melbourne: Tennis Australia. Retrieved from https://www.tennis.com.au/about-tennis-australia/reports-and-policies/annual-report

Tennis Australia. (2019a). Disciplinary policy. Retrieved from https://www.tennis.com.au/wp-content/uploads/2019/02/TA-Disciplinary-Policy-2019.pdf

Tennis Australia. (2019b). Member protection policy. Retrieved from https://www.tennis.com.au/wp-content/uploads/2019/02/TA-Member-Protection-Policy-2019.pdf

TIU. (2016, 27 January). Terms of reference announced for independent review of integrity in tennis. Tennis Integrity Unit – Media Release. Retrieved from www.tennisintegrityunit.com/media-releases/terms-reference-announced-independent-review-integrity-tennis

TIU. (2017, 2 July). Isaac Frost provisionally suspended from playing professional tennis. Tennis Integrity Unit – Media Release. Retrieved from https://www.tennisintegrityunit.com/storage/app/media/Media%20Releases/Isaac%20Frost%20provisional%20suspension.pdf

TIU. (2017, 19 July). Tennis Integrity Unit briefing note – July 2017. Tennis Integrity Unit. Retrieved from www.tennisintegrityunit.com/media-releases/tennis-integrity-unit-briefing-note-july-2017

TIU. (2020a) Tennis anti-corruption program. Tennis Integrity Unit. Retrieved from www.tennisintegrityunit.com/storage/app/media/TIU%20Documents/TACP.pdf

TIU. (2020b). Investigations and sanctions. Tennis Integrity Unit. Retrieved from https://www.tennisintegrityunit.com/investigations-and-sanctions

UNODC. (2013). *Criminalization approaches to combat match-fixing and illegal/irregular betting: A global perspective.* United Nations Office on Drugs and Crime. Vienna: United Nations.

UNODC. (2016). *Resource guide on good practices in the investigation of match-fixing.* United Nations Office on Drugs and Crime. Vienna: United Nations.

Vedelago, C. (2020, 27 June). Victoria police cracks alleged international tennis fixing syndicate. *The Sydney Morning Herald.* Retrieved from https://www.smh.com.au/national/victoria-police-cracks-alleged-international-tennis-fixing-syndicate-20200627-p556sz.html

Walker, M. (2006). *Moral repair: Reconstructing moral relations after wrongdoing.* Cambridge: Cambridge University Press.

Walsh, C. (2016, 6 May). Tennis Australia's Ann West on front foot in tackling corruption. *News Limited.* Retrieved from https://www.news.com.au/sport/tennis/tennis-australias-ann-west-on-front-foot-in-tackling-corruption/news-story/b50754422a975ea02ab1646378e3c330

Wood, J., Howman, D. and Murrihy, R. (2018, March). Report of the review of Australia's sports integrity arrangements. Report No 12074. Retrieved from https://www1.health.gov.au/internet/main/publishing.nsf/Content/63F0A5D7BDA5A0B5CA2582CF0005E6F9/$File/HEALTH-RASIA-Report-Acc.pdf

10 The fight against corruption in Vietnamese football

A closer look at typical corruption cases, causes and possible solutions

Thi My Dung Nguyen and Simon Gardiner

Vietnamese football has unfortunately been subject to significant levels of corruption. The most common form of corruption found has been match-fixing, often connected with betting. In the autobiography of the former Vice President of the Vietnam Football Federation (VFF), Ngo Tu Ha, who was in charge of organising VFF competitions, Mr Ngo revealed: 'in the 1990s … there was corruption of all forms, including match manipulation by teams, players in domestic football competitions' (Ngo, 2018). Strong action has been taken by the VFF in imposing sanctions on individuals and teams where there was suspicion of match manipulation based on the reports about the match and other relevant evidences. These actions, however, have not totally eliminated corruption, and this chapter makes further recommendations for restoring trust in Vietnamese football.

Typical corruption cases in Vietnamese football

In the last 15 years, several betting-related match-fixing cases involving Vietnamese players in men's football, competing at the international level, were discovered (H.B., 2014). Two cases are of note and illustrative of the types of challenges facing the VFF.

Case study SEA Games 2005 – Fix

During the football competition in the South East Asian Games (SEA Games) 2005 in the Philippines, seven national players of the Vietnamese men's team were involved in a fix. One of the players (X) was the instigator, who contacted a gambler to discuss the result of the match between the national teams of Vietnam and Myanmar. He encouraged six other players to fix the match result at one goal difference for Vietnam.

On the day of the match, the Vietnamese team scored the first goal of the match. After the goal was scored, the players, who agreed to fix the match result, played below their normal level of performance and tried to keep the ball on the Vietnamese half of the field. They passed the ball so slowly that, although there were some opportunities created, no further goals were scored. The opponent, Myanmar, was the weaker team in the match and could not score a goal. The result of the match was 1–0 for Vietnam and money was paid to the players involved (approx. US$ 1,000 each) by the gambler through an arrangement made by the instigator X (VNS, 2005).

This fixed arrangement was discovered through the presence of a police official. For many years, it had been the practice that each time a Vietnamese sports team travelled for competition, the Ministry of Police sent a police official to assist in security arrangement and to monitor any unsporting behaviour. In this case, the police official received news about contact between a gambling broker with some of the players. Before the match, the official warned the team management about a possible match manipulation conspiracy. After the match, the player who scored the goal, who was not part of the gang, reported information about the conspiracy to the team manager. Thereafter, the police investigation, and subsequent criminal prosecution against the players involved, was conducted. The instigator X was convicted and sentenced to six years of imprisonment, which was reduced to four years by the court of appeal. The other six players were given suspended sentences of between two years, and two and a half years, for the offence of 'organising gambling'. The role of the seven players in this case was to fix the match result, but this act is not a specific offence under the criminal law. For the misconduct of match-fixing, they were only liable for sport sanctions under the VFF disciplinary regulations. However, manipulating the match result at the request of, and in return for, the benefit of the gambler, the players involved were prosecuted for 'organising gambling' (VFF, 2007; T.T. & N.T., 2017).

After serving three years of the four-year sentence, player X, the instigator and main contact with the illegal betting broker in the 2005 case, was released from the prison ahead of time because of good behaviour. Following his release, X is reported to have experienced a difficult period. In speaking to reporter Lan Phuong ten years later, he stated that: 'there had been time when I was very lonely because nobody trusted me anymore. I wished that a team would give me a chance to join the team but nobody offered and all refused' (L.P., 2015).

Case study AFC Cup 2014

Almost a decade later, players from the Vissai Ninh Binh Football Club (VNBFC) from Vietnam were found to have been involved in match-fixing and betting in relation to their matches in the men's Asian Football Confederation club competition, AFC Cup (VNS, 2014; Hoang and Le, 2016).

Three days prior to the match between VNBFC against Malaysian side, Kelantan Football Club, at the team hotel in Malaysia, one VNBFC player (Y), gathered a group of eight other players, to discuss a plan. Y had contacted an illegal betting broker in Vietnam before the trip to prepare the fix. The plan was to place a spot bet for a minimum of two goals to be scored in the first half of the match against Kelantan on 18 March 2014. The total amount intended to be wagered by the players was two billion dong (approx. US$100,000). The agreement was that, whether the result was either a loss or a win, the amount won or lost on the spot bet would be divided equally among the players. Y then contacted the illegal betting broker to place the bet as agreed. However, at the suggestion of the broker, the bet was placed on the total number of goals. There had to be a minimum of three goals scored in the match. This meant that if there were less than three goals in the match (scored by either team), the players would lose the wager. If there were three goals in total, then they would receive nothing. If there were more than three goals scored (in total, to either side), then the players would win the bet. The total amount of the bet placed was set at one billion and 20 million dong (about USD 51,000). If the players won the bet, they would gain 800 million dong (about US $40,000) to share between them. Y informed the players and requested them to try to score as many goals in the match as possible to ensure the number of goals required to win the bet. The players rationalised that this was not cheating, as playing to win is their aim anyway. The result of the match was 3–2 for VNBFC. The players therefore also won the amount of 800 million dong, which was later divided between the nine players involved in the conspiracy. The four players who played the majority of the match received more money than the five who were on the bench (Nguyen, 2014).

Before the match, the club manager had become suspicious after receiving information that some players had a relationship with illegal betting brokers and were concerned that other players might be enticed to manipulate the match result and place a bet on the result of the match (B.P., 2014). The players were monitored, and the concerns reported to the Ninh Binh province police to investigate the suspect players, including Y. The investigation revealed the conspiracy and there was a criminal prosecution. Y was sentenced to 30-months imprisonment and the other players were given between 24 and 27 months suspended sentences by the Ninh Binh provincial court under Article 248 of the Criminal Code for gambling (T.T., 2014). In addition, the VFF disciplinary committee found all the players in breach of Article 55 of the VFF disciplinary regulations for match-fixing and gambling and imposed lifetime bans from all football activities (H.M., 2014).

Unlike the situation in the SEA Games 2005 case mentioned above, where the players involved fixed the match, but did not place a bet themselves on the result, the players of VNBFC both fixed the match result, and placed a bet on the result. They therefore committed the disciplinary offences of match-fixing and gambling at the same time. The key difference between the case studies is that, in the SEA Games case, the corrupted players agreed to play below their normal level of performance to achieve the fixed result, which is against the 'spirit of sport', while the VNBFC players tried to score more goals, which is the normal aim when taking part in a match. However, in both cases, their actions were not just for sporting results but for material gain from betting. This type of match-fixing could not be easily achieved unless they were playing against a weaker opponent. Against a stronger opponent, the fix could be achieved through causing more total goals to be scored by committing fouls leading to penalty kicks being awarded for the opposing team, or by scoring 'own goals'.

In these case studies, there was an insider instigator, who had some form of connection with the betting brokers, who planned and induced other players to be part of the betting-related match-fixing plan. The players involved in those cases have broken the work ethics of players, breached the football rules, that they must not bet on their own games and must report any approaches of match-fixing. Through match-fixing, the players have jeopardised the integrity of football and caused distrust in the sporting public.

Issues which gives rise to corruption

There are many factors which may cause an athlete to become involved in corruption which adversely threatens the integrity of sport. The following have been identified in relation to betting-related match-fixing cases in Vietnamese football.

1. Inadequate training and education on work ethic and sport values: Young footballers in Vietnam are developed mainly at sports training centres and football clubs. They receive inadequate education on the value of sport and work ethics, where the focus is more on training sport-specific skills. Naivety about the outcome of match-fixing due to a lack of awareness can be seen from the police interviews conducted with some of the national players involved in a SEA Games fix. The players said that they thought if they agreed to place a bet on the result of the match to earn some money where they would also win the match, then where was the harm? (A.P., 2005). The players did not appear to consider that once they agreed to fix a match result for an advantage, there would be future implications. For example, it does not seem to have occurred to any of the players, that after winning the bet, this illegal conduct can be used as leverage by the betting broker to force them to do it again; effectively blackmailing them to keep the secret.
2. Vietnamese betting culture: even though gambling was illegal under the law of Vietnam for a long time and has only recently been permitted under strict legal conditions, illegal betting is very popular in the country. Betting on sport attracts many people, especially with the development of online betting platforms where it is very easy to place a bet without regard to the national law, as the Internet has no national boundaries. Each football season, the police in Vietnam have prosecuted many cases of illegal gambling. Recently, two of the former high-ranking police officers in charge of fighting cybercrime, were arrested and criminal proceedings have been opened against them for their involvement in organised crime connected to illegal betting (VnExpress, 2018). However, it can be argued that the information that is known is only the tip of the iceberg. As can be seen with the amount of money bet in each world cup season, there are many illegal betting brokers (AFP., 2018). Players, as well as match officials, are often targeted by these brokers for betting-related match-fixing.
3. Lack of alternate leisure activities: due to the irregular timing of training and competitions, and the player payments received, many players do not work or study. They prefer using their mobile phones for personal entertainment, rather than reading, painting or doing other healthier leisure activities in their free time. The coach of the U23 national team of Vietnam once mentioned in an interview that he would like to give each player a TV so that they could use it for playing

games on big screen instead of using the small screens of their phones (CafeF, 2018). Even though playing phone games can be a form of entertainment, and helps to reduce stress after training and competition, they can also be used to access betting platforms (see for example, Deans et al., 2016). Betting advertising frequently appears while users are accessing games and entertainment websites on the Internet. This can lead to players becoming addicted to betting and/or being approached by betting brokers, and potentially betting on their own matches or coming under the influence of betting brokers.

4. The temptation to spend more than they earn: some players suddenly find themselves comparatively rich overnight through receiving large signing fees and bonuses (Tran, 2014). Without adequate financial education and support, this practice may lead to the habit of spending without thinking. Not having a proper financial plan has led many athletes to spend more than they earn. Even without a career interrupting/ ending injury, this habit can make athletes vulnerable to the lure of gambling activities to earn more money. The consequent connection with gambling crime syndicates may lure them into creating or agreeing to a match-fixing proposition (see also Chapter 12 Ordway and Lenten, this volume).

Difficulties faced by sports associations and authorities in detecting and dealing with corruption

Corruption as a phenomenon that by its very nature is invariably concealed, and sports associations have ineffective measures and tools to monitor and discover it. In many cases, betting-related match-fixing was discovered by general police investigations of organised criminal gangs which led to information related to sports players or officials who had relations with illegal betting brokers. There were also cases in which suspicious players or officials, after being approached and confronted by their club or the federation, disclosed concerns about the corruption. However, this is only a rare occurrence, in part because players and officials were afraid of revenge by those benefiting from the corrupt acts. There is also evidence that individuals might not be aware of the obligation to report incidents of corruption under the rules; they wrongly believed that if they rejected the bribe and did not participate in the match-fixing, then that was enough. In a number of cases of corruption identified and decided under the disciplinary procedure in football, the simple and similar answers from match officials and players were to the effect of: 'I thought if I did not accept the offer then I did nothing wrong.'

Sports associations enjoy autonomy and independence in their organisation and activities under the law. In turn, the law provides for the right of the sports associations to deal with disciplinary matters under the association's rules and regulations. This practice may lead to the sports associations keeping information about corruption within the association. They avoid reporting breaches of the law to the authorities, in order to protect their officials and players. There is also a well-founded fear that once the authorities conduct investigation, there might be other wrongdoing found, and the reputation or brand of the sports association can be badly affected.

Measures put in place to restore trust by Sports associations (the VFF and clubs)

Recognising the real threat of corruption, which jeopardises the integrity of football and causes loss of trust, action has been taken by the sport authorities, namely the VFF as well as the football clubs, in order to educate the players, to monitor and report the suspicion of match-fixing and to sanction infringers. These actions are aimed at preventing, exposing wrongdoing, sanctioning those involved. This sends a strong message that corruption will not be tolerated, and that trust must be regained or football will lose its supporters.

The VFF and the organisers of professional leagues in Vietnam, the Vietnam Professional Football Company (VPF), have cooperated closely with the police authorities working in anti-corruption. The VFF signed an agreement for anti-corruption in football with the Vietnam Criminal Police Department (C45), in 2008 (VFF, 2010). Each year, the VFF and VPF organise training activities for all match officials of the professional leagues prior to the season and request the clubs, officials and players to sign an anti-corruption commitment. Every time the national team is in either training camp and travel for competition, special monitoring measures are implemented with the participation of the team manager, the coach and also the police force. Workshops on anti-corruption have been conducted with the participation of international organisations, such as Interpol, FIFA, AFC (Asian Football Confederation), and local sports authorities to discuss anti-corruption measures.

The cooperation between sports authorities, the VFF and the police force has proved to be effective in general. The VFF has had particular success in the investigation into betting-related match-fixing cases such as that involving Vissai Ninh Binh FC. When VFF received information of possible corruption cases, they would inform the police department in charge of sports-related matters and the police force will carry out the necessary investigation. This approach is generally more effective compared to the investigation by VFF as the police force has the right to use professional methods of investigation and have access to more information on illegal brokers or gamblers. Cases prosecuted and criminal sanctions imposed on offenders also serve the purpose of education and prevention. These cases are used as examples to instruct players and officials that offences committed in sports activities could lead to imprisonment and other sanctions under the criminal law, not just disciplinary sanctions.

Additionally, football clubs and academies have paid attention to the comprehensive education of young players. Hoang Anh Gia Lai Football Club in the V-League is a typical example of the type of clubs which have invested in developing young players and provided the players also with continuing education, including the opportunity to study at the sports university in Vietnam (Hoang Anh Gia Lai Football Club, 2018). Opportunities are also created for them to train and play abroad with professional teams to have better career development. Talented players are identified and nurtured in a good training and competitive environment. Remunerations and benefits of players were also well taken care of so players could focus on training and competition. The young players of Hoang Anh Gia Lai got support everywhere they go (D.A., 2014), Football fans generally of many clubs love the way they play and behave in and out the field of play and believe that they have done their best to perform in the match. This shows how importance trust is, even if you cannot always perform well, you still have the support.

Another club in the V-League, Hanoi Football Club is doing a good job in this talent identification and nurturing (T.H., 2018). Many players of Hanoi Football Club have been called to the national U20, U23 and senior national team to represent the country in international competitions, and they are role models and good examples for younger players to follow. These practical steps helped to develop a generation of players who focus on training and education for better performance, building good image and reputation for exploitation of commercial rights and getting a chance to represent the country in international arenas. They are therefore likely to be less attracted to wrongdoings in sport (H.L., 2019).

The devotion of the young players also showed in the results of the national youth and senior teams where the teams achieved many good results in international arena under the leadership of great Korean head coach Park Hang-seo in all competitions in the regional and continental levels during the last two years. When the national U23 team won the silver medals of the U23 AFC Football Championship in 2018, millions of Vietnamese came out of their homes, waited for the players and cheered them along their way from airport to the city. What is normally a 30-minute trip from the airport to city became a five-hour journey with people cheering to show their love to the team. The sponsors also strongly supported the national teams, the development of youth competitions, as well as national leagues. In return, the sponsors want the commitment from the sports organisers and the teams to zero-tolerance to corruption (Do, 2019).

Recommendations

As laid out in the previous section, action has been taken by the sports authority and the VFF, in cooperation with the relevant police force, to fight corruption at a national level, to educate young players and to regain the trust of supporters. However, it is also necessary to ensure that at the grassroots level, in training centres and football clubs, where players are trained and work, action is taken to prevent and detect corruption. There have continued to be suspicions about corruption cases in amateur football competitions and youth football competitions in recent years (Do, 2019). It is argued that measures must be strongly imposed to show the fans and the sponsors, anti corruption behaviour; and for the players to really understand and avoid being corrupted to protect their image, career and the trust of supporters. The adoption of good policy and practice across several sports and related research findings (see for example ITF, 2008; European Commission, 2019) has suggested restoring trust can be best carried out in three main ways.

1. Education and communication

Education for players about sports values and ethical principles is important to encourage behaviour which could help to prevent and eliminate corruption in football and in life. Open communication among team members, between players and their coaches, managers on how to prevent corruption should be encouraged to create understanding and exchange to avoid committing offences and support early warning and report of corruption. In both cases mentioned earlier, all players, except one, approached by the instigators agreed to be part of betting-related match-fixing conspiracy and none of them reported the approach. This occurred despite there being national laws preventing gambling related match-fixing, and football rules requiring athletes to report any approaches. This indicates that education on the ethical issues around corrupt activities together with the law and rules still needs to be strengthened to create an intrinsic anti-corruption behaviour.

2. Assistance and support to players

Players are targets of crime syndicates and betting people who want to have the game results fixed for their benefit. Not all players are well equipped with a knowledge of grooming techniques, have a promising future in football, a strong reputation to protect, and a solid income to help them to resist the financial offers from corrupting influences. Helping athletes to develop a strong career, to focus on the betterment of sport performance and results, and on legal ways of earning money, with the emphasis on encouraging good practices are important to prevent corruption.

Training centres and football clubs should put in place mechanisms and officials in charge of support the well-being of athletes; ranging from analysing their sport and non-sport talents; creating programmes on sport and life skills, including pursuing alternate educational programmes; advising and counselling athletes in career development in sport and post-retirement. See for example the Australian Institute of Sport (AIS) Wellbeing and Engagement team and resources (https://ais.gov.au/health-wellbeing/awe). Internal networks encouraging exchanges of information and social activities among team members on various subjects would also be beneficial. This helps establish a culture of sharing and helping each other in times where individuals are facing difficulties in sport and in life. Assistance in financial planning should also be supported (pay can be divided into salary, bonus, financial assistance for higher education) (A system for post-retirement funds is set out in Chapter 12 Ordway and Lenten, this volume). Ideally, players should be supported to continue higher education and take training courses on various subjects to improve their knowledge, job opportunities and legal sources of income.

The Ministry of Culture, Sport and Tourism, the Vietnam Olympic Committee and the VFF need to collaborate on establishing a fund from a range of sources to create a resource centre to support all elite athletes (male and female). Successful players, the VFF and sponsors may all be mobilised to contribute to the funds in order to provide scholarships, sponsorships, and loans for athletes who wish to continue their study in sport and other fields for career development. Also, importantly, funding can provide support and assistance to former players to become coaches, trainers, referees, administrators and other relevant roles in the sports industry.

Athletes should be required by their training centres and clubs to keep themselves up to date with information about corruption issues. This includes the duty to report, avoid associating with people who could induce them into corrupt activities, and to educate themselves about the causes and consequences of corruption. They should also be encouraged to reach out for help from their family, club and sports association if they face difficulties in sport, or in life. Although it has been argued that generally young men have a heightened interest generally in gambling (Hing et al., 2016), athletes, if aware of the dangers, may be more inclined to avoid choosing betting as a form of entertainment or a source of income.

Both recommendations one and two focus on the underlying need to bring about measurable change in the cultural framework of sport that prioritises moral-based integrity that focuses on moral and psychological values that are key to dialogue and open-relationships inside and outside the organisation (see Walker, 2002; Gardiner et al. 2016; Harvey & McNamee, 2019).

A key future development is for a players' union to be established to represent and protect players' rights and benefits, to provide help and support to players in need of, and among others, educate and support player in career development, and promote an anti-corruption behaviour among the players. Collective representation of athletes has been a general development across different sports as they develop in size and undergo systemic changes such as professionalisation (Dabscheck, 1994; Schwab, 2018).

3. Rules and regulations, reporting and investigation, disciplinary and criminal actions

At training centres and clubs, there must be consistent rules and regulations on disciplinary and ethical issues. Currently, the VFF club licensing regulations are divided into four categories (A-D). Level A is the highest, mandatory, level that must be met by the clubs to be granted licences to take part in the men's premier division, V-League, competition. One of the lower C level criteria is that the clubs must have rules and regulations on disciplinary and ethical issues. Under category A and B, not meeting such criteria will mean the licence will not be granted. A failure to meet category B requirements means that a licence may be granted with sanctions. It is recommended that the criteria relating to anti-match-fixing should be moved to category A, as it is important for disciplinary and ethical rules be applied in a standardised manner at club level. The sanctions be imposed will then also send a strong message of zero-tolerance to corruption.

The VFF should consider appointing a fulltime integrity officer, to receive and provide all requests for information and assistance on drafting and implementation of anti-match-fixing rules and regulations; to initiate and follow up with investigation and actions in corruption cases reported or discovered.

The tools for reporting information about possible corruption cases also are needed to be created allowing the anonymous report of corruption. Any allegations can then be monitored and followed up with investigatory steps by integrity officers of the federation. Lessons on the whistleblowing system established in the Czech Republic (as outlined in Chapter 8 by Ondráčková and Verschuuren, this volume) could be applied in Vietnam. There is a strong argument that an independent national body, similar to that established in Australia on 1 July 2020 (Sport Integrity Australia), responsible for anti-corruption in sport should be established to carry out these functions. Collaboration with the national body in cooperation with integrity officers in sports organisations, such as outlined in the Tennis Australia example (in Chapter 9 by Harrison and Moller, this volume) could also be useful. In this way, the relevant authorities can follow up with procedures and sanctions under the sports rules and the criminal law (AFC, 2017). This third recommendation reflects a top-down regulatory approach employing both the internal sporting rules and external legal rules that reflects the recent Council of Europe regulatory framework that should be constructed to engage effectively with corrupt manipulation of sports events (Serby, 2015).

Conclusion

Football brings many positive values and enjoyment to the supporters, especially in a country where fans are crazy for football like Vietnam. However, this is very closely linked to the perceived honesty in the sport performance and the key characteristic of competitive sport, the 'uncertainty of outcome' (Gardiner et al., 2012; Pielke, 2013). Fans watch football to enjoy and appreciate the true efforts of the players and teams. They do not come to the football field to watch 'a prescripted and determined play'. Corruption, in the form of taking a material gain from betting on a fixed sport results, jeopardises the integrity of the sport, ruins the good values of honesty and fair play, and causes distrust in football fans. In recent history in Vietnam, match-fixing, bribery, violent conduct and other forms of wrongdoing by players, officials caused a significant reduction in the number of spectators to attend matches of the national football league. Only recently, through young players demonstrating genuine participation and effort in every international match, has the number of football fans coming back to the stadiums for national league matches increased to show their support for this new generation of players. In response, anti-corruption actions must be planned and carried out systematically and consistently at all levels to effectively combat corruption and restore the trust of football fans.

The first step should be focusing on developing generations of football players, from young children to adult professional players, and incorporate their careers as they become coaches or officials, to understand the values of football. Detecting and sanctioning wrongdoing should be the last step. Everyone involved in football must be clear about their responsibilities and duties to safeguard the integrity of football, which will in turn protect their career in football and their well-being in life.

Anti-corruption is an important task which requires the contribution of the whole society for the advancement of sport and return benefits to the society. Better athletes, more transparent and honest competitions will lead to true enjoyment of the people who participate in and support sport competitions. This includes upholding true values for entertainment and development of human physical and mental health. Hand in hand with sporting integrity and the growth of the social values of sport, commercial integrity of sport is vital. External organisations that provide marketing and sponsorship support must be confident that their investment is helping to promote these positive characteristics of sport and that corrupt activities are being robustly engaged with.

Questions

- i *Trust loss* – In whom (or, in which group) has trust been lost in this case?
- ii *Trust correction* – How, if attempted, has the restoration of trust been tried?; and;
- iii *Lessons learned* – How could the lessons from this case be applied to other sports, nations, states, other districts for the same sport, or other sports to prevent a further loss of trust or at least to restore trust?

References

AFC. (2017). The AFC Integrity App (current version: 1.2.5.1-FTR updated February 2020). The Asian Football Confederation. Retrieved from https://play.google.com/store/apps/details?id=ag.sportradar.mobile.radar.afc&hl=vi

AFP. (2018, 24 June). Vietnam busts US$26 million online betting ring: State media. *Vietnam Investment Review News*. Retrieved from https://www.vir.com.vn/vietnam-busts-us-26-million-online-betting-ring-state-media-60415.html

A.P. (2005, 23 December). Quoc Vuong Van Quyen khai gi trong trai giam. *Nguoi Lao Dong News*. Retrieved from https://nld.com.vn/the-thao/quoc-vuong–van-quyen-khai-gi-trong-trai-giam-137323.htm

B.P. (2014, 1 May). Vụ tieu cuc ơ Ninh Binh co dien tien nhu the nao. *Tien Phong News*. Retrieved from https://www.tienphong.vn/the-thao/vu-tieu-cuc-o-ninh-binh-co-dien-tien-nhu-the-nao-701480.tpo

CafeF. (2018, 5 September). HLV Park Hang-seo cuc tam ly, tang cac cau thu mon qua bat ngo truoc khi tro ve CLB. *CafeF News*. Retrieved from http://cafef.vn/hlv-park-hang-seo-cuc-tam-ly-tang-cac-cau-thu-mon-qua-bat-ngo-truoc-khi-tro-ve-clb-20180905095436774.chn

D.A. (2014, 15 September). Khan gia Viet Nam khong quay luong lai voi bong da dep. *VOH online*. Retrieved from https://voh.com.vn/the-thao/khan-gia-viet-nam-khong-quay-lung-voi-bong-da-dep-167421.html

Dabscheck, B. (1994). Early attempts at forming soccer player unions in Australia. *Sporting Traditions*, 10(2), 25–40.

Do, H. (2019, 20 February). V_League co nha tai tro moi: 'Chung toi chi can khong tieu cuc'. *Zing News*. Retrieved from https://news.zing.vn/vleague-co-nha-tai-tro-moi-chung-toi-chi-can-khong-tieu-cuc-post918324.html

Do, H. (2019, 29 December). Canh sat dang dieu tra nghi van tieu cuc tai giai U19 quoc gia. *Zing News.* Retrieved from https://news.zing.vn/canh-sat-dang-dieu-tra-nghi-van-tieu-cuc-tai-giai-u19-quoc-gia-post1030538.html

Deans, E. G., Thomas, S. L., Daube, M., & Derevensky, J. (2016). 'I can sit on the beach and punt through my mobile phone': The influence of physical and online environments on the gambling risk behaviours of young men. *Social Science & Medicine*, 166, 110–119.

European Commission. (2019) Erasmus+ Sport cluster meeting on 'The integrity of sport': Final report. Retrieved from https://eacea.ec.europa.eu/sites/eaceasite/files/brochureclustermeetingsport_2019_web.pdf

Gardiner, S., Welch, R., O'Leary, J., Boyes, S., & Naidoo, U. (2012). *Sports law* (4th ed.). Abingdon: Routledge.

Gardiner, S., Parry, J., & Robinson, S. J. (2016). Integrity and the corruption debate in sport: Where is the integrity? *European Sport Management Quarterly*, 17(1), 6–23.

Harvey, A., & McNamee. M. (2019). Sport integrity: Ethics, policy and practice: An introduction, *Journal of Global Sport Management*, 4(1), 1–7.

H.B. (2014, 4 April). Nhung vu ban do rung dong lang bong da Viet Nam. *Kenh 14 News.* Retrieved from http://kenh14.vn/sport/nhung-vu-ban-do-rung-dong-lang-bong-da-viet-nam-2014041103379961.chn

Hing, N., Russell, A. M., Vitartas, P., & Lamont, M. (2016). Demographic, behavioural and normative risk factors for gambling problems amongst sports bettors. *Journal of Gambling Studies*, 32(2), 625–641.

H.L. (2019, 23 October). Voi the he 'khong doi:lua' cua Quang Hai, Ha Noi FC se mo ra mot ky nguyen moi cho bong da Viet Nam. *Kenh 14 News.* Retrieved from http://kenh14.vn/voi-the-he-khong-doi-lua-cua-quang-hai-ha-noi-fc-se-mo-ra-mot-ky-nguyen-moi-cho-bong-da-viet-nam-20191022183533332.chn

H.M. (2014, 25 December). VFF treo gio vinh vien 9 cau thu Ninh Binh ban do. *Dan Tri News.* Retrieved from https://dantri.com.vn/the-thao/vff-treo-gio-vinh-vien-9-cau-thu-ninh-binh-ban-do-1420167491.htm

Hoang Anh Gia Lai Football Club. (2018, 10 October). Players of Hoang Anh Gia Lai attending the ceremony for their new term of academy at the university of sport. *Hoang Anh Gia Lai FC YouTube channel.* Retrieved from https://www.youtube.com/watch?v=e520h8rdGlo

Hoang, T. & Le, L. (2016, 18 March). Former Dong Nai captain gets 6 years in football match-fixing scandal. *Thanh Nien News.* Retrieved from www.thanhniennews.com/sports/former-dong-nai-captain-gets-6-years-in-football-matchfixing-scandal-60106.html

International Tennis Federation (ITF). (2008). Environmental review of integrity in professional tennis. Retrieved from www.sportingintelligence.com/wp-content/uploads/2011/01/Integrity-in-tennis.pdf

L.P. (2015, 19 July). Cuu tien ve Quoc Vuong: toi chua gia nhung nhung gi toi trai qua con hon ca mot cuoc doi. *Thanh Nien News.* Retrieved from https://thethao.thanhnien.vn/bong-da-viet-nam/cuu-tien-ve-quoc-vuong-toi-chua-gia-nhung-nhung-gi-toi-trai-qua-con-hon-ca-mot-cuoc-doi-51415.html

Ngo, T. H. (2018, 31 May). The auto-biography: Trai bong lan giua doi:toi: Mot minh chong lai … 'mafia'. *Thanh Nien News.* Retrieved from https://thethao.thanhnien.vn/bong-da-viet-nam/tu-truyen-trai-bong-lan-giua-doi-toi-mot-minh-chong-lai-mafia-87910.html

Nguyen, T. C. (2014, 12 April). Lo dien ke dau so va danh sach cac cau thu ban do cua V. Ninh Binh. *Thethao247.vn.* Retrieved from https://www.tinmoi.vn/toan-canh-vu-ban-do-o-vninh-binh-da-co-danh-sach-den-011301687.html

Pielke, R.Jr. (2013, 19 February) Does uncertainty of outcome define sport? *The Least Thing*. Retrieved from http://leastthing.blogspot.com.au/2013/02/does-uncertainty-of-outcome-define-sport.html

Schwab, B. (2018). Embedding the human rights of players in world sport. *The International Sports Law Journal*, 17(3–4), 214–232.

Serby, T. (2015). The Council of Europe convention on manipulation of sports competitions: The best bet for the global fight against match-fixing? *The International Sports Law Journal*, 15 (1), 83–100.

T.H. (2018, 13 September). Bau Hien: 2 den 3 nam nua Quang Hai se toi nhung doi: hang dau Chau A. *Zing News*. Retrieved from https://news.zing.vn/bau-hien-2-den-3-nam-nua-quang-hai-se-toi-nhung-doi-hang-dau-chau-a-post876689.html

Tran, H. (2014, 26 August). Cau thu ca do dung loi gia dinh vao. *Thethao Vanhoa News*. Retrieved from https://thethaovanhoa.vn/bong-da-viet/cau-thu-ca-do-dung-loi-gia-dinh-vao-n20140826001418288.htm

T.T. and N.T. (2007, 26 January). Vu cac cau thu U13 ban do: 6 nam tu giam cho Quoc Vuong, cac cau thu con lai huong an treo. *Thanh Nien News*. Retrieved from https://thanhnien.vn/thoi-su/phap-luat/vu-cac-cau-thu-u23-ban-do-6-nam-tu-giam-cho-quoc-vuong-cac-cau-thu-con-lai-huong-an-treo-277861.html

T.T. (2014, 25 August). Tuyen an nhom 9 cau thu Ninh Binh ban do. *An Ninh Thu Do News*. Retrieved from https://anninhthudo.vn/phap-luat/tuyen-an-nhom-9-cau-thu-ninh-binh-ban-do/567392.antd

VFF. (2007, 20 March). Cong bo cac muc ky luat cac cau thu dinh dang den tieu cuc tai SEA Games 23. *VFF website*. Retrieved from https://vff.org.vn/cong-bo-cac-muc-ky-luat-cac-cau-thu-dinh-dang-den-tieu-cuc-tai-sea-games-23/

VFF. (2010, 26 April). VFF and police authority signed agreement to cooperate in anti-corruption in football. *VFF website*. Retrieved from http://en.vff.org.vn/news/vff-and-c14-sign-co-ordination-regulations-of-anti-corruption-in-football-906.html

VnExpress. (2018, 6 April). Vietnam's former police chief arrested in multi-million-dollar gambling case. *VnExpress International News*. Retrieved from https://e.vnexpress.net/news/news/vietnam-s-former-police-chief-arrested-in-multi-million-dollar-gambling-case-3733301.html

VNS. (2005, 22 December). Star striker held for SEA Games match-fixing. *Viet Nam News –The National English Language Daily*. Retrieved from http://vietnamnews.vn/sports/149451/star-striker-held-for-sea-games-match-fixing.html#SpSDEKjQTO5dzRK1.97

VNS. (2014, 26 August). Ninh Binh players sentenced to jail. *Vietnam News –The National English Language Daily*. Retrieved from http://vietnamnews.vn/sports/259325/ninh-binh-players-sentenced-to-jail.html#TORz86K9H0RmrYQQ.97

Walker, M. (2002) *Moral repair: Reconstructing moral relations after wrongdoing*, Cambridge: Cambridge University Press.

11 Restoring trust in football through behavioural advocacy

A case study from Nigeria

Bob Olukoya and Aderonke Ogunleye-Bello[1]

Introduction

The purpose of this chapter is to apply the case study of a Nigerian football coach recorded collecting a bribe to illustrate how *moral repair* (Walker, 2001) and *ethics of care* (Gilligan, 1982) can be complementary to the predominantly punitive and retributive justice system in Nigeria. Football is no doubt the most popular sport in Nigeria and it unifies the nation the way nothing else does (Omilana, 2018). The Super Eagles and the Super Falcons (male and female national team respectively) are well loved and have enjoyed great successes in Africa and on the world football stage (Asokan, 2010). However, both football leagues in Nigeria are currently going through a challenging period mainly due to historical integrity issues that have led to sponsor and fan apathy. Football coaches in Nigeria, especially with the national teams, are high-profile individuals and subjected to public scrutiny, especially during the countdown to continental and international tournaments. The dominant narrative within the media and amongst fans is that the selection process had been corrupted and players are chosen based on their willingness to bribe the coach (Nwosu & Ugwuerua, 2015).

This chapter is focused on a case study relating to a coach of the Super Eagles found to have been bribed, and how he was addressed by the responsible football federation. Did this response restore trust? What other step(s) could have been taken in attempting to restore trust? The chapter will conclude with recommendations on what could be done to discourage similar behaviour in future promoting values such as care, remorse, ethics and virtue-based rules at its core.

The case study: Salisu Yusuf

Nigeria, in the wider context is a country that is tough on societal ills with an unforgiving penal system. While capital punishment remains on the books, the prison service was recently renamed the Nigerian Correctional Service (NCS), partly in recognition of the fact that there is the need to move towards rehabilitation and away from punishment and retributive justice (Afilaka, 2019).

This is a case study of a Nigerian coach recorded collecting a bribe from undercover reporters posing as football agents. The subject of the sting, Mr Salisu

Yusuf, was a respected assistant coach of the Super Eagles (Nigerian senior men's national football team). He was also in charge of the Nigerian U/23 men's team. In July 2018, the news broke that Yusuf had been caught accepting a 'bribe' – US $1,000 – from undercover journalists. Posing as football agents, the journalists paid the bribe on the pretence that it was to facilitate the selection of two players into the B-Team of the Super Eagles scheduled to represent Nigeria at the 2018 edition of the African Nations Championship. Yusuf also agreed in the video to accept a financial payoff if the players in question eventually secured transfers to foreign clubs as a result of their exposure in the Championship (Sulola, 2018).

Conviction and punishment

After an inquiry by the disciplinary committee, it was found that Yusuf had breached his duty as a senior coach and had brought disrepute to football and his employer – the Nigeria Football Federation (NFF). It was further found that the decision to accept the cash was a deliberate one, and not merely an error of judgement as suggested by some of Yusuf's advocates (Ugbane, 2018). Yusuf was subsequently banned from all sporting activities for one year and fined US$5,000. He protested his innocence throughout the trial and was fiercely supported by the highly influential Nigerian Football Coaches Association (NFCA).

The NFCA representatives claimed that the hearing was unnecessary and supported the view that the cash was a gift, as contemplated within Article 20(1) of the FIFA and NFF Code of Ethics, which provided that gifts and other benefits were permitted where the gift is 'symbolic or trivial value and would not create a conflict of interest'. However, Article 20(2) clarified that gifts 'shall' not be accepted if there is any doubt as to their purpose or intent. The disciplinary committee held that the coach ought to have rejected the gift (Olawale, 2018).

Public opinion

Yusuf's one-year ban and fine by the disciplinary committee was viewed by the public, the media and other external football stakeholders as unusually lenient and a: 'mere slap on the wrist' (Udoh, 2018, p. 1). While the gift giving culture in Nigeria has been described as including 'polite corruption' (Brownsberger, 1983), it is also clear that people: 'know the difference between a polite gratuity and a bribe' (Salisu, 2000, p. 6). The public perception in Nigeria was also that the NFF and its disciplinary committee were too eager to close the case and 'move on' with the hope that the public would sooner, rather than later, forget the saga.

The reverse, however, was the case, as the public opinion continued to build against the NFF. This was exacerbated as Yusuf, who was viewed as a role model within and outside football, did not show any remorse (Edefe, 2019). Journalists tied this case back to a previous incident in 2016, involving the highly rated Daniel Amokachi, former captain and coach of the Super Eagles. Amokachi disclosed at the time that young footballers (U/17 cadre) invited to the national camp were required by the coaches to part with at least N250,000 (700 USD) each in order to make the team (Ochayi, 2016). The NFF did not take Amokachi's revelation seriously and never investigated the claim. Rather, the NFF and the NFCA at the time, defended their coaches and demanded empirical evidence from Amokachi (Ugbane, 2016). The authors observed that, had the NFF taken the allegations from Amokachi seriously and instituted an inquiry or review similar to the Wood Review (2018) in Australian sport, the Yusuf saga might have been averted. This was predicated on the fact that issues of bribe-taking would have been in the forefront of public discourse and might have influenced Yusuf's judgement.

After Yusuf was sentenced, the public was of the opinion that the NFF had again missed an opportunity to use the case of a very popular coach, who had obviously erred, to lead the advocacy for the restoration of trust and confidence in Nigerian football. The NFF was further criticised for not being proactive, especially as the chairman of the ethics committee publicly declared that Yusuf committed a moral wrong rather than a legal wrong (Editor, 2018). No lasting measures were put in place by the NFF to forestall or dissuade other coaches, players and their agents from future moral breaches.

To balance the leniency perceptions of the public, an analysis of the options open to the NFF disciplinary committee reveals that the committee has limited powers in sentencing. The FIFA rules (FIFA, 2019) regulating breaches of Art 20 (1) and (2) provided for a ***maximum*** fine of CHF10,000 (US$10,000 approximately) and a ban from all football activities for two years for a first-time offender (repeat offenders gets a maximum of five years) (Art 20(3)). Yusuf, as a first offender, receiving a US$5,000 fine and one-year ban represents a 50% reduction in the recommended tariff. The disciplinary committee and the NFF justified the reduced sanction on the fact that the coach was previously of unblemished character and that the players in question were an automatic pick for the national team anyway (Okeleji, 2018).

Based on the public reaction described above, the punitive and retributive focused judicial system in Nigeria had not satisfied the yearnings of some of its critical stakeholders (the fans). Can the moral repair concept and Ethics of Care theory fill in this gap?

Moral repair

Margaret Walker argues that moral repair is 'an unavoidable human task' given that our human fallibility is replicated through traditional restorative justice processes. Reparations can strengthen individual dignity and mutual trust in the wake of serious wrongdoing (Walker, 2006, p. 6). At the most basic level (everyday practice), moral repair is simply a response to wrongdoing (Walker, 2001), such as through an offending party offering an apology to the offended party and guaranteeing not to repeat the behaviour in question. Mere apology might not suffice in such circumstances and retributive justice may also be impracticable. Therefore, reparative effort, which includes a complex process of the acknowledgement of wrongdoing and the desire to re-establish broken trust in order to forge better relationship between the offender and the offended groups might be desirable

(Brännmark, 2008). For example, moral repair can be applied within the context of historical injustices spanning generations that have damaged relationships, such as the slave trade and the apartheid regime in South Africa. In Australia, a National Sorry Day has been held each year since 1998: 'This day gives people the chance to come together and share the steps towards healing for the Stolen Generations, their families and communities. Stolen Generations refer to Indigenous Australians who were forcibly removed from their families and communities' (Passi, 2013).

Ethics of Care theory

The Ethics of Care was developed out of the identity and moral development research by Carol Gilligan (1982). It is premised upon the fact that humans are inherently relational, responsive, connected and interdependent (Walker, 2006). Sometimes referred to as feminist ethics (Bogaert & Ogunbanjo, 2009), due to its focus on care and compassion rather than justice-based rules. Gilligan posits that morality based on pursuit of justice alone was incomplete and likely to become oppressive and damaging (Pettersen, 2011). In the same vein, critical ethicist Nel Noddings also contributed to the theory by promoting the view that values such as care, ethics, trust, mutual consideration and solidarity should be embedded within the justice system (Noddings, 1984, p. 2). Higher standards of responsibility, Noddings claimed, are usually associated with people with a moral duty of care, in contrast with people merely under legal obligations (1984, p. 2). She went further to argue that the law in most cases simply forbade people from acting in a particularly harmful way, whereas moral obligations include both refraining from acting in a harmful manner, and also providing help to others whenever needed. Care, empathy and relationship building are at the core of the theory (Held, 2005; Slote, 2007).

In applying the principles of moral repair and Ethics of Care to the case study, there are two critical stages. The first is to establish the existence of a moral wrongdoing, and identify the perpetrator, beneficiaries and victims. It is evident by virtue of the pronouncement of the disciplinary committee that trust had been broken or, at very least, damaged. The coach was found to have brought the game into disrepute (Okeleji 2018). The breach was made public which means that it impacted on the broader footballing community so that fans, players, parents of children playing, the NFF and football stakeholders including licensees, broadcasters and sponsors are all victims. Yusuf was both the perpetrator (although on this occasion, not the initiator) and sole beneficiary – however, under different circumstances, there could be multiple parties, i.e. multiple perpetrators and beneficiaries.

The second stage is to formulate a clear pathway in dealing with the wrongdoing. The options include doing nothing and allow the wrongdoing to fade away or either to forgive or make amends (Walker, 2006). The first option is rarely recommended. The victim(s) is/are at the heart of the forgiveness pathway. According to Walker: 'forgiveness is a variable human process and a practice with distinctive versions' (2006, p. 152) and the mode and manner of forgiveness is solely at the discretion of the victim(s). Walker was careful not to provide a definitive explanation of forgiveness. Rather, she acknowledged three definitive features of forgiveness that have been commonly discussed by other writers. Forgiveness is predicated upon 'getting past resentment'; 'restoration of relationship' or 'permanently settling or fixing a past wrong' (Walker, 2006, p. 169). Walker's position was that forgiveness can endure even if all the three features of forgiveness remain indeterminate. None should be insisted upon as a prerequisite for forgiveness. Each individual and community has their peculiar way of forgiving, which must be respected. Recalling that the victims in the case study were football stakeholders and the NFF, the key question is, who then forgives Yusuf and how is the forgiveness determined and translated? These will be discussed further below.

The third pathway to moral repair is making amends, which is firmly within the realm of the wrongdoer. Making amends is described by Walker as: 'intentional reparative action by party or parties who acknowledge responsibility for wrong, and whose reparative actions are intended to redress that wrong' (2006, p. 191). These could range from a straightforward public apology to engaging in behavioural change advocacy as previously mentioned. The most important aspect is that amends are made to the victims with a view to trust restoration.

Why is trust important in sport?

The uniqueness, or as described by Bruyninckx (cited by Nehme & Ordway, 2016, p. 208), the 'exceptionalism' of sport, is well recognised. The Nice Declaration on Sport (European Council, 2000) introduced the term 'specificity of sport' in reference to sport's special characteristics (Smith & Stewart, 2010, p. 2). This uniqueness, according to Hoye et al. (2008, p. 507), transcends consumer behaviours, relationship between sport and government, regulatory regimes, strategy, organisational structure, human resource management, organisational culture, governance and performance management, etc. Sport has become a protected 'social institution' (Smith & Stewart, 2010), despite its capacity to generate huge commercial resources, based on its necessity for competitive balance and uncertainty of outcomes (Zimbalist, 2002; Szymanski, 2006; Healey, 2012). These dual concepts form the bedrock of professional sport and have driven the drama, passion and rivalry that has transformed sport, especially team sports such as football, into the global, entertaining and economic phenomenon that it is today (Buraimo & Simmons, 2008, p. 146). The challenge, as identified by Nehme & Ordway (2016), is that if the social contract, or social licence (outlined in Chapter 5 Jamieson and Ordway, this volume), is breached through any attempt to tinker with the competitive balance or uncertainty of outcome, then trust in sport is destroyed. In this setting, if the outcomes of games are pre-determined, or players are selected by how much they can pay, not by how well they can play, then sport is robbed of its spontaneity, integrity, appeal and meaning (Szymanski, 2006). It is paramount that trust is preserved, and sport administrators put measures in place that will dissuade behaviour that undermines trust at all levels. Relating this to the case study of Yusuf, receiving money in order to field players, as already established, is a fundamental breach of trust, which can potentially affect the competitiveness or otherwise of the teams involved.

Pre-condition to restoring trust: Addressing the culture of deviancy

In responding to breach of trust issues, it is pertinent to adopt a holistic stance (Harley, 2012), bridge communication gaps (Chambers & Craft, 1998), review existing systems and explore ways of rebuilding trust within the affected community (the football ecosystem). The first step then is to examine whether a culture of deviancy exists within the football community and hierarchy:

(i) Response from the Offender (Yusuf): The national team coaches are high-profile and widely regarded, fairly or otherwise, as role models for other coaches and players alike. In this case study, despite being the second highest ranked football coach in Nigeria, Yusuf did not appear to show any remorse before or after his sanction. It is also telling that none of the commentators, nor Yusuf himself, seemed concerned that coaches would agree to meet with 'player agents', despite stating upfront in the videoed meeting that their mission was to undermine his decision-making process as a coach.

Remorse on the part of the wrongdoer is a critical condition precedent to the application of the moral repair (making amends) and the Ethics of Care theory. However, the NFF cannot force the coach to feel or demonstrate genuine and sincere remorse as contemplated by Gilligan and Walker. If the wrongdoer does not show remorse, it is likely to reflect a personal unwillingness to repair trust and may be evidence of a culture that trivialises ethical imperatives and ignores deviant behaviour, which needs to be addressed.

(ii) Response from the Senior Coach (Gernot Rohr): Not only did the senior coach, Rohr, not show any genuine outrage, he publicly supported Yusuf as a victim of entrapment (PH, 2018). Ignoring the FIFA Code of Ethics, which applies to coaches (FIFA, 2019), Rohr also did not report the meeting to his employer or to the numerous anti-bribery agencies in Nigeria (such as the Independent Corrupt Practices Commission – ICPC). Rohr may have been concerned that as he had only been in the country since 2016 (Ayinor, 2016), and if he 'made waves' his contract may have been terminated. The alternate argument is that, as a senior German coach for over 20 years, Rohr would have been aware of the zero-tolerance policy on corruption in football, and what his obligations were (Ordway, 2014). If Rohr knew that Yusuf had been approached, it should also have been mandatory that Rohr report it to the NFF and FIFA (Hill Commandment 4, Pielke, 2011).

(iii) Response from the Nigerian Football Coaches Association (NFCA): While some stakeholders may feel it is entirely appropriate for the NFCA to stand by their member in the wake of the public outcry that followed the release of the video recording, others may believe that the NFCA responsibility was to back those coaches who are ethical, and would not have accepted the bribe. Instead, the NFCA spokesperson at the time described the gift as 'trivial'. The NFCA agreed that the behaviour of Yusuf 'dents' the reputation of their association but stated that they did not think the integrity and reputation of football was negatively affected (Udo-Okpo, 2018). The NFCA clearly exhibited a high level of tolerance for deviance and contributed to creating a culture of impunity and cheating.

(iv) Response from the NFF: The NFF followed its own rules and that of FIFA in diligently investigating the matter in relation to Yusuf (but not Rohr as mentioned above). However, there was public outcry when the one-year ban and $5,000 fine was announced. As set out above, the NFF were unable to clearly communicate the restrictions placed on the domestic tribunal by the FIFA regulations, and why it was felt that a 50% reduction in the FIFA recommended sanction was appropriate. The challenge for the NFF position became even stronger when Yusuf was first restored to his old job after his ban was served, and then was seconded by the NFF to oversee the affairs of a Nigerian club in the prestigious Confederation of African Football (CAF) Confederation Cup, after that team parted ways with their manager (Oyeleke, 2019). These decisions poorly reflected on the supposed conscience of football in Nigeria.

(v) Response from the fans, sponsors and other external stakeholders: The public outcry and media attention around this case study indicated that there was a trust deficit between the NFF and some of its external stakeholders, especially the fans, which in turn had led to a disconnect between the two. It was clear that the fans wanted more than a 'box-ticking' disciplinary process. However, as illustrated above, the NFF appeared to prioritise addressing the issue in a timely manner, rather than the substantive causes. While an argument about fairness for people having the opportunity to make amends and get on with their lives after serving their sanction is acknowledged, the NFF, in reinstating Yusuf to his old job without having accepted responsibility for his actions, means that the NFF's efforts were significantly undermined.

This case also highlighted a missed opportunity for the government, sponsors and broadcasters to influence the action taken by the NFF. While there may still be a view that: 'Most Nigerians continue to question government's involvement in sports matters that they believe should be left for the private sector', the fact is that the NFF is reliant on government funding and that: 'The National Sports Policy of Nigeria highlights the obligations of the federal government in sports, including football, with an emphasis on the administration, management and sponsorship' (Okolie-Osemene & Okoh, 2014, p. 5).

Recommendations

One popular way to demonstrate the rebuilding process is to sanction the offender. In this case study, the NFF punished Yusuf. However, as already discussed, sanctioning one individual offender alone is insufficient to repair the damage done, particularly where there was widespread belief that this incident was merely one of many other cases that had gone undetected and/or unpunished. Therefore, additional ways to renew and promote integrity, fairness, solidarity, responsibility and respect are needed to restore trust in Nigerian football. A holistic (Ordway & Opie, 2016), Ethics of Care approach, including behavioural integrity awareness campaigns, ethical training, and establishing a code of ethics is recommended to achieve moral repair and to restore trust to Nigerian football as follows.

1. Behavioural awareness advocacy

It is clear from the foregoing that rules, regulations or codes cannot be the only solution to Nigeria's integrity problem. Rather, the challenge is ensuring that rules, codes and regulations are understood and adhered to. In this case study, the fact that Yusuf continues to insist that the money he collected from the undercover reporter was merely 'symbolic and of trivial value', as provided in the FIFA codes, could be a product of ignorance and lack of appreciation of the importance of 'letter and spirit' of the law. If a high-profile football coach and administrator of his calibre can get it so wrong, then hundreds of local coaches throughout Nigeria may act in similar manner (if not worse).

As a result, there is an urgent need for the Integrity Unit of the NFF to embark on sustained anti-corruption awareness throughout the country. The advocacy must be focused, friendly and in multiple languages. The content needs to be geared towards educating all stakeholders, from the grassroots to the professional level, on the damaging effect that deviant behaviour, no matter how petty, can have on the game and their careers. For instance, major sponsors had abandoned Nigerian football partly due to the accumulation of integrity challenges, which includes match-fixing, age fraud, nepotism, funds mismanagement, electoral malpractices and breaches of contract (Ifetoye, 2019). If these sponsors refuse to return to Nigerian football, the loss will be felt by everyone, especially those at the community level. The message must also be clear about what people should do when they witness or become aware of unethical behaviour. If this advocacy is well planned and implemented, it will go a long way in restoring trust and rebuilding the image of Nigerian football.

2. Regular training and coaching conferences

These are essential for coaches irrespective of status. With global technological advancement, coaching has become more scientific and many Nigerian coaches could benefit from training that better equips them for the job and raises their level of technical competence. Online training, face-to-face conferences and awareness-raising, regarding the dangers of corruption and of negligence in their coaching work, could improve their ethical competence and renew their commitment to the job. This will strengthen their moral fibre to be able to resist desperate players and agents who may offer gifts and a percentage of their wages in order to curry favours and/or be selected as one of the first 11 players in the team.

3. Code of ethics

To support these measures, the NFF needs to strengthen its code of ethics for its members, particularly including the referees and the NFCA, to guide them on how to behave professionally and promote fairness. This can support the work of every member, official and coach at all levels in Nigeria. All coaches should sign the code of ethics at the time of accepting their contracts. Stiff penalties must be spelt out for deviant behaviour, such as bribe-taking (Hill argues for life bans: Commandment 5, Pielke, 2011). As part of the code of ethics, a comprehensive coaching policy for football should be developed for the country, to ensure that a high level of technical competence is achieved alongside with deepened ethical awareness.

A separate code, supported by ethical training, could also be provided for match and player agents. This guidebook can be used by every agent and would constitute a germane part of the roadmap to sustainable football development. The understanding of the need for this clarity is not new internationally (e.g. Dee, 1992; Kelly & Chatziefstathiou, 2018). In line with the FIFA Code of Ethics, the NFF Code must also cover player and match agents and clearly spell out their obligations, such as found in the Football Federation of Australia [FFA] Code of Conduct:

> A Player, an Official and an Agent must not:
>
> (a) accept bribes through the offer, promise or acceptance of any Benefit in return for violating his or her duties; or
> (b) provide for a Benefit any information concerning a Club, its team's actual or likely composition, the form or injuries of Players or possible tactics (other than in connection with a bona fide media interview). (FFA, 2017, Art 4.2)

Having such commonalities in the way everyone works would be good for the industry and help to promote fairness, solidarity and respect from juniors all the way up to the national women's and men's representative teams. (Further discussion on the drafting of Codes of Ethics can be found in Chapter 4 by Riedl, this volume.)

4. *Timely payment of salaries and allowances*

As demonstrated by the research of Declan Hill, the adequacy and timeliness of remuneration is crucial to ensure robust integrity (Commandment 3, Pielke, 2011). Predominantly in Africa, and Nigeria in particular, salaries and allowances of coaches and at times players are left unpaid for several months, usually caused by the mismanagement of funds or sponsors defaulting on payments. There is also no state sponsored social or financial support for citizens on low income or the unemployed. Therefore, if coaches and other sports professionals are not paid on time, it has profound and fundamental effects on these players and their families. Nigerian teams have had a long history of protesting to bring attention to these contractual breaches (e.g. Ndlovu, 2002; Waldstein, 2014), including at the Premier League level (Okolie-Osemene & Okoh, 2014). As recently as 2019, both the Super Eagles and the Super Falcons had to threaten strike action in order to receive their promised payments (Okeleji, 2019). Whilst not justification to resort to criminality or deviant behaviour, it would be self-defeating for the NFF to embark on behavioural awareness advocacy whilst basic contractual terms remain unfulfilled.

5. Clear guidance on accepting gifts

The NFF, as part of its oversight function, must set out clear guidelines on when it is appropriate to accept as gifts, and from whom gifts can be accepted. Unsolicited gift offering and acceptance is normal in the wider Nigerian society and it is unrealistic to expect football to be an exception. This cultural norm was clearly demonstrated in the attitude of Yusuf and the NFCA. This ambiguity can be removed by the NFF through either banning the acceptance of gifts – solicited or otherwise by its coaching staff – or outlawing the acceptance of cash and establishing a threshold on non-cash gifts (e.g. N 3,000 or $10). It would have been interesting to note what the reaction would have been if only the conversation, but no evidence of cash, had been recorded.

Conclusion and final considerations on restoring trust

A single solution to the challenges of bribe-taking and other deviant behaviour in Nigerian football cannot produce the desired result. A multifaceted and holistic approach involving all stakeholders is required. Starting from the national coaches, who occupy a special position of trust that must not be abused nor utilised for personal gain, the NFF must be alive to its responsibilities as the regulator of football in Nigeria and the coaches' employer. To be effective, the recommendations discussed above need to be implemented and communicated throughout all levels of the game.

More importantly, when breaches of the rules inevitably occur, a balance is needed: while punishment and retribution may be appropriate, the breach cannot be treated with levity. Rather, a robust inquiry into why the wrongdoing happened and the factors responsible must be conducted. The immediate acknowledgement that trust has been broken, and an understanding that it can be mended through the care and just moral repair process is crucial. The interests of the victim in the breach must always be paramount; in this case the loyal fans. Above all, regular behavioural advocacy for coaches and agents aimed at consistently orientating them on the highest standards of professional and social behaviour, supported by a code of ethics embedded into their job descriptions and accreditation processes, will go a long way to restoring trust.

Questions

i *Trust loss* – In whom (or, in which group) has trust been lost in this case?

ii *Trust correction* – How, if attempted, has the restoration of trust been tried?; and;

iii *Lessons learned* – How could the lessons from this case be applied to other sports, nations, states, other districts for the same sport, or other sports to prevent a further loss of trust or at least to restore trust?

Note

1 The authors are grateful to the feedback on this chapter provided by Kemi Ogunyemi, Catherine Ordway, Stirling Sharpe and Richard Lucas.

References

Afilaka, T. (2019, 17 August). The Nigerian correctional service: What's in a name change? *Cobra Review*. Retrieved from https://cobrareview.com/nigerian-correctional-service-name/

Asokan, S. (2010, 15 June). World Cup 2010: Super Eagles allow hopes to soar in land of so little. *The Guardian*. Retrieved from https://www.theguardian.com/football/blog/2010/jun/15/nigeria-world-cup

Ayinor, P. (2016, 5 August). BREAKING: NFF picks Gernot Rohr as Super Eagles coach. *The Punch*. Retrieved from https://punchng.com/nff-picks-gernot-rohr-super-eagles-coach/

Bakare, T. (2018, 24 July). Nigerian Coach caught on tape taking bribe. *The Guardian*. Retrieved from https://guardian.ng/sport/nigerian-coach-salisu-yusuf-caught-on-camera-taking-bribe/

Bogaert, K. D., & Ogunbanjo, G. A. (2009). Feminism and the ethics of care.*South African Family Practice*, 51(2), 116–118.

Brännmark, J. (2008). Moral repair: Reconstructing moral relations after wrongdoing – by Margaret Urban Walker. *Theoria*, 74(2), 169–172. doi:10.1111/j.1755-2567.2008.00015.x

Brownsberger, W. N. (1983). Development and governmental corruption – Materialism and political fragmentation in Nigeria. *The Journal of Modern African Studies*, 21(2), 215–233.

Buraimo, B., & Simmons, R. (2008). Do sports fans really value uncertainty of outcome? Evidence from the English Premier League. *International Journal of Sport Finance*, 3(3) 146–155.

Chambers, H., & Craft, R. (1998). *No fear management*. Boca Raton, FL: St. Lucie Press.

Dede, S. (2018, 9 May). 'A slap in the wrist': Twitter reacts to NFF's one-year ban for Nigerian coach. *Pulse.ng Newspaper*. Retrieved from https://www.pulse.ng/sports/football/salisu-yusuf-a-slap-in-the-wrist-twitter-reacts-to-nffs-one-year-ban-for-nigerian/d9n8ngp

Dee, P. T. (1992). Ethical aspects of representing professional athletes. *Marq. Sports LJ*, 3, 111.

Edefe, E. (2019, 12 September). [Nigeria] Nobody is removing Imama, He remains the chief coach of U23 and WAFU bound team – NFF. *ZoneFoot*. Retrieved from https://zonefoot.net/2019/09/12/nigeria-nobody-is-removing-imama-he-remains-the-chief-coach-of-u23-and-wafu-bound-team-nff/

Editor. (2018, 6 September). Ethics committee: Why Salisu got lenient punishment. *Football Live.ng*. Retrieved from https://www.footballlive.ng/ethics-committee-why-salisu-got-lenient-punishment/

Eludini, T. (2018, 24 July). Super Eagles Coach Salisu Yusuf caught receiving bribe. *Premium Times*. Retrieved from https://www.premiumtimesng.com/sports/football/277573-super-eagles-coach-salisu-yusuf-caught-receiving-bribe.html

European Council. (2000). *Nice declaration: Declaration on the specific characteristics of sport and its social function in Europe*. Nice: European Council.

FFA. (2017, 1 September). Code of conduct. Football Federation Australia [FFA]: Sydney. Retrieved from https://www.ffa.com.au/sites/ffa/files/2017-09/National%20Code%20of%20Conduct.pdf

FIFA. (2019, 1 August). FIFA: Code of ethics. Fédération Internationale de Football Association [FIFA], Zurich. Retrieved from https://resources.fifa.com/image/upload/fifa-code-of-ethics-2019.pdf?cloudid=fmhdml5mjqynrljmmsut

Gilligan, C. (1982). *In a different voice*. Cambridge, MA: Harvard University Press.

Harley, M. (2012). *The ripple effect' process: An introduction to psycho-emotional-education* (1st ed.). London: Balboa Press.

Healey, D. (2012). Governance in sport: Outside the box? *The Economic and Labour Relations Review*, 23(3), 39–60.

Held, V. (2005). *The ethics of care: Personal, political, and global*. Oxford Scholarship Online. Oxford University Press.

Hoye, R., Nicholson, M., & Smith, A. (2008). Unique aspects of managing sport organizations. In C. Wankle (Ed.), *Sage handbook of 21st century management* (pp. 501–509). London: Sage Publications.

Ifetoye, S. (2019, 26 April). Why private sponsorship of football clubs is failing in Nigeria. *The Guardian*. Retrieved from https://guardian.ng/sport/why-private-sponsorship-of-football-clubs-is-failing-in-nigeria/

Kassy, O. (2018, 5 September). NFF ethics committee ban, fines Salisu Yusuf. *PTV*. Retrieved from https://ptvng.com/nff-ethics-committee-ban-fines-salisu-yusuf/

Kelly, S., & Chatziefstathiou, D. (2018). 'Trust me I am a football agent'. The discursive practices of the players' agents in (un) professional football. *Sport in Society*, 21(5), 800–814.

Ndlovu, R. (2002, 8 January). Overseas football: Nigeria's players strike. *The Telegraph*. Retrieved from https://www.telegraph.co.uk/sport/football/international/2428213/Overseas-Football-Nigerias-players-strike.html

Nehme, M., & Ordway, C. (2016). Governance and anti-doping: Beyond the fox and the hen house. In U. Haas & D. Healey (Eds.), *Doping in sport and the law*. London: Hart Publishing Bloomsbury. doi:10.5040/9781509905911.ch-011

Noddings, N. (1984). *Caring: A feminine approach to ethics & moral education*. Berkeley: University of California Press.

Nwosu, O., & Ugwuerua, E. (2015). Nigerian football federation, corruption and development of football in Nigeria. *International Journal of Physical Education, Sports and Health*, 3(1), 376–382.

Ochayi, C. (2016, 19 October). Corruption killing sports in Nigeria, Amokachi alleges. *The Vanguard*. Retrieved from https://www.vanguardngr.com/2016/10/corruption-killing-sports-nigeria-amokachi-alleges/

Okeleji, O. (2016, 23 December). Former captain Daniel Amokachi in Nigeria cash-to-play claims. *BBC Sport*. Retrieved from https://www.bbc.co.uk/sport/football/38405425

Okeleji, O. (2019, 29 June). Africa Cup of Nations: Nigeria players' strike averted after payment. *BBC Sport*. Retrieved from https://www.bbc.co.uk/sport/football/48812533

Okolie-Osemene, J., & Okoh, R. I. (2014). The role of Nigeria Football Federation in the denouement of premier league seasonal disputes: Issues and prospects. *Recreation and Society in Africa, Asia and Latin America*, 5(1). Retrieved from https://www.researchgate.net/publication/337290821_The_Role_of_Nigeria_Football_Federation_in_the_Denouement_of_Premier_League_Seasonal_Disputes_Issues_and_Prospects_The_Role_of_Nigeria_Football_Federation_in_the_Denouement_of_Premier_League_Seasonal

Olawale, O. (2018, 5 September). Nigeria Football Federation Ethics and Fair Play Committee ban Salisu Yusuf for collecting bribe. *Sport Flames*. Retrieved from www.sportflames.com/2018/09/nigeria-football-federation-ethics-and.html?utm_source=feedburner&utm_medium=feed&utm_campaign=Feed%3A+Sportflamescom+%28SportFlames.com%29

Omilana, T. (2018, 11 June). Football stands as a unifying force against constant divides – Dr Boer. *The Guardian Newspaper*. Retrieved from https://guardian.ng/sport/football-stands-as-a-unifying-force-against-constant-divides-dr-boer/

Opara, J. (2017, 18 May). NFF slashes coaches' salary arrears. *Vanguard News*. Retrieved from https://www.vanguardngr.com/2017/05/nff-slashes-coaches-salary-arrears/

Ordway, C. (2014). Why this Australian supported Germany to win the World Cup. *Sport & EU Review*, 6(2), 6–11. Retrieved from www.sportandeu.com/wp-content/uploads/2014/12/SportEU-Review-vol-6-no-2-November-2014.pdf

Ordway, C. & Opie, H. (2016). Integrity and corruption in sport. In N. Schulenkorf & S. Frawley (Eds.), *Critical issues in global sport management* (pp. 60–85). Abingdon: Routledge.

Oyeleke, S. (2019, 4 December). Fans to NFF: Withdraw Salisu from Rangers. *The Punch*. Retrieved from https://punchng.com/fans-to-nff-withdraw-salisu-from-rangers/

Passi, C. (2013, 22 May). National Sorry Day: An important part of healing. Reconciliation Australia. Retrieved from https://www.reconciliation.org.au/national-sorry-day-an-important-part-of-healing/

Pettersen, T. (2011). The ethics of care: Normative structures and empirical implications. *Health Care Analysis*, 19(1), 51–64. doi:10.1007/s10728-010-0163-7

PH. (2018). Gernot Rohr speaks on Salisu Yusuf collecting bribe from Super Eagles players. *Nigeriana News*. Retrieved from https://nigeriana.news/gernot-rohr-speaks-on-salisu-yusuf-collecting-bribe-from-super-eagles-players.html

Pielke, R. (2011, 29 August). Declan Hill's ten commandments for anti-corruption. *The Least Thing*. Retrieved from https://leastthing.blogspot.com/2011/08/declan-hills-ten-commandments-for-anti.html

Salisu, M. (2000). Corruption in Nigeria. Lancaster University Management School Working Paper 2000/006. Retrieved from https://eprints.lancs.ac.uk/id/eprint/48533/1/Document.pdf

Slote, M.(2007). *The ethics of care and empathy*. New York:Taylor & Francis.

Smith, A., & Stewart, B. (2010). The special features of sport: A critical revisit. *Sport Management Review*, 13(1), 1–13. doi:10.1016/j.smr.2009.07.002

Sulola, R. (2018, 24 July). Salisu Yusuf, Super Eagles coach, caught on camera taking 'bribe'. *The Cable NG*. Retrieved from https://www.thecable.ng/video-salisu-yusuf-super-eagles-coach-caught-camera-taking-bribe

Szymanski, S. (2006). The economic evolution of sport and broadcasting. *The Australian Economic Review*, 39(4), 428–434. doi:10.1111/j.1467-8462.2006.00432.x

Udo-Okpo, I. (2018, 24 July). Nigerian coaches pledge full support for embattled Salisu Yusuf. *TODAY.ng*. Retrieved from https://www.today.ng/sport/football/nigerian-coaches-pledge-full-support-embattled-salisu-yusuf-135742

Udoh, C. (2018, 6 September). Salisu Yusuf's punishment is a mere slap on the wrist. *ESPN Football*. Retrieved from https://www.espn.co.uk/football/nigeria/story/3625186/nigeria-coach-salisu-yusufs-punishment-a-mere-slap-on-the-wrist

Ugbane, D. (2018, 5 September). Super Eagles assistant coach Salisu Yusuf banned for bribery. *ESPN Soccer*. Retrieved from https://www.espn.com/soccer/nigeria/story/3624326/super-eagles-assistant-coach-salisu-yusuf-banned-for-bribery

Waldstein, D. (2014, 30 June). African teams head home, cash in hand. *The New York Times*. Retrieved from https://www.nytimes.com/2014/07/01/sports/worldcup/world-cup-2014-african-soccer-overshadowed-by-protests.html

Walker, M. (2001). Moral Repair and Its Limit. In T. Davis & K. Womack (Eds.), *Mapping the ethical turn: A reader in ethics, culture and literary theory* (pp. 110–127). Charlottesville: University of Virginia Press.

Walker, M. (2006). *Moral repair: Reconstructing moral relations after wrongdoing*. Cambridge: Cambridge University Press.

Wood, J., Howman, D. and Murrihy, R. (2018, March). Report of the review of Australia's sports integrity arrangements. Report No 12074. Retrieved from https://www1.health.gov.au/internet/main/publishing.nsf/Content/63F0A5D7BDA5A0B5CA2582CF0005E6F9/$File/HEALTH-RASIA-Report-Acc.pdf

Zimbalist, A. (2002). Competitive balance in sports leagues. *Journal of Sports Economics*, 3 (2), 111–121. doi:10.1177/152700250200300201

12 Could conditional retirement funds restore trust following the Tandy match-fixing case in rugby league?

Catherine Ordway and Liam Lenten[1]

Introduction

Public confidence in sporting performances the world over has taken a serious dent as a result of a range of corruption scandals, including major investigations exposing widespread doping and match-fixing cases. A study commissioned by UK Anti-Doping in 2017, also reflecting the findings of surveys conducted by consulting firm PwC in recent years, found that athletes, members of the public and those working inside international federations, are very concerned by the perceived: 'lack of trust in sports governing bodies' (ComRes, 2017; PwC, 2017, p. 7 and p. 15; PwC, 2019, p. 12).

It has been a decade since the then International Olympic Committee President, Jacques Rogge, declared that: 'We have made doping a top priority, and now there is a new danger coming up that almost all countries have been affected by and that is corruption, match-fixing and illegal gambling' (Associated Press, 2011, para 2). Researchers including Declan Hill (2008, 2013) have reported widespread spot and match-fixing across a range of sports. In 2014, Patrick Jay from the Hong Kong Jockey Club estimated then that there was one trillion US dollars involved in sport gambling (Oke, 2014). Sport organisations, governments, law enforcement agencies and international bodies have been working together to understand how to detect and deter match-fixing (e.g. UNODC, 2016), and thereby, restore the sporting public's trust in the industry.

Margaret Walker states that the concept of: 'moral repair aims at reinstating moral terms and replenishing our trust and hope in them and in ourselves' (Walker, 2001, p. 115). In sports besieged by match-fixing allegations, such as tennis, cricket and association football [soccer], a range of strategies designed to strengthen the robustness of the sports and restore trust in the sporting public are being implemented. In this case study, research by economists into retirement incentives (referred to as 'conditional superannuation') in anti-doping is considered within a match-fixing setting. Conditional superannuation, or delayed retirement benefits, is proposed as one strategy to incentivise athletes to avoid engaging in a range of corrupt, criminalised behaviour, including match-fixing.

'Superannuation' is an Australian term, and the Australian Taxation Office defines it as: 'A system where money is placed in a fund to provide for a person's retirement. Often shortened to "super"' (https://www.ato.gov.au/Super/). In other parts of the world, systems where employers contribute a portion of the employee's salary into a fund that cannot be accessed until a defined date into the future may be known as a pension plan or a retirement fund. For example, in France (https://www.cleiss.fr/docs/regimes/regime_france/an_3.html) and the United Kingdom refer to variations on a 'workplace pension scheme' (https://www.gov.uk/workplace-pensions-employers), while the United States of America uses the short-hand reference to their Internal Revenue Code article, the '401(k) Plan', to mean the equivalent (https://www.irs.gov/retirement-plans/401k-plans).

In this chapter, the conditional superannuation strategy is considered against the scenario involving the Australian National Rugby League (NRL) player, Ryan Tandy, who was convicted of match-fixing offences, to see whether this could be a useful approach to restore trust in this sport. Through this analysis, using the SCCORE model (Vousinas, 2019), it will be suggested that further research is warranted to examine whether there are scenarios, including those involving vulnerable athletes, in which this novel conditional superannuation solution could be beneficial in restoring trust in sport.

Motivations for match-fixing: Using espionage and fraud models

Researchers such as Caneppele et al. (2020) recommend that: 'researchers should make a more systematic effort to establish a sport fraudsters typology' (p. 13). In attempting to understand why athletes become involved in match-fixing, it is useful to consider behavioural motivation models for crimes, such as fraud, unauthorised leaking of sensitive/confidential information, treason and corruption. It is interesting to contemplate whether the emotions invoked in representing your team (club/nation) can be equated from a psychological and sociological perspective to the loyalty expected of workers in high-security clearance positions in major corporations, the military (Connor, 2010; Connor et al. 2019) and government. For example, the Australian Government Protective Security Policy Framework (2018) includes 'Loyalty' as one of the required integrity character traits:

> Loyalty – a commitment to Australia and the democratic processes of the Australian Government. Loyalty is not confined to the nation but also includes the objectives, ethos and values of the working environment (strong political views incompatible with the Australian democratic system of government may put a person's loyalty in doubt). (Australian Government, 2018, Annex A: Personnel security adjudicative guidelines 2(f), p. 22)

Similarly, athletes accepting bribes to alter the 'uncertainty of outcome' requirement of sport (Pound, 2011, p. 2; Pielke, 2013), has been seen as an act of disloyalty: 'To many, match-fixing undermines some sporting values such as integrity, loyalty, fair and open contests (i.e. fair play), sportsmanship, and respect for others' (Huggins, 2018, p. 126; Veuthey, 2014, p. 97 citing UEFA Disciplinary Regulations). It should be noted, however, that where the organisation, and/or the senior leadership team, promotes a culture of corruption, complying with that culture may in fact be demonstrating loyalty to that club or team, even if not to the sport as a whole (e.g. Duncan, 2018; Lee, 2017; Chapter 7 by Nichol, Solomon and Kawai, this volume).

Early psychology research by Rotter (1966) on the internal and external 'locus of control' has inspired several models in a range of settings, including to help explain espionage and treason (e.g. Stone, 2001). The 'attractive simplicity' (Eoyang, 1994, p. 72) of the well-known 'MICE' model, motivations of Money, Ideology, Coercion (or Compromise), and Ego (or Excitement), is now described by some authors as 'having out-lived its usefulness' (Burkett, 2013, p. 7). Burkett (2013) prefers Cialdini's 'principles of influence', or RASCLS framework, in his context of recruiting US Central Intelligence Agency (better known as CIA) agents: Reciprocation, Authority, Scarcity, Commitment and consistency, Liking, and Social proof. Cialdini later updated this framework to include a seventh principle, 'Unity' (Cialdini, 1984; 2016).

In the sport integrity context, perhaps these national security intelligence models can usefully be applied to 'cheating to win' through doping and 'cheating to lose' via match-fixing (Ordway & Opie, 2016). Particularly in team sports, the war/sport metaphor has long been used in both the military context and throughout sport journalism and the industry to promote:

> … the values of hegemonic masculinity (i.e., aggression, competition, dominance, territoriality, instrumental violence) as desirable and essential to the social order while at the same time, either explicitly or implicitly, marginalizing other types of masculinities within the culture (i.e., protest masculinities, pacifist and profeminist masculinities, weak and emotionally vulnerable masculinities). (Jansen & Sabo, 1994, p. 10)

'Warspeak' perpetuates the myth of organised team sport being a 'matter of life or death' (Segrave, 1997). In the context of the COVID-19 pandemic, the Australian Rugby League Commission Chair, Peter V'Landys, appealed for the sport to return to play and receive government funding ahead of other businesses impacted, stating that: 'An Australia without rugby league is not Australia' (NRL, 2020). Perhaps if the current Australian Prime Minister, Scott Morrison can be described as a 'high-identifying fan' (End et al. 2003), and therefore more amenable these arguments, it provides an explanation as to why this professional high contact collision sport was permitted to resume against the physical distancing requirements imposed on the rest of society (and before any women's or grassroots sports, museums, art galleries or live music venues (Halloran, 2020)). If there are major segments of the community then who believe that elite male sport is an 'essential service' to the community, equated with national security, then applying espionage models to match-fixing may not be too much of a stretch.

The application of this research to the national security and fraud models (e.g. Kranacher et al., 2010) is also relevant because, in many parts of the world (e.g. Italy, Portugal, Spain, Britain, Bulgaria, Poland (Homewood, 2011) and Germany

(Keidel, 2017)), and in the case study here, match-fixing cases are prosecuted through criminal fraud provisions (Police v Tandy, 2011; DPP (NSW) v Elias, 2013, pp. 71–4; noting that this has been replaced in Australia with 'cheating at gambling' provisions; Thorpe, 2014). Most recently, Vousinas (2019) proposed the SCORE model (which he expanded to become SCCORE). This model promotes the theory that people involved in fraud, and similar crimes, do so based on the following motivations: Stimulus; Capability; Collusion; Opportunity; Rationalisation and/or Ego.

Whether the war/sport metaphors and the promotion of hyper-masculinity in sport has had any impact on both the reluctance of whistleblowers in sport, and the low/no recorded match-fixing cases involving female athletes (despite its high risk on account of the pay inequity; Douglas, 2016; Kubbe et al., 2019), remains to be analysed by others. What is known is that athletes are driven to perform through both intrinsic and extrinsic motivations (Vallerand, 2007), triggers for cheating in sport vary, and a greater understanding of those triggers can support risk-reduction strategies.

In relation to 'cheating to win', research has indicated that some athletes choose to engage in doping behaviour in order to achieve, any/all of the following: a) qualify for elite sport at entry level, b) recover from injury, c) maximise success and earning power, and d) prolong careers and avoid an early retirement (Morente-Sanchez & Zabala, 2013; Overbye et al., 2013). As also could be expected, athletes believe that doping is more prevalent than the general population does. The study by Stamm et al. (2014) found that this was particularly the case for sub-elite athletes, which they dubbed the 'performance oriented leisure athletes' (POLAs), as compared with elite athletes and the general population. This is relevant, as it ties back into Cialdini's (2016) concept of 'Social proof', meaning that athletes will justify using performance-enhancing drugs if they believe that other athletes are also doping (Hutchinson et al., 2018).

In addition, research now increasingly recognises that elite athletes are highly prone to mental health challenges, including acute psychosocial issues, depression, anxiety, personality disorders, self-harming and suicidal ideation (Rice et al., 2016; Purcell et al., 2019), especially as athletes contemplate retirement (Smith & McManus, 2008; Rens, 2017). Sports physicians are also aware that these mental health issues are linked to substance abuse (usually alcohol, through binge drinking, and illicit drugs), often as a means of self-medicating (Harcourt, 2019).

Consistently, a factor for athletes involved in either doping or match-fixing is financial vulnerability, even for high-profile elite athletes. A recent survey of Olympic athletes has found that 58% of athletes responding said they did not consider themselves financially stable, and only 6% had access to retirement funds (Global Athlete, 2020, pp. 6, 8). There is also support for the correlation in cheating by older (hence near to retirement) athletes (Hill, 2013; Šindelář, Lenten, & Libich, 2021), which can also be related to the financial vulnerability indicator and lack of post-retirement options (Stambulova & Ryba, 2013).

Case study: Ryan Tandy and the National Rugby League [NRL]

This case study has been chosen to consider how conditional superannuation as a trust restoration methodology may be applicable for vulnerable athletes, including those with financial challenges, gambling, and addictions to prescription and illicit drugs, such as the now deceased, former Australian rugby league player, Ryan Tandy. It is fair to have characterised Tandy as a 'workman' in his chosen career as a professional rugby league athlete. His teammates classed Tandy as: 'a toiler with a big engine' (Brett Clarke cited by Feneley, 2014a). His talents enabled him to make a living from his craft, but he did not play a starring role in any of the NRL teams he served over his seven-year playing career. Tandy did, however, develop several antisocial habits. In turn, this created a vulnerability to be exploited, and adversely impacted on his ability to be the elite athlete and good citizen he might otherwise have been. The relevant timeline as described by his biographer, Josh Massoud, is as follows:

- *5 June 2010: Ryan Tandy moved to Sydney to join the Canterbury-Bankstown Bulldogs* [NRL team]. *Tandy places his first bets with John Schell* [jockey manager] [including on the NRL; Massoud, 2014, p. 38]
- *18 June 2010: Tandy makes his NRL debut for the Bulldogs against the Gold Coast at Suncorp Stadium. He also has a multibet with Schell that includes a Bulldogs win, in breach of the NRL rules that prohibit players from betting on games they participate in. Tandy later claims the bet was placed on behalf of flatmate, Saleh.*
- *17 August 2010: Schell informs Bulldogs officials about his dealings with Tandy and the footballer's* [rugby league player's] *$30,300 gambling debt.*
- *18–21 August 2010: More than $30,000 worth of straight-out and multibets are placed on North Queensland to open the scoring with a penalty goal in their round 24 clash against Canterbury in Townsville.* ['Those involved in the fix stood to win over $100,000 on Tabcorp, an Australian sports betting agency' Opie & Lim, 2018, p. 72 F/N8.]
- *21 August 2010: Spooked Tabcorp officials shut down the first scoring option market at 4.30pm and inform the NRL.* [Game kicked-off at 7.30pm] *Tandy hands over possession and concedes a penalty in the opening 90 seconds to present the Cowboys with an ideal opportunity to open the scoring with a penalty goal. North Queensland utility Anthony Watts declines the attempt at goal and the hosts instead open the scoring with a try.*
- *22 August 2010: Tandy tells Bulldogs football* [rugby league] *manager Alan Thompson about $75,000 in personal debt he'd like consolidated in an advance on his next contract …*
- *6 October 2011: Tandy is convicted of match-fixing. He announced an immediate appeal to the NSW District Court. He is fined $4,000 and given a twelve-month good behaviour bond …* ['Tandy was found unsuitable for community service because of his recovery from knee surgery' Davies, 2011]
- *2 December 2011: Tandy is found guilty on one of four charges of lying to the NSW Crimes Commission – namely, his betting activities with Schell …*

- *13 January 2012: sentenced to six-month Intensive Correction Order* (Massoud, 2014, ix–xii).
- *19 January 2012: Tandy's appeal is dismissed.* [Tandy was charged and convicted in 2011 of the criminal offence 'attempting to dishonestly obtain a financial advantage by deception'. As the bets had failed, the criminal charges related to an attempt. Tandy was the first person in Australia to be found guilty of match-fixing conduct (other than in animal racing incidents). The Court described the crime as involving 'significant organisation and ... a significant level of criminality'. He was banned from rugby league for life. (ABC/AAP, 2014, 29 April); Police v Tandy (2011)]
- *28 April 2014: Carol Tandy, Tandy's mother, found Tandy's body at home. It is believed that Tandy unintentionally took a fatal dose of pain-killing medication. This cannot be verified as Mrs Tandy has not released the Coroner's report. It is noted that: 'Tandy was experiencing immense back pain that required surgery'* (Massoud, 2014, pp. 251–3).

If the SCCORE model is applied to Tandy's life choices and behaviour, with the benefit of hindsight, there are several indicators that point to Tandy's vulnerability in being recruited to implement a match-fixing scam. Whether his vulnerability could have been reduced or supported through a wide-ranging athlete welfare system is beyond the scope of this chapter. For example, it is not clear why Tandy's lawyer advised Tandy to stop seeing his counsellor, Rob Brown, and the Club did not insist that counselling continue as a term of Tandy's contract (Massoud, 2014, p. 89). Measures to strengthen intrinsic motivators should be the first focus to support anti-corruption efforts. This chapter is looking at one extrinsic motivator in isolation in what should be a holistic package. It is proposed here that one of the mechanisms that could have changed Tandy's behaviour, or that of future players like him, is a conditional superannuation provision in his professional playing contract.

Application to the Tandy scenario

All of the SCCORE model indicators were in place in the lead up to Tandy's involvement in the match-fixing event, i.e. Stimulus; Capability; Collusion; Opportunity; Rationalisation and Ego. This also echoes the work of Gelles (2006; cited by Schwartz, 2007), who states that the first of the: 'Three Critical Factors and Traits Lead to Treasonous Betrayal' is: 'a personality or character weakness, such as antisocial tendencies or narcissism, that causes a predisposition to maladjusted counterproductive behavior' (Schwartz, 2007, p. 68). Rather than it being a personality weakness, Tandy's psychologist (Brown) believes that:

> When his father died, [Tandy] found that being emotionally exposed was dangerous. But by putting his emotions to one side, he also became isolated and at risk of making poor decisions. He was also drawn to risk-taking, and there was no one there to stop him. (Massoud, 2014, p. 244)

Journalist, Rick Feneley summarised Tandy as: 'the kid who 'oozed confidence' … verging on cockiness … the off-the-cuff comedian, the prankster who drove the school tractor into the creek at [his] High [school]' (Feneley, 2014a,b). Tandy's extroverted, rule-breaking life is well-documented; from adventures involving running naked in public (Massoud, 2014, pp. 74–5), writing off a car whilst under the influence of cocaine (Massoud, 2014, pp. 227–8), or posing nude for the national portrait prize (Massoud, 2014, pp. 73–6).

Tandy's relationship with integrity could be described as casual at best: he admitted to regularly being part of a group of rugby players who swapped urine samples to hide their illicit drug habits (Massoud, 2014, pp. 22–3). It is also alleged that, in January 2014, Tandy was involved in a kidnapping to settle a drug debt for someone else (Feneley, 2014b; Massoud, 2014, p. 252). Tandy's response to his father's death, when Tandy was 14 years old, was to begin gambling and illicit drug use a few years later: 'unknown to most, Tandy had a long-standing gambling habit which would be the catalyst for a life that spiralled out of control …' 'It's been a pattern for his whole life, even going back as far as the early 2000s when he played for the (St George) Dragons … He had to go to the extent of the CEO to look after his rent, look after his groceries, and then pay him what was left, just to make sure that he had those needs met' (Welch, 2014, quoting Moussoud).

In line with the SCCORE motivations, Gelles also identifies: 'a personal, financial, or career crisis puts an individual with these weaknesses under great stress, triggering more obvious counterproductive behavior often observed by friends, co-workers, or a supervisor'. (Schwartz, 2007, p. 68). In Tandy's case, he was devastated when:

> In April 2010, an NRL investigation found the [NRL club Melbourne] Storm had cheated by paying its players $1.7 million more than the salary cap over five years. The club was stripped of its 2009 and 2007 premierships. 'He [Tandy] was a shattered man,' [Brett] Clarke recalls. Tandy's pay-packet was modest but he became collateral damage – 'the toiler at the bottom of the pyramid' – in the salary cap scandal. 'Ryan lost his contract, his security and the culture of the team he loved. It's like taking a child away from his family.' (brackets added; Feneley, 2014b)

Without self-medicating, Tandy was unable to keep playing. He became addicted to stimulants and pain-killing medication to ensure he received his wage and had his contract renewed each year: 'Painkillers had allowed the journeyman footballer [rugby league player] to play on with injuries because, unlike the superstars, he could not afford to miss games' (Feneley, 2014b). Even without the gambling addiction, Tandy was under financial stress. Tandy described himself in his last interview on 23 April 2014 as: 'a bloke on minimum wage' (Massoud, 2014, p. 249). On the night of the match involving the fix, Tandy reflected that:

> I injured my sternum playing for Melbourne [Storm] early that year and they had a special guard made for me that I wore through 2010. Some matches I'd need an injection to take the field, and I took painkillers no matter what. On

> that night I remember having two Tramadol tablets. I also had three No-Dose pills and a can of Red Bull … just to get me charging. People might think that's strange for players to take so many stimulants, but lots do it … Fans have no idea how tough the game is, particularly when you play week in and week out for six months. You need help to get through. (bracket added; Massoud, 2014, pp. 49–50)

In what turned out to be his final interview, Tandy articulated the impact that being in constant debt had on him:

> I've woken up on most mornings with doubts or demons. In recent years it's often been about debt and how on earth I will pay them all back … I still believe I can wake up one morning and not be in debt. (Massoud, 2014, pp. 249; 251)

In line with the risk indicator outlined by Gelles above, no one from the club, the NRL, Tandy's coach, teammates or friendship group:

> recognize the signs of a serious problem, and they decide they don't want to get involved or assume that someone else will take care of it. As a result, no one intervenes to help resolve the problem, and the individual's behavior spirals out of control. (cited by Schwartz, 2007)

In Tandy's case, an NRL investigation was conducted into what the club knew, and whether the club had played an enabling role, rather than adequately supporting his welfare. By the time the investigation had taken place, one of the key club officials had been promoted into the NRL Chief Executive role, and the investigation exonerated the club (ABC/AAP, 2014, 10 May; NRL, 2014). This finding not only raises questions on the independence of the process, it demonstrates a missed opportunity for the NRL to learn from errors made, and to deeply consider how clubs and the NRL can better support their 'assets' (Ordway & Opie, 2016).

The vulnerabilities of athletes are exploited in a range of ways, and financial vulnerability is identified as a particularly successful lever. Athletes needing money are more likely to be motivated to accept the 'easy' money offered. Professor Jack Anderson, observed that:

> Elite players in well-paid leagues, for example the English Premier League, are unlikely to be targeted in this regard, unless they have a gambling problem or related debts. These players are well paid, but players further down the leagues and into the semi-professional leagues may be more susceptible. Further, in a league that has salary caps where leading players are well paid and the remainder of the roster may not be, the resulting inequality might heighten the latter's vulnerability to illicit betting approaches. (Anderson, 2011, p. 3)

Tandy played in a league with salary caps and received a much lower salary than his teammates. Criminologist, Samantha Bricknell, also identified the financial element in the environmental conditions in the recent Australian match-fixing cases citing:

> the minimal salary offered by the Victorian Premier League [association football/ soccer] was likely to be a motivating factor for participation in the alleged match-fixing scheme involving the Southern Stars players and coach [club in the Victorian Premier League], and the combination of a tight network with a strong gambling culture provided the setting for the Tandy spot-fix. (brackets added, Bricknell, 2015, p. 5. See also Murnane & Moller, 2018)

Where sport organisations are unwilling to proactively support athletes like Tandy, it is interesting to consider whether it could be imposed. For example, the new Australian match-fixing legislation could include a similar provision to that found in the UK *Bribery Act* 2010 (s.7). This legislation includes an offence of failing to prevent bribery. The defence open to the commercial organisation charged is to demonstrate that it: 'had in place adequate procedures designed to prevent persons ... from undertaking such conduct' (UK Ministry of Justice, 2010). The new Australian legislation could provide a positive obligation on sports organisations to demonstrate that their policies and processes were reasonable to prevent match-fixing.[2] This could include a range of programmes and initiatives, including conditional superannuation.

Conditional superannuation research

The 2017 article by one of this chapter authors, Dr Liam Lenten, and his economist colleagues concludes by suggesting that the conditional superannuation:

> mechanism might prove to be a promising addition to help attenuate other sport challenges ranging from corruption, off-field transgressions, violence against women, gambling, and perhaps even impoverished retirement. One potential avenue for exploration would link conditional superannuation to sport corporate social responsibility. (Lenten et al, 2017, p. 602)

For those not with a retirement income included in their package, conditional superannuation can be seen, from an Ethics of Care approach (Gilligan, 1982), as a mechanism to alleviate the financial stress for athletes during their post-athletics career. It is argued that this is, therefore, also an appropriate risk management strategy to reduce the vulnerability of athletes to seek or accept financial incentives (bribes) to alter the outcome of a match, provide insider information, or otherwise impact on the uncertainty of an aspect of the competition. It will be considered whether, in the fact scenario of the Tandy case, conditional superannuation could be one of the factors to reduce the risk of match-fixing by vulnerable athlete employees playing a professional team sport.

Wu et al. (2020) took up the challenge originally suggested by Maennig (2002) by designing an economic experiment to test whether a conditional superannuation scheme could reduce the risk of athletes doping to prolong their athletic careers. Maennig suggested that, rather than introducing fines, which were difficult to enforce:

> One solution to the problem of the implementation of penalties could be for a large part of the sponsoring money to be paid into funds that would then be paid out at the end of a—doping free—sporting career. Any penalties for doping offences would then be paid from the funds of the individual athletes involved. The incentive not to become involved in doping would be particularly great, especially for such 'long-serving' athletes as those mentioned above who at present are hardly affected by competition bans (and who in any case have a greater motivation toward doping, given that it is often more difficult for them to keep up with the younger athletes). (Maennig, 2002, p. 81)

In this proposed version of the conditional superannuation model, the mechanism needs to be supported by the relevant player association and then detailed in player contracts. Sponsors can also include conditional super provisions into their sponsorship/endorsement contracts with the individual players/teams that they sponsor. As Šindelář & Lenten (2020) identified in the anti-doping setting focused on by Wu et al. (2020) and Lenten et al. (2017):

> Superannuation could potentially have two positive effects. Firstly, it mitigates the end-game problem; and secondly, it reinforces the current ban system and increases costs of doping for all athletes–young and old. The superannuation scheme proposal has the potential to be a complementary tool in the arsenal of anti-doping measures. (Šindelář & Lenten, 2020, p. 23)

These economists suggest that a mandatory conditional superannuation scheme could be established for both sport organisations and athletes to demonstrate publicly their support for 'clean' sport. This strategy provides the opportunity for athletes to have, colloquially, 'skin in the game' and 'put their money where their mouth is'.

Male professional rugby league players in Australia currently have access to three forms of post-career funds:

1 **Super**: As employees of NRL clubs, mandatory Australian Government superannuation is paid as part of their employment package and becomes available once the player reaches the age requirement (usually 65 years old). It is compulsory for employers to make superannuation contributions for their employees on top of the employees' wages and salaries. The employer contribution rate has been 9.5% since 1 July 2014, and has gradually increased until it is planned to be 12% by 2025.

2 **Retirement**: The current Collective Bargaining Agreement 2018–2022 (CBA) increased the Retirement Account to $12,750 per annum flat fee per

player (increasing by $250 each year) for the top 30 players per NRL club (RLPA, 2017). Players are eligible for this Retirement Account amount as soon as retire, whether by choice or by injury, including the scenario whereby they are not offered another NRL contract and play in the lower reserve grade.

3 **Hardship**: The CBA introduced the Injury Hardship Fund, which is a benevolent fund for players who are seriously injured while playing (15M AUD over the term of the CBA) (RLPA, 2017). It was used to pay the players during the COVID-19 pandemic lockdown (RLPA, 2020).

It is proposed here that the terms of the NRL Retirement Account should include an additional condition, that is if the player is convicted of a sport integrity offence, such as match-fixing or other forms of fraud, then that player's retirement savings would be confiscated from the date of the offence. It should be considered whether the Retirement Account fund is a sufficient motivator, or whether the mandatory employee super should also be included in the forfeiture, as is the case in other industries involving trust and national security, set out below.

In the event of the Retirement Account amount being forfeited in this manner, any confiscated funds could be redistributed as agreed with the Rugby League Players Association (RLPA), including: back to the impacted players by effectively increasing the Retirement Account (which may also incentivise whistleblowing); diverting it into the NRL Injury Hardship Fund; including in the NRL Integrity Unit for future integrity-proofing work; and/or redistributing the money into programmes for underfunded/emerging athletes (e.g. junior women's teams).

For the NRL to restore trust then, some of the options to be put to the RLPA as part of the next round of CBA negotiations may include:

a Increasing the amount placed into the Retirement Account to balance the imposition of this additional condition. The current CBA provides players with 29.5% under the Revenue Share Model. An incentive to agree to this condition may require something in the order of 32%. It is hard to know how realistic this option will be given the negotiations that have taken place due to the suspension of the 2020 competition and reduced broadcasting rights deal in response to the coronavirus pandemic (RLPA, 2020). Once the financial position for Clubs and the NRL improves in future years, then this position could be reviewed.

b A players' total superannuation (including both compulsory employee superannuation, and the Retirement Account fund) can be seized from the date the player is found to have been match-fixing (or committing other forms of fraud) under the proposed national, or existing State/Territory, match-fixing legislation and/or the player's employment contract.

c Once players advise in writing that they have officially retired, where there have been no match-fixing or other specified crimes committed by the player, then these additional funds would be made available to the player after an agreed period. It would defeat the purpose of the paternalistic Retirement Account fund to make players wait the ten years outlined in the World Anti-Doping

Code (2015); however, perhaps 12 months would be sufficient, even noting the experience in anti-doping that: 'A number of events in the past have demonstrated that it can sometimes take a long time before sophisticated doping schemes are uncovered' (WADA, n.a.). The new organisation, Sport Integrity Australia, could be tasked with providing the 'clearance' after the specified period, for the conditional superannuation funds to be released.

Conditional superannuation in other industries

In a range of other Australian industries, (which has a legislated retirement superannuation system in place for all employees), a finding of corrupt behaviour and/or serious misconduct may mean that some/all of the employee's retirement income is forfeited. This means that there are already a variety of situations where superannuation and other termination payments are delayed and/or forfeited wherever conduct is investigated, and a conviction recorded through the criminal law processes.

The classes of employees who have this conditional superannuation requirement in place include: those people in positions of trust, including Australian Federal Police (AFP) employees (sworn and unsworn officers) (Australian Federal Police Act, 1979 (Cth) [AFP] Part VA), and defined 'accountable persons' within the banking industry as recommended by the Australian Financial Services Royal Commission (APRA, 2020; Banking Act 1959 Part IIAA). These provisions may also be extended as a result of the recent High Court decision in *Australian Securities and Investments Commission v King* (2020). The Court held that a person who has the capacity to significantly affect the financial standing of a company may be held to be an 'officer' as defined by the Corporations Act, even if they do not hold or occupy a named office or recognised position in a corporation. Commonwealth public servants hold national security clearances (see discussion above), and therefore a conviction of a corruption offence(s) and a sentence of more than twelve months imprisonment also attracts the: 'forfeiture and recovery of employer-funded superannuation benefits' (Crimes (Superannuation Benefits) Act, 1989 (Cth) [CSB Act]; Australian Government, (n.a.)). The process for the recovery of funds under the *AFP Act* and the *CBS Act* are set out in the Commonwealth Director of Public Prosecutions (CDPP) *National Legal Directions* (2016).

Where match-fixing offences already attract criminal sanctions under State legislation in Australia (Opie & Lim, 2018), the soon-to-become national legislation (Department of Health, 2019), could similarly include conditional superannuation in its terms.[3] As set out above, this legislation could also place a positive obligation on Clubs and other sport organisations to put in place procedures designed to prevent vulnerable athletes from engaging in match-fixing.

Would conditional superannuation have influenced Tandy's decision to match-fix?

The key question is whether this conditional retirement benefit provision would be enough to influence players not to become involved in match fixing. Whether conditional superannuation could have reduced the risk of Tandy agreeing to be involved in match-fixing is purely speculative, particularly given Tandy's documented impulsiveness, risk-taking and addictive personality (outlined above). It is also difficult to hypothesise without knowing the percentage of funds that the condition would have applied to.

If the Retirement Account had been in place at the current rate during Tandy's seven-year career, he would have been eligible for more than 90,000 AUD upon his retirement. Tandy would have needed to consider his promised cut of the match-fixing winnings (as well as its probability of success), the size of his debts and the perceived likelihood of being convicted for the offence in determining whether going ahead with the scam was worth the risk.

Having been in the NRL system for several seasons by the time of his 2010 transfer to Canterbury-Bankstown, Tandy's accumulated withheld conditional superannuation amount could have been sufficient to close his existing debt, with some to spare. If Tandy had been aware that this amount would have been available to settle his debts upon retiring from the NRL, and considering his ongoing injuries, perhaps that knowledge may have discouraged him from ultimately participating in the intended fix and brought forward his retirement from the sport.

Challenges to the conditional approach

One criticism of promoting this conditional superannuation approach, which has also been levelled at the Banking Executive Accountability Regime (outlined above), is that it may be too complex and expensive to administer (Australian Law Reform Commission, 2019). Ideally, this approach, where it is included in the proposed national match-fixing legislation, and in player and sponsorship contracts, could be supported by improved detection and fast-tracked legal processes, together with the seizure of unlawfully obtained assets, so that fewer athletes will benefit from ill-gotten financial gains post-retirement. However, given that the broader superannuation system in Australia is now firmly the status quo without employer peak bodies questioning the administration cost aspect, it can be assumed that the sports industry, and the regulators (including Sport Integrity Australia) will have the resources to oversee such a system.

Another concern warranting further research is whether extrinsic, rather than intrinsic, motivators are more effective in changing behaviour long-term (e.g. Van der Linden, 2015), and whether these results can be extrapolated to the elite athlete population. It would be of immense interest to see whether the results (using undergraduate university students) of Wu et al. (2020) could be generalised to a professional or semi-professional athlete subject sample. Hoffer and Giddings (2015), for example, found significantly different results between the athlete and non-athlete samples in their (unrelated) economic experiment. The behavioural motivations between the genders, and different cultural groups, also warrant further study.

It is also questionable if athletes from lower socio-economic groups, particularly those supporting extended family members, could be influenced by a 'save for tomorrow' philosophy instead of spending now on material goods, drugs and supporting close and extended family members as part of creating a 'good life' for themselves. The research by Chávez Villegas (2020) on: 'development and criminology which seeks to understand aspirations and how individuals conceptualize a "good life" and addresses the role of unfulfilled aspirations in the onset of criminal behaviour' provides some very useful points of similarity and areas to continue research, particularly where sport is used by athletes to get themselves, and their families, out of lower socio-economic groups.

With strong echoes from the Tandy case, where he found himself constantly in debt through over-spending on material goods, Chávez found that in the young offenders she studied: 'there is a greater inclination toward accumulating material items and luxury goods' including branded clothing and shoes, jewellery, cars, flat screen TVs, drugs, alcohol and cigarettes (Chávez Villegas, 2020, pp. 338–41). In this way, choosing to spend on expensive clothing and all the material trappings of players earning far more than Tandy was, rather than on education or healthcare, indicated, like the Mexican offenders in the Chávez study, that Tandy was seeking 'social mobility' and the 'good life'. In what should be a strong recommendation for NSOs and player associations worldwide to make increased efforts to facilitate post-sport readiness and education while playing, Chávez also found that:

> offenders placed greater importance on having a tertiary education or a profession in comparison to non-offenders (23.9% vs. 7.8%) … Unfortunately, there was also high agreement amongst offenders as to the lack of opportunities to access tertiary education, with almost half (44.3%) mentioning that they had no opportunities to have a professional career prior to their engagement in delinquent activity. (Chávez Villegas, 2020, p. 337)

Perhaps if Tandy had been more strongly encouraged to seek a trade or other professional qualifications this would have made a positive influence on his life.

Another similarity with the Tandy case is the importance of family, particularly his mother, in his life. As sports are now professional, and no longer purely the luxury of the 'leisure classes', and predominately populated by white, upper or middle class boys from private or independent schools (also known as 'Great Public Schools' or GPS), then the aspirations and motivations of families from different cultural and socio-economic groups also need to be considered when developing policies of this kind. For families in many parts of the world who have the opportunity to send their children (usually boys) overseas to work in sport or other industries: 'Migration decisions are usually shaped within family contexts, as migrants leave to meet certain family expectations directed at improving the living standards of those who remain at home and the lifestyle and income of the migrants' (Connell, 2010, p. 122). As Peter Horton points out in the rugby union context:

> For Pasifika and Maori boys living in Australia and in New Zealand this process often begins with gaining a football-based scholarship in a private school or a centre of sporting excellence in the state system. They must then advance to a state rugby academy and then gain a professional contract. Many are thus

> directed in life to gain a 'contract' and obviously the odds of actually getting a contract are painfully low, as they are in all professional sports globally. If a young Pasifika man achieves such a goal and even if he receives a basic salary he would immediately be in a position to help support his family and he would be obliged to do so. (Horton, 2012, p. 2,398)

For these young men, the discussion around the benefits of an additional superannuation or retirement income will have more nuanced implications:

> For a Pasifika man, whether attempting to pursue a professional sporting career directly from one of the Pacific Islands, on the rebound from New Zealand or Australia or as a second or even third generation immigrant in Australia or New Zealand, they will do so with the knowledge that their success, both in the sporting and financial sense will be a success for their family and the wider community. They will, as working adult males, be expected to 'put in' to the family coffers and probably to their church; thus if they have the opportunity through hard work and training to achieve even a modest 'contract' in a second division French team or the like, the pressure of being a breadwinner and of 'intergenerational reciprocity' will have to be considered seriously. (Horton, 2012, p. 2400)

Many Pasifika and Maori players, which make up more than a third of Australian senior and junior rugby league teams, measure their success through spiritual connection and a sense of fulfilling their masculine identity, rather than seeking individual affirmation through material goods: 'achieved success, bringing prosperity to his entire *aiga*, more so spiritually and emotionally, rather than in terms of materialistic gains' (Panapa & Phillips, 2014, p. 1380). For all athletes, particularly those spiritually motivated, it should also be considered whether the additional 'punishment' of withholding a portion of their superannuation could adversely impact on their mental health through an added sense of shame, particularly if it also brings shame on their extended family and broader community.

It could be argued that, rather than using a form of restorative or reparative justice (such as proposed by Braithwaite, 1989; Walker, 2010), this policy contributes to a form of degradation which may further ostracise athletes. In a worst-case scenario, this financial deprivation and sense of shame may lead some athletes to consider suicide. An alternative perspective is that providing athletes with an incentive to resist involvement in match-fixing is a positive reinforcement of sport integrity educational messages. Future research in applying restorative justice measure to professional sport would be interesting to consider in this context (e.g. MacPherson & Kerr, 2019; See also Chapter 11 Olukoya and Ogunleye-Bello, this volume).

Conclusion

It is proposed in this chapter, that conditional superannuation is an additional possible solution worth considering, to add to the standard motivators delivered through education, to empower individuals to be 'good citizens' and make the 'right' decisions to achieve a redefined 'good life'. It aims to find a balance between developing positive relationships based on trust and applying appropriate regulatory constraints and powers. In considering how the sport of rugby league in Australia, and professional sports around the world, could restore trust in the sporting public, the Tandy case study is a useful one. While not reinforcing the benefits of extrinsic regulatory constraints unreservedly, this scenario nonetheless serves to add weight to the substance behind the economic intuition underpinning this innovative policy augmentation proposal and provides another 'tool' to add to the anti-corruption-in-sport 'toolbox'.

Questions

- i *Trust loss* – In whom (or, in which group) has trust been lost in this case?
- ii *Trust correction* – How, if attempted, has the restoration of trust been tried?; and;
- iii *Lessons learned* – How could the lessons from this case be applied to other sports, nations, states, other districts for the same sport, or other sports to prevent a further loss of trust or at least to restore trust?

Notes

1 The authors are grateful for the ideas and critiques provided by colleagues on aspects of this chapter: Adam Masters, Nicholas Sellars, Hayden Opie, Kath Hall, Richard Keegan, Tracey Dickson, Monique Hennessy and Adrian Turner.
2 This recommendation was included as a public response to the Australian Sports Integrity Taskforce on 2 April 2020 (ID: ANON-YQCZ-QT45-N)
3 This recommendation was included as a public response to the Australian Sports Integrity Taskforce on 23 March 2020 (ID: ANON-YQCZ-QT4F-6).

References

ABC/AAP. (2014, 29 April). Former NRL player Ryan Tandy found dead from reported drug overdose. *ABC News*. Retrieved from www.abc.net.au/news/2014-04-28/ryan-tandy-dies/5416398

ABC/AAP. (2014, 10 May). NRL reportedly investigating Todd Greenberg over knowledge of Ryan Tandy's gambling on rugby league games. *ABC News*. Retrieved from www.abc.net.au/news/2014-05-10/nrl-investigating-greenberg-over-tandy-allegations-report/5444154

Anderson, J. (2011). Combating serious crime and corruption in sport: International and comparative perspectives. Briefing Paper: Workshop Queensland Cricketers Club, Brisbane, 27 July, ARC, Centre of Excellence in Policing and Security (CEPS), Nov 2011 (issue 6). Retrieved from https://prism.ucalgary.ca/handle/1880/49800) [Also republished as Anderson, J. (2012). Gambling-led corruption in international sport: An Australian perspective. The International Sports Law Journal, (1–2), 3–7.]

Associated Press. (2011, 14 July). Corruption next fight. *ESPN*. Retrieved from http://espn.go.com/olympics/story/_/id/6768358/jacques-rogge-says-match-fixing-gambling-big-fights-sports

Australian Federal Police Act 1979 (Cth). Canberra. Retrieved from https://www.legislation.gov.au/Details/C2019C00012/Html/Text#_Toc534640275

Australian Government. (n.a.) Crimes superannuation benefits. Attorney-General's Department, Canberra. Retrieved from https://www.ag.gov.au/Crime/federal-offenders/Pages/crimes-superannuation-benefits.aspx

Australian Government. (2018). 12 Eligibility and suitability of personnel. Protective Security Policy Framework, Attorney-General's Department, Canberra. Retrieved from https://www.protectivesecurity.gov.au/sites/default/files/pspf-persec-12-eligibility-suitability-personnel.pdf

Australian Law Reform Commission. (2019, 19 December). The Banking Executive accountability regime: An alternative model of individual liability for corporate fault. Retrieved from https://www.alrc.gov.au/news/the-banking-executive-accountability-regime-an-alternative-model-of-individual-liability-for-corporate-fault/

Australian Prudential Regulation Authority (APRA). (2020). Banking Executive accountability regime. Canberra. Retrieved from https://www.apra.gov.au/banking-executive-accountability-regime

Australian Securities and Investments Commission v King (2020). *HCA* 4. Retrieved from https://cdn.hcourt.gov.au/assets/publications/judgment-summaries/2020/hca-4-2020-03-11.pdf

Banking Act, Cth (1959). Banking Executive accountability regime (BEAR), Part IIAA. Canberra. Retrieved from https://www.legislation.gov.au/Details/C2018C00331

Braithwaite, J. (1989). *Crime, shame and reintegration.* Cambridge: Cambridge University Press.

Bricknell, S. (2015). Corruption in Australian sport. *Trends and Issues in Crime and Criminal Justice*, 490, 1. Retrieved from: https://apo.org.au/sites/default/files/resource-files/2015/02/apo-nid52991-1148731.pdf

Burkett, R. (2013). An alternative framework for agent recruitment: From MICE to RASCLS. *Studies in Intelligence*, 57(1) (Extracts, March 2013), 7–17. Retrieved from http://opencda.com/wp-content/uploads/2014/01/Burkett-MICE-to-RASCALS.pdf

Caneppele, S., Langlois, F., & Verschuuren, P. (2020). Those who counter match-fixing fraudsters: Voices from a multistakeholder ecosystem. *Crime, Law and Social Change*, 74, 1–14.

Chávez Villegas, C. (2020). Poverty, aspirations, and organized crime in Ciudad Juárez, Mexico. *Victims & Offenders*, 15(3), 330–349. doi:10.1080/15564886.2019.1694114

Cialdini, R. B. (1984). *Influence: The new psychology of modern persuasion.* New York: Morrow.

Cialdini, R. B. (2016). *Pre-suasion: A revolutionary way to influence and persuade.* New York: Simon & Schuster.

Commonwealth Director of Public Prosecutions (CDPP). (2016, 5 December). National legal directions. Canberra. Retrieved from https://www.cdpp.gov.au/sites/default/files/NLD%20-%20Restraint%20action%20and%20enforcement%20of%20recovery%20orders.pdf

ComRes. (2017, 10 July). UK anti-doping – Doping in sport report. Retrieved from https://www.comresglobal.com/wp-content/uploads/2017/07/UKAD_Doping-in-sport.pdf

Connell, J. (2010). Pacific islands in the global economy: Paradoxes of migration and culture. *Singapore Journal of Tropical Geography*, 31(1), 115–129.

Connor, J. M. (2010). Military loyalty: A functional vice? *Criminal Justice Ethics*, 29(3), 278–290.

Connor, J., Andrews, D. J., Noack-Lundberg, K., & Wadham, B. (2019). Military loyalty as a moral emotion. *Armed Forces & Society*. doi:0095327X19880248.

Crimes (Superannuation Benefits) Act, Cth [CSB Act]. (1989). *Canberra*. Retrieved from https://www.legislation.gov.au/Details/C2014C00437

Davies, L. (2011, 6 October). Ryan Tandy found guilty of trying to fix 2010 match between Canterbury Bulldogs and North Queensland Cowboys. *Daily Telegraph*. Retrieved from https://www.dailytelegraph.com.au/sport/nrl/ryan-tandy-nrl-match-fixing-scandal-court-case/news-story/207a9bde6b09a4a7cbe255a527ad388c

Department of Health. (2019). Safeguarding the integrity of sport – the government response to the Wood Review. Canberra. Retrieved from https://www.health.gov.au/resources/publications/safeguarding-the-integrity-of-sport

Director of Public Prosecutions (*DPP*) (*NSW*) *v Elias* (2013). NSWSC 28. Retrieved from https://www.austlii.edu.au/cgi-bin/viewdoc/au/cases/nsw/NSWSC/2013/28.html?context=1;query=tandy%20%202011%20%20;mask_path=

Douglas, L. (2016). 'Say it ain't so … Josephine?': The risk of match-fixing in women's sport. *The ANZSLA Commentator*, 97, 29.

Duncan, S. K. (2018). Acting as one: Understanding the actions of the banned Essendon 34. *Sport in Society*, 21(3), 529–545.

End, C. M., Kretschmar, J., Campbell, J., Mueller, D. G., & Dietz-Uhler, B. (2003). Sport fans' attitudes toward war analogies as descriptors for sport. *Journal of Sport Behavior*, 26 (4), 356–367.

Eoyang, C. (1994). Models of espionage. In R. Carney, C. Eoyang and T. Sarbin (Eds.), *Citizen espionage: Studies in trust and betrayal* (pp. 69–91). Westport, CT: Praeger.

Feneley, R. (2014a, 21 June). Inside Ryan Tandy's fretful final hours. *Illawarra Mercury*. Retrieved from https://www.illawarramercury.com.au/story/2367159/inside-ryan-tandys-fretful-final-hours-photos/

Feneley, R. (2014b, 21 June). The real Ryan Tandy. *The Sydney Morning Herald*. Retrieved from https://www.smh.com.au/sport/nrl/the-real-ryan-tandy-20140616-3a6fu.html

Gilligan, C. (1982). *In a different voice*. Cambridge, MA: Harvard University Press.

Global Athlete. (2020, 24 February). 2020 Survey results: Athlete rights, athlete welfare, athlete representation. Retrieved from https://static1.squarespace.com/static/5c8a203ac46f6d6629eac1f4/t/5e4fecb29963cc36ec44b04f/1582296243015/Global+Athlete+Survey+Results+Rights+Welfare+Compensation.pdf

Halloran, J. (2020, 30 May). What about us? Women fight to share the stage in sport's return. *The Australian*. Retrieved from https://www.theaustralian.com.au/sport/nrl/what-about-us-women-fight-to-share-the-stage-in-sports-return/news-story/171ac172a5211becf606d16f97fd5b5c

Harcourt, P. (2019, 7 May). *ASADA leadership in sport conference*. Canberra.

Hill, D. (2008). *The fix: Soccer and organized crime*. Toronto: McClelland & Stewart.

Hill, D. (2013). *The insider's guide to match-fixing in football*. Toronto: Anne McDermid & Associates.

Hoffer, A., & Giddings, L. (2015). Exercising willpower: Differences in willpower depletion among athletes and nonathletes. *Contemporary Economic Policy*, 34(3), 463–474.

Homewood, B. (2011, 29 September). Europe 'in danger' as match-fixing cases grow, claims Platini. *Independent*. Retrieved from https://www.independent.co.uk/sport/football/news-and-comment/europe-in-danger-as-match-fixing-cases-grow-claims-platini-2362503.html

Horton, P. (2012). Pacific islanders in global rugby: The changing currents of sports migration. *The International Journal of the History of Sport*, 29(17), 2388–2404, doi:10.1080/09523367.2012.746834

Huggins, M. (2018). Match-fixing: A historical perspective. *The International Journal of the History of Sport*, 35(2–3), 123–140.

Hutchinson, B., Moston, S., & Engelberg, T. (2018). Social validation: A motivational theory of doping in an online bodybuilding community. *Sport in Society*, 21(2), 260–282.

Jansen, S. C., & Sabo, D. (1994). The sport/war metaphor: Hegemonic masculinity, the Persian Gulf War, and the new world order. *Sociology of Sport Journal*, 11(1), 1–17.

Keidel, C. (2017, 14 September). A guide to Germany's new criminal law against betting fraud and match-fixing in sports. *LawInSport*. Retrieved from https://www.lawinsport.com/topics/sports/item/a-guide-to-germany-s-new-criminal-law-against-betting-fraud-and-match-fixing-in-sports

Kranacher, M. J., Riley, R., & Wells, J. T. (2010). *Forensic accounting and fraud examination*. Hoboken, NJ: John Wiley & Sons.

Kubbe, I., Alexander, A., & Wängnerud, L. (2019). The effect of gender on corruption: Sorting out explanations for gender differences with new experimental research. QOG. The Quality of Government Institute, University of Gothenburg. Retrieved from https://gupea.ub.gu.se/bitstream/2077/62809/4/gupea_2077_62809_4.pdf

Lee, P. C. (2017). Understanding the match-fixing scandals of professional baseball in Taiwan: An exploratory study of a Confucianism-oriented society. *European Sport Management Quarterly*, 17(1), 45–66.

Lenten, L. J., Smith, A. C., & Bayer, R. C. (2017). Adding conditional superannuation to the antidoping policy mix. *Journal of Sport Management*, 31(6), 591–604.

MacPherson, E., & Kerr, G. (2019). Sport fans' responses on social media to professional athletes' norm violations. *International Journal of Sport and Exercise Psychology*, 13, 1–18.

Maennig, W. (2002). On the economics of doping and corruption in international sports. *Journal of Sports Economics*, 3(1), 61–89.

Massoud, J. (2014). *The penalty*. Sydney: Allen & Unwin.

Morente-Sanchez, J., & Zabala, M. (2013). Doping in sport: A review of elite athletes' attitudes, beliefs, and knowledge. *Sports Medicine*, 43(6), 395. Retrieved from http://pilarmartinescudero.es/bibliografia_dopaje/australianos/actitudesdopajeZabala.pdf

Murnane, K., & Moller, J. (2018). On the frontline: The role and operations of the Victoria Police Sporting Integrity Intelligence Unit ('SIIU'). In S. Steele, & H. Opie (Eds.), *Match-fixing in sport* (pp. 187–203). Abingdon: Routledge.

NRL. (2014, 16 May). Greenberg cleared over Tandy betting allegations. National Rugby League. Retrieved from www.nrl.com/greenberg-cleared-over-tandy-betting-allegations/tabid/10874/newsid/78500/default.aspx

NRL. (2020, 15 March). ARLC and NRL COVID-19 update. National Rugby League Media Release. Retrieved from https://www.nrl.com/news/2020/03/15/arlc-and-nrl-covid-19-update/

Oke, F. (2014, 26 June). The football fix. *The Stream, Al Jazeera*. Retrieved from http://staff.stream.aljazeera.com/story/201406262041-0023881?qt-more_from_the_stream=0

Opie, H., & Lim, G. (2018). The Australian legal framework for countering match-fixing. In S. Steele & H. Opie (Eds.), *Match-fixing in sport* (pp. 59–74). Abingdon: Routledge.

Ordway, C., & Opie, H. (2016). Integrity and corruption in sport. In N. Schulenkorf & S. Frawley (Eds.), *Critical issues in global sport management* (pp. 60–85). Abingdon: Routledge.

Overbye, M., Lykke Knudsen, M., & Pfister, G. (2013). To dope or not to dope: Elite athlete's perceptions of doping deterrents and incentives. *Performance Enhancement and Health*, 2(3), 119.

Panapa, L., & Phillips, M. (2014). Ethnic persistence: Towards understanding the lived experiences of Pacific island athletes in the National Rugby League. *The International Journal of the History of Sport*, 31(11), 1374–1388. doi:10.1080/09523367.2014.924105

Pielke, R.Jr. (2013, 19 February). Does uncertainty of outcome define sport? *The Least Thing*. Retrieved from http://leastthing.blogspot.com.au/2013/02/does-uncertainty-of-outcome-define-sport.html

Police v Tandy. (2011, 12–13 September). Unreported. Downing Centre Local Court (NSW), Wahlquist J.

Pound, R. (2011, 3 October). Responses to corruption in sport, play the game conference. Retrieved from www.playthegame.org/fileadmin/image/PTG2011/Presentation/Richard_Pound_2011.pdf

Purcell, R., Gwyther, K., & Rice, S. M. (2019). Mental health in elite athletes: Increased awareness requires an early intervention framework to respond to athlete needs. *Sports Medicine-Open*, 5(1), 46.

PwC Sports Surveys. (2017). Sports: the most disrupted of all industries? Retrieved from https://www.ecaeurope.com/media/4148/pwcs-sports-survey-2017.pdf

PwC Sports Surveys. (2019). Sports industry: time to refocus? Retrieved from https://www.pwc.ch/en/publications/2019/PwC-Sports-Survey-2019-web.pdf

Rens, N. M. (2017). Changes in fame and fortune: A phenomenological study of professional athletes entering retirement. UST Research Online, University of St. Thomas, Minnesota. Retrieved from https://ir.stthomas.edu/cgi/viewcontent.cgi?article=1088&context=caps_ed_lead_docdiss

Rice, S. M., Purcell, R., De Silva, S., Mawren, D., McGorry, P. D., & Parker, A. G. (2016). The mental health of elite athletes: A narrative systematic review. *Sports Medicine*, 46(9), 1333–1353.

RLPA. (2017, 2 November). Key outcomes achieved in the CBA: Collective bargaining agreement 2018–2022. Rugby League Players Association. Retrieved from https://www.rlpa.com.au/key-outcomes-achieved-cba/ (Infographic: https://www.rlpa.com.au/infographic-collective-bargaining-agreement-2018-2022/).

RLPA. (2020, 3 April). RLPA and NRL reach agreement. Rugby League Players Association. Retrieved from https://www.rlpa.com.au/rlpa-and-nrl-reach-agreement/

Rotter, J. B. (1966). Generalized expectancies for internal versus external control of reinforcement. *Psychological Monographs, 80*(1), 1–28. Retrieved from https://pdfs.semanticscholar.org/161c/b7ac92d7571042bb11ebdaaa1175be8079f8.pdf?_ga=2.177951141.1677183275.1581554625-801290576.1581554625

Schwartz, J. M. (2007). Exploring the mind of a spy. *The Forensic Examiner*, Spring, 67–68.

Segrave, J. O. (1997). A matter of life and death: Some thoughts on the language of sport. *Journal of Sport and Social Issues*, 21(2), 211–220.

Šindelář, J., & Lenten, L. J. A., & Libich, J. (2021). What do elite athletes' leaked blood samples reveal about doping incentives? Retrieved from https://liamlenten.files.wordpress.com/2020/03/c5a0indelc3a1c599-and-lenten-2020.pdf

Smith, J. L., & McManus, A. (2008). A review on transitional implications for retiring elite athletes: What happens when the spotlight dims? *The Open Sports Sciences Journal*, 1(1). Retrieved from https://benthamopen.com/contents/pdf/TOSSJ/TOSSJ-1-45.pdf

Stambulova, N. B., & Ryba, T. V. (Eds.). (2013). *Athletes' careers across cultures*. London: Routledge.

Stamm, H., Lamprecht, M., & Kamber, M. (2014). Attitudes towards doping – A comparison of elite athletes, performance oriented leisure athletes and the general population. *European Journal for Sports and Society*, 11(2), 171–189.

Stone, L. A. (2001). A two-factor motivational theory for spying behavior. *Psychology of Espionage Reports*, 2. Retrieved from www.home.earthlink.net/~lastone2/espionage.html

Thorpe, D. (2014). The efficacy (and otherwise) of the 'new' sport anti-corruption legislation. *Victoria University Law and Justice Journal 4*(*1*), 102. Retrieved from https://www.austlii.edu.au/au/journals/VicULawJJl/2014/9.pdf

UK Ministry of Justice. (2010). The Bribery Act 2010: Quick start guide. Retrieved from https://www.justice.gov.uk/downloads/legislation/bribery-act-2010-quick-start-guide.pdf

UNODC. (2016). Resource guide on good practices in the investigation of match-fixing. United Nations Office on Drugs and Crime. Retrieved from https://www.unodc.org/documents/corruption/Publications/2016/V1602591-RESOURCE_GUIDE_ON_GOOD_PRACTICES_IN_THE_INVESTIGATION_OF_MATCH-FIXING.pdf

Vallerand, R. J. (2007). Intrinsic and extrinsic motivation in sport and physical activity. In G. Tenenbaum & R. C. Eklund (Eds.), (2007). *Handbook of sport psychology* (pp. 59–83). Hoboken, NJ: John Wiley & Sons. Retrieved from https://www.academia.edu/download/48438018/935385808Handbook_of_Sport_Psychology_1.pdf#page=82

Van der Linden, S. (2015). Intrinsic motivation and pro-environment behaviour. *Nature Climate Change*, 5, 612.

Veuthey, A. (2014). Match-fixing and governance in cricket and football: what is the fix?. *The International Sports Law Journal*, 14(1–2), 82–114.

Vousinas, G. L. (2019). Advancing theory of fraud: The S.C.O.R.E. model. *Journal of Financial Crime*, 26(1), 372–381.

WADA. (n.a.). 2015World Anti-Doping Code. World Anti-Doping Agency. Retrieved from https://www.wada-ama.org/en/questions-answers/2015-world-anti-doping-code

Walker, M. U. (2001). Moral repair and its limits. *Marquette University e-Publications@Marquette*, Milwaukee, WI. 1-1-2001. Retrieved fromhttps://epublications.marquette.edu/cgi/viewcontent.cgi?referer=&httpsredir=1&article=1151&context=phil_fac

Walker, M. U. (2010). *What is reparative justice?* Milwaukee, WI: Marquette University Press.

Welch, D. (2014, 9 May). Ryan Tandy: Disgraced NRL footballer's gambling led to his career, life unravelling. *ABC News* (online). Retrieved from www.abc.net.au/news/2014-05-08/gambling-led-to-nrl-footballer-ryan-tandys-life-unravelling/5440368

Wu, Q., Bayer, R. C., & Lenten, L. (2020). Conditional pension funds to combat cheating in sporting contests: Theory and experimental evidence. *Journal of Behavioral and Experimental Economics*, 89, 101537.

13 Restoring trust in the horse racing industry

Fine Cotton and the complexities of gambling, organised crime and entrenched corruption

Genevieve Lim and John Young

Introduction

The employment of horse substitution in the case of Fine Cotton has left an indelible mark on the history of horse racing in Australia, not only because of the farcical execution of the fix, but because it acutely exposed entrenched corruption in the Queensland gambling industry and law enforcement agencies. While the events of the case took place in 1984, it still attracts widespread media and public commentary today. It was recently listed as #5 of 'The ten most cringe-worthy moments in Australian sport' (Holden, 2020) and inspired a book in 2019 (Hoysted & Shiel, 2019). The effect of the Fine Cotton affair still reverberates in the public consciousness and valuable insights may be drawn from the way the corruption presented and the penalties that were imposed on implicated parties.

Many people, including champion tennis player and pay parity advocate, Billie Jean King, have observed that: 'sport is a microcosm of society' (SI Staff, 2010), in that sport possesses the same characteristics and patterns of behaviour as broader society, but within a contained sphere of influence. In the case of Fine Cotton, however, society at large invaded the sporting competition space, bringing influence and conduct beyond the control of sporting regulators. It provides an interesting juxtaposition to other sport case studies, demonstrating that restoring trust in sport may be messy and complicated, involving multiple sectors of the community.

The substitution of a faster horse for a reputedly slow one has been a favoured technique of horse racing corrupters for many decades, before the advent of implanted digital chips to verify horse identities. Known as 'ring-ins' these substituted horses could often effectively masquerade as another horse to bring gambling windfalls to those in the know, by virtue of capitalising on long odds (Cripps, 1990). 'Odds', in gambling as in statistics, is the numerical description of the likelihood of a specified possible event expressed as a ratio. The toss of a coin, to land as either 'heads' or 'tails', is said to be 'even odds'. 'Long odds' means that a positive outcome is unlikely. Shakespeare's character Lord Bardolph in *King Henry IV* reflected that they: 'Knew that we ventured on such dangerous seas / That if we wrought out life 'twas ten to one' (Shakespeare, 1623, Act I Scene 1 lines 181–2). In gambling terms then, when the bookmaker believes that a registered horse is very unlikely to win the race, they will offer 'long odds' or a large pay out if that horse performs better than expected.

Fine Cotton case study

The case of Fine Cotton has become infamous due to the poor resemblance of the ring-in to the original horse, the ineptitude of the fix and the vast numbers of people who knew of it and bet accordingly, reducing the long odds of the gambling variable and compromising the fix. Fine Cotton was a brown gelding with a record of poor performances and was eligible to race in a restricted class, having had few significant results. A syndicate, led by bloodstock agent and convicted fraudster John Gillespie, purchased a superior performing horse, *Dashing Solitaire*, as a ring-in for the strikingly similar horse, Fine Cotton. Gillespie had already been implicated in a horse substitution that failed and a suspected plot to substitute a different horse which was thwarted by a period in jail (Ashforth, 2002a). Gillespie had purportedly arranged the syndicate on the instructions of underworld gangster Mick Sayers, in part to generate funds to repay a large debt Sayers owed to illegal bookmaker, George Freeman. Sayers' involvement has never been formally confirmed. He was gunned down in his driveway in 1985 and his murder remains unsolved (Reilly, 2010).

In the lead up to the target event, the 2 Novice Handicap at Eagle Farm Racecourse in Queensland, Dashing Solitaire was injured and unable to race. The syndicate persisted with the planned substitution, purchasing a lighter brown horse, Bold Personality, which was an open class animal with a history of much better performances than Fine Cotton. Bold Personality was significantly lighter in colour than Fine Cotton and did not bear the distinctive white markings on his hind legs. Conspirators John Gillespie, trainer Hayden Haitana, and businessman Robert North attempted to dye the animal with brown hair dye (inadvertently turning him orange) and painted his hind legs with house paint, after forgetting to bleach them white using peroxide.

Betting on Fine Cotton commenced at the long odds of 33/1. In the lead up to the race, a large volume of betting on Fine Cotton to win caused the total win pool to increase above normal expectation. This 'betting plunge' forced all bookmakers to shorten Fine Cotton's win odds to 7/2 and lengthen the odds of all other horses in the race to protect their race investment. It is widely believed that both Gillespie and Haitana spread the word that Fine Cotton was a certainty to win: Haitana through a propensity for gossip over beer, and Gillespie for an agreed share of the gambler's winnings (Ashforth, 2002a). The investment in betting on Fine Cotton to win occurred not only at Eagle Farm Racecourse, but at other gambling establishments throughout the country, and overseas, raising the suspicions of the racing stewards. It is notable that large bets were placed on the inauspicious animal by very experienced and usually discerning gambling operators such as on-course bookmakers Robbie and Bill Waterhouse, and an unlikely punter, Mona Lewis, the mother of the then Queensland Police Commissioner, Terry Lewis. The involvement of these bettors, the volume of gambling and the value of bets provided Queensland racing stewards with a strong indication that inside knowledge of the fix was widespread. Further, extensive betting on this minor race by the gambling community, members of the government and the police force presented damning evidence of collusion between these sectors.

Bold Personality, masquerading as Fine Cotton, narrowly won the race, edging out the horse Harbour Gold. Trainer, Haitana, had placed a 50 AUD bet on Harbour Gold, suggesting a lack of belief in the success of the substitution (White, 2010). Suspicious stewards suspended payment of bets shortly after the race after shouts of 'ring-in' were made by the public and paint was noticed running down Bold Personality's hind legs. The substitution was discovered, Haitana absconded from the racetrack and 'Fine Cotton' was disqualified. All bets stood: runner-up Harbour Gold was determined the winner at 5/1, and the many individuals who had invested in Fine Cotton and caused the betting plunge lost their money.

The subsequent inquiry by the Queensland Turf Club resulted in bans for six people. Further prosecution led to jail terms for the executors of the fix: Haitana, Gillespie and North. In addition, high-profile betting service operators, Bill and Robbie Waterhouse, were banned from Australian racetracks for life for their prior knowledge of the fraud, although both have always denied inside information or any relationship to the fix. Authorities were convinced that the Waterhouse men were behind the ring-in and focused on gamblers connected with the men who had bet large sums. Robbie Waterhouse testified that he had not facilitated betting in relation to Fine Cotton, seeking to protect client Gary Clarke who had sought his assistance to place a 50,000 AUD bet on the horse anonymously. The intermediary for this bet, Ian Murray, lied to the Australian Jockey Club, claiming the bet as his, but told the subsequent Racing Appeals Tribunal that he had placed it at Waterhouse's request. The origin of the bet was found to be Mick Sayers, facilitated by Clarke, then Waterhouse and placed by Murray. His lying under oath exposed, Robbie Waterhouse was convicted for false testimony, but was found not guilty of any deeper role in the fraud. During the trial Gillespie testified that Sayers had orchestrated the scheme and that Waterhouse had not been involved (Ashforth, 2002b).

In his 2009 autobiography, Bill Waterhouse asserts that he and son Robbie were made scapegoats by the Australian Jockey Club which was embarrassed by the horse substitution scandal (Waterhouse, 2009). Until this point, there had not previously been a charge of 'prior knowledge' (what would be considered as 'misuse of inside information' in a present-day context). It was alleged that the complaint was created to exclude the powerful Waterhouses, denying both men their livelihoods (Martelli, 2009).

In 2010 Gillespie asserted that the substitution was never intended to succeed, and that he had correspondingly betted heavily on *Harbour Gold*, the clear favourite who was eventually awarded the race after Fine Cotton's expulsion (Shand, 2010). He maintained that after serving five months in custody and two years of home detention (of a four-year sentence) he was released from prison to enjoy the 1.8 million AUD proceeds from the corruption. Doubt has been cast on this account and on Gillespie's credibility, but it remains an interesting theory and an example of how gambling odds in racing may be manipulated for large payouts.

The case of Fine Cotton caused outrage producing front page news stories for many weeks and resulted in a loss of trust in the integrity of racing and gambling. Following the scandal, the betting public became more likely to heavily scrutinise all races that involved winning horses that had large odds movements. In recent times, the TAB (Tabcorp Holdings Limited – the leading gambling operator for racing in Australia) has publicly broadcast large bets placed on each race. This public scrutiny has placed increased pressure on racing stewards in each state to protect the integrity of racing.

The nature of the deception and the impact on trust

The nature of the originating corruption was a deception at its simplest level – representing one thing as another – for financial gain through the competition and the related betting market. The corruption was compounded, however, by the numbers of people who were aware of the deception and exposed their knowledge through betting. While all corrupt actions are not necessarily illegal (Miller, 2018, p. 6), in this occurrence the behaviour of the arrangers of the fix and the government officials who placed bets with at least suspicion, if not knowledge of the fix, were illegal. The corruption therefore is both personal – the fraud of individuals – and institutional (Miller, 2018, p. 9). The integrity values within law enforcement were so weak that Queensland officers chose to bet on the fix, rather than prevent its commission. Finally, a significant proportion of the racing gambling community across Australia demonstrated a willingness to bet on inside information of a fraudulent activity, rather than reporting it to racing stewards. While not illegal, the fact that the betting plunge occurred on Fine Cotton and so many people sought to capitalise on the deception, signifies dubious values in relation to knowledge of corrupt conduct in the racing gambling community more broadly.

Further, the conduct was not the result of random opportunism, but had its origins in organised crime. The corruption occurred in the context of what is thought to be a previously planned fix that went awry: horse trainer George Brown allegedly refused to execute a ring-in involving a horse called Risley, and his badly tortured body was subsequently found in his burnt out vehicle in April 1984, four months before the Fine Cotton affair (Ashforth, 2002a). Haitana has asserted that he did not want to execute the fix but was threatened with a similar fate to Brown if he did not proceed (Thompson 2016). Rather than being a prank executed by larrikins, the Fine Cotton affair was more likely a desperate venture orchestrated by individuals coerced by organised criminals. Its clumsy execution may be attributed to a fearful commitment to the plan in the face of misfortune, rather than bumbling ineptitude.

The circumstances of the Fine Cotton case may be contrasted with a human racing example, that of the Antonich brothers at the Stawell Gift, known as Australia's richest footrace. Scott Antonich was the favourite to win the 1988 event, and his enterprising coach Sam Martin saw an opportunity to make gains on the associated betting market by manipulating public perception. He charged Scott's low profile identical brother, Paul, with the task of conspicuously consuming meat pies and beer on the morning of the event, steadily generating longer odds on his brother's performance as gamblers assumed it was the athlete behaving inappropriately in preparation for the upcoming race. Paul left the public arena, and then Scott materialised for the actual event, winning convincingly and securing $33,000 in gambling profit for his coach in a favourable betting market (McIver & Tran, 2018).

In that example, while a substitution appeared in the event lead up intended to influence spectators, the correct participant completed the race. Although the manipulation of gambling odds may arguably have been dishonest, it was not illegal. It was a true example of larrikin behaviour resulting in dubiously acquired financial gain. By contrast, the substitution of another horse for Fine Cotton was dishonest, illegal, and inspired by fear and greed. The horse race was compromised by criminal and corrupt police networks, which served to spread the planned illegal conduct information. This combination was destructive to the reputation of the racing industry and regulatory controlling bodies alike.

Horse racing suffers more damage from race-fixing than other sports, due to its reliance on gambling for survival (Brooks et al., 2013). If gamblers do not believe in the spectacle of racing they will not gamble on the outcomes. The damage to trust in the Queensland racing industry was significant, due to the nature of the corruption and the number of parties who engaged with the conduct at some level; from the few implicated in masterminding and orchestrating the fix to the great many with prior knowledge who placed enough bets to cause a blatantly suspicious betting plunge. Not only did the Chief Commissioner of Police place a 5000 AUD bet through his mother, members of the Queensland Police Fraud Squad also placed numerous bets and there was a large contingent of off-duty Brisbane detectives present at Eagle Farm on the day of the race. The event magnified the damage to civic trust in the Queensland government and its institutions. The exposure of the fix and the identities of those individuals who placed bets, and by implication those who had prior knowledge of the corruption, damaged the reputation of not only the racing industry but the broader arms of the Queensland civic system. While it is not always unexpected for a 'stitch-up' to occur within a horse racing competition, the event demonstrated that the entire legal order was tainted and exposed deeper institutional corruption.

Horse substitution was not unheard of before Fine Cotton, and it is difficult to tell how often it was successfully perpetrated before technological advances made it a form of corruption unlikely to succeed. The most famous of these was the horse Erbie, which had an official record of 23 wins but is thought to have accrued at least a further dozen victories masquerading as a different horse across Australia in the 1930s (Hunt, 2012). Some cases of substitution were uncovered when the individuals involved allowed greed to push the substitution too far, to the point where the explanation for a miraculous change in performance became obvious. For example, the case of Fine Cotton may be contrasted with that of Regal Vista, occurring over a decade previously. Used car dealer Rick Renzella meticulously planned the fix, setting up the details over several months. He purchased the poor performing horse, Royal School, and entered him in four races in

Gippsland, Victoria in quick succession, where the horse achieved two second lasts and two last results. He also purchased Regal Vista, a classy performer with a solid record, who looked strikingly like Royal School but for a scarred rump. Renzella then entered 'Royal School' in a race at Casterton in country Victoria, with the expectation that stewards would be unlikely to attend, and that the fix would be further buried in a betting variable called a 'daily double' in which the bet was teamed with a result in another race.

Renzella successfully executed the substitution on race day and Regal Vista came home first in the guise of Royal School, bringing more than 30,000 AUD in gambling profit (a significant sum in 1972). While there were allegations of a ring-in on the day, the registration papers for the horse matched his brand. Officials referenced these papers with official records of Royal School's brand days later and the registration papers were exposed as fraudulent. Renzella, the trainer, the jockey and two others were banned by racing authorities and prosecuted for fraud. Renzella was jailed for two years (Hunt, 2013).

Fine Cotton differs from Regal Vista, in that a popular urban racecourse, rather than a remote county location, was selected for the target event. It is not evident that falsification of the horse's identity extended beyond a poor attempt at physical verisimilitude. What made Fine Cotton infamous was the poor orchestration of the corruption and the very large numbers of people affected, through a significant betting pool, and the large number of participants. It is a further irony that a great many of the people who gambled on Fine Cotton are likely to have had inside information about the fix, or at least that some corrupt conduct had been perpetrated to give the horse an edge, lost their money when the fix was exposed. Renzella managed to keep his plans to substitute the horse secret and to capitalise fully on long odds, without knowledge of the 'certain win' spreading through the racing community.

It is interesting to consider this old Fine Cotton case through the lens of modern scholarship in relation to sport integrity. Recent research has characterised corruption as behaviour attributable to 'bad apples' (corrupt individuals and groups), 'bad barrels' (corrupt organisations) and 'bad orchards' (corrupt systems) (Roberts & Bolton, 2018, p. 144). Many sports corruption scandals in recent history may be attributed to 'bad barrels', that is, the culture and leadership of high-profile international sporting organisations, such as the Federation International de Football Association (FIFA), the International Association of Athletics Federations (IAAF) and the Union Cycliste Internationale (UCI) (see Roberts and Ordway Chapter 6, this volume).

In the case of Fine Cotton, one particularly 'bad apple', Sayers, set in train two courses of conduct: the purchasing of the horses and orchestration of the substitution through Gillespie, Haitana and North, and the placing of a large bet on the relevant race through Clarke, Waterhouse and Murray. The plot's organised crime origins transitioned seamlessly into the racing and gambling environments, in which operatives were easy to identify and then engage assistants. The ease with which both racing and gambling industries were accessed for corrupt purposes suggests that both were pre-existing 'bad orchards' to a certain degree and predisposed if not to enable corrupt activities, at least not to unduly challenge their execution.

There is no suggestion that racing authorities were aware of or complicit in the fix, or that a transparently 'bad barrel' was an operative factor in the corruption. Corruption researchers, however, debate the extent to which corruptors should be considered isolated agents making rational means-end calculations, and the weight to be given to external social, economic and cultural features of the environment in which the corruption occurred (Gottschalk, 2012, p. 43). It would be interesting to contrast, for example, the susceptibility of infiltration by match-fixers in a different sport in another jurisdiction during this era. Fine Cotton made transparent not only the dearth of integrity protocols and values within the Queensland racing and gambling industries, but also the intimate relationship of corrupt conduct information holders with a corrupt law enforcement system in Queensland ('bad orchard'). While space does not permit a detailed discussion of corruption theories in relation to the chain of conduct in the Fine Cotton scandal (for further analysis on this point see Bayley and Egle, Chapter 3 this volume), consideration must be given to the likelihood that the culture of the racing industry at that time played a role in enabling the corruption.

In planning the fix, Haitana, North and Gillespie, through their lived experience in the racing industry, must have considered that, although the rules existed, they did not apply to them, were not sincerely upheld or would not be rigidly enforced. North has publicly stated that he 'wasn't really worried to be honest. I thought it would blow over. I certainly didn't think I'd ever be arrested for it because I thought "well I haven't backed the horse"' (Nolan, 2019). His words indicate that he did not appreciate the harm in his actions within the broader racing context and did not consider it likely that investigations and prosecutions would be comprehensively carried out. Considering the intimacy of key Queensland law enforcement personnel with the racing and gambling industries and organised crime identities, North's beliefs were rational. If the rules were transparently ignored in relation to the big operators, it would be easy to believe that no one would come after the individual who merely stabled a ring-in at his property and helped prepare the horse for substitution in a race. Perhaps the underlying reason for Fine Cotton's infamy is not the damage the scandal caused to the integrity of racing, but the exposure of broken social contracts within the broader Queensland regulatory environment. (Note 'social contracts' / social licences discussed further in Jamieson and Ordway, Chapter 5 this volume).

The response from the authorities

Thoroughbred, harness and greyhound racing industries differ from other Australian sports in that they are subject to significant government regulation by entities created under statute. As horse racing has historically been staged for the purpose of providing a subject for betting, special rules and tribunals have evolved to facilitate its governance (Thorpe et al, 2018, p. 372). Due to the strong connection between the industry and gambling, sport integrity is an essential commercial imperative – betting will not occur where gamblers consider that the spectacle is corrupt. Australian governments also fund safety and integrity processes within these industries, providing stewards with significant investigatory powers and a range of penalties for racing specific corruption. Correspondingly, the racing industry enjoys greater regulatory infrastructure than, for example, Olympic sports, and government is directly involved in regulatory oversight.

While there had been a small number of known cases involving ring-ins within the racing industry before, the case of Fine Cotton made transparent the high levels of corruption within police and government, facilitating organised crime in the racing industry. Important steps were taken by government and media institutions in subsequent years to address these, culminating in the *Royal Commission of Inquiry into Possible Illegal Activities and Associated Police Misconduct*, which became known as the Fitzgerald Inquiry, commencing in 1987. The result of the Fitzgerald Inquiry was the resignation of the Queensland Premier Joh Bjelke Peterson, jail terms for three Ministers (but not then racing Minister Russ Hinze) and for the Police Commissioner, Terry Lewis (Queensland Government, 1989). Hinze was reputedly involved in numerous corrupt activities and was charged five years later with receiving illegal payments in exchange for abusing his position, however, he died from bowel cancer before being brought to trial.

Racing authorities banned six individuals from Australian racetracks for life for participation in, or knowledge of, the conspiracy: bookmakers Bill and Robbie Waterhouse, trainer Hayden Haitana, socialite Robert North, salesman John Dixon and electrician Tommaso Di Luzio. The latter three were involved in preparing and transporting the horses for the fix. The Waterhouse men had their ban lifted after 14 years, and Haitana eventually had his racetrack ban from racetracks lifted in 2013, nearly 30 years after the incident.

The prosecution of Bill and Robbie Waterhouse appears to have been a high-profile reprimand designed to provide the appearance of a strict and uncompromising response from the racing industry to the scandal. However, the action had a narrow connection to the criminal elements that perpetrated the fraud, and despite strong belief that the Waterhouses had a bigger role in the fix, nothing could be proven. Robbie Waterhouse was found to have lied to authorities under oath about whom he placed bets for and was sanctioned with eight months of weekend detention at Long Bay prison in Sydney (Nolan, 2019). The 14-year racetrack ban appears to have been ‘making an example’ rather than a protective measure to uphold racing integrity. The incident also resulted in criminal prosecutions of the perpetrators. Haitana received a six-month sentence and Gillespie a four-year sentence (he served six months and two years under house arrest). Gillespie subsequently resumed an illustrious career in fraud, including tax evasion, peddling a unproven and non-existent anti-wrinkle cream, famous artwork scams (Chang, 2016) and issuing passports for a fictitious South Pacific dominion (Ashforth, 2002b).

In the intervening years since the Fine Cotton scandal, numerous operational processes have been instituted in the horse racing industry to ensure that the identities of horses can be easily and conclusively verified and to minimise the corruption of horses and jockeys on race day. The Australian Rules of Racing (ARR) (Racing Australia, 2020) is a set of rules which are consistently refined and are backed by statute in Australian jurisdictions in conjunction with their 'local rules'. Many of the rules implemented since 1984 would make it difficult or impossible to substitute a horse in the manner that occurred with Fine Cotton, such as the horse registration, ownership, leasing and traceability requirements. These include the requirement to brand and microchip a horse upon registration which allows horse identities to be verified before all races (Racing Australia, 2020, ARR 29).

These measures have been very effective in determining an equine competitor's identity. Ashforth observed that:

> Nowadays, with every race studied, the ringer is an endangered, if not an extinct species. Every horse born in Great Britain or Ireland since January 1, 1999 has an identifying microchip injected deep in its neck. Taking it out, and replacing it with another, would not be easy. Every horse's passport is checked on its debut, on its first appearance after a change of trainer, or if the horse is dope tested, and there are also random checks. Improvement in form or evidence of a betting coup can trigger a passport check. The day of the ringer may be over. (Ashforth, 2002b)

Other important operational measures inhibit criminal collusion at the racetrack, such as the rule prohibiting the carrying of electronic devices, including mobile phones, while riding (Racing Australia, 2020, ARR 113) and the absolute prohibition on electronic devices in certain parts of the track, including the mounting yard, scales area and jockey's room (Racing Australia, 2020, ARR 218). British Horseracing introduced a limited place and time for jockeys to use their mobile phones on race day, known as the 'phone zone', from as early as 2003 (BHA, 2003). In addition, the investigatory powers of Australian stewards include the ability to examine any horse, including by taking samples, to seize and examine phones, computers or electronic devices and to search any licensed person or their gear (Racing Australia, 2020, ARR 22).

Since the Fine Cotton scandal, significant improvements have been made in governance and integrity within the racing industry. Racing Victoria has provided a strong racing integrity model for thoroughbred racing in Victoria, but other Australian states and territories have varying views of the necessity for this approach. 'Fair Racing for All' seeks to: 'promote a responsible culture of fair play, ethical behaviours and respect' (Racing Victoria, 2019, p. 3). The initiative is based on seven areas: values and behaviour, compulsory personal development, enhanced licensing standards, updated penalties and whistleblowing, improved information-sharing, investment infrastructure and technology and transparency in thoroughbred sales. This model would have been useful in addressing the fact situation in Fine Cotton. In particular, the ability of any participant in the fix or a member of the public who was aware of the intended corrupt conduct to anonymously report the plan through a sporting integrity hotline would have been helpful. A primary executor of the corruption, Haitana, has stated that he did not want to perpetrate the substitution, but felt that he had no choice as his life would be endangered if he did not proceed. Haitana has also stated that he felt unable to go to police with his information, due to the close relationship between Queensland police and organised crime. An anonymous whistleblower mechanism, independent of the racing authority (and in this case, potentially Queensland police) (such as described in Chapter 8 by Ondráčková and Verschuuren, this volume), would have provided an important avenue to receive information from individuals such as Haitana about proposed illegal activities.

Australian jurisdictions have invested significant resources into integrity investigations in the last three decades. The development of agencies such as the Victorian Sports Integrity and Intelligence Unity also support racing integrity through specialised investigatory teams, in close collaboration with Victoria Police (see also Murnane & Moller, 2018). In 2019, NSW police agreed to deploy a senior detective with the NSW racing regulator to facilitate collaboration between these agencies and improve integrity investigations (Roots, 2019). In Queensland, integrity within three animal racing codes is managed by the Queensland Racing Integrity Commission, an independent body created to oversee integrity and welfare standards for racing animals and participants. The increased development of racing integrity infrastructure in each jurisdiction signifies an appreciation of integrity practices being central to the quality of competitions and the ability of the industry to survive. While a better developed integrity strategy and enhanced investigatory capacity may not have prevented an incidence of horse substitution, such as Fine Cotton, renewed focus on these areas decreases the likelihood of these events occurring in the future.

Alternative approaches to restore trust

It is difficult to determine what alternative response racing authorities could have made beyond enforcing lifetime racetrack bans for those found guilty of the fix. Any lesser penalty would have substantially undermined confidence in the integrity of the organisation and racing. The betting plunge on the novice handicap race in which Fine Cotton participated was significant for the time (1.5 million AUD), and it was important that perpetrators of the fix be denied the opportunity to participate in the racing community. Their removal was essential to maintain public confidence, regardless of whether their moral culpability for the fix was diminished by acting under duress applied by organised crime identities. As duress was not established in the criminal trials, it was not considered in disciplinary proceedings. Haitana had his lifetime ban lifted some 30 years after the event, to enable him to attend racecourses for recreation, rather than to participate in the industry. It seems unlikely that lifting the ban after this length of time in these circumstances would undermine the reputation of the racing industry.

The lifetime racecourse ban of bookmakers Bill and Robbie Waterhouse on the grounds of a disciplinary charge that had not been prosecuted before ('prior knowledge') may have worked against racing authorities. After all, many people, including other racing industry participants, demonstrated that they possessed 'prior knowledge', although few were so closely connected to the source of the plot. Singling out the Waterhouse men for the harshest penalty available suggested unfairness and gave the impression of desperation. Rather than a public demonstration of punishment, it might have been more effective for racing authorities to look at the culture of information exchange, the laws and practices of gambling and to champion improved regulation and operational measures to constrain the sharing of corrupt conduct information. In many ways the Waterhouse ban perpetuated the long media cycle around the scandal and exacerbated a poor public perception. The bans were lifted, not without controversy, after 14 years, enabling both men to resume gambling operations in relation to racing.

Measures could have been implemented to foster a culture of trust with racing authorities, whereby industry participants could be confident that information provided would be dealt with effectively and confidentially. This may have alleviated some of the negative sentiment surrounding the return of the Waterhouse men to racetrack gambling, where many of the older betting operators remembered that they had been willing to take an unfair advantage in their dealings with the industry (Ashforth, 2002b).

Interestingly, the failure of the substitution and the fact that all bets stood after Fine Cotton's disqualification meant that a number of individuals who had knowledge of the corruption and sought to use this knowledge for gains on the gambling market, actually ended up losing their investment. The distribution of this form of 'just deserts', however, does not remedy the damage to others who acted in good faith, whether through placing a bet without insider knowledge, or preparing a horse for competition where it was believed that a fair playing field existed.

While penalties were issued under the criminal law system to the individuals who executed the fix (but not necessarily those who instructed that it occur), it is not clear that moral wrongs were effectively addressed. Walker has discussed the concept of moral repair as requiring: 'the restoration or reconstruction of confidence, trust and hope in the reality of shared moral standards and of our reliability in meeting and enforcing them' (Walker, 2001, p. 120). In this case study the broader issue of social repair was not acknowledged and the silence of authorities in relation to the systemic corruption exposed by the scandal perpetuated cynicism about the Queensland racing industry and local law enforcement.

Ultimately, it would have been impossible to restore trust in the racing industry without the Queensland Royal Commission into broader corruption within government institutions. This scandal is unique in its complex connections between the sport, organised criminals and the regulatory bodies. It may be argued that a more thorough investigation of the corruption may have uncovered details that would have distributed legal culpability for the fix differently. It seems likely that there was little appetite to look closely at the personalities which may have encouraged the syndicate to arrange the substitution and their broader relationships in the community, and this was the ultimate failing of corrective action to restore public trust in the integrity of racing.

As described above, racing integrity measures are not consistent across Australian jurisdictions. Racing and gambling within Australia are primarily regulated within each state and territory, rather than by the federal government. Greater participation by federal authorities may have the effect of protecting the horse racing industry from corruption which is linked to integrity failures of the state and territory regulatory systems. It is interesting to note that the sports integrity regime being implemented from recommendations made in the recent 'Review of Australia's Sports Integrity Arrangements' (the Wood Review) will not be extended to animal racing (Wood et al., 2018). The recommendations include important match-fixing offences which will apply across the country, and most importantly in those state jurisdictions in which specific match-fixing laws do not exist.

While states and territories staunchly defend their authority to regulate animal racing, it seems like a missed opportunity not to include them in federal sports integrity initiatives. These initiatives would complement their regulatory machinery, such as the above-mentioned criminal laws relating to corruption in sport, integrity whistleblowing mechanisms and enhanced criminal intelligence capabilities. Additional tools developed through the National Integrity in Sport Unit, such as the anti-match-fixing Code of Conduct, would be a helpful addition to racetrack agreements, emphasising: 'knowing the rules, avoiding betting on your sport, protecting sensitive information, refusing to match-fix and reporting approaches' (Commonwealth of Australia, 2016). This is particularly the case now that insider information can be more readily exploited, for example through betting exchanges, such as Betfair, offering a betting product that was not available at the time of Fine Cotton: 'lay' bets. To 'lay' a bet is betting that your horse or team will lose, rather than to 'back' that competitor to win (Betfair n.d.). Participation from the federal government in this industry would also be protective against fraud in racing which has connections to corrupt state or territory governments, as in the case of Fine Cotton.

Conclusion

Sport appears to operate within a world and according to rules of its own, but is very much a product of broader society, including its darker elements. Some sports, particularly those in which gambling is a cornerstone and organised crime has an interest, are subject to external interference which is difficult for sports controlling bodies to combat. With continuing technological advancement in a globalised world, corrupt conduct for gains on the gambling market will be increasingly difficult to detect and address. The Fine Cotton affair is a colourful example of the extent to which nefarious elements may be involved in sporting corruption.

Sports controlling bodies operating in these environments face unique challenges and must work closely with law enforcement agencies and government regulators to provide the best protective measures for the integrity of their competitions. Corrupt conduct in these sports may often result in criminal as well as sporting offences. In conditions where the integrity of those government entities may be compromised, sport controlling bodies will have few avenues left open to them, but must continue to strive for thorough investigations, comprehensive rules and well formulated operational measures. State and territory racing authorities would be aided in protecting the integrity of their competitions by explicit and consistently implemented integrity initiatives, such as the model in Victoria, and by inclusion in the proposed federal sports integrity regime.

Questions

i *Trust loss* – In whom (or, in which group) has trust been lost in this case?
ii *Trust correction* – How, if attempted, has the restoration of trust been tried?; and;
iii *Lessons learned* – How could the lessons from this case be applied to other sports, nations, states, other districts for the same sport, or other sports to prevent a further loss of trust or at least to restore trust?

References

Ashforth, D. (2002a, 23 January). Great racing scams: Fine Cotton, 'Ring-in' that was destined to fail from the outset. *The Racing Post*. London. Retrieved from https://www.thefreelibrary.com/Great+Racing+Scams%3a+Fine+Cotton%2c+Part+1+-+%60Ring-in'+that+was+destined … -a082055907

Ashforth, D. (2002b, 24 January). Great racing scams: Witch hunt that led to 17 years in the wilderness. *The Racing Post*. London. Retrieved from https://www.thefreelibrary.com/GREAT+RACING+SCAMS%3a+Witch+hunt+that+led+to+17+years+in+the+wilderness.-a082086330

Betfair. (n.d). Exchange: What does the term 'lay' mean and what is a lay bet?. Help Topics, Betfair. Retrieved from https://en-betfair.custhelp.com/app/answers/detail/a_id/417/~/exchange%3A-what-does-the-term-lay-mean-and-what-is-a-lay-bet%3F

BHA. (2003, 16 September). Jockey Club to introduce amended mobile phone restrictions. British Horseracing Authority. Retrieved from https://www.britishhorseracing.com/press_releases/jockey-club-to-introduce-amended-mobile-phone-restrictions/

Brooks, G., Aleem, A., & Button, M. (2013). Fraud and corruption in horse racing. In *Fraud, corruption and Sport* (pp. 107–122). London: Palgrave Macmillan.

Chang, C. (2016, 6 April). The rundown Aussie hotel linked to global Panama Papers scandal. News.com.au. Retrieved from https://www.news.com.au/finance/money/tax/the-rundown-aussie-hotel-linked-to-global-panama-papers-scandal/news-story/4d201c21fd9faeaafb681fc0a6a39e79

Commonwealth of Australia. (2016, 1 August). '13. Annexure D - Code of Conduct'. Anti-match-fixing policy template. National Integrity in Sport Unit, Department of Health. Retrieved from https://www1.health.gov.au/internet/main/publishing.nsf/Content/Anti-match-fixing-policy-template~Anti-match-fixing-policy-template-annexured-code-of-conduct

Cripps, C. (1990). *Racetrack ring-in and rorts*. (2nd ed.). Chelsea, Victoria: Vetsport Promotions.

Gottschalk, P. (2012). Rotten apples versus rotten barrels in white collar crime: A qualitative analysis of white collar offenders in Norway. *International Journal of Criminal Justice Sciences*, 7(2), 575–590.

Holden, D. (2020, 10 April). The ten most cringe-worthy moments in Australian sport. *The Roar*. Retrieved from https://www.theroar.com.au/2020/04/11/the-ten-most-cringe-worthy-moments-in-australian-sport/

Hoysted, P., & Shiel, P. (2019). *The Fine Cotton fiasco*. North Sydney: Random House Australia.

Hunt, E. (2012, 5 November). Racing's 'ring-in king' Erbie, a galloper that ran under several names in the 1930s. *The Herald-Sun*. Retrieved from https://www.heraldsun.com.au/news/law-order/racings-ring-in-king-erbie-a-galloper-that-ran-under-several-names-in-the-1930s/news-story/7cb9416c531d52df9a42e666537ccf0c

Hunt, E. (2013, 31 October). How Regal Vista became Royal School in racing ring-in scandal. *The Herald-Sun*. Retrieved from https://www.heraldsun.com.au/news/law-order/regal-vista/news-story/2ed07c8ab569035a90c420c7a95897a7

Martelli, J. (2009, 25 September). Bookmaking legend Bill Waterhouse tells about Fine Cotton affair. *The Daily Telegraph*. Retrieved from https://www.dailytelegraph.com.au/sport/superracing/bookmaking-legend-bill-waterhouse-tells-about-fine-cotton-affair/news-story/09051eae9717688f393daef0b2e285e9?sv=cfb04f33261a5e58e437fa24984ecead

McIver, D., & Tran, D. (2018, 30 March). Stawell Gift: How the Antonich twins used a meat pie to stage one of the race's greatest coups. *ABC News*. Retrieved from https://www.abc.net.au/news/2018-03-30/stawell-gift-scott-antonich-twins-1988-meat-pie-coup/9604972

Miller, S. (2018). Corruption. In E. Zalta, *et al.* (Eds.), *Stanford encyclopaedia of philosophy*. Stanford: Stanford University Press.

Murnane, K., & Moller, J. (2018). Preventing match-fixing and promoting integrity in sport: Reflections on experiences in Australia, Japan and Korea. In H. Opie & S. Steele (Eds.), *Match-fixing in sport: Comparative studies from Australia, Japan, Korea and Beyond*. Abingdon: Routledge.

Nolan, D. (2019, 4 November). 'Sick of the lies': Why man jailed over Fine Cotton scandal broke three-decade silence. *Channel 9 News*. Retrieved from https://www.9news.com.au/national/fine-cotton-scandal-robert-north-speaks-exclusively-a-current-affair/d9d6dedf-5137-45d9-bb57-d9a3c1a2a92e

Queensland Government. (1989). *Royal Commission of Inquiry into possible illegal activities and associated police misconduct* (the Fitzgerald Inquiry). Retrieved from https://www.ccc.qld.gov.au/sites/default/files/Docs/Publications/CCC/The-Fitzgerald-Inquiry-Report-1989.pdf

Racing Australia. (2020). *Australian Rules of Racing* (ARR). Retrieved from https://www.racingaustralia.horse/uploadimg/Australian_rules_of_Racing/Australian_Rules_of_Racing_01_January_2020.pdf

Racing Victoria. (2019). Fair racing for all. Retrieved from https://racingvictoria.com.au

Reilly, T. (2010, 9 December). Richards accused of being a hard man in the past. *Sydney Morning Herald*. Retrieved from https://www.smh.com.au/national/nsw/richards-accused-of-being-a-hard-man-in-the-past-20101208-18px8.html

Roberts, S., & Bolton, C. (2018). Approaches to compliance and reform. In L. Kihl (Ed.), *Corruption in Sport: Causes, Consequences and Reform* (pp. 144–155). Abingdon: Routledge.

Roots, C. (2019, 12 October). Racing NSW and police join forces to rein in cheats. *The Sydney Morning Herald*. Retrieved from https://www.smh.com.au/sport/racing/racing-nsw-and-police-join-forces-to-rein-in-cheats-20191012-p5302v.html

Shakespeare, W. (1623). *Henry IV, Part II*. First Folio.

Shand, A. (2010, 23 May). Bungled Fine Cotton con a 'double sting'. *Perth Now*. Retrieved from https://www.perthnow.com.au/news/wa/bungled-fine-cotton-con-a-double-sting-ng-697090ba73e0a0ae358d1c493d6645e5

SI Staff. (2010, 30 November). Billie Jean King: In her own words. *Sports Illustrated*. Retrieved from https://www.si.com/sportsperson/2010/11/30/billiejeanking-sportsman

Thompson, A. (2016, 16 April). Unsolved murder of horse trainer George Brown torments Jean O'Leary, 82. *Port Stephens Examiner*. Retrieved from https://www.portstephensexaminer.com.au/story/3852914/its-torture-gruesome-cold-case-torments-grieving-sister/?cs=4152

Thorpe, D., Buti, A., Davies, C., & Jonson, P. (2018). *Sport law* (3rd ed.). Sydney: Oxford University Press.

Walker, M. U. (2001). Moral repair and its limits. *Marquette University e-Publications@Marquette*, 1-1-2001. Retrieved from https://epublications.marquette.edu/cgi/viewcontent.cgi?referer=&httpsredir=1&article=1151&context=phil_fac

Waterhouse, B. (2009). *What are the odds?*Sydney: Random House Australia.

White, S. (2010, 13 August). Hayden Haitana still paying for the Fine Cotton betting scandal. *The Advertiser*. Retrieved from https://www.adelaidenow.com.au/ipad/hayden-haitana-still-paying-for-the-fine-cotton-betting-scandal/news-story/425a1ac75c8aeea1b117355931a638d8

Wood, J., Howman, D., & Murrihy, R. (2018, March). Report of the review of Australia's sports integrity arrangements. Report No 12074. Retrieved from https://www1.health.gov.au/internet/main/publishing.nsf/Content/63F0A5D7BDA5A0B5CA2582CF0005E6F9/$File/HEALTH-RASIA-Report-Acc.pdf

14 Restoring trust in sport

Lessons learnt

Catherine Ordway[1]

Where should we best invest our combined energies and focus for the future? The most sobering realisation for many sport fans throughout the COVID-19 lockdown is that sport is not 'essential' in the same way our front-line health workers, emergency services and teachers are. The view represented by the often-quoted Bill Shankly (former Liverpool Football Club manager), paraphrased as espousing that football (and perhaps all sport) is more important than matters of life and death (Bona, 2015), has been brought sharply into focus. Despite the fact that community-level competitions, professional leagues, World Championships, Grand Slams, Grands Prix, Tours and even the Tokyo 2020 Olympic Games have been postponed or cancelled, and travel restricted, the emerging evidence suggests that corruption in all its forms has continued unabated while our collective eyes have been 'off the ball'. For instance, it appears that 'cheating' – whether through doping, fraud, money laundering, bribery and/or match-fixing – has found new footholds in fantasy sports or online gaming (commonly referred to as 'e-sports'), or have flourished elsewhere in the absence of drug testing or other external scrutiny.

As was outlined at the outset, the focus for this book in solving the 'pandemic' of corruption in sport has been to consider how trust is impacted by corruption. There are many options for research, collaboration and policy development in combatting corruption and in restoring trust in sport. The challenge is to identify how we can be most 'effective' (Anstiss, 2020 quoting Moya Dodd), and what the levers, motivators and areas of concentration might be. One key challenge facing all sport researchers, and as outlined in Chapter 13 by Lim and Young in the case of Fine Cotton, is that sport is only one part of the fabric of society, and:

> Corruption can also be endemic and ingrained within certain sports and sporting associations. This is made all the more complex when the sport is encompassed within countries and regions where corruption is tolerated and indeed incorporated within the societal framework. (BaMaung & Cuddihy, 2018, p. 115)

While acknowledging this challenge, this book has focused on restoring trust in the chosen sports corruption case studies through an Ethics of Care [EoC] perspective (Gilligan, 1982). As set out below, an EoC approach provides an opportunity for leading sports organisations to restore trust in a public that wishes to believe again in the ideals promised by competitive sport.

The recent article by Ransom & Barsuhn (2020) concluded by echoing the sentiments of many contributors in this space, including the authors in this book, by making the following recommendations about how legitimacy and trust could be re-established in sport:

1 *Work collaboratively to:*

 (i) create governance and policy education courses;
 (ii) network and information share;
 (iii) develop a practical, balanced, transparent and consistent scorecard/ rubric – to assist decision-making e.g. major event bids/ large scale public infrastructure.

2 *Accountability structures and sanctions – through international conventions/ Codes of Conduct* [paraphrased – Ransom & Barsuhn, 2020, p. 144].

These are not new observations, and much of the work aimed at achieving these outcomes has been improving over recent decades. Yet as demonstrated in Chapter 2 by Caneppele, Cinaglia and Langlois, 'sport corruption' is increasingly being reported. The Database of Corruption Cases in Sport (DACCS) research project identified six general categories of corruption in sport: (a) manipulation of competitions, (b) doping, (c) event bids, (d) contracts, (e) elections, and (f) 'all other sporting cases related to corruption that do not fit the previous typology'. In this book, the case studies reviewed have fallen into the DACCS categories as follows: (a) manipulation of competitions: through sumo wrestling in Japan (Chapter 7 Nichol, Solomon and Kawai), tennis in Australia (Chapter 9 Harrison and Moller), football in Vietnam (Chapter 10 Thimydung and Gardiner) and rugby league in Australia (Chapter 12 Ordway and Lenten); and (b) doping: through British road cycling (Chapter 6 Roberts and Ordway) and Russian biathlon. In Chapter 4, Erika Riedl outlines the accusations of bribery against the International Biathlon Union (IBU) associated with both DACCS (b) doping and (c) event bids categories. The bribery is alleged to relate to the IBU's treatment of Russian biathlete doping cases, and in the 2016 decision to award the 2021 World Championships to Tyumen, Russia despite the International Olympic Committee's edict following the McLaren Report into systemic doping at the 2014 Sochi Olympic Winter Games.

Chapter 3 (Bayley and Egle) looks at DACCS category (d) contracts and 'procurement corruption' in relation to the PyeongChang 2018 Olympic Winter Games. Close friends of the President of South Korea, and Olympic sponsor executives, were found guilty of corruption following a range of charges involving abuse of power, extortion, bribery and fraud in connection with projects such as building facilities and national sport development programmes. These forms of corruption went far deeper than the Games and led to the impeachment of President Park.

In Chapter 11, Olukoya and Ogunleye-Bello, refer to the various forms of corruption that have beset Nigerian football, including DACCS category (e) elections, observing that: 'Match fixing, age fraud, nepotism, funds mismanagement, electoral malpractices and breaches of contract' have caused sponsors to walk away from the sport (p. 183). DACCS category (f) 'all other sporting cases related to corruption that do not fit the previous typology' could be expected to include the selection bribery case studies featured in ice hockey in the Czech Republic (Chapter 8 Ondráčková and Verschuuren) and in football in Nigeria (Chapter 11 Olukoya and Ogunleye-Bello), the abuse of power through over-reach by the World Anti-Doping Agency (Chapter 5 Jamieson and Ordway) and horse substitution in Chapter 13 (Lim and Young).

The world is no longer naïve nor blinkered to corruption and manipulation in sport – we have a good understanding of the dimensions of the problem. The question then is one of *how* to create greater accountability, responsibility and transparency where decision-makers and power players in sport are unwilling, voluntarily, or unaware of what is required, to be a force for positive change. This draws on the 'four levels of teaching' as originally described by Broadwell (1969) as: the conscious competent; the unconscious competent; the conscious incompetent and the unconscious incompetent. If applied in the sport integrity regulatory setting, the challenge is how the traditional 'carrots and sticks' (Montague, 1849, p. 139) motivation approach applies where integrity is not merely a skills acquisition process but has an ethical and values foundation. What sanctions are appropriate for the intentionally corrupt (conscious and unwilling incompetent)? How best can we persuade and educate the unintentionally corrupt (unconscious but willing incompetent) to create a culture of integrity?

Vertical and horizontal integrity system weaknesses

As observed by Riedl in Chapter 4, 'corruption cases are the most difficult to prosecute, especially since in most cases both parties are happy with their 'deal', e.g. the one offering the bribe and the one taking the bribe. The need for people to come forward and 'blow the whistle' is therefore crucial in many cases' (p. 54). Unfortunately, without sophisticated and robust whistleblowing systems of the kind described by Ondráčková and Verschuuren in Chapter 8, and initiated by Tennis Australia (mentioned by Harrison and Moller in Chapter 9), other than through the efforts of professional and diligent investigative journalists, there are few places for whistleblowers to turn. Some courageous athletes have chosen to speak publicly, at great personal cost, to expose the corruption, including cover ups and criminal behaviour, by people involved in sport who were in positions of trust; most recently representing Russian athletics and US gymnasts.

There are a range of settings where this connection between athlete welfare and integrity should be examined through future research. Internationally, the extensive publicity surrounding shocking allegations in a range of sports has put the focus on inappropriate behaviour in elite sport. The sentencing of Dr Nassar in January 2018 (Perry, 2018), following the Daniels Report (2017) involving 265 gymnasts, and evidence of the abuse of US swimmers over decades (Reid, 2018), and the surrounding cover-up by the sports organisations themselves, demands that more is done to restore trust in sport leadership. There have also been independent cultural reviews looking at men's cycling in the UK (Phelps, 2017) leading to the broader *Organisational Culture in Sport* review (ICSA, 2018) relating to the Team Sky case study featured in Chapter 6 by Roberts and Ordway. Also, 80 football coaches have been convicted of child sexual abuse, while police continue to investigate the 2800 historic abuse reports to their hotline (BBC, 2018). An independent review of UK Gymnastics was launched in July 2020 (UK Sport, 2020), and on behalf of Australian Gymnastics the same month (Australian Human Rights Commission, 2020). Similarly, in US college sport, there is a growing awareness that a system built on the financial exploitation of vulnerable athletes is at extreme risk of on-field and off-field corruption (Kupfer, 2018; Ordway and Lenten Chapter 12). Brooks et al. (2013), for example, has reviewed the 'points shaving' and 'tanking' practices in US college basketball (Brooks et al., 2013, pp. 123–38). While it is noted that corruption is 'not endemic' in college sport yet (Brooks et al., 2013, p. 127), it is suggested that the recent changes to US State sport gambling laws (Gouker, 2018) will only increase the opportunities for, and ultimately, the prevalence of, match-fixing offences, particularly if the welfare needs of college athletes are not urgently addressed.

A number of cultural reviews into the Australian Institute of Sport and the culture of Australian sports have also been conducted over the years relating to issues of leadership, bullying allegations, poor off-field behaviour by athletes and on field cheating, including: the Black Report into drug use (1989), the women's artistic gymnastics (Opie, 1995), men's road cycling (Anderson, 2004; Wood, 2013), men's cricket (The Ethics Group, 2018) and the Australian Olympic Committee (The Ethics Group, 2017). Swimming Australia has also faced challenges relating to its male team members (Bluestone Edge, 2013; Smith, 2013), and the inappropriate behaviour by elite coaches (e.g. Scott Volkers: Keith, 2018). The Australian Royal Commission (2017) publicly reviewing *Institutional Responses into Child Sexual Abuse*, resulting in a report into 'Sport, recreation, arts, culture, community and hobby groups', created more discussion around what is expected of organisations who have a legal and moral duty to care for young people. At the same time, Australian tennis player Jelena Dokic published her story about family violence perpetrated by her father (and coach) (Dokic & Halloran, 2017). Tennis Australia was aware of Jelena's abuse, and questions remain about what more could have been done by the organisations and institutions when Jelena was an adult and refusing assistance. A spotlight is also being shone on the practice internationally of trafficking promising child athletes in a range of sports (from football, to athletics to ice skating (Gordon, 2016; Halloran & Linden, 2020), and what implications these kinds of athlete welfare issues have for sport, and integrity, more broadly.

A novel approach has been outlined by Ordway & Opie (2016) which links the anti-corruption model of asset protection (ACLEI n.d.) with Hill's research into the exploitation of athlete vulnerabilities in match-fixing (Hill, 2008; Hill, 2013) to suggest that a holistic athlete welfare approach can support other anti-corruption strategies:

> Integrity in the organisation can be seen as an asset in the same way as both athletes and staff need to be developed and empowered by their sports within an integrity framework. In his book, The Insider's Guide to Match-Fixing in Football, Declan Hill (2013) went further by arguing that the first priority [in protecting integrity] is to address baseline survival issues. Hill called on sports organisations to reduce integrity risks through providing for the athletes' welfare, paying them appropriately and on time and supporting vulnerable athletes (e.g., those with gambling and prescription drug addictions). WADA has also funded a number of important social science studies into doping athletes' motivations and rationale in order to assist in shaping the education and welfare programs (Moston, Engelberg, & Skinner, 2015). It is clear from both WADA's and Hill's research that financial rewards are motivators both in cheating-to-win (doping) and cheating-to-lose (match-fixing) scenarios which leads to the conclusion that measures aimed at minimising the financial vulnerability of players will, at least in some cases, head off such cheating activity. (Ordway & Opie, 2016, pp. 52–3, brackets added)

This then replaces the purely economic devaluation of athletes as 'assets' with a humanistic, inclusive, EoC, wellness focus. This approach is in line with the rise of athlete activism and an acknowledgement that human rights must take priority over commercial interests (e.g. Schwab, 2017; Schwab, 2018; Freeburn, 2018; WADA, 2020). It is also reflected in the most recent initiative of the Australian Institute of Sport, through the work of the Athlete Welfare & Engagement team (AIS, 2020).

Another area ripe for further research, linking athlete welfare and sports integrity, relates to the growth of women's sport. One question to explore further is whether the under payment and/or the increased injury rates may impact on the susceptibility of women to match-fixing and other forms of corruption (Douglas, 2016; Didulica, 2019). The concussion research on male athletes is clear (Greenhow & East, 2015), and more work is being done on whether this is directly replicated in female athletes (Aubusson, 2018). As part of a broader demonstration that athlete welfare is paramount to sports organisations, leaders need to be assessing the training and game-day impacts on male and female players to determine whether, as a minimum, rule changes (Blair, 2018), or at the extreme, new 'gender blind' (sex inclusive: Hargreaves, 2002) sports need to be developed to ensure that sport continues to be physically safe, and safe from integrity risks.

The accountability action taken by the World Anti-Doping Agency (WADA) in relation to the international athletics federation (IAAF, now World Athletics) and the Sochi 2014 Olympic Winter Games, following the systemic doping exposed by the German ARD documentary-makers, laid bare the weaknesses in both the World Anti-Doping Code, and in the international sport accountability system both vertically and horizontally. Despite what were undoubtedly expensive, time-consuming and personally harrowing independent investigations, the issues surrounding the State-sanctioned doping programme in Russia have not been resolved and trust has not been restored in Russian sport and, some critics would argue, in WADA and, more broadly, in Olympic administration and governance. (It should be noted by way of contrast, as discussed elsewhere, World Athletics has made impressive headway to restore trust in the governance of its sport (e.g. Ordway, 2021; Riedl Chapter 4)). It is too early to tell how successful these measures will be.

Similarly, despite authorities in Switzerland and the US engaging in globally publicised raids resulting in arrests and prosecutions of influential and executive members of the international federation for football (FIFA) in 2015, these matters have also not been finalised. The social media evidence is that while fans of the game don't appear to care much about the corruption issues at the top (Hölzen & Meier, 2019), there remains misgivings about whether the new administration is able to deliver a culture that is markedly different from the past. Gianni Infantino was voted into the FIFA Presidency in 2016, having worked for the European Confederation, UEFA, since 2000. Infantino was UEFA secretary general from 2010, and then effectively took over the presidency once Michel Platini was banned by FIFA in 2015 for 'Offering and accepting gifts and other benefits' (FIFA Governance, 2015). One of Infantino's key election promises was to implement the FIFA Reform Committee's proposals (FIFA, 2015). The day after Infantino had told the FIFA Congress in Paris in 2019 that: 'the days of scandal were over, one of his vice presidents, the head of African soccer (Ahmad Ahmad), was arrested and questioned by French financial prosecutors' (Panja, 2019). Then in July 2020, the Swiss federal prosecutor opened an investigation against Infantino in relation to his dealing with the former Swiss attorney-general dating back from 2015 (Panja, 2020).

In international weightlifting, then President, Tamás Aján, clearly felt so secure in his 45-plus year control of the IWF that, without a hint of irony or self-awareness in his role as primary protagonist, in 2011 he openly called upon the EU Commissioner to create an agency against sports corruption, stating that:

> There is no sports organisation today where the appointment to important posts would not be tainted by corruption. In some countries, money seems to be growing on trees, and these countries can buy positions in places where they have no professional influence. (quoted by Andersen, 2020)

Despite financial irregularities being publicly identified from 2013 (Hartmann, 2013), an independent investigation (headed by Richard McLaren) was not launched until after ARD again aired an exposé documentary in 2020 (Seppelt et al., 2020). These examples provide support for calls for a broad international sport integrity and anti-corruption watchdog to restore trust in sport.

Education based on an Ethics of Care (EoC) approach

> The secret to success [in life] is to stay in love. Staying in love gives you the fire to ignite other people, to see inside other people, to have greater desire to get things done than other people. A person who is not in love doesn't really feel the kind of

> excitement that helps them to get ahead and to lead others and to achieve. I don't know any other fire, any other thing in life that is more exhilarating and is more positive a feeling than love is. (Quoting then Brigadier General John H. Stanford in Kouzes & Posner, 1992, pp. 479–80).

The EoC approach promotes the idea of bringing more love and care back into our communities, and in this case, our sports organisations. It may seem over-simplified, but the approach promotes a proactive response based on the fundamental values of sport. It is argued throughout this book that educating children on respect, ethical decision-making and how to be a good citizen will have much greater long-term benefit than spending more money on criminalisation, courts, invasive anti-doping methodologies and increased law enforcement powers in match-fixing and anti-corruption.

The authors here have called for better and more targeted educational resources in sport. It is recommended that sport anti-corruption educators draw upon the lessons learnt in the anti-doping space to consider developing education tools applicable to the age and role of sport actors based on the five approaches identified by Backhouse et al. (2014) (also set out in Jamieson and Ordway in Chapter 5) as follows:

> (1) 'knowledge-focused (e.g., side effects)'; (2) 'affective-focused (e.g., targeting feelings of value and self-worth)'; (3) 'social skills training (e.g., assertiveness, decision-making, and resistance to peer pressure)'; (4) 'life skills training (e.g., multicomponent: social skills, personal skills, and knowledge)'; and (5) 'ethic- and value-based (e.g., against the rules, fair play, honesty, and integrity)' (Backhouse et al., 2014, p. 53).

Harrison and Moller in Chapter 9 outline Tennis Australia's education framework focused on athletes, support personnel, parents, officials, staff and volunteers (including parents of 'ballkids'): 'providing practical examples through a blended learning experience, including online and face-to-face workshops' (p. 157).

In Chapter 10, Thimydung and Gardiner recommend that the Vietnamese football authorities actively promote open communication between players, coaches and managers about how match-fixing occurs, what the early warning signs are and outlining their reporting responsibilities. Riedl in Chapter 4 refers to this as creating a 'a robust "speak-up" culture' (p. 54, quoting Aiolfi, 2019). Nichol, Solomon and Kawai in Chapter 7 recommend 'ethics training for new *sumo*'. Similarly, for Nigerian football, in Chapter 11, Olukoya and Ogunleye-Bello suggest that behavioural integrity awareness campaigns and ethical training is needed from the grassroots to the professional levels for coaches and players through online and face-to-face mediums, which should be 'focused, friendly, and in multiple languages' (p. 183).

In Chapter 3, Bayley and Egle propose that educational measures based on the principles of New Ethical Leadership and action-logics, particularly when applied to major event organising committees, should be aimed at:

i building an explicit culture of integrity and trust: As conflicts of interests were identified as a major contributor to the wrongdoing exposed surrounding the South Korean Winter Olympic Games, Bayley and Egle recommend education measures to clarify what is meant by conflicts of interest in procurement, particularly where benefits are sought for friends and family.

ii harnessing the power and influence of positional authority: The education measures for leaders and decision-makers should be aimed at learning how to model and promote ethical behaviour. Through scenario planning and what the authors refer to as 'heat events', leaders can be trained to create and enforce a culture of integrity and trust. Heat events are complex situations that disrupt and disorient habitual ways of thinking. Through a critical analysis approach, these discussions create new norms, new processes, ethical frameworks and procurement and integrity policies within teams, while balancing the need for results in very tight timeframes.

iii supporting external scrutiny to avoid an environment where insiders cannot see and/or challenge the integrity gap: It is necessary for sport organisations to be willing to both look to other sports, and outside sport, for transferrable learnings about integrity and trust. Ideally, external scrutiny would not just include learnings, but allow for external, transparent oversight to ensure that ethical standards were being developed and upheld. (pp. 38–41).

Recommendations beyond education

That is not to say that, for those not acting as good citizens in sport, that detection and sanctioning measures are not warranted – they are. Education measures that are not supported by sanctions are likely to be perceived as hollow and inauthentic. What is promoted here is that an equal emphasis is placed on educating stakeholders on positive values and fostering a culture of integrity at every level of the sport ecosystem.

As we have seen in responses to the COVID-19 lockdowns around the world that have focused political effort on the health priorities for the community, and also through support for movements bringing awareness to gender equality through #MeToo and anti-racism in #BLM (Black Lives Matter), is that there have been outstanding examples of fairness, inclusion, love and kindness demonstrating that 'we are all in this together'. Efforts directed towards alleviating unfairness in all its forms will bring about the greatest change, starting with poverty, racism, genocide, sexism, prejudice, injustice and greed. Sport organisations exist as part of the community, not in a vacuum, and must play their part in this cultural change. Most positively, we have increasingly heard the athletes' voices seeking influence on broader societal issues, as well as on the areas that directly impact on their lives and their rights. It is hoped that an EoC approach grounded in fairness as proposed here will create a sense of ownership, rather than a mere licence to play, in all stakeholders, to strengthen these integrity efforts.

The importance of values-based education, from a restoring trust perspective, through schools and throughout the entire sport ecosystem is now increasingly being recognised by national Olympic committees and national anti-doping organisations. To support these deterrence efforts, improved coordinated information-sharing and rule enforcement approaches are now also being developed at the national and international levels. An examination of these current models therefore deserves attention to determine where these arrangements might be strengthened.

Harrison and Moller in Chapter 9 outline the importance of sports organisations and law enforcement agencies working collaboratively in the case study involving combatting match-fixing through sharing information between Tennis Australia and the Victoria Police.

Both Nichol, Solomon and Kawai in Chapter 7 and Olukoya and Ogunleye-Bello in Chapter 11 recommend establishing a code of ethics for Japanese *sumo* and Nigerian football respectively. This recommendation is examined in detail by Riedl in Chapter 4 through the codes in the Winter IFs, resulting in suggested methods for strengthening the codes through clarifying: jurisdiction, including event bidding processes and procurement provisions (as outlined in Chapter 3 Bayley and Egle); rules for defined conduct (wrongdoing); sanctions for rule breaches; obligations to report any alleged breach of the rules; mandated cooperation with investigations and providing evidence where requested; integrity and vetting checks; conflict of interest disclosures; investigation procedures; independence in sanctioning bodies and the ability to hand down binding rulings. The importance of ensuring that rules of this nature are appropriately tailored to allow for a discretion to be exercised for non-elite athletes is addressed in Chapter 5 Jamieson and Ordway.

Nichol, Solomon and Kawai in Chapter 7 also outline sport-specific rule changes to reduce the risk of throwing matches in *sumo*. As was introduced in the Australian Football League, for example, to reduce the risk of 'tanking' individual matches towards the end of the season to give teams a better standing in the 'draft' (Lenten et al., 2018), Nichol, Solomon and Kawai recommend reforming the *sumo* promotion rules based on an overall win/loss record, rather than a tournament win/loss record. Nichol, Solomon and Kawai also consider who else benefits from fixing in *sumo*, which is in line with the approach under the World Anti-Doping Code in applying sanctions to athlete support personnel, in recommending that stable masters should also receive bans. However, an additional challenge to changing this customary practice is it is also noted that the fixing in *sumo* is not related to gambling, but instead has become a cultural norm for wrestlers to trade or buy wins to avoid injuries or to prevent demotion. The *sumo* elders, through the wrestling association, as custodians of the sport, may be reluctant to ban this practice as 'that is the way it has always been done'.

Intersection with governance, culture and integrity

In response to the review into sport integrity in Australia in 2018, known as the 'Wood Review' (Wood et al., 2018), the Australian Government introduced wide-ranging amendments to the *Australian Sports Anti-Doping Authority Act*. The centrepiece was to establish Sport Integrity Australia, which commenced on 1 July 2020, to bring anti-doping, match-fixing and athlete safeguarding efforts together under one entity.

'Sport integrity' is defined in the positive: 'the manifestation of the ethics and values that promote community confidence in sport' (ASADA Amendment Act, 2020 s.4; NISU, 2016). As noted in the introductory chapter to this book, Chapter 1 Ordway and Lucas, this definition does not assist to identify wrongdoing, or to clarify the relationship with corruption in sport. The 'threats to sports integrity' are defined as including (and not limited to) member protection, 'cheating to win' (doping) and 'cheating to lose' (match-fixing) (Ordway & Opie, 2016; Ordway, 2018) as follows:

a the manipulation of sporting competitions; and
b the use of drugs or doping methods in sport; and
c the abuse of children and other persons in a sporting environment; and
d the failure to protect members of sporting organisations, and other persons in a sporting environment, from bullying, intimidation, discrimination or harassment (ASADA Amendment Act, 2020, s.4).

It is not clear whether the non-exclusive list of 'threats' under the Sport Integrity Australia legislation is intended to also incorporate broader anti-corruption threats to sport, as defined by Miller (2018) and the DACCS research project outlined above, such as corruption associated with event bids, elections or contracts (e.g. major procurement processes in the Chapter 3 Bayley and Egle case study). While the responsibility for oversighting good governance remains with Sport Australia, it will be interesting to watch in the next phase of Sport Integrity Australia's evolution, how the intersection of poor culture and poor governance translating into sport integrity may be addressed through transparency and accountability.

Both Bayley and Egle in Chapter 3 and Lim and Young in Chapter 13 examine the anti-corruption research into 'bad apples' (corrupt individuals and groups), 'bad barrels' (corrupt organisations) and 'bad orchards' (corrupt systems). The McLaren Report (2020) into international weightlifting provides an insight into how a 'bad apple' contributes to creating a toxic culture ('bad orchard'):

> The control exerted by Dr Aján was absolute and infamous. At a macro level, he manipulated the EB, Member Federations and staff to acquiesce whatever authority they may have been able to exert in their respective roles. The either tacit acceptance or wilful blindness to Dr Aján's methods of control has exposed systemic governance failures at the highest levels of the IWF. Those who challenged him were punished or bullied. Any conduct at the highest levels of a federation that permits the rule by fear, deception and corruption to satisfy personal desires, acts to the detriment of the sport's key stakeholders: the athletes. (McLaren, 2020, pp. 18–19)

One challenge for sport is how behaviour identified by the forms of corruption such as fraud, bribery, nepotism and cronyism can be addressed; all of which were identified by McLaren in examining how millions went missing from international weightlifting bank accounts.

A leadership culture based on fear and retribution to ensure critics are silenced is also alleged at the highest levels of the Olympic movement (Weinreich, 2020). Weightlifting appears to be a sport corrupted from within, rather than being infiltrated by external nefarious parties. One of several recommendations to support a strong ethical culture is to ask staff and stakeholders, including athletes, whether they fear retribution, punishment, bullying or loss of access to discretionary favours, if they speak up (Ethisphere, 2020).

Directly addressing the vulnerabilities of athletes and others within the sport ecosystem has been examined in Chapter 12 by Ordway and Lenten. Athletes are vulnerable for a range of reasons, including addictions, secrets, poverty and greed. Using the men's professional sport of rugby league in Australia as a case study, an incentive-based strategy, conditional retirement funds, was examined to hypothesise whether addressing financial vulnerabilities may make some athletes less susceptible to the risk of match-fixing.

In Chapter 6 Roberts and Ordway, a number of recommendations were made that can be more broadly applied to sport organisations seeking to restore trust, namely: (a) time – both in timeliness of response and playing the long game; (b) transparency and consistency; (c) redress and remorse; and (d) walking the talk, which includes the role of sponsors in supporting sport integrity. The need for greater transparency is also highlighted in the recommendations by Jamieson and Ordway in Chapter 5. In the case study involving a recreational athlete in New Zealand, it is recommended that the exercise of discretion by national anti-doping organisations under the World Anti-Doping Code should be clarified to restore trust, and the Social Licence to Operate, and thereby assist to focus anti-doping efforts on 'cheating' and corruption in sport.

Similarly, the response to the selection bribery scandal engulfing ice hockey in the Czech Republic was for the national ice hockey federation to establish a formal cooperation agreement and a whistleblowing hotline with the national chapter of Transparency International (TI). As outlined by Ondráčková, from TI, and Verschuuren in Chapter 8, TI then collects and reviews reports, but also coordinates integrity awareness programmes and acts as a mediator and adviser for those within the sport facing challenging integrity issues. Lim and Young in Chapter 13 suggest that a similar hotline for the horseracing industry would have provided an alternate avenue to reporting the horse substation to the police.

Hotlines now exist in the horse racing industry, and as outlined in a recent report into the harness racing industry, complaints received are: 'assessed and go through an intelligence process and [are] then managed internally and subsequently investigated if that is required'. It is recommended that further: 'consideration could be given to the appropriate thresholds or factors that would justify further investigation, including assessing whether complaints coincide with trends in other key indicators' (Harness Racing Victoria, 2020, p. 36). The key indicators identified 'of the effects of corrupt activity in harness racing when measured to determine variations against past levels and against any movements in industry averages', in addition to wagering data, include:

> overall race entries; entries per race; number of races per meeting; number of meetings per year; racecourse attendance levels; number of registered trainers in the relevant area; number of horses in work with the registered trainers; [and] ... the number and type of complaint made by participants about alleged corrupt practices in the industry. (Harness Racing Victoria, 2020, pp. 4–5)

Many of these indicators may also be applied beyond animal racing into other sports to detect whether confidence, and trust, is declining due to corrupt practices.

Ideas for future endeavours

Based on the case studies outlined, to restore trust in sport, further areas for research, policy development and resourcing are recommended as follows:

- establishment of an international equivalent of Sport Integrity Australia or a sport ombudsman;
- resourcing and legal protection for (a) whistleblowers and (b) investigative media;
- resourcing and support for a collaborative approach with national prosecutors and law enforcement agencies to enable action to be taken against the perpetrators, enablers and those failing to act on sport corruption and athlete welfare issues, including auditors and board members failing to exercise their fiduciary duties (e.g. Global Athlete, 2020);
- accountability through (a) legal and (b) sport investigations leading to proportionate sanctions and other restorative action; this may include fines and/or repayment of stolen funds into ethical education and research programmes;
- examining and strengthening the national anti-corruption laws implementing UNCAC (UN, 2005), UNTOC (UN, 2003) and other international conventions to ensure that the sport industry is included (Passas & Ordway, 2016) (e.g. recent compilation of the national anti-bribery laws undertaken by the UNODC);
- supporting the people of integrity working within corrupt, bullying environments controlled by fear e.g. counselling fund to support their psychological well-being;
- ethical leadership training supporting recruitment, nomination and 'good character' reference processes to ensure that people of integrity are elected and appointed into decision-making positions;
- publishing an 'integrity' equivalent of the WADA Prohibited Association list;
- research into ethical decision-making and accountability, for example, examining leadership decisions and hosting right decisions; noting that transparency in voting is a first step (e.g. for the first time, following the vote for the FIFA WWC 2023 in 2020, the bid each of the delegates voted for was published);

- research into the link between athlete welfare and integrity with a view to developing policies with a human rights, inclusive, EoC, wellness focus (e.g. Newton, 2019; UNDP, 2019);
- strengthen codes of ethics (for example, an investigation could not be conducted into former IWF President under the IOC Code of Ethics following his resignation (IOC, 2020)); and
- work collaboratively with sponsors to require accountability and to strengthen ethical culture in the individuals and organisations they support.

Conclusion

The title of Stephen Covey's book *From Effectiveness to Greatness* (Covey, 2013), expanding upon the Jim Collins mantra that 'Good is the enemy of the great' (Collins, 2001), might well describe the biggest challenge for people seeking to support sport integrity and restore trust to sport. Corruption in sport is a 'wicked' problem on a worldwide scale. Rather than throw up our hands in the air declaring that it is 'all too hard', the challenge is to focus our efforts on the most effective levers – those interventions that are most likely to have the greatest positive effect. Marking the four years since *The Copenhagen Declaration* (2016), international anti-doping leaders reiterated their support for the following levers:

- greater autonomy of WADA and the anti-doping system – particularly with greater independence from sports organisations;
- improved governance and transparency at WADA;
- increased encouragement, support, recognition and protection of whistleblowers;
- support for investigations and adequate sanctioning power (CCES, 2020).

Many of the recommendations made here reflect these same levers, namely: independence, good governance and transparency, protection for whistleblowers, meaningful penalties and support for well-trained investigators. In addition, it is clear that the key to a strong integrity framework is to develop ethical leaders and 'good citizens' who live the fundamental values of sport of friendship, health, vitality and joy while building strong communities founded on honesty and integrity. It is well established that sporting organisations which manifest principles of good governance are less likely to experience integrity issues. Good governance in this context often refers to leadership, transparency and accountability. What has not been focused on significantly to date is linking a strong integrity culture with well-being, fairness and inclusiveness (from membership, playing rules, decision-making and match-day official roles, disciplinary procedures, transition post-sport and the distribution of profits). It is proposed here at an EoC approach will create a sense of ownership by all stakeholders (a proprietary relationship with the sport, rather than a licence to play), which will in turn further strengthen integrity efforts. The challenge for future research is to determine whether the solutions proposed herein can be measured and demonstrated to support, and develop, ethical leaders and positively influence sports integrity. If we achieve that then, as described by Collins (2001), we can reflect on having had a meaningful life in that we: 'had a hand in creating something of intrinsic excellence that makes a contribution … [and] gain that deepest of all satisfactions: knowing that your short time here on this earth has been well spent, and that it mattered'.

Note

1 The author would like to thank a number of colleagues whose thoughts and ideas have contributed to this chapter: Jack Anderson, Genevieve Lim, Richard Lucas, Adam Masters, Matt Nicholl, Nick Sellars and Bill Turner.

References

Aiolfi, G. (2019). Protecting whistleblowers in Switzerland: Can a speak-up culture and self-reporting framework help? Retrieved from https://www.baselgovernance.org/news/protecting-whistleblowers-switzerland-can-speak-culture-and-self-reporting-framework-help

Andersen, J. S. (2020, 9 June). The man who blew the whistle on his own corruption. *Play the Game.* Retrieved from https://www.playthegame.org/news/news-articles/2020/0645_the-man-who-blew-the-whistle-on-his-own-corruption/

Anderson, R. (2004). *Report to the Australian Sports Commission and to Cycling Australia.* Australian Government, Department of Communications, Information Technology and the Arts, Canberra. Retrieved from https://www.clearinghouseforsport.gov.au/Library/archive/digital_archive/cycling/anderson_report_2004

Anstiss, S. (2020, 14 July). Moya Dodd. Fearless women in sport series. *The Game Changers Podcast.* Retrieved from https://thegamechangers.libsyn.com/moya-dodd

Aubusson, K. (2018, 9 February). Greater risk of concussion for women, experts warn as codes beckon women to contact sports. *The Sydney Morning Herald.* Retrieved from https://www.smh.com.au/sport/greater-risk-of-concussion-for-women-experts-warn-as-codes-beckon-women-to-contact-sports-20180209-h0vuxe.html

Australian Commission for Law Enforcement Integrity (ACLEI). (n.d.). Key concepts. Retrieved from www.aclei.gov.au/Pages/Corruption-Prevention/Key-concepts.aspx

Australian Human Rights Commission. (2020, 4 August). Information: Independent review of gymnastics in Australia 2020. News. Retrieved from https://humanrights.gov.au/about/news/information-independent-review-gymnastics-australia-2020

Australian Institute of Sport (AIS). (2020). Athlete wellbeing and engagement: Beyond the podium. Retrieved from https://www.ais.gov.au/health-wellbeing/awe

Australian Sports Anti-Doping Authority (ASADA) Amendment (Sport Integrity Australia) Act 2020. Commonwealth of Australia. Retrieved from https://www.legislation.gov.au/Details/C2020A00011https://www.legislation.gov.au/Details/C2020A00011

Backhouse, S. H., Collins, C., Defoort, Y., McNamee, M., Parkinson, A., Sauer, M.*et al.* (2014). *Study on doping prevention: A map of legal, regulatory, and prevention practice provisions in EU, 28.* Luxembourg: European Commission. Retrieved from http://eprints.leedsbeckett.ac.uk/753/1/doping-prevention-report_en.pdf

BaMaung, D., & Cuddihy, J. (2018). Corruption: The exposure and exploitation of human vulnerabilities. In E. Campbell & N. Lord (Eds.), *Corruption in commercial enterprise* (pp. 117–135). Abingdon: Routledge.

BBC. (2018, 5 December). Eighty sports coaches convicted of child sex abuse, says Offside Trust. *BBC Sport*. Retrieved from https://www.bbc.com/sport/football/46453955

Black Report. (1989, May). *Interim report: Drugs in sport*. Commonwealth of Australia. Retrieved from https://www.aph.gov.au/Parliamentary_Business/Committees/Senate/Environment_and_Communications/Completed_inquiries/pre1996/drugsint/index

Blair, A. (2018, 28 September). Mick Malthouse slammed by AFLW star Moana Hope after speech. Retrieved from https://www.news.com.au/sport/afl/mick-malthouse-slammed-by-aflw-star-after-sickening-speech/news-story/c300644e31649176f6918b6af78d5ff3

Bluestone Edge. (2013, 19 February). Culture review into Australian Olympic swimming. Retrieved from https://www.clearinghouseforsport.gov.au/Library/archive/digital_archive/swimming/A_review_of_culture_and_leadership_in_Australian_Olympic_Swimming.pdf

Bona, E. (2015, 29 September). Bill Shankly remembered: 11 brilliant quotes from Liverpool's iconic manager. *The Liverpool Echo*. Retrieved from https://www.liverpoolecho.co.uk/news/liverpool-news/bill-shankly-remembered-11-brilliant-10156199

Broadwell, M. M. (1969, 20 February). Teaching for learning (XVI.). *The Gospel Guardian*, 41, 1–3a. Retrieved from www.wordsfitlyspoken.org/gospel_guardian/v20/v20n41p1-3a.html

Brooks, G., Aleem, A., & Button, M. (2013). *Fraud, corruption and sport*. Basingstoke: Palgrave Macmillan.

CCES. (2020, 4 September). International anti-doping leaders stand with athlete community in calling on WADA to go further and faster with meaningful anti-doping reform. Canadian Centre for Ethics in Sport. Retrieved from https://cces.ca/news/international-anti-doping-leaders-stand-athlete-community-calling-wada-go-further-and-faster

Collins, J. (2001). *Good to great: Why some companies make the leap and others don't*. New York: Harper Business.

Covey, S. R. (2013). *The 8th habit: From effectiveness to greatness*. New York: Simon & Schuster.

Daniels, D. J. (2017, 26 June). Report to USA Gymnastics on proposed policy and procedural changes for the protection of young athletes. Retrieved from https://usagym.org/PDFs/About%20USA%20Gymnastics/ddreport_062617.pdf

Didulica, J. (2019). Changing the game: The legal framework for the laws of the game, management of human performance data and related safety considerations in women's professional sport. *Int Sports Law J.*, 18(3–4), 114–135.

Dokic, J., & Halloran, J. (2017). *Unbreakable*. Sydney: Random House.

Douglas, L. (2016). 'Say it ain't so … Josephine?': The risk of match-fixing in women's sport. *ANZSLA Commentator, The*, 97, 29.

Ethisphere. (2020). Measuring ethical culture. Ethisphere's 2020 Culture Benchmark Data Set. Retrieved from https://ethisphere.com/wp-content/uploads/Ethical_Culture_Infographic_2020-f.pdf

FIFA. (2015, 2 December). 2016 FIFA reform committee report. Retrieved from https://resources.fifa.com/image/upload/1514-proposals-of-the-2016-fifa-reform-committee.pdf?cloudid=npyfsjqt5diw9ncaxpyw

FIFA Governance. (2015, 21 December). Independent ethics committee bans Joseph S. Blatter and Michel Platini. Media Release. Independent Ethics Committee Adjudicatory Chamber. Retrieved from https://www.fifa.com/who-we-are/news/independent-ethics-committee-bans-joseph-s-blatter-and-michel-platini-2747411

Freeburn, L. (2018). Fundamental aspects of regulatory power in international sport. In L. Freeburn (Ed.), *Regulating international sport* (pp. 6–49). Leiden: Brill Nijhoff. Retrieved from https://minerva-access.unimelb.edu.au/bitstream/handle/11343/197924/Lloyd%20Freeburn_Thesis%20Final%20Jan%202018.pdf?sequence=1&isAllowed=y

Gardiner, S. (2018). Conceptualising corruption in sport. In L. A. Kihl (Ed.), *Corruption in sport: Causes, consequences, and reform*. Abingdon: Routledge.

Gilligan, C. (1982). *In a different voice*. Cambridge, MA: Harvard University Press.

Global Athlete. (2020, 5 June). Global athlete calls on the International Weightlifting Federation (IWF) to implement independent athlete oversight as a result of the McLaren independent investigation. Media Release. Retrieved from https://globalathlete.org/our-word/iwf-mclaren-report

Gordon, A. (2016, 24 May). VICE sports Q&A: How big of a problem is youth trafficking in soccer? Retrieved from https://www.vice.com/en_uk/article/aebg5e/vice-sports-qa-how-big-a-problem-is-youth-trafficking-in-football

Gouker, D. (2018). Sports betting Bill Tracker. *Legal Sports Report*. Retrieved from https://www.legalsportsreport.com/sportsbetting-bill-tracker/

Greenhow, A., & East, J. (2015). Custodians of the game: Ethical considerations for football governing bodies in regulating concussion management. *Neuroethics*, 8(1), 65–82.

Halloran, J., & Linden, J. (2020, 24 August). Katia Alexandrovskaya tragedy: Be grateful for the abuse skater told. *The Australian*. Retrieved from https://www.theaustralian.com.au/sport/katia-alexandrovskaya-teen-ice-star-who-fell-through-the-cracks/news-story/7f36d9d95250c48ea3a713ed748188a9

Hargreaves, J. (2002). *Sporting females: Critical issues in the history and sociology of women's sport*. Abingdon: Routledge.

Harness Racing Victoria. (2020, 1 September). The effects of corrupt activity, perceptions of corrupt activity and of integrity interventions in harness racing. News, Integrity Matters. Retrieved from https://www.thetrots.com.au/news/integrity-matters/world-first-study-into-effects-of-corrupt-activity-and-perceptions-of-corrupt-activity-in-harness-racing/

Hartmann, G. (2013, 14 May). IWF president under suspicion of financial mismanagement. *Play the Game*. Retrieved from https://www.playthegame.org/news/news-articles/2013/iwf-president-under-suspicion-of-financial-mismanagement/

Hill, D. (2008). *The fix*. Toronto: McClelland & Stewart.

Hill, D. (2013). *The insider's guide to match-fixing in football*. Toronto: Anne McDermid & Associates.

Hölzen, M., & Meier, H. E. (2019). Do football consumers care about sport governance? An analysis of social media responses to the recent FIFA scandal. *Journal of Global Sport Management*, 4(1), 97–120.

Institute of Chartered Secretaries and Administrators (ICSA). (2018). Organisational culture in sport: Assessing and improving attitudes and behaviour. Retrieved from https://www.icsa.org.uk/assets/files/policy/research/Organisational-culture-in-sport.pdf

International Olympic Committee (IOC). (2020). IOC 'ETHICS' TEXTS COLLECTION – 2020. Retrieved from https://www.olympic.org/code-of-ethics

Keith, B. (2018, 9 November). Olympic swim coach Scott Volkers will stand trial on sex abuse charges. Retrieved from https://swimswam.com/olympic-swim-coach-scott-volkers-will-stand-trial-on-sex-abuse-charges/

Kouzes, J. M., & Posner, B. Z. (1992). Ethical leaders: An essay about being in love. *Journal of Business Ethics*, 11(5, 6), 479–484.

Kupfer, T. (2018, 2 March). The NCAA must reform itself or die. *National Review*. Retrieved from https://www.nationalreview.com/2018/03/ncaa-college-athletics-corrupt-student-athlete-model-must-reform/

Lenten, L. J., Smith, A. C., & Boys, N. (2018). Evaluating an alternative draft pick allocation policy to reduce 'tanking' in the Australian Football League. *European Journal of Operational Research*, 267(1), 315–320.

McLaren, R. (2020, 4 June). Independent investigator report to the Oversight and Integrity Commission of International Weightlifting Federation. McLaren Independent Weightlifting Investigation. Retrieved from https://mclarenweightliftingenquiry.com/wp-content/themes/mclarenweightlifitingenquiry/assets/mclaren-independent-investigator-report-iwf-final.pdf

Miller, S. (2018, 21 September). Corruption. *Stanford encyclopedia of philosophy*. Stanford University Press. Retrieved from https://plato.stanford.edu/archives/win2018/entries/corruption/

Montague, E. P. (1849). *Narrative of the late expedition to the Dead Sea: From a diary by one of the party*. Carey and Hart. Retrieved from https://archive.org/details/narrativelateex00unkngoog/page/n161/mode/2up

Moston, S., Engelberg, T., & Skinner, J. (2015). Self-fulfilling prophecy and the future of doping. *Psychology of Sport and Exercise*, 16, 201–207.

Newton, A. (2019). *The business of human rights: Best practice and the UN guiding principles*. Abingdon: Routledge.

NISU. (2016, 3 August). National Integrity of Sport Unit. Australian Government, Department of Health. Retrieved from www.health.gov.au/internet/main/publishing.nsf/content/national-integrity-of-sport-unit

Opie, H. (1995). *Report of the independent inquiry into women's artistic gymnastics at the Australian Institute of Sport*. Australian Sports Commission. Available from https://catalogue.nla.gov.au/Record/2350710

Ordway, C. (2018). Sports integrity: Legislating into a position of strength. *World Sports Advocate*, 16(9), 16–19.

Ordway, C. (forthcoming, 2021). *Gender equality achieved through crisis: Football Federation of Australia (FFA)* (manuscript submitted for publication).

Ordway, C., & Opie, H. (2016). Integrity and corruption in sport. In N. Schulenkorf & S. Frawley (Eds.), *Critical issues in global sport management* (pp. 60–85). Abingdon: Routledge.

Panja, T. (2019, 6 June). FIFA vice president detained by the French police. *The New York Times*. Retrieved from https://www.nytimes.com/2019/06/06/sports/fifa-ahmad-ahmad.html

Panja, T. (2020, 30 July). FIFA president Gianni Infantino faces criminal investigation. *The New York Times*. Retrieved from https://www.nytimes.com/2020/07/30/sports/soccer/fifa-gianni-infantino-investigation.html

Passas, N., & Ordway, C. (2016). Sports corruption: Justice and accountability through the use of the UNCAC and the UNTOC. UNODC. Retrieved from https://www.researchgate.net/publication/311937014_Sports_Corruption_Justice_and_Accountability_through_the_use_of_UNCAC_and_the_UNTOC

Perry, K. (2018, 24 January). USA Gymnastics statement regarding Nassar sentence. USA Gymnastics. Retrieved fromhttps://usagym.org/pages/post.html?PostID=21228

Phelps, A. (2017, 15 July). Independent review into the climate and culture of the World Class Programme (WCP). Retrieved from https://www.sportsthinktank.com/research,116656.html

Ransom, H., & Barsuhn, A. (2020). More than a game. *Harvard Kennedy School Review*. Retrieved from https://issuu.com/harvardkennedyschoolreview/docs/2020_edition, p140–145

Reid, S. M. (2018, 30 July). 100s of USA swimmers were sexually abused for decades and the people in charge knew and ignored it, investigation finds. Retrieved from https://www.ocregister.com/2018/02/16/investigation-usa-swimming-ignored-sexual-abuse-for-decades/

Royal Commission. (2017). *Final report 'Sport, recreation, arts, culture, community and hobby groups' V14, Institutional responses into child sexual abuse*. Retrieved from https://www.childabuseroyalcommission.gov.au/sites/default/files/final_report_-_volume_14_sport_recreation_arts_culture_community_and_hobby_groups.pdf

Schwab, B. (2017). When we know better, we do better: Embedding the human rights of players as a prerequisite to the legitimacy of lex sportiva and sport's justice system. *Md. J. Int'l L.*, 32(1). Retrieved from https://core.ac.uk/download/pdf/147107125.pdf

Schwab, B. (2018). Celebrate humanity: Reconciling sport and human rights through Athlete activism. *J. Legal Aspects Sport*, 28, 170.

Seppelt, H., Hartmann, G., & Butler, N. (2020, 15 January). Geheimsache Doping: Der Herr der Heber (Doping Top Secret: Lord of the Lifters). ARD. Retrieved from https://www.sportschau.de/weitere/geheimsachedoping/video-geheimsache-doping—der-herr-der-heber–100.html

Smith, W. (2013). Independent review of swimming. Retrieved from https://www.clearinghouseforsport.gov.au/__data/assets/pdf_file/0009/768627/Independent_Swimming_Review_FINAL_2013.pdf

The Ethics Group. (2017). Australian Olympic Committee culture alignment. Retrieved from https://ethics.org.au/casestudy/australian-olympic-committee-case-study/

The Ethics Group. (2018, 29 October). Australian cricket – A matter of balance. Retrieved from https://apo.org.au/node/199701

UK Sport. (2020, 16 July). UK Sport and Sport England to co-commission review into allegations of athlete mistreatment in gymnastics. Retrieved from https://www.uksport.gov.uk/news/2020/07/16/gymnastics-review

United Nations (UN). (2003). Convention Against Transnational Organized Crime. Retrieved from https://www.unodc.org/unodc/en/treaties/CTOC/signatures.html

United Nations (UN). (2005). United Nations Convention Against Corruption (UNCAC). United Nations. Retrieved from https://www.unodc.org/unodc/en/corruption/uncac.html

UNDP. (2019, 22 November). Gender dimensions of the guiding principles on business and human rights. UN Development Programme. Retrieved from https://www.undp.org/content/undp/en/home/librarypage/democratic-governance/gender-dimensions-guiding-principles-on-business-n-human-rights.html

Weinreich, J. (2020, 3 April). IOC president holds on to power while federations face financial problems. *Play the Game*. Retrieved from https://playthegame.org/news/comments/2020/0999_ioc-president-holds-on-to-power-while-federations-face-financial-problems/

Wood, J. (2013, 14 January). Cycling Australia review. Australian Government, Department of Health. Retrieved from https://www1.health.gov.au/internet/main/publishing.nsf/Content/cycling-australia-review-index/$file/cycling-australia-review-20130111.pdf

Wood, J., Howman, D., & Murrihy, R. (2018, March). *Report of the review of Australia's sports integrity arrangements, report No 12074*. Australian Government, Department of Health. Retrieved from https://www1.health.gov.au/internet/main/publishing.nsf/Content/63F0A5D7BDA5A0B5CA2582CF0005E6F9/$File/HEALTH-RASIA-Report-Acc.pdf

World Anti-Doping Agency (WADA). (2020). *Athletes' Anti-Doping Rights Act*. Retrieved from https://www.wada-ama.org/sites/default/files/resources/files/athlete_act_en.pdf

Index

For Product Safety Concerns and Information please contact our EU
representative GPSR@taylorandfrancis.com
Taylor & Francis Verlag GmbH, Kaufingerstraße 24, 80331 München, Germany

www.ingramcontent.com/pod-product-compliance
Lightning Source LLC
LaVergne TN
LVHW021121300926
849160LV00010B/816
9780367616922